Shame and Honor

SHAME
AND
HONOR

A Vulgar History
of the Order of the Garter

STEPHANIE TRIGG

PENN

UNIVERSITY OF PENNSYLVANIA PRESS

PHILADELPHIA

Published by
University of Pennsylvania Press
Philadelphia, Pennsylvania 19104-4112
www.upenn.edu/pennpress

Printed in the United States of America on acid-free paper
10 9 8 7 6 5 4 3 2 1

Library of Congress Cataloging-in-Publication Data
Trigg, Stephanie.
Shame and honor : a vulgar history of the Order of the
Garter / Stephanie Trigg. — 1st ed.
p. cm.
Includes bibliographical references and index.
ISBN 978-0-8122-4391-8 (hardcover : alk. paper)
1. Order of the Garter—History.   2. Orders of knighthood
and chivalry—Great Britain—History.   I. Title.
CR4827.T75 2012
929.7'10941—dc23
2011044323

For Paul James and Joel Trigg

Contents

Introduction

It's a nice piece of pageantry which I think a lot of people enjoy. . . .
Rationally it's lunatic but in practice everyone enjoys it I think.
  —HRH Prince Philip, Duke of Edinburgh, in *The Queen's Castle*

They wear trailing mantles of blue velvet lined with white silk, a red velvet hood pinned to the right shoulder with a red sash draped across the body, and a black velvet hat piled high with white ostrich feathers. On the left shoulder, their mantles are adorned with a large embroidered scutcheon featuring a red cross surrounded by a motto in gold letters. A white silk ribbon is tied in a bow on each shoulder, and a heavy enamel and gold chain is draped around the neck, weighted further with an enamel model of a knight slaying a dragon. A long golden cord with large tassels is tied and looped so that one end sits lower than the other, as it has done since the fourteenth century. Underneath this elaborate costume, they wear a gray suit, or a long white dress. This is the modern medievalism of the Most Noble Order of the Garter in the twenty-first century (figure 1).

As the members of the Order of the Garter move slowly down the hill from the keep at Windsor Castle to St. George's Chapel they are accompanied by the cheers and applause of the crowd on either side, the music of military bands, and the click of cameras. The procession is led by the military knights of Windsor and the officers of arms; it moves slowly, in deference to both the crowds and the age of some of its members. Several, indeed, have already been driven down the hill. When the Garter Companions appear, the newest members come first, and the last to pass by is the Queen, the train of her mantle held by two young pages. The long parade winds into the south side of the chapel, and the crowd settles down on the grass to listen to a broadcast of the service, following along with the help of the printed glossy guide. The sound quality is terrible. After an hour or so, there is more movement. The

Figure 1. Prince Andrew and Prince Edward in the Garter procession, 2009.
Photographer Chris Jackson. © Getty Images.

procession leaves the chapel down the broad steps on the west side, and the members climb into cars or open carriages for the trip up the hill. Women in elaborate hats and dresses and men in morning suits emerge from the chapel, enjoying their turn to be the object of the gaze of tourists, royalists, and photographers. An academic observer (and amateur photographer) is also there to observe the procession. The crowds on the lawns are all dressed rather more practically, wearing comfortable shoes and standing amid the clutter of folding chairs and picnic lunches (figure 2).

The annual procession of the Order of the Garter is one of the principal events in the ritual year of the English monarchy. Like many examples of proud display and ritual practice in the royal calendar, the procession represents a symbolic inheritance from the Middle Ages. The Order was founded in the 1340s, and has a more or less continuous history of activity, though the Garter procession in its current form at Windsor Castle dates from a postwar revival in 1947. The robes and regalia worn by the Companions represent an accretion of styles from different centuries. Carrying the weight of medieval tradition, the procession provides an excellent opportunity for loyal subjects to feast on the visible accessibility of the royal family and the other members of this elite chivalric order. It offers a perfect blend of royal tourism, heritage culture, celebrity culture, and the magnificent costumes of medievalist dress-ups, yet Garter Day is a less familiar spectacle than the daily Changing of the Guard at Buckingham Palace. In contrast to that daily fixture of London's international tourist calendar, the annual procession at Windsor attracts a higher proportion of English visitors and dedicated royalists who demonstrate their affinity with the royal family and their comprehension of the day's significance by ordering tickets in advance and making the hour-long train journey from Waterloo Station in London to Windsor. Lining the route, the crowds are players in the ritual performance, for a procession needs an audience in the way the changing of the guard does not. As they clap and cheer the familiar faces of the royal family and past prime ministers, and acknowledge the less familiar members of the Order, these visitors are also taking part in an act of medievalism, celebrating the modern ritual of the medieval Garter.

Apart from its ornate costume, one of the most striking things people remember about the Order of the Garter is its putative foundation myth. According to this story, the Order was founded by Edward III to honor an embarrassing occasion. The king is said to have been dancing with a lady, perhaps the Countess of Salisbury, when the garter holding up her stocking fell to the floor. As the courtiers laughed at her distress, the chivalrous or enamored

Figure 2. Guests at Garter service. Photo by the author.

king is said to have retrieved the garter and tied it around his own leg, declaring "Honi soit qui mal y pense" (*Shamed be he who thinks evil of this* or more proverbially, *Evil be to him who evil thinks*) and promising to found an order of knighthood in honor of the garter that would become so famous that all those now laughing would want to join it.

This story of a medieval royal scandal about sex and underclothes has often been dismissed as a fantastic or romantic invention, but it has nevertheless given rise to a long and beloved tradition. Again and again, the venerable history of the Garter returns to this mythical moment of ritual disruption. There have been many attempts to displace this scandalous narrative with a series of more palatable explanations of the Order's origins, but such attempts have been largely unsuccessful: there is something pleasant, even gratifying to the popular imagination and to the national mythology about finding a desiring royal body and an embarrassing wardrobe malfunction at the heart of one of the monarchy's proudest rituals. Even when the Order's official and apologetic historians dismiss this story as a romantic fiction, attempting to control the irreverent mythologies of popular medievalism, they are condemned to a similar logic as they repeat the story in order to transcend it. Like the king in the Garter myth, they seek to transform this trace of medieval frivolity into something nonmedieval, something that will endure without embarrassment into a future, modern temporality.

The Order of the Garter was established in the fourteenth century, but it resonates both backward and forward in time. Historical accounts of its foundation are contradictory, but all indicate a commemorative function of some kind, in memory of an event at Edward III's court, Richard I's crusading heroics, or Arthur's Round Table. The Order also anticipates its own futurity, especially through its enigmatic motto. In its first, immediate setting, this little French text anticipates a querulous response to the English chivalric order, but it also knowingly generates centuries of puzzled speculation about its meaning. Those centuries of speculation, along with the transformations of the Order's ritual forms, have the effect of destabilizing the "medieval" qualities of the Order, as it takes on a double life as a historical phenomenon and as an ongoing project of medievalism.

This book traces those cultural, symbolic, and narrative transformations. I have joined together a series of diachronic and thematic approaches to the long and varied traditions of the Order to compile a cultural history of this medieval institution and its survival into contemporary culture, long after the social and political forces that framed its formation have disappeared. It would be misleading in the extreme to suggest that modern chivalric orders now carry the same cultural, social, or political importance they did in the past: the contemporary dynamics of shame and honor, for example, are almost unrecognizable from medieval and early modern codes. But it is precisely because this Order, with a more or less continuous history from the 1340s to the present, has had to make so many accommodations with its medieval origins that it poses such an intriguing set of questions and problems about the afterlife of the medieval in postmedieval culture.

A repeated theme of *Shame and Honor* will be the necessary tensions between the Order's periodic appeals to its medieval foundations, on the one hand, and its insistence, on the other, that it can update itself and remain responsive to the ever-changing imperatives of modernity. Much of the Order's official discourse is careful to position it between these two poles. There is also a significant strand of laughter, or a sense of the ridiculous, that threads through the Garter's history from the foundational myth right through to contemporary meditations on its practices.

A recent television documentary offers a characteristic moment. The Duke of Edinburgh, Prince Philip, as Ranger of Windsor Great Park, is our host and guide over the vast estates and elaborate interiors of the castle. Much of the second part of the three-part series is concerned with the preparations for the annual feast, procession, and service in St. George's Chapel for the Order of the Garter, and the duke comments casually on the festivities, "It's a nice piece of pageantry which I think a lot of people enjoy. . . . Rationally it's lunatic but in practice everyone enjoys it I think." His remarks are typical of the low-key, chatty style of his commentary throughout the program, but they draw loosely on a long tradition and a powerful structure of thought and feeling about the Order of the Garter and perhaps also about English eccentricity as part of the national character. Where Edward III's motto boldly dares the casual observer to mock or find fault with royal practice, the Duke of Edinburgh expresses, in a more faltering way, a sense of the ridiculousness of the ritual, and a more superficial sentiment: popular enjoyment. The two men share a consciousness that the royal court can be seen as ridiculous, but they resolve that tension in different ways. The medieval king proudly forces a hierarchical division between insiders and outsiders, whereas the modern consort appeals tentatively to a much broader sense of a public audience on whose behalf he projects the enjoyment of spectacle.

At one level, the duke's words seem refreshingly candid and surprisingly modern, and to this extent, give voice to one of the oppositions that structure this book. The medieval ritual of the Order of the Garter—and all that it represents for English heritage culture, historical tradition and royal tourism—is charismatic and intriguing in its remoteness from everyday reality; but by the same token, it also threatens to seem laughable. Along with other activities of the English royal family and the monarchy in general, it invites curiosity and tremulous interest, helping to sell millions of newspapers and attracting millions of visitors to Britain, visitors who in turn spend millions of pounds on royal tourism and royal souvenirs. Like many other royal ceremonies, the Order of the Garter is both a time-honored tradition and a media circus. No matter that the monarchy is regularly derided or dismissed as irrelevant to contemporary British culture and society: such ceremonies and processions are popular features of traditional English heritage and play an important role in the nation's image and economy, both domestically and internationally.

As a member of the Order, and as a rational modern subject, the duke is perfectly able to keep these two views in comfortable suspension with each other. He seems to experience no personal contradiction or threat to his selfhood in dressing up in a long blue velvet robe and hat with flamboyant white ostrich feathers to parade from one part of his castle to another in front of thousands of royalist fans, to take part in a religious service that many believe commemorates a light-hearted exercise in fourteenth-century chivalric manners.

It is easy for an outsider to look dispassionately or critically at the elaborate forms of royal pageantry and find them "lunatic" or laughable. It is more surprising to find this attitude voiced by one of the most privileged players in such pageantry, although the duke's insouciance is matched by his sense of the enduring popularity of the tradition. Similarly, another television program commemorating the Queen's eightieth birthday in 2006 shows John Major, the former prime minister, being presented with his Garter star by the Queen in a private ceremony. "I love the story," he says. "Yes, it's fun, isn't it?" she replies benignly, as she pins the star on his jacket.[1]

The dualism voiced here—I love its importance, but I can see it is also ridiculous—is analogous to the logic of the fetish, in which the inanimate object both does and does not stand in for the absent body, generating its own rituals of desire. This logic is played out at several historical and cultural levels in the Garter's traditions. In the Garter myth itself, the king's desire and the possibility of heterosexual scandal are strategically transformed into an expression of the ideals of chivalric brotherhood. And in the long history of the Order, the story of the woman's garter, while often dismissed as a trivial trace of medieval gossip, nevertheless enjoys great popularity, especially in England, as a powerful sign of the medieval past, reminding us of all that seems quaint or unfamiliar about the Middle Ages. At the same time, the Order of the Garter remains the rarest and most elevated sign of royal favor in the modern honors system, the greatest distinction a monarch can bestow, even if lesser awards to musicians, actors, and athletes receive greater coverage in the press. The distinctive regalia of the Order can function as fetish objects, too, either in their highly decorated form (spelling out the words of the Garter motto in hundreds of diamonds, for example) or in the increasingly rare sight of a ribbon or buckle tied below the knee over white court stockings. Similarly, the honor of belonging to such an order can quickly give way to a sense of the ridiculous or, at least, the irrelevantly archaic. The cultural and social history of the Order of the Garter cannot be written simply from within, then, as has often been the case. This is a tradition of ritual practice whose meaning has developed and changed over the centuries in constant dialogue between insiders and outsiders, through different layers and levels of understanding, interest, sympathy, or contempt.

The Order's Companions may speak lightly of the Garter, as we have just seen, but they speak as insiders or initiates. By way of contrast, the Duke of Edinburgh's comments are counterpointed in the same program by the far more reverential remarks of the Queen's Master of Ceremonies, Colonel Sir Malcolm Ross, who is responsible for making sure that the Garter procession at Windsor runs smoothly. He speaks of it as "a magnificent and very ancient procession, full of really the most distinguished people in the country, one way and another." He is obviously less willing or able to express a sense of the Garter procession as "lunatic." For such household officers, the pageant is coded much more firmly as work. The "enjoyment" of which the duke speaks is not experienced equally by everyone: it is the product of scrupulous and achingly detailed labor. In the same documentary, for example, Garrison Sergeant-Major Billy Mott checks that the heels of the guards lining the route are perfectly aligned with the curb, while the staff setting the table for the Garter feast take pains to position the olive oil for the Prince of Wales's place setting, even as it disturbs the symmetry of the butter dishes for everyone else. This exception, the accommodation of personal preference in a highly regimented and ritualized celebration, is willingly incorporated into the preparations. Such a tiny example may seem to indicate merely the indulgence of a fussy eater, but it also signals the ritual's capacity to respond to modern (sophisticated) taste. It is one of the many ways in which the Order of the Garter willingly proclaims its readiness to reconcile medieval traditions with the imperatives and innovations of modernity.

The significance of the Order of the Garter in contemporary culture is highly uneven. As a persistent reproduction of medieval tradition it is a key component of a lucrative tourism industry that depends heavily on heritage culture. The Garter is lauded as the preeminent rank of the English honors system, though its political and diplomatic significance is much reduced from previous centuries. Its numbers are tightly restricted, and it is both starkly elitist and socially remote from most of our daily realities, although it might also have seemed that way, once, to the daughter of an English grocer, Margaret Thatcher, and the New Zealand beekeeper, Edmund Hillary, who came to adorn its ranks as the 980th and 981st Companions, respectively, in 1995. It is easy to see the Companions' blue robes and ostrich feathers as the trappings of a hopelessly archaic remnant of past glory; to dismiss the Order's survival as a historical accident; and to regard the whole affair as no more than a vestigial trace of a defunct empire. Indeed, there is a sustained tradition of mocking and ridiculing the Order for its rituals and robes, a tradition we will have occasion to visit in later chapters.

It is also easy to translate this exclusiveness into a version of conspiracy theory. When we think of the Order of the Garter, or rather, when I have mentioned my work on this book over the past few years, the response has often been to ask: "Isn't it some sort of secret society?" And indeed, the Order often features in some free-wheeling associations between Freemasonry, demonic worship, right-wing conspiracy theory, and the Illuminati.[2] The Garter is also sometimes associated with witchcraft, and there is a slender tradition (to be considered in Chapter 2) arguing that Edward III's choice of the emblem indicates his support for a native English Wiccan tradition.

More recently, in the space where conspiracy theory meets tabloid gossip, there was also speculation around the time of Prince Charles's second marriage that he had asked the Queen to make Camilla, Duchess of Cornwall, a member of the Order, and that his mother had refused, though it is presumably only a matter of time before the duchess is elevated by Elizabeth, or by Charles, on his succession, to the position of Lady Companion (such as Baroness Thatcher) or Lady of the Garter (such as Princess Anne). It was also widely rumored in Australia, in 2008, to considerable public amusement, that former prime minister John Howard, whose government had recently lost office, might be made a Companion of the Order, and wear its robes and plumes, though this rumor seems to have had little currency in the United

Kingdom. Such rumors and backstories about the filling of Garter vacancies are the stuff of both history and fiction. Many readers will recall Plantagenet Palliser's dilemma in Anthony Trollope's novel *The Prime Minister* (1876) whether to uphold tradition and recommend his own name to the Queen, or the names of various other, less deserving members of the peerage.

The Garter attracts only a small number of conspiracy theories, relative to those that surround the medieval church and the Catholic Church, for example, but Dan Brown's *The Da Vinci Code* and a range of similar films and fictions testify to the appeal of the darker versions of medievalism that throw a colorful tint over the Order and other similar institutions, insisting on their arcane mysteries. Umberto Eco describes the appeal of this version of the Middle Ages: "An eternal and rather eclectic ramshackle structure, swarming with Knights Templars, Rosicrucians, alchemists, Masonic initiates, neo-Kabbalists, drunk on reactionary poisons sipped from the Grail, ready to hail every neo-fascist Will to Power."[3] For Eco, this is "the Middle Ages of so-called *Tradition*, or of occult philosophy (or *la pensée sapientielle*)."

"Tradition" is a concept that will feature largely in this book, though not always in the sense Eco invokes. The Order of the Garter can certainly function as a filter for gossip, conspiracy theories, and fantasy; and its role in the cultural formation of what Nickolas Haydock calls "the medieval imaginary" is one of my main concerns.[4] But Eco's sense of "tradition" here is a relatively unhistorical one ("an eternal and rather eclectic ramshackle structure"), framed more by his taxonomy of the various cultural revivals or "dreams" of the Middle Ages—his famous "ten Little Middle Ages"—than by the continuity of historical rituals such as the Garter's. Instead of seeing "tradition" as a species of medievalist revival, I turn his reasoning around in order to argue that the medieval past plays an important, unacknowledged role in structuring our understanding of English cultural tradition, especially in the area of heritage culture. "Tradition" thus appeals to a cosmology or worldview in which temporal continuity and the repetition of ritual practice are meaningful signs of a greater truth: a vision of an ordered social world.

More specifically—and this is the central rationale for this book—the Order of the Garter, while undeniably an elite institution directly affecting only a handful of individuals at any given time, is symptomatic of the diverse, fluctuating, and ongoing life of medieval traditions in postmedieval culture. The Order has for centuries been the object of serious historical study by antiquarians and scholars of heraldic ceremonial, but it is also associated with heritage culture that is often coded as popular and commercial.[5] I argue that we can understand the dynamics of English cultural heritage with greater precision by examining the treatment of its medieval components, using analytical frames drawn from the study of ritual practice and medievalism. Thus, when I use the term "modernity," I mean not that the "modern" has *replaced* the "traditional" but rather that the social world has a different *dominant* sense of time, space, and embodiment. Medieval tradition now sits inside this social frame, domesticated and routinized as medieval*ism*.

The Order is an ideal phenomenon for such a study of continuity and social change, as it offers an example of medieval ritual practice that extends from the 1340s to the present day, even if there have been long periods of abeyance in its elections and the performance of some of its rituals. On the one hand, it deserves to be read in historical, cultural, and imaginative terms. It cathects much of our fascination with royal spectacle, personality, and performance, a fascination that is played out in poetry, fiction, music, art, and gossip, as well as in the more formal discourses of heraldry and history writing. But on the other hand, the Order also has much to tell us about the way Edward III's foundation has been transformed, reinvented and revived over the intervening centuries, and the way this medieval institution expresses both continuities and discontinuities with the past. I read its history, then, as a species of medievalism: the conscious or unconscious practice of, and interest in, medieval culture. Because the Order has a continuous if uneven history, it provides a unique record of changing attitudes to medieval traditions, and the various attempts to revive and reform those traditions. At different periods in this long history, the dominant forces of English culture and society have sought to express different relationships with the medieval past, through the performance of rituals that necessarily invoke or make connections with that past. I thus use the 650-year history of the Order as a bridge between two disciplines that have sometimes seemed antithetical: medieval studies (the study of medieval texts and cultures) and medievalism studies (the study of postmedieval revivals or reprises of those cultures).[6] In many respects, the distinction between these two disciplines is barely sustainable: for one thing, a long tradition of ritual practice like the Order of the Garter helps us see how hard it is to declare the end of the medieval and the beginning of medievalism.

Unlike the literary, visual, and historical texts that are the usual objects of research in medievalism, the Order of the Garter offers an example of medievalism as a tradition of ritual practice and behavior. Its traditions are not even or stable, though, and my argument does not depend on a pattern of unbroken continuity. Periodically, the Order revises its formal statutes and makes changes to update its regulations, customs, and costumes, and there have also been several periods where the Order's traditions and rituals have sunk into disuse or been deliberately suspended. These changes constitute an intriguing register of the way the monarchy thinks of itself and its relation to its medieval past, over periods of civil and national war, religious strife, and longer patterns of social and cultural change. The Order sees itself as honoring its ritual traditions, but also as open to progressive stages of renewal in response to changing social expectations. As we will see in Chapter 5, however, it is also possible to write its history as one of disruption, decay, and radical reform. My principal concern throughout this book is with the changing valencies and representations of the medieval origins of the Garter in various discourses about its history and traditions. As the Order of the Garter is revived, reformed, and modernized, it bears the weight of both its medieval origins *and* later revivals, reformations, and modernizations. At any given moment, it is both medieval and modern, and many other things besides. It thus exemplifies the capacity of medievalism and its multiple, contradictory temporalities to destabilise a simple linear model of temporal and cultural progress.

In a recent essay, Louise D'Arcens coins the term "*para*modern" to describe the way premodern culture is sometimes invoked in contemporary critical theory, as "a premodern existing not before the modern, but alongside it and within it as a trace, a simultaneous presence and absence."[7] Drawing on Bruce Holsinger's concept of "theoretic medievalism," D'Arcens remarks: "Conceived as paramodern, the medieval period is thus in a synchronic rather than diachronic relationship with the modern."

I draw loosely on D'Arcens's insights here to suggest that the Order of the Garter similarly destabilizes diachronic history. Given its changing appearance over time, we might conceptualise the Order of the Garter as an example not of the "paramodern" but of the "paramedieval." The effect, however, is very different. My argument in *Shame and Honor* is that the medieval content of the fetish and its rituals actually lives on today as tradition, but that it is at the same time reformed in terms of modern sensibilities and temporalities. It is thus both synchronic *and* diachronic.

The Order of the Garter sometimes appears in medieval guise, then, but for most of its history, its clothes, feasts, and processions offer a layered mixture of inherited tradition, contemporary fashion, and deliberate revivalism.[8] Amid such contradictory markers of multiple temporalities, the medievalism of the Garter is manifested as a kind of "paramedieval," whereby its medieval origins sit "alongside it and within it as a trace, a simultaneous presence and absence."

Accordingly, this book works against conventional chronologies by suggesting that the postmedieval history of the Order of the Garter can help us understand its origins, most obviously in Chapter 2, which explores some of the deeper anthropological meanings of the Garter myth, but also in other chapters that explore the ritual life of medievalist objects, clothes, and patterns of behavior.

Shame and Honor investigates the ongoing cultural life of the Order of the Garter from the 1340s into the first decade of the twenty-first century. While there is a considerable body of historical material that discusses the Order, its practices are normally most fascinating not to outsiders but to itself, and those followers most in sympathy with its ideals or the symbolic, cultural, and traditional authority it seems to confer. The Garter's historians, heralds, followers, and modern Society of Friends are intimately and passionately concerned with its own traditions, its origins, its regulations, its dress code, and its membership: who was let in and why; and sometimes, who was expelled. Most histories of the Order are celebratory, written from the inside, as it were, or by admiring outsiders. They are concerned principally with setting the Order of the Garter at the heart of an ancient chivalric tradition, with extolling the continuities of this English order, or with tracing the biographies of its thousand-odd Companions. Recent years, however, have seen a number of more impartial scholarly studies, and I have drawn gratefully on them, particularly on those that focus on the specific details and politics of appointments to the Order and its role in court and state politics.[9]

Shame and Honor starts from different premises. While it is interested in the historical and political context of the Garter rituals, it is more closely concerned with the historiography of ritual practice: the different ways people think, talk, and write about the performance of those rituals, and especially the extent to which they are seen, or thought of, as medieval or medievalist, at different periods and in different contexts. Its concerns, then, are rarely biographical or straightforwardly sequential. Rather, cultural history and poetics take center stage here, as a means of measuring and analyzing the changing medievalism of the Garter.

Throughout its 650-year history, the Order has often performed a strategic balancing act between its appeal to the longevity of its medieval traditions and the question of its political, religious, and social relevance to the present. At other times it has been profoundly unconcerned with how it has been perceived by outsiders. The Order of the Garter has been written about, painted, and recorded in many forms. It has been heavily regulated, neglected, reviled, ridiculed, and revived. Above all, it has been performed and embodied in a range of fashions and styles, many of which actively downplay its medieval origins. In its current manifestation, the Garter represents neither a straightforward survival nor a simple revival of medieval practice.

Although its membership is tightly restricted, the Order nevertheless generates enormous symbolic resonance, and so the commentaries around its rituals offer a rich symptomatic register of social and cultural sensibility about the monarchy, about the nation, and about the relationship of the medieval past to the present.

Reading and analyzing the cultural history of this medieval institution thus calls for a flexible approach. As a "long history," *Shame and Honor* has affinities with other cultural histories that stretch from the present back to the Middle Ages, like studies of Chaucer's literary reception or Arthurian tradition. But it is not a straightforward or comprehensive narrative of the Order's history. Like my book on Chaucer's reading history, *Congenial Souls*, this book is what I call a *symptomatic long history*; it is especially interested in those moments when the Order of the Garter turns to examine its own traditions, or when changes in its rituals foreground the tension between inherited medieval tradition and the impulse to modernize those traditions.[10] Unlike Chaucer, however, the Order of the Garter has not generated a tradition of familiarity with a medieval figure. The presiding tropes in this tradition are not the sense of *knowing* Chaucer across the ages. Instead, they are tropes of *not* knowing, of mysterious and occluded origins and secret ritual practices.

As a study of changes in ritual practice, structural patterns are of greater importance than, for example, a prosopographical study of Garter membership, although I will sometimes consider the selection of members and the individual passage of several Companions into—and out of—the Order. To help orient readers to the overall shape of the Garter's long history, Chapter 1 presents an outline of the main features and changes in the Order's history, but I make a point of resisting the conventional diachronic narratives that characterize most celebratory and biographical accounts of the Garter. Unlike most such accounts, *Shame and Honor* also foregrounds imaginative literature and popular culture throughout.

In this book I deliberately set selected aspects of the Order's official history against some of the less official stories and patterns of its reception. I follow several partial diachronic trajectories in the first part and develop a number of thematic clusters in the second. I make no claim to offer a disinterested or comprehensive narrative; indeed, I often use as starting points those moments, events, or images that seem to jump out in their bizarreness and oddity. I also foreground the various manifestations of shame and honor in the Order's practices and its history, in contrast to the official insider's emphasis on the honor the Garter bestows and celebrates. The history offered here is thus a "vulgar history" in two senses. First, it is neither continuous nor comprehensive, but moves between historical and thematic approaches, bypassing the commemorative impulses of official histories and embracing many of the contingent aspects of ritual practice. Nor does this book examine all the literature, art, music, and drama associated with the Garter, but selects from a range of familiar and less well known texts. Second, *Shame and Honor* returns repeatedly to the myth of the woman's dropped garter, so often dismissed as a "vulgar" invention, both in its content, and in the form of its dissemination through gossip and rumor. The improper nature of this story is a means of exploring the persistent connections between the popular imagination, sexuality, and medievalism, writing from a position outside the official discourse of the Order.

Beyond the vulgar history of the Garter, this has also become a book about temporality and cultural allusion, the capacity of the Order, its costumes, its motto, and its practices to set up patterns of reference and allusion that move us back and forth in time, in and out of the charmed circle of "proper" or "historical" understandings of the Garter. The Order of the Garter struggles to speak directly to most of us. Yet as a survival of a medieval fraternity, its political and cultural traditions and the power structures they represent invite us to contemplate the ongoing life of the medieval into modernity and postmodernity, and that remains the ultimate aim of this book.

The book is organized in three parts. The first, "Ritual Histories," proceeds roughly chronologically. Chapter 1 introduces the concepts of ritual criticism, mythic capital, and medievalism. Reading the Order as a form of medievalist ritual practice allows me to focus attention on discussion of the medieval origins of the Order in Chapters 2 and 3, not simply as a historical question of sources and their witness, but also as an example of the curious, diverse, and ongoing life of the medieval. Chapter 2 explores what we know of the Order's first founding and the ritual meanings of its central mythology. Chapter 3 considers the first few hundred years of Garter histories, and the way those histories treat the medieval past.

The second part, "Ritual Practices," is organized more thematically. Three chapters range widely, back and forth between the fourteenth and twentieth centuries. Chapter 4 considers the concept of shame that shadows much of the

Order's ritual practice, a concept that makes it almost impossible to say where the medieval ends and the modern begins in Garter history, or where a Renaissance or modern understanding of shame replaces a medieval one. Chapter 5 examines the nature of ritual reform and change, the discourses used by the Order of the Garter when it engages most self-consciously in ritual criticism. Chapter 6 focuses on the embodied performance of the Order, in the fashions and regalia worn by its men and women, the ritual life of queer and gendered bodies, and the importance of the pictorial and visual tradition in the construction of the medieval.

The third part, "Ritual Modernities," in chapter 7, integrates these two approaches in order to consider the history of the Garter in the twentieth and twenty-first centuries, examining the implications for medievalism in the transition from the dominance of the modern to the emergence of the postmodern. The chapter analyzes this most medieval order's perpetual struggle for modern legitimation in the context of a faltering modernity, growing disenchantment with the authority of traditional symbols, and the increasingly blurred distinction between the historical Middle Ages and the compelling narratives and structures of medievalism.

PART I

Ritual Histories

Chapter 1

Ritual Theory and Medievalism

> On receipt of the command from Her Majesty I will proceed to the
> Legislative Assembly where the door is slammed in my face.
> —Australian state of Victoria's parliamentary Black Rod, 1954

The startling sentence that provides the epigraph to this chapter appears in
a typescript of several pages in the parliamentary archives of the Australian
state of Victoria.[1] The typescript probably dates from 1954, when the newly
crowned Queen Elizabeth II was making her first tour of Australia. The type-
written instructions seem to have been prepared by the Usher of the Black
Rod in preparation for the Queen's opening of the Victorian Parliament, on
a rare visit from the head of state. The text sets out the procedure, modeled
on Westminster parliamentary custom, whereby Black Rod summons the
members of the lower house to join the upper for a joint sitting to open
the parliamentary term. Calmly the document anticipates an act of violence
against its narrator.

This text represents a kind of fold or wrinkle in time. It brings together a
fourteenth-century institution with a seventeenth-century crisis at the twentieth-
century high point of royal popularity. The office of Black Rod was inaugurated by Edward III at Windsor in the 1350s, and was associated directly with
the Order of the Garter by 1399.[2] The Usher of the Black Rod is the chief officer in English and Commonwealth parliaments, a role matched in the United
States by an officer with the equally medieval title of Sergeant at Arms. Black
Rod's rejection by the lower house is of more recent origin and dates from the
dramatic events of 1642, when Charles I entered the chamber of the House
of Commons with an armed guard, seeking to arrest five of its members. The

attempt failed, and the members escaped. Since then no monarch has entered the Commons chamber during proceedings, a convention that in Australia is maintained both in the Federal Parliament and in those state parliaments that have two houses (all except Queensland). In this "Westminster tradition" the Usher of the Black Rod summons the members of the lower house to a joint sitting at the opening of every parliamentary session, but the door is customarily closed against him or her. He or she raps three times on the door with the rod of his or her office and gains admittance to deliver the invitation. The members then proceed to the upper house, although the manner of their moving sometimes reflects the tradition of rivalry between the two houses: there is a convention in Westminster, at least, according to which the members do not hasten but proceed quite slowly, to signal their legislative independence from both the monarch and the House of Lords.[3] It is a form of ceremonial practice in which many take great delight: the thirty-ninth session of the Victorian Parliament had already been opened by the Governor of Victoria in December 1952 after the general election, but the session was prorogued so that the time-honored ritual, with its tangible links to seventeenth-century England, could be performed again to celebrate the Queen's presence as head of state.[4]

This is the world of ritual practice, where actions that might seem either bizarre or perfectly ordinary in everyday reality are planned with formal precision and performed with great solemnity, where careful consideration is given to the smallest details and variations, and where active pleasure is taken in rehearsing gestures and words that might commemorate deeds, events, and words that took place or were spoken long ago. In this world time slows down, both to ensure that all parts of the ritual are enacted fully and to allow for communal meditation on the significance of the actions and events being recalled. It is a world where future events are predicted with the absolute certainty of the normative, cosmologically weighted present tense and passive voice: "where the door is slammed in my face." More specifically, it is the world of *historical* ritual practice, strongly mediated by cultural memory of a specific event, although ritual repetition has the distinctive capacity to transfigure what may be unpleasant, awkward, or embarrassing into something pleasant, formulaic, and honorable. The instructions prepared by the Victorian Black Rod in 1954 belong firmly to this world. Lovingly, the document embraces the idea of an insult or public shaming in the service of tradition and the fulfilment of the ritual. As we will see again and again in the history of the Order of the Garter, ritual practice often works to turn a moment of disruption, social embarrassment, or shame into the honor of immaculate theatrical or ritual performance.

I begin with this example for several reasons. I do not mean to suggest that the Order of the Garter currently enjoys the same authority as it did in the fourteenth century, or that the lines of continuity between the Order's first foundation and this colonial iteration are unbroken. In truth, they are worlds apart. Nevertheless, Black Rod's instructions are a symptomatic instance of Garter cultural history, from which it will be possible to tease out a number of questions and problems that thread through this book. I have also chosen an instance of ritual practice that is very far in geographical, historical, and cultural terms from the conventional starting points, trajectories, and parameters of Garter histories, as a sign of my own attempt to disrupt the rituals of conventional Garter historiography.

This chapter introduces some of the problems and challenges of the long history of the Garter, and some of the interpretive strategies that frame its discussions. It concludes with a brief history of the Order, to provide a diachronic frame for the work of subsequent chapters.

Rods and Rituals

In the world of ritual practice, the door *not* being slammed in Black Rod's face would represent an infraction of the customary rules and a transgression of the ritual norm. Most discussions of ritual stress their repetition and continuity, as if their meaning and significance emerge naturally from those elements that are successfully repeated on subsequent occasions. But the world of ritual practice is often also marked by disruption. Many will immediately think of Franz Kafka's parable of the leopards who break into the temple and drink from the sacrificial chalices so regularly that this incursion becomes predictable and is incorporated into the ceremonial ritual.[5] Kafka's parable has often been taken up by literary critics and theorists to deconstruct the once stable hierarchy of primary text and secondary commentary, but it also applies in quite practical terms to many rituals. The slamming of the door against Black Rod is a good example of a singular act of violence becoming a celebrated component of traditional practice. We might even argue that the myth of the dropped garter operates in the same way: the social ritual of a court dance threatens to collapse into chaos and disorder until the king rescues the occasion and promises to found a chivalric order in honor of the moment.

Moments of disruption are also of central importance to the practice of ritual commentary, although this importance sometimes emerges retrospectively.

For example, Paul Strohm shows how, after the deposition of Richard II, the pro-Lancastrian Adam of Usk "recalled" three incidents at Richard's coronation that he read as prefiguring the king's calamitous end: the boy had lost one of his coronation shoes, one of his golden spurs had fallen off, and a gust of wind was said, however implausibly, to have blown the crown from his head at the banquet. Strohm describes Usk's "imaginative construct, weaving actual and invented details into an explanatory pattern," whereby prophecies about the king's downfall were seen as starting to come true from the moment of the boy's coronation.[6] Thus the shameful aberration of a poor reign is absorbed into a grander narrative of national history and prophetic wisdom. In the same way, the "shameful" story of the Countess of Salisbury's garter will be absorbed into the rich contradictory traditions and modern reiterations of the Order.

Much later, and from the secondary perspective of ritual commentary, a messy performance can become an object lesson in a study of national character. James Robinson Planché, who was made Rouge Croix herald in 1854, writes of a bungled ceremony in 1856 that was designed to celebrate the peace between England and Russia after the Crimean War. As the junior pursuivant, Planché was supposed to demand entrance to the city of London at Temple Bar, but on his arrival, he found the gates on which he was supposed to knock had never been closed. "I was, consequently, obliged to send a trooper to call them back, and get the stupid people, whose business it was, to shut the gates in my face, that I might knock at them and have them opened again by the City Marshal, with the usual formalities, in obedience to my instructions."[7] Insisting on its repetition and correct performance may weaken the ritual somewhat, but it also underlines the commemorative symbolism of the protocol: the autonomy of the city. Planché introduces this anecdote with an intriguing reflection on the current state of English heraldic ritual and its implications for national identity: "It would have been quite un-English if such a ceremony had passed off without a blunder of some sort; and a most ludicrous one took place on this occasion." Even when the ritual performance fails it is still possible to recuperate a different version of honor by appealing to national sentiment and identity.

Planché's gloomy expectation of a ceremonial blunder may come as a surprise to those who associate English protocol with perfected form and military precision. It certainly contrasts with Victorian Black Rod's careful instructions in 1954. But as David Cannadine has demonstrated, the latter part of the nineteenth century and the early part of the twentieth saw dramatic improvements in the smooth performance of royal and parliamentary ritual, in both the United Kingdom and its former colonies.[8] I return to this aspect of royal ritual in Chapter 5.

The Victorian parliamentary document still seems strange. Black Rod's instructions set out what will happen and what he must do, although the ceremony is probably the best known of all his duties. The text renews the ritual in the present tense, independent of any given performance, and offers up its own distinctive language for commentary. The most significant word is the vehement "slammed." In contrast to the formal language of "receiving" commands and "proceeding" to the lower house, this vigorous instruction recalls the highly charged emotions that gave rise to the original action being commemorated ten thousand miles away and three hundred years later. The sound of slamming doors reverberates across space and time, but the text reminds the participants that ritual actions are best performed with dramatic immediacy. The passage of centuries should not seem to dilute the force of the action or its significance: by slamming the door, the members of the lower house can rehearse or perform the anger of their precedessors at the threat to parliamentary privilege in 1642. And by commemorating the action in equally strong language, this informal little document stakes its own claim to be considered part of the ritual and its associated traditions of rehearsal and performance. Its first-person narration, moreover, adds a singular dimension to the customary impersonality of historical ritual practice.

But as we will see repeatedly, rituals are often disrupted and changed. The Victorian Parliament had been inaugurated in 1856 but instituted the office of Black Rod only in 1951, just three years before the Queen's visit, when the Parliament celebrated the centenary of its first Legislative Council. The three-year-old Rod was of an elaborate design (including a bas-relief of St. George and the Dragon underneath its base), but the tip was made only of gold-covered plaster affixed to the wooden shaft. A wooden cap had been planned to protect the tip but was not ready, and the plaster tip would have shattered if it had struck the door. An information brochure from the Parliament tells us what happened in 1951: "Mr. Tierney strode to the door and, as had his predecessors since 1856, he instead struck the door three times with the heel of his shoe, thereby preserving the plaster Rod."[9] There are two historical paradoxes here: first, even without the office or the instrument of Black Rod, the Parliament had been practicing the ritual of summoning and rejection; and second, even though an Usher of the Black Rod had been appointed, his symbolic instrument of office could not be used for its most famous act.[10]

Mr. Tierney kicking at the door is exactly the kind of improvisation that characterizes mythological tradition, especially in Lévi-Strauss's reading, where the *bricoleur* fashions new ritual practices from what is at hand (or in this case, on foot), even if by doing so he seems to depart from tradition. The textual commentary here deepens and enhances this *bricolage*, transforming it into its own venerable century-old tradition: Black Rod "strode" to the door (there is no room for hesitancy in ritual performance), and when it was closed against him "struck" the door with his foot "as had his predecessors since 1856." As we find with many rituals, there is no single or pure tradition for Victoria's Black Rod. Original moments are layered over and over with subsequent variations in practice and meaning, whether motivated or contingent, while the language of reportage from within the ritual institution seeks to preserve the liveliness and immediacy of repeated actions.

The office of Black Rod is best known now for this commemorative ritual that carries the burden of substantive tension between the two Houses of Parliament (a tension that is a feature of Australian legislature and politics, since there is no guarantee that the government formed in the lower house will have a majority in the upper). Like many such offices in Commonwealth parliaments it has its origins in medieval court practice. In 1361 Walter Whitehors or Withors was granted 12d. per day to bear the Black Rod before the College of St. George's Chapel at Windsor when the King was present. The Usher of the Black Rod soon became the principal Usher in England. His formal duties included carrying the rod of his office before the King and the college at Windsor, and on rare occasions he would be called on to tap the shoulder of any knight who was to be degraded or dismissed from the Order of the Garter. His principal function, however, was to "keep the doors" of the Chapter House of the Order (or wherever the chapter was meeting) and also of the monarch's Council and Parliament.[11] If the Usher was not already a knight, he was knighted upon his appointment. This office has persisted from the medieval period into modernity, while its ushers and rods, its officials and ritual objects, multiplied across the British Empire and Commonwealth as a significant link with an English past and the constitutional traditions (and tensions) of its Parliament.

These links are not straightforward, of course; the customary uniform of the Usher is often a version of seventeenth-century court dress, known as Windsor Court Uniform, while most Black Rods and maces in Commonwealth parliaments in Australia, Canada, and elsewhere register subtle differences from their original by using native timbers and ornamental designs drawing on native flora (for example, fiddleback blackwood for Victoria's Black Rod, instead of Westminster's ebony).[12]

On February 12, 2008, for the first time in Australian history, Aboriginal leaders were invited to offer a "Welcome to Country" at the opening of the Federal Parliament. The juxtaposition could not have been more striking between Matilda House-Williams, in her possum-skin cloak, and the Usher of the Black Rod, Andrea Griffiths, striding in her neat black suit from the upper house to beat on the doors of the lower, her heels clicking authoritatively across the empty hall. The next day, representatives of the Stolen Generations (Aboriginal children taken from their families and placed in institutional care or foster families) accepted the apology for past laws and practices and the "pain, suffering, and hurt" inflicted on generations of Aboriginal families. The apology was offered on behalf of the Parliament and the government by the prime minister, Kevin Rudd. During the ceremony the Speaker of the House was presented with a coolamon (a long, multipurpose bowl sometimes used for carrying babies), and at least one broadcaster speculated that this might now take its place with the ceremonial mace on the table between the two sides of the House when it is in session.[13] This commemorative coolamon is made of glass and is currently on public display in Members' Hall, along with the "Apology Manuscript," an illuminated vellum manuscript of the prime minister's speech, prepared by calligrapher Gemma Black to commemorate the national apology: a further example of the naturalized association of public ceremonial with the art and culture of the Middle Ages.[14]

It is easy to see how institutions and rituals can change, and yet still allude to older medieval origins. If a female Black Rod, eschewing the traditional breeches, long coat, marcasite buckles, and lace jabot and cuffs, beats on the door of the lower house chamber to commemorate a seventeenth-century parliamentary crisis, she is building yet another layer onto medieval and early modern tradition. This dialectic between old and new, medieval and modern, is a feature of both Garter history and medievalism more generally. These fragments from the Australian history of Black Rod remind us that medievalism continues to inform the way modern culture thinks about and reinvents tradition at the highest level of government.

When we think of medievalism it is easy to focus on its most obvious manifestations in fantasy film and fiction, in Gothic revival architecture, the costumes and armor, the arts and crafts of reenactment groups, and the perpetual reinvention of the medieval in opera, ballet, art, television, fashion, and advertising. But in addition to providing conceptual structures, narratives, and images to the worlds of the historical imagination and of fantasy, medievalism also permeates many public and state rituals. Moreover, in its most general form as the idea and the practice of looking back to the medieval past, medievalism also has important precursors in the Middle Ages. The Order of the Garter can play an exemplary role in demonstrating the longevity but also the traditional and modern dynamics of those traditions. A few years prior to founding the Order in 1348, Edward III also founded a Round Table at Windsor as a deliberate and self-conscious Arthurian revival and a fulfilment of his grandfather's Arthurian aspirations.[15] This provided a framework and a context for the much more successful Order of the Garter. These two closely associated institutions show us how deeply medievalism is entrenched within some of the earliest origins of English court ritual. Even the Garter's medieval rituals, then, are medievalist.

Ritual Theory, Medievalism, and Mythic Capital

Medievalism is often defined by its secondary nature and status. Its texts, images, and objects not only come after the historical Middle Ages; they are also usually characterized as derivative, imperfect imitations or copies, hopelessly seeking to recapture the plenitude of a lost past. In scholarly terms, too, medievalism is often seen as the poor relation of traditional medieval studies, a secondary and intellectually impoverished field when compared with an apparently more robust scholarly discipline. Medieval purists will not often admit to a prejudice against popular culture, but there is little doubt that a conventional cultural hierarchy continues to structure the status of medieval literature and popular medievalism as objects of scholarly inquiry. Much recent work in the field of medievalism studies attempts to bring the study of medievalist texts into closer relationship with medieval studies proper, and to articulate a more productive relationship between the two academic fields. Medievalism studies have also begun to engage in more robust debate over questions of periodization, especially the various critical and ideological investments that insist on the radical difference or alterity between the medieval and the early modern. Medievalism studies also foreground the ontological and epistemological issues at stake in the rigorous separation of medievalism from the medieval.[16] In what sense can the Middle Ages be said to be completely in the past, for example, when we still regularly use the adjective "medieval" as a disapproving synonym for outdated forms of modern technology or the religious and cultural practices of our enemies?[17]

These are complex questions for historical, literary, and cultural studies, with the potential to destabilize some persistent disciplinary and temporal hierarchies between the historical past and the present, between high culture and popular culture, and between historical events and ongoing ritual practice.

The relationship between tradition, modernity, and medievalism is a complex one for the Order of the Garter as a medieval institution that has survived into the present. An instructive instance is the question of the Garter's medieval origins. For a cultural institution that prides itself on its longevity and historical continuity, the Order of the Garter's origins are surprisingly obscure, the subject of heated debate among its early historians in the sixteenth and seventeenth centuries. Neither its chief insignia—the blue Garter—nor its enigmatic motto yields its significance or meaning with ease to the casual observer, while appeals to historical record or the motivations of Edward III, the Order's founder, provide answers that are either problematic or unpalatable to many inquirers. The traditional explanation—that Edward III founded the order in honor of a garter he had courteously retrieved after it had fallen from a lady's leg as she was dancing—is recounted in great detail in Joanot Martorell's fifteenth-century romance, *Tirant lo Blanc*, though this work was not widely circulated. The sixteenth-century historian Polydor Vergil offers a similar explanation in his *Anglica Historia*, but many later historians and antiquarians have been scathing in their dismissal of his account, largely because Vergil says he takes popular tradition as his source. It is not clear whether Vergil knew Martorell's romance. No specific occasion for its founding is mentioned in any of the Order's early records, and many commentators remain reluctant to associate this great chivalric order with such a "vain and idle romance," as Peter Heylyn called it in 1652. There are a number of medieval analogues that lend the story greater plausibility, but regardless of the truthfulness of this account, the story of the lady's garter persists in the popular historical imagination as a powerful myth of origins. For this reason, it plays a major part in the cultural history of the Order, though this role has not always sat comfortably with the Garter's military and diplomatic orientation. These disputed origins will help us consider the shape and the limits of the medieval, as well as the ways in which the medieval is used, again and again, to bolster modernity's sense of itself as *non*medieval, whenever it exercises critical judgment about the medieval past. This question is taken up in Chapter 3.

A related set of tensions is played out in the perpetual negotiations

between ritual repetition and change in the Order. The Order prides itself on
its continuity, or at least its longevity, but oscillates between wanting to appeal
to medieval tradition and wanting to "renew" its rites to suit the demands of
modernity. We may read these dynamics in reforms to the electoral process, the
periodic revival of its ceremonial processions, and changes to the clothes and
fashions that are worn to accompany the insignia. The reforming process becomes most urgent in moments of constitutional and religious crisis, as in the
reigns of Edward VI and Mary Tudor, as well as the interregnum in the seventeenth century, or whenever this chivalric, ostensibly military order is presided
over by a queen, as in the sixteenth, nineteenth, and twentieth centuries. On
a smaller scale, too, the Order periodically undergoes moments of uncertainty
or anxiety over its traditional inheritance, an anxiety that finds expression in
piecemeal changes to ritual dress, behavior, or rules about membership.

The Order has a long history of interrogating and modifying its own
rules. For example, how close did a Companion need to pass by St. George's
Chapel at Windsor before he was obliged to come and hear Mass there? What
did a Companion have to do to be expelled from the Order? What kind of
clothing is appropriate to wear with a blue garter tied below one's left knee, or
above one's left elbow? What role could women play in the nation's preeminent chivalric order of knighthood? How many of his sons and foreign allies
could a king nominate as Companions?

The medievalism of the Garter, then, is not simply derivative, not simply
a set of modified repetitions of a medieval inheritance. In debates about such
minutiae, the medieval origins of the Order are often problematic. At times
they appear to be venerable sources of authority; at times they seem merely
arcane or even downright embarrassing. The cultural valency of the Middle
Ages similarly rises and falls according to whether the Order's medieval past is
valued as a tradition to be revived, recovered, and lovingly rehearsed, or deval-
ued as the archaic remnant of a bygone era, to be superseded by such actions
and reforms as will demonstrate the modernity and contemporary relevance
of the institution. The Order has developed some very distinctive conventions
and patterns for the performance of its rituals, from its royal ceremonies and
processions to its procedures of election, selection, investiture, and installation of Companions; its rites of degradation and dismissal; and its insignia,
robes, and conventions of dress. Over its long history, the Order has learned
how to manage several different religious, cultural, and gendered inflections
of the Order instated under a succession of kings and queens; how to preside
over its rich cultural life; how to manage the political vicissitudes of its patron

saint, George; and in particular, how to develop the processes and procedures by which it can reform and renovate itself. There is thus an elaborate form of cultural and temporal exchange between the Order of the Garter and those who observe it, whether in sympathy, with dispassionate historical interest, or with mockery. With every procession, with every new appointment, and also with every cultural allusion, joke, or historical study, the Order of the Garter has the potential to reshape our understanding of both the Middle Ages and modernity.

Of course, there are many differences between the cultural forms of the Middle Ages and those of postmedieval times. The Order is founded on an unambiguous contrast between chivalric honor and shame, but the nature of the honor and shame it bestows or withholds has been dramatically transformed over the centuries. There is a world of difference, for example, between the shame visited on a fifteenth-century Companion dismissed from the Order and formally "degraded" before being executed for treason against a king whose right to rule he disputed, and the shame experienced by a Japanese emperor whose letter of appointment to the Order was quietly annulled by royal dispensation in 1941.

As with many other royal institutions, the Order's chief significance in the cultural and social life of the nation in the twenty-first century lies in its symbolic force as a historical tradition, deriving its authority as much, if not more, from its longevity as from the political or social authority of its membership. Its annual procession at Windsor, all blue velvet cloaks and white ostrich feathers, is a significant component of the royal and heritage tourism industry, worth millions of pounds to the British economy. As a form of ritual, the Order of the Garter has far more observers than participants. From the outside, whether one stands with the royal fans to watch the procession pass by or scans the images that circulate the globe within minutes of the Queen's passing, it looks a lot like dressing up, wearing the elaborate costumes of a bygone era for mysterious purposes comprehended fully only by the insiders, but making a grand spectacle, a sign of "tradition" and "ceremonial" of the kind it is generally agreed the English are now expert in.[18] The Order compels attention as a form of ritual practice, though without inviting participation or communal sharing of its rites.

In contrast to many religious, political, or social rituals (for example, coronations, elections, and royal weddings), the Order of the Garter does not offer the kind of social cohesion that many anthropologists and sociologists emphasize as the effect or the aim of ritual practice. Its full ceremonies and rites are hardly the stuff of prime-time television coverage or widespread social identification with the monarchy: rather, they are reported as ceremonial curiosities, glimpses into the lives of the royal family, or sightings of past prime ministers or newly installed members.

Nevertheless, they do participate in a limited degree of social modelling. As Edward Muir comments in his study of early modern ritual practice, "When public officials calmly walk in an ordered procession they model the behavior expected of them in the conduct of the affairs of state."[19] In the same vein, Roy Strong describes the ritual significance and "glittering, glamorous, effulgent" spectacle of the Queen's coronation in 1953 as "the perfect microcosm of a country that has always opted for evolution and not revolution."[20] Muir explains, however, that it is sometimes hard to tell whether rituals "model" idealized behavior or "mirror" the reality of behavior: "Rituals tend to blur these two processes, which is perhaps the very source of the creative tension in rituals, the tension between a conservative mirroring of what is and the utopian behavior of what might be."

For Mircea Eliade, ritual abolishes history, replacing linear time with circular time, suspending "profane time and duration."[21] The opposition he assumes here is unduly simplified: much of the cultural weight of historical, commemorative rituals, at least, depends on the multiple layering of different linear and circular temporalities. Nevertheless, traditional time as such is more obviously evident in religious rituals that express spiritual or eschatological truths for their participants, or even a coronation ceremony, which seeks to be a moment of national union. In contrast, the Order of the Garter is coded as both historical and commemorative, on the one hand, and allegorical and timeless, on the other. Its medievalism is similarly tied to the Middle Ages while also offering a shifting, mutable signifier, available for the endless reinventions of postmedieval culture. The Garter's traditional symbols affirm its behavior, while the fact that its members are selected on "merit," subject to the will of the Sovereign, disqualifies it from any symbolic, unifying national or microcosmic role. The Order's rituals participate in a national mythology similar to that of a coronation ceremony, but they are very different from more inclusive social or political rituals like elections, national sporting events, or royal weddings, funerals, and coronations that strive to incorporate the citizens into the communal or sacred participation in the idea of the state. Because the Order of the Garter is so restricted, because it is inextricably tied to its contested medieval origins, and because its political and strategic role has been almost completely displaced by its importance on the calendar of royal tourism, it hardly participates in the same kind of nation formation as these festivals of broader interest. On the other hand, its more restricted field of ritual performance is complemented by a rich mythical narrative and a powerful cultural afterlife in the tradition of medievalism.

As is the case with many rituals, the origins of the Garter are disputed, but in all the rival accounts of its inaugural moments, there is a structural insistence on the King's secular power to make meaning from a small, even trivial event or item, whether this is a woman's garter or, as many insist, a small strap or miniature buckled belt. This transformation of a small object is one of the hallmarks of ritual practice. The Order's forms are embedded in religious tradition, but the question of origins always returns us to the resolutely secular and rarefied world of medieval chivalry, where a buckled belt or a woman's garter or sleeve can inspire a knight to greater heights of chivalric display and military strength.

The play between the historical and the mythic dynamics of the Order's origins is ongoing. Whatever the truth about Edward III's designs, the dominant myth that circulates about the founding moments cannot easily be dismissed. It thematizes courtly laughter at the lady's and then at the king's expense, but ends with his immediate and dramatic reclamation of his own authority. It is a story of risk that is quickly and safely resolved. Yet the consistent pattern of reluctance to give credence to this story is part of a different, secondary history of perpetual risk to the dignity of the Order and the narrative and symbolic danger of its popular myth of origins. Retrospectively, the weird temporalities of medievalism and the undiminished popularity of this story allow us to see that its mythical transfiguration of the quotidian may even partly account for the longevity of the Order itself, not just its social and cultural resonance. A persistent structural theme in the Order's history is the juxtaposition of the triviality of the countess's garter and the obliqueness of the Order's motto against the formal dignity of most of its proceedings and their repetition across the centuries.

Even setting aside the question of origins, the Order must constantly traverse the liminal territory between the solemn and the trivial. Its Companions transcend the possibility of laughter at their outlandish costumes by their silent invocation of the Order's tradition and longevity. All rituals are susceptible to critique for their arcane qualities, their insistence on elaborate formalities and symbolic practices that threaten to obscure their original meaning or intent. In Protestant culture, in particular, it is difficult to separate the social criticism of ritual from the Reformation suspicion of ornate, ritualized worship. These divisions and tensions are crucial components of ritual and mythological practice, though the official discourse of the Order makes no such concessions. Accordingly, its attempts to regulate its own mythologies and to reform itself from within constitute a fascinating sequence of engagements with the medieval past and its meaning for the present.

The field of ritual theory is a relatively new one. There is much debate in the fields of anthropology, sociology, religious studies, and literary studies about what constitutes a ritual: the relationship between ritual and belief, and between ritual and ceremony. Is ritual behavior primarily expressive or performative? What is the role of the individual or socialized body in such rituals? Or the role of the ritual scholar as impartial observer or as audience?[22] These debates are often played out in the intersection between "history" and "cultural memory" studies, and equally fraught dialogues between history and a cluster of disciplines from anthropology and sociology to religious studies and philosophy.[23]

Under the influence of Michel Foucault, Pierre Bourdieu, and others, contemporary ritual theory often moves beyond the classical study of the rites of tribal societies or religious and spiritual ritual to direct its attention to modern secular and political practices, from the public drama of political campaigns to the quotidian routines of work practices.[24] I do not attempt in this book to synthesize these developments or to propound a new theory of ritual practice as such. Rather, I work outward from a very restricted set of historical rituals dating back to the middle of the fourteenth century to examine the implications of chivalric ritual practice for the ongoing life of medievalist tradition and heritage in English culture.

The role of the medieval in the understanding of English tradition and heritage, across a range of cultural forms, representations, and practices, is not always fully recognized. The medieval, for example, makes very few appearances in Raphael Samuel's *Theatres of Memory,* David Lowenthal's *The Past Is a Foreign Country,* or Paul Connerton's *How Societies Remember.* In his essay in Hobsbawm and Ranger's *The Invention of Tradition,* David Cannadine is little interested in the medieval aspect of the rituals that revived the public image of the British monarchy in the years before World War I.

By training and inclination, my work springs from the central concerns of literary and medievalism studies, but I draw close inspiration from Ronald Grimes's *Ritual Criticism* and his attention to the way groups analyze and criticize their own rituals, even if textuality is not his chief focus. Grimes names as "ritual criticism" the endless cycles of debates and discussions *about* rites and ceremonies, by both the participants in and the observers of such ritual events.[25] Such discussions are seen not as extraneous commentary *on* the ritual but as part of the ritual itself. Ritual criticism is not only the preserve of academic or professional discourse from outside, from an anthropological or sociological perspective; it is also the practice of commentary, reform, and evaluation from within, among the participants and members of the group, at all levels from the most formal legal statute concerning the coronation of a monarch to the drawn-out planning of a wedding and its postmortem with friends and family over the photographs and videos afterward.

Grimes's insights into ritual criticism inform my reading of the Order's historical traditions, helping me analyze its verbal, textual, and visual memorials in a way that I hope is attentive to the ritual dynamics of the Order and the way it negotiates change, especially with reference to its medieval traditions. But I draw a rather wider frame of reference, in that I am not principally concerned with the Order's membership and the performance of its rituals of installation and its annual feast and procession at Windsor. I am also interested in the broader cultural context in which the Order and its medieval origins are discussed by outsiders—and not just academic commentators—in all historical periods. I am interested in the contribution of this medieval ritual to our understanding of medievalism.

"Medievalism" is a troublesome term in some disciplinary and institutional contexts, being used variously as (1) a synonym for medieval studies, (2) the uncritical invocation of the medieval as a cultural ideal, and (3) a more neutral term to name the study of such invocations. Its problematic nature is symptomatic of its utility, though, for its uncertainty suggests precisely that shifting territory between the purely historical and the mythical invocation or deployment of the historical that I have in mind. Alternatively, we might say that medievalism mediates between the official documented history of the medieval period and the subsequent popular understanding or knowledge of that history and between the idea of the medieval as a historical and as a mythological or cultural category. I am particularly interested in the multiple temporalities of medievalism: the way we carry medieval forms into a sequence of different presents, with all the cultural and ideological contradictions this entails. The Order of the Garter's long history of ritual practice confounds any easy historical opposition between the medieval and the postmedieval, as successive traditions and modifications of tradition are layered over each other, producing the curious temporalities of medievalism. This is particularly visible in the history of Garter costume, as we will see in Chapter 6. More generally, medievalist texts and practices do not simply "represent" the medieval past; they actively shape our memories of that past and its relationship to the present.

A fittingly trivial but telling example is provided by Sellar and Yeatman, who in 1931 published their parodic spoof of English history books, *1066 and All That*, which defines history as "all the parts you can remember." Their page on the Order of the Garter (figure 3) shows a king kneeling at the feet of an embarrassed court lady whose garter has fallen to her ankle, whereupon the king "made the memorable epitaph: 'Honi soie qui mal y pense' ('Honey, your silk stocking's coming down')" and gave the offending courtiers the Order of the Bath ("an extreme form of torture in the Middle Ages").[26] So powerful is

Figure 3. "Honey, your silk stocking's coming down." © Methuen & Co.

this story in the history of everything the English student remembers that it also appears on the frontispiece, as "Magna Garter," with the king raising his hands in titillated delight at the sight of an elegant lady lifting her gown to reveal the garter in place below her left knee (figure 4).

This pleasure in the more salacious aspects of the Garter myth reminds us that sex and vulgarity are precisely what we do remember about history, about royal history in particular (even though we might "misremember" the spelling or translation of a heraldic motto). Unofficial histories like this play a powerful role in both the national memory and the medievalist imagination, and

Figure 4. Magna Garter. © Methuen & Co.

cannot easily be ignored. At its best, the study of medievalism helps us make sense of what we like to remember about the medieval past and what we like to forget. Ritual practice, similarly, is closely concerned with commemoration: the remembering and the forgetting of ritual components.

This book, then, is not a purely anthropological study of the meaning of the Garter rituals. Nor is it a historical, diachronic study of all the changes in those rituals over six and a half centuries. It ranges freely and unevenly across those centuries, picking out particular moments where the Garter traditions examine themselves or undergo minor or radical change, or when historians, heralds, artists, poets, and novelists invoke the Order's imagery or rituals. This book does not provide comprehensive discussion of the Order's membership, or a systematic account of its development, or of all the changes in its forms, costumes, and processes of election. But it does seek to make sense of this survival of medieval court practice through many great vicissitudes, testing the thesis that this continuous ritual form, for all its exceptionality and marginality, nevertheless helps us chart the work of medievalism: what we *do* with the medieval, and how we measure its value in and influence on postmedieval culture.

The Order and its historians do not acknowledge it, but the disputes and disagreements about its origins have the important effect of enhancing what I call the Order's "mythic capital." A metaphorical spin-off from Pierre Bourdieu's notion of symbolic capital, mythic capital is a way of conceptualizing and measuring the exchange value of cultural institutions that invoke a significance deeper and more resonant than a simple historical or contemporary political one, either by deliberate analogy with other religious, national, or ethnic traditions, or as in the case of the Garter, through the mystification—the mythmaking—of origins.[27] The fact that the Garter's origins are now unrecoverable with certainty has the effect of enhancing both its mystique and its historical distance: its past promises to shade off beyond historical into mythic time, implying a kind of human truth about the behavior of the king and the lady. The mythic incident is explicable both as an example of medieval courtesy—the royal defiance expressed in the French motto—*and* as a generous act of social grace: after such embarrassment, such rescue and such honor. Each time the origins of the Order are disputed, mythic capital is accumulated. Even, or perhaps especially, when its participants and adherents find the story of the lady and her garter "lunatic," this builds up the mystery and the mythic force of the Order.

The process of accumulating mythic capital is not a conscious one. Nor was it a possibility during the medieval era of the Garter. It is only when the medieval threatens, or promises, to disappear from view, only when a sense of modernity is layered over inherited, traditional forms, that the possibility of accruing symbolic capital from historical uncertainty arises. It is furthermore a paradoxical concept: to draw self-consciously upon mythic capital is to dissolve its power, resulting in such decidedly *un*mythical comments like the Duke of Edinburgh's description of the ritual as "lunatic," or Black Rod's pedantic instructions to himself. I use the term to accentuate the twinned effect of collective, institutional action and the cultural allusions and citations that constitute the Garter's cultural history. In this process, the medieval components of the Order are often deployed in ways that transcend their historical context and shift into the mythical realm. A telling sign of this shift is the uncertainty over the identity of the woman at the heart of the foundational myth: whom does the phrase "the Countess of Salisbury" truly name? Eliade remarks upon the "anhistorical [*sic*] character of popular memory, the inability of collective memory to retain historical events and individuals except insofar as it transforms them into archetypes," and suggests that this "mnemonic lacuna" might even reveal the secondary character of historical, as opposed to mythic, narratives.[28] The general vagueness about the identity of this woman is a register of the story's shift from medieval historical time into the mythic time of medievalism.

In such mythical contexts, if the word "medieval" is invoked, it is rarely with any historical precision, any more than it is in the imaginary medieval origins of the seventeenth-century Order of the Thistle, or the vaguely medieval conception of the eighteenth-century Order of the Bath.[29] This will come as no surprise to scholars of medievalism, who know that "the medieval" can name both a precise historical moment *and* a mythic structure and context. It is more problematic for the purists of historical medieval studies, who prefer to see their period free from its mythical and popular culture associations. However, it is an important part of the work of medievalism studies to find ways of balancing the rival historical and mythical claims of medievalism.

Very rarely does the Order of the Garter invoke its mythological aspect explicitly. For the most part, it is comfortable with the image of itself as a historical entity, or as a form of contemporary practice. In its self-conscious rules and regulations, in its religious and ritual practices, in its various acts of religious and political reformation, it customarily presents itself as a medieval English tradition whose origins and continuance derive from the specific acts of historical individuals, especially its kings and queens. Yet many of its structures accord closely with mythological or social rituals conducive to being read in anthropological terms. Such readings are unusual: the reception and scholarly discussion of the Order take place within a relatively restricted range dominated by historians, heralds, and scholars of court politics, whose preoccupations are principally with royal polity, the prosopography of the Order's membership, and so on. Beyond the world of heraldry and scholarship, however, there are a number of other attitudes to the Order, some of which we will have occasion to consider at greater length in this book, in the work of the poets and novelists who glorify or mock the Order's traditions, individuals, and practices; the painters and cartoonists who depict its members in flattering or less than flattering ways; the writers of memoirs; the satirists and gossips; the journalists who present thirty-second summaries of the Order's traditions and regalia when introducing a news item. Paying critical attention to the Order's mythologizing and ritual aspects makes it possible to move with some freedom between these positions: one does not have to be a royalist, or to *believe* in the Order, to write about it, or to find it a fascinating object of study.

Ritual History

The intricacies of individual Garter appointments lie outside my concerns in this book, and I do not present a continuous chronological history of the Order. Nevertheless, in spite of my desire to break with the ritual historiography of the Garter, it may still be useful for me to outline the Order's chief features and key transitional moments, to provide some points of orientation for the chapters that follow.

Since its foundation in the 1340s the Order of the Garter has been the highest honor in the gift of the Sovereign. Membership has normally been restricted to twenty-five Companions at any one time, in addition to the Sovereign, though numbers in the ranks have occasionally swelled with the inclusion of additional appointments from within the royal family, from the ranks of European royalty, and with the inclusion of the Emperor of Japan, Yoshihito, in 1912. The appointments of foreign members—sometimes called "Stranger Knights"—are often occasions of major diplomatic missions abroad or receptions in England, particularly at Windsor. In the fourteenth and fifteenth centuries, wives and daughters of the Garter knights were often given Garter robes, and may have taken part in some of its festivities, but such appointments ceased in the reign of Henry VIII, and this custom was not revived until 1901, when Queen Alexandra joined the order. It was only in 1987 that women were able to become full Companions of the Order, joining the women of the royal family who have been invited to join as supernumerary members.

It is important to distinguish between the more or less unbroken tradition of appointments to the Order (Prince William became its thousandth Companion in 2008) and the much greater variation in the political and social importance of the Order, and even the performance of its most important celebrations and rituals. The Order's history can appear deceptively continuous, particularly when it is celebrated in the list of members whose names decorate St. George's Hall at Windsor Castle, or in the twenty-two-page appendix of Begent and Chesshyre's study. The history of its ritual practice, and indeed the history of its social, political, and cultural impact, is much more diverse.

For example, there are three phases in the full process of becoming a member: election or appointment to the Order; investiture, in which the Sovereign presents the new member with the regalia of the Order and dubs as a knight any who do not already enjoy that honor; and finally, the "installation" of new knights, when they are escorted to their allotted stall in the choir during the annual service at St. George's Chapel, currently held in June. However, there are many periods in Garter history where installations were not held at all, when the elaborate services and feasts were not held. There was a lapse of thirty years in the last three decades of the eighteenth century—years marked by episodes of George III's illness—when the number of knights who had been formally installed in the Chapel was reduced to six, though others had received their insignia directly from the hands of the Sovereign. In 1801, the King issued letters patent to twenty-one knights, including six of his sons, dispensing with their installation so that they could still enjoy the full honors and privileges of the Order.[30] But between 1805 and 1948 there were no further installations. Instead, Companions were merely "invested" in private ceremonies or at court, although these ceremonies were often quite lavish, especially for foreign members. In 1906, Edward VII invested King Hakon of Norway with the Order of the Garter at Windsor Castle, in a grand ceremony "on exactly the same lines as when the Emperor Napoleon and King Victor Emanuel were invested there."[31]

Annual meetings have not always been held, either, while the procedures for electing and appointing knights of the Garter have also varied. Most dramatically, during the interregnum, Charles II dispensed with the regular elections. He nominated sixteen knights of the Garter while he was in exile, deferring their installations until after his restoration to the monarchy in 1660, when he inaugurated one of the most magnificent periods of Garter ceremonial. But the system of election has often not been fully observed. The earliest surviving statutes, from 1415, refer to the "election" of knights, and elections on different models have been held at different times, but it was always understood that the Sovereign "was not required to select the candidate with the most votes."[32] Some detailed records of voting patterns still survive in the Garter archives (the latest are from 1790 and 1791), but Queen Victoria, most notably, showed little interest in holding elections, and the last formal election was held in 1860. Recommendations for new members were received from the prime minister, sometimes on the advice of Parliament, but it was not until 1953 that Elizabeth II formally abandoned elections and affirmed the Sovereign's right to "declare" new members Knights Companions.

Such cycles of institutional and ritual change move more slowly than cycles of institutional politics: successive monarchs and royal dynasties have made dramatically different use of the Order and the potential it offers for distributing shame and honor. At times these activities have taken place in a festive atmosphere of chivalric revivalism; at other times the demands of court or of national or international relations have propelled a more actively political deployment of the honors system.

Edward III designed the Order of the Garter to provide an occasion for chivalric display at home, and to consolidate military achievement abroad, as he pressed his claim to the French crown. But as Hugh Collins has shown, even in the first phase of its history the Garter was also "an instrument of political patronage," in which military and chivalric considerations were often mixed with political ones when it came to making appointments.[33] As the war with France gave way to the wars of succession between the Lancastrians and the Yorkists, membership of the Order, and the possibility of being dismissed or degraded from it, became increasingly politically motivated.

Henry VII and Henry VIII both drew on the Garter's Arthurian associations to bolster the Tudor claims to the royal succession, though Henry VIII increasingly used the Garter as a political reward for loyal courtiers, especially the members of his Privy Chamber. In contrast, Elizabeth I's Privy Chamber was largely female, and so she used membership in the Garter as her father had used the Privy Councillors: as a privileged group of advisers.[34]

The early Stuart court maintained the traditions of Tudor chivalric culture, but Charles I allowed the practice of tournaments to lapse, as these outward manifestations of military medievalism became increasingly unfashionable. Instead, the Carolingian court celebrated "not merely martial valour but sacred loyalty and idealised moral virtue."[35]

After the Restoration of the monarchy in 1660, Charles II used the Order to reward those who had remained loyal to him, and reinstituted many of its most lavish customs, ceremonials, and costumes. This was also the period in which Elias Ashmole, Windsor Herald at Arms, compiled his magisterial history of the Order, *The Institution, Laws and Ceremonies of the Most Noble Order of the Garter*, published in 1672. Ashmole was concerned to restore stability and continuity to the Order, and in part as a result of his history, the "institutional and ceremonial framework of the Order was hardly altered at all during the century following the Restoration."[36]

The decades after the Restoration also saw the institution of the Order of the Thistle under James II in 1687 (revived again under Queen Anne in 1703), complete with its imaginary medieval origins; and in 1725, the Order of the Bath, under George I, on the inspiration of John Anstis, Robert Walpole, and the Duke of Montagu. Anstis himself wrote the *Observations Introductory to an Historical Essay upon the Knighthood of the Bath* in 1725, a year after he had published his heavily annotated two-volume edition and translation of the Latin Register of the Garter, the Black Book (*Liber Niger*) compiled in the reign of Henry VIII and currently held at Windsor.

The Order of the Bath at least had medieval antecedents in the medieval ceremony of knighthood, attested and vividly illustrated in the late fifteenth- and early sixteenth-century manuscript of John Writhe's *Garter Book*.[37] One of the intentions behind the foundation of the Order of the Bath was to relieve pressure on the restricted numbers of the Order of the Garter; the new order was conceived in part as a stepping-stone to the older and more prestigious order of knighthood.[38] Appointments to all three Orders—Garter, Thistle, and Bath—were in high demand in this period. Matikkala coins the phrase the "Chivalric Enlightenment" to describe this century, from 1660 to 1760, a period that witnessed "a government-supported rhetorical and antiquarian notion of chivalry, which aimed at historical accuracy but was not meant to be taken literally."[39]

This was nevertheless a period of considerable instability in English politics, especially in the relationships between the monarch and an increasingly dynamic and contested parliamentary party system. Cannadine reminds us that "even if the text of a repeated ritual like a coronation remains unaltered over time, its 'meaning' may change profoundly depending on the nature of the context."[40] Conventional Garter histories that only look inward, to the text and scripts of ritual performance, sometimes give a distorted view of the "continuity" of the Order.

By way of a contrasting example, R. O. Bucholz draws attention to the transitional nature of Queen Anne's reign, half-way through the century of Matikkala's study. On her accession, and in the first few years of her reign, the Queen used royal progresses, Garter services, and ceremonies of thanksgiving for military victories, often modeled on Tudor pageantry, in an attempt to lift the monarchy above partisan politics and to generate "widespread participation and apparent popular approval [for] a regime fighting a costly and often unpopular war."[41] Yet as the Queen's health deteriorated—her gout making public appearances almost impossible—and as her finances suffered in the expense of a war on foreign soil, more and more public events were canceled. Moreover, in Bucholz's words, the experience of attending her impoverished court at St. James "may actually have undermined, for those members of the ruling class who did so, the very sentiments of loyalty and reverence that the queen's out-of-doors appearance was designed to instill."[42] Bucholz suggests that Anne both looked back to an era of past chivalry while also inadvertently prefiguring a modern era, "presiding over a court that embodied the middle-class values of thrift, sobriety, moderation, and decorum."[43]

The ceremonial history of the Order of the Garter underwent severe disruption in the eighteenth and most of the nineteenth centuries, a period in which the love of pageantry espoused by the medieval, Tudor, and Stuart regimes and their autocratic rulers fell out of favor. The Hanoverian monarchs did occasionally conduct formal Garter ceremonies, including the degradation of James Butler, Duke of Ormonde, in 1716, and the elaborate service in which George II assumed his royal stall in St. George's Chapel in 1728.[44] A number of significant foreign appointments were made during the eighteenth and nineteenth centuries, too, but as the eighteenth century stretched into the nineteenth, the elaborate forms of British royal ceremonial—and not just for the Order of the Garter—began to give way to a much more problematic configuration.

Cannadine draws out the paradox by which, during the first three quarters of the nineteenth century, the British monarchy wielded so much "real, effective political power" that public displays of that power became unacceptable. As the influence of the Crown was perceived to grow, the monarchy became increasingly unpopular. The press was in the main hostile to the monarchy, which was regularly the object of satire and critique, while sales of the few commemorative volumes celebrating royal occasions were very low. The church was suspicious of elaborate ritual; there was little interest in the composition of original music, and the city of London, with its narrow streets, hardly lent itself to public processions. As Cannadine remarks, "Under these circumstances, great royal ceremonies were not so much shared, corporate events as remote, inaccessible group rites, performed for the benefit of the few rather than the edification of the many."[45] There was no "coherent ceremonial language, as had been the case in Tudor and Stuart times, and as was to happen again towards the end of the nineteenth century."[46] The years following the death of Prince Albert in 1861 saw the "nadir" of royal ceremony in England.

In the last few decades of the nineteenth century, however, as Queen Victoria became less politically active, as the parliamentary electorate grew steadily in numbers, and as royal occasions now attracted the added luster of *imperial* ones, there was a dramatic shift toward enhanced public ceremonials, a progression that received added impetus from the Diamond Jubilee of Victoria in 1887 and the coronation of Edward VII in 1902. Cannadine charts the increasingly formal, carefully organized processions and royal occasions of the twentieth century, as the monarchy adapted older ceremonial forms, invented new traditions, and harnessed the new media of radio and, later, television, aided by an increasingly reverential, even obsequious press.

The history of the Garter cannot always be mapped exactly onto these developments: for one thing, its ceremonies are always more restricted than coronations or Accession Day parades. Victoria had been willing to dispense with the holding of elections, and often, indeed, the chapters of the Order: these rituals did not undergo the spectacular renewal of the increasingly polished performances of imperial parades. For example, the Garter feast of 1805 was the last to be held according to the traditional pattern. Formal dinners were held in the 1830s, but not again until 1912, 1913, 1914, and 1937. After the war, the Garter procession and service at St. George's at Windsor in 1948 was preceded by a formal luncheon, and this pattern has remained in place ever since as by far the most prominent of Garter celebrations.[47]

The history of the Order, then, is a history of perpetual revivals and renovations, particularly as both the monarchy and the medievalism of chivalric orders enjoy patterns of renewed fashion and popularity. The conventions of Garter historiography tell a similarly uneven story. As a chivalric order, the Order of the Garter has been supported and maintained from its inception by the heralds and officers who continue to marshal its activities and record its deeds from year to year in its Register and other annals, recording its feasts and chapters, its services and charitable works. Its historiographic traditions have thus been marked from the beginning by the decorums of heraldic service: a strong degree of sympathy and identification with chivalric ideology.

Elias Ashmole, Lancaster Herald, and John Anstis, Garter King of Arms, compiled their important and comprehensive studies of the Order in 1672 and 1724, respectively, while George Beltz compiled his *Memorials* of the Order in the role of Lancaster Herald in 1841.[48] More recently, Peter Begent, the heraldic adviser to the dean and canons at Windsor, and Hubert Chesshyre, the secretary of the Order, in 1999 published a comprehensive and fully illustrated study of the Order to commemorate its six hundred and fiftieth year. As we might expect, these studies are principally commemorative, as they celebrate and sometimes glorify the Garter's traditions. In their love of heraldic detail, the biographies of Companions, and the minutiae of changes to regulations and practices, they present histories that sustain and promote the Order as a continuous form of traditional practice, often to the exclusion of the broader social and political contexts in which the monarchy sometimes struggles to maintain its customary dignity and authority. These studies are not without moments of critical distance, however, and in many of these histories there is discernible an acute degree of separation between the knightly companions and the heralds who serve them. Begent and Chesshyre's history is, for example, as interested in the heralds and officers of the Order as it is in its Knight Companions, and includes a welcome chapter on the modern artists and craftsmen who have been responsible for the stall plates, banners, and crests that adorn St. George's Chapel. The prevailing theme of most such commentary, however, is the persistence of the Order's ideals through the ages, in a fashion that seems to celebrate difference but that subordinates it to the idea of overall continuity.

Several recent studies are more firmly framed by modern historiographic and prosopographical conventions: books by Hugh Collins (2001) and Antti Matikkala (2008) focus on the periods 1348–1461 and 1660–1760, respectively, and tend to emphasize the strategic deployment of the Order's honors and the politics of individual appointments.[49] Both are right to distinguish their studies from the work, in Collins's words, of those "antiquarians who, fascinated by the complexities of the order's ceremonial structure, sought to evaluate the institution as an expression of the chivalric ethos."[50] Nevertheless, perhaps as a result of their insistence on a harder-edged political assessment, neither of these studies pays much attention to the mythological structures of the Order, or the cultural implications of the Order for the traditions of medievalism. Also worthy of mention is D'Arcy Boulton's comprehensive and comparative study of late medieval European chivalric orders, *Knights of the Crown*.[51]

There are also many other smaller-scale studies that examine the use made of the Garter by different monarchs or in specific dynastic or court contexts, or that investigate its origins, and I will make reference to many of these in later chapters. There are also a number of biographical studies of Garter knights.

My chief concern in this book, however, is to use some of the records and histories of the Order of the Garter for a somewhat different use: to elucidate the role of this medieval chivalric order and its ritual forms in the cultural history of England, and especially to test the changing valencies of the Order's fourteenth-century origins—their value as mythic capital—in postmedieval culture, from the fifteenth century through to the twenty-first. This involves reading strategies drawn from a number of different fields: from heraldry and national history, from literature and the visual arts, and also from medievalism studies. My analysis also directs attention to the way histories have been written, while seeking to engage with the interplay between medieval myth and political ritual at different stages in the Order's history.

In most scholarly studies of the Order, imaginative literature has been emphatically subordinated to historical analysis, while literary references to the Garter have been read as of interest only insofar as they shed light on the Order's founding. In addition to these early works (Joanot Martorell's *Tirant lo Blanc*, *Wynnere and Wastoure*, *Sir Gawain and the Green Knight*), I consider a range of other texts that celebrate or allude to the Garter in ways that are often symptomatic of broader attitudes to royalty, court life, or medieval tradition. My concept of "literature" here is broad indeed, and embraces historical, antiquarian, and heraldic discourse as well as poems, novels, and dramatic texts that are either centrally or only marginally concerned with the Order. These texts help us contrast the "official" discourse about the Garter with the liminal or marginal texts that refer, often quite knowingly, to its rites and conventions. It is a distinctively national literature, a literature that celebrates or satirizes, from a position of knowing familiarity, the particular rites of English heritage. Scottish, Australian, or American literature of the Garter is rare indeed.

I have already mentioned the authoritative genealogy of historical studies of the Order. I have frequent and grateful recourse to these studies, while at the same time I also diagnose some of the habitual patterns—the ritual performances—of such histories. For example, there is a very strong compulsion

in the work of Anstis, Ashmole, and Beltz, shared by many chivalric and heraldic historians, to name and list all the members of the Order. The heraldic
records of the College of Arms have many such records, while the stall plates
of St. George's Chapel and the wooden panels in St. George's Hall at Windsor
Castle similarly commemorate individual members. However, it is difficult to
put together a list of perfect accuracy at any one time, especially if we try to
enumerate the ladies of the Order, whose participation, until very recently,
has been much more tangential. Add to this the confusion over names and
titles, the sons who succeed their fathers and attain higher and higher rank;
the painfully discreet silence over knights who were degraded and dismissed
from the Order; the question of how we should count "stranger" or foreign
knights, or the additional Hanoverian princes whose inclusion pushed the
number of knights out well beyond twenty-five, and it becomes surprisingly
hard to come to an accurate count.[52] However, this very difficulty produces its
own ritual pleasures: the production of lists and illustrations of coats of arms
is the very business of heraldry and heraldic scholarship, while the dispute
over whether Prince William is or is not the thousandth member is a pleasant
one for enthusiasts. At another level again, it is also amusing to mock one's
own obsessions. James Gillespie writes a telling footnote that encapsulates
the pleasures here. Referring to the lists of Beltz, Fellows, and Nicolas, he
comments, "All these lists of the Ladies of the Garter are imperfect. I shall
pass over the specifics lest I be accused of the anal-erotic fixations common to
prosopographers."[53]

The Order of the Garter plays an important role in symbolizing national
identity, although this role has changed substantially over the centuries, and
according to the viewer's perspective: whether one is a tourist in search of
heritage culture, a royalist in search of a glimpse of a favorite member of
the royal family, a republican, or a feminist or socialist critical of the Order's
elitist privilege. Its annual procession at Windsor before thousands of royal
fans barely enacts the kind of "national communion" or "social solidarity," in
Kertzer's phrase, that royal weddings, jubilees, and funerals can still generate, though it certainly still alludes to such a possibility, performing it for a
small group of enthusiasts.[54] In its medieval origins, the Order of the Garter
was driven in part by the desire for conspicuous, even ostentatious display, a
tradition that was maintained well into the seventeenth century. Its rituals and
practices became more privatized then, but from the middle of the twentieth
century, public display became important once more. Given the venerable
history of the Order and the limited numbers of members (after more than

six hundred and fifty years, the Order has recently named only its thousandth Companion), the Order has always been more observed, painted, and written about than participated in. This makes it a particularly rich topic for combining approaches from literary and cultural history as well as ritual theory and medievalism.

Chapter 2

Origins

Motto, Emblem, and Myth

The best-known story about the origins of the Order of the Garter is also the most contentious. A king retrieves a garter that fell from a lady's leg as she was dancing, ties it around his own, and silences the laughter of his courtiers by promising to form a chivalric order in honor of the occasion. This narrative's mythic resonance derives in part from the way it foregrounds its own etiology, but as many times as this story is told it is derided, dismissed, or flatly rejected. The postmedieval reception history of this story, which was not widely circulated as a written text before the middle of the sixteenth century, will be the subject of Chapter 3. But what do we know about the "real" origins of the Order?

None of the early official records or statutes refers to any particular occasion that might have motivated Edward III to found the Order of the Garter, but this omission has never been problematic. If anything, the silence of the early records has been an enabling aspect of the Order's structure and status as national myth. Far from casting doubt on its authenticity or diminishing the pleasure of its rituals, the uncertain origins of the Garter enhance its mythic capital in postmedieval culture. The putative originary moment is also thereby dehistoricized, sent into a kind of mythic temporality, beyond written records. There is general agreement now among scholars about the date of the Order's foundation, but debate persists in both scholarly and popular contexts about the origins and meaning of the Garter emblem and Edward's elliptic motto. In the ritual sphere, this mystery has the dual effect of affirming the sheer longevity of the Order's medieval traditions, and enhancing the aura of "romance" engendered by the infamous story about Edward and the countess, an aura that is regularly conjured up even by those who dispute the veracity of the story.

This chapter is principally concerned with the cultural meanings generated by and ascribed to the origins of the Garter's rituals. Its ultimate guiding question is a methodological one. What difference does history—or, indeed, historical uncertainty—make to ritual meaning? The first section of the chapter examines the forms of heraldic display by which the Garter insignia are disseminated in the fourteenth century, and the second considers some of the archival and literary evidence from the first hundred years after the Order's inception, and some recent hypotheses about its origins. The third section focuses on the motto itself, especially the cultural, social, and ritual work it performs. The fourth section is more hypothetical, returning to the putative scene of chivalric rescue to explore its ritual implications and symbolic structures.

Heraldic Display

The story about the King and the lady's garter may be the one most commonly associated with the Order of the Garter in popular opinion, but it is a divisive story. Many official accounts of the Order are skeptical about its authenticity, but are equally drawn both to its charms and to its capacity for building mythical and romantic capital. Given that so many histories of the Order are written from a position *within* or in close sympathy with the Order, it seems proper to begin with the problem of the "real," to ask if there is any kind of knowable historical core at the heart of the myth. Can we identify a historical event that might have generated alternative explanations and engendered the mythic structure we recognize today?

Most straight histories of the Order begin with this question of origins, but the historical records frustrate such searches. Indeed, reading through the primary archive and the secondary commentary and critique on this topic is an object lesson in the difficulties of historical reconstruction. Sometimes it is possible to put the surviving fragments together to make a plausible narrative or historical sequence of events. So, too, we may guess at the political and social role the Order may have fulfilled in its first years, from the many lists and records that tell us who was appointed to its membership.[1] However, there are large gaps and omissions in the records and the early narrative accounts of the Order. One of the problems that besets any attempt to ascertain the precise date and circumstances of the Order's first founding (if indeed there *was* such a singular occasion) is that eventually, no matter what path of inquiry we take, we come up against the question of the King's motivation and the mystery of his design of emblem and motto. Weirdly, we are left guessing in a manner predicted by the motto itself, *Honi soit qui mal y pense*: Shamed be he who thinks evil of it. The question of what that "*y*," the "it," refers to has become the central problem of the Order's early history. Like the confounded courtiers, we are not equal to the King's larger vision. In saying this, I do not wish to be understood as either glorifying the King or abjecting the work of modern scholarship and our attempts to understand the past. However, while the uncertainty about the Order's origins may seem a simple matter of lost or missing evidence, we may still acknowledge that the uncertainty—let us call it the undecidability—of the Order's origins might actually be integral to the mythic structure and resonance of the Order.

Beyond the motto itself, a first hint that this refusal to explain might be structural comes from the surviving statutes. Few of the early records survive. Lisa Jefferson has recently identified Manuscript Arundel 48 in the College of Arms as the oldest surviving copy of the statutes. The manuscript dates from 1415, more than sixty years after the Order was founded.[2] Jefferson argues that the text represents a reordering and clarification of existing statutes under the governance of Henry V. The oldest version of the Order's Register (a record of meetings and elections) dates only from 1416, and may well have been the first of its kind. Henry was the first of many monarchs who sought to reform and regularize the Order, and to institute new ways of keeping track of changes in its ritual practice, but his revised statutes make no mention of any occasion of the Order's founding.

The ritual theorist might suggest that formal statutes and written records of rituals are generally more concerned with articulating synchronic systems and regulations than with tracing historical origins. Even if earlier statutes came to light they would probably still not provide the explanation so desperately sought by the historian: it seems unlikely that Henry would have *removed* something of that magnitude, and no other later version bears any trace of such an explanation. As I suggested earlier, from the mythological perspective, the absence of a historical date or specific occasion enhances the ritual's mythic capital, allowing for the greater participation in mythic structures, above and beyond merely historical or commemorative rituals.

This is not to diminish the importance of the statutes or the Register. The proliferation of statutes (at least one copy for every member) and the number of variants (in Latin, French, and later in English), with varying layers of deletions and amendments, is ample testimony to the ritual compulsion to copy and refine the procedures of the Order. We will have occasion in later chapters to discuss a number of the variations they record, though their complex textual history is a separate study in its own right.[3] The statutes rehearse in scrupulous detail the requirements for the celebration of the feast of St. George, the electoral procedures of the Order, the rules of precedence, the maintenance of the poor knights, canons, and vicars at Windsor, the instructions for summoning the knights to a feast, the rules for the wearing of Garter robes and garters (and the various penalties for infringing these rules), the numbers of masses to be sung on the death of a Companion (according to his rank: a very generous one thousand for a king, down through to one hundred for a knight bachelor), and other matters. But they are synchronic and prescriptive in their concerns, rather than offering a historical account. The preamble to the 1415 statutes explains merely that Edward III formed the Order, which was dedicated to the Virgin Mary and to St. George, in the twenty-third year of his reign; and later versions repeat the same formula, gradually adding longer and more general histories of knighthood and chivalry. This practice extends into the *Liber Niger*, the records of the Garter produced under Henry VIII; and also into the work of later historians of the order, such as Elias Ashmole's 1672 *Institution, Laws and Ceremonies of the Most Noble Order of the Garter: A Work furnished with variety of matter, relating to honor and noblesse*, weighing in at more than eight hundred and fifty pages: and John Anstis's two-volume edition and translation of the *Liber Niger* (incomplete, but already heavy with weighty supplementary material), published in 1721.

It is thus worth distinguishing between the ritual needs of the Order and the historical, political, and cultural interests of its commentators in clarifying its historical origins and tracing its institutional history.

To compound the difficulties in trying to elucidate this early history, for many years there was also uncertainty about the founding date. The 1340s saw a flurry of chivalric activity in the warring nations of England and France, and this may account for some of the confusion. Many of the chroniclers appear to confuse the founding of the Round Table with that of the Order of the Garter. Jean Froissart, for example, conflates the foundation of the Order with the tournament Edward III held at Windsor in 1344, celebrating his triumphant campaign in Brittany in the previous year.[4] Edward announced at this tournament that he planned to revive an Arthurian court at Windsor, complete with a new building and a Round Table to hold the prospective three hundred knights, a number of suitably romantic dimensions.[5] The

festivities were to be tied to the feast of Pentecost, another Arthurian allusion. Events in the ongoing, expensive war with France intervened, however,
to delay this foundation, and this Round Table never met, being gradually
displaced by the more restricted Order of the Garter. Juliet Vale suggests, indeed, that Edward may have decided to distance himself from the Arthurian
story and its ending in betrayal and defeat; that he "may also have recognised
the fundamental tension between the Arthurian Round Table, with parity
between hundreds of members, and the prestige that he wished to accrue to
himself as sovereign, which was most effectively achieved through exclusivity
and elitism."[6]

In the absence of any direct record of the Order's first meeting, or any
contemporaneous account of Edward's motivations in adopting the motto or
insignia of the Order, scholars turn to the royal Wardrobe accounts, which
offer rich and detailed testimony to the production of many garters on clothing, banners, and ceremonial bedclothes between 1345 and 1349 (at which
point there is a gap in the records until 1361). These records and accounts are
not known for the force of their narrative or explanatory drive, and it is sometimes difficult to know how to interpret them. One of the earliest is a list of
materials supplied to the king's armorer, John of Cologne: "For making two
Streamers of worsted, one of Arms quarterly, and the other of Arms quarterly,
with the Image of St. Lawrence worked in the head, one white pale, powdered
with blue garters [*pouderata cum garteriis bluettis*]; and for making two short
Streamers of the King's Arms, quarterly; and for making two Guidons of the
same Arms of the King."[7] Nicholas Harris Nicolas thought these streamers
were for a procession in honor of St. Lawrence, but Juliet Vale has argued
from the number of pieces required that they were much larger, and would be
more fitting for a ship: "Certainly the nature of the items and the quantities
in which the items were supplied suggest the full heraldic panoply for a large-
scale expeditionary force rather than any domestic ceremony or tournament."[8]
Vale suggests the garter was being used as a decorative device from the beginning of the campaign that would include Edward's stunning victory at Crécy
in 1346. In the absence of such an image, she imagines its impact: "Against
the bed of state and dressed himself in the same blue fabric, shimmering with
gold embroidery and hundreds of silver-gilt buckles and pendants, [Edward]
must have seemed not only the image of kingly splendour, but the very per-
sonification of his claim. The eye of the observer was assaulted with Edward's
pugnacious assertion: 'Hony soit q' mal y pense.'"[9] Edward was soon distributing the Garter as the sign of the most preeminent order of chivalry. There

seems little doubt that whatever the occasion or the timing of the Order's inauguration, it was closely associated with the King's war effort. The foundational members, for example, had all served with the King in France, and the Order became "a sophisticated instrument of patronage in monarchical relations with the nobility."[10] As Hugh Collins writes: "In founding a secular fraternity, Edward III had sought to harness the cult of chivalry as a means of galvanizing aristocratic support behind the war in France. With its enigmatic and consciously romantic associations, the order served to glamourize both the ongoing conflict and those who participated in it."[11] In Collins's reading of the surviving records, the most decisive date for the Order's inauguration is 6 August 1348, when the King issued letters patent outlining his plans to restructure the chapel at Windsor castle, rededicated to St. George and the Blessed Virgin, and with provision for twenty-four alms knights, twenty-four secular priests, and other officers, suggesting "that the college of St George was instituted as a complement to the order of the Garter."[12] This followed a tournament at Windsor in June of that year. It seems that the first formal celebrations of the Feast of St. George were held on April 23, 1349, at Windsor. The Wardrobe accounts record that John of Cologne, the king's armorer, provided "six garters and twenty-four robes powdered with garters bearing the motto of the Order, together with matching altar hangings for the Chapel."[13] It is worth recalling that from the very beginning of its formal institution, the Order had strong religious affiliations, and most of the early statutes are concerned with religious observance.[14]

As Vale suggests, conspicuous display was a driving force in the court culture of Edward III, well before the foundation of the Order.[15] In this heraldic context, the generation of verbal, visual, and gestural signs was paramount. These signs were sometimes religious but often social, generating both vertical and horizontal lines of heritage and allegiance. Edward fostered a court culture of conspicuous consumption and the visual enforcement of an English team identity. The metaphor of the team is appropriate here even if we do not accept with Nicolas and Vale that the original Garter members constituted two tournament teams under the respective leadership of Edward and his son the Black Prince.[16]

The Order of the Garter capitalized on Edward's own love of the tournament, as well as the deep history associated with King Arthur, known both for uniting Britain and for his great European conquests. Edward was a medieval master of medievalism, harnessing the fashionable recuperation of Arthurian style in the service of his own national ambitions and imperial aspirations, following a similar kind of cultural policy, in this regard, as his grandfather, Edward I, had done.[17]

In its social form, then, the Order of the Garter reaches back to an even earlier mythical construct, the idea of the preeminent king surrounded by the best knights. The Garter has always been very restricted in its numbers. Edward's first foundation was limited to twenty-six knights, including the Sovereign, and the numbers have only rarely gone much higher than that, depending on whether "foreign" or "stranger" knights are to be counted in the number of Companions, and how many members of the royal family are included. Just as Arthur attracted ambitious knights to come and be tested and approved by the Round Table, so too did Edward hope to draw knights to him and to the cause of his French war, as well as rewarding those who had already fought in it. Its original members included "the chief commanders of the English armies in the Crécy campaign."[18]

A significant aspect of the Order of the Garter, like many other chivalric or courtly forms in this period, was the audience for such display, especially the women of the court. In the Arthurian romances and in countless manuscript illustrations it is the Queen and her ladies who observe and judge the knights. So too in the late medieval tournament, much of this display is for the benefit of the women observers. Certainly the tournament could not take place without them, and they often participated in its processions, feasts, and other celebrations, both in historical fact and in the works of literary and artistic imagination that portrayed many such festivities.[19] Edward's Round Table invokes the literature and mythology of Arthurian tradition.

Conversely, the female narrator of the fifteenth-century poem *The Floure and the Leafe* records her discussion with the "faire lady" who describes the Garter knights and the Nine Worthies as deriving "their triumph eke and marshall glory" from their devotion to the green laurel. Women play a crucial role in this context, circulating information and stories about chivalric honor.[20] When Gawain returns to Camelot at the end of *Sir Gawain and the Green Knight* the lords and ladies of the court all agree to wear the green baldric as a mark of honor.[21] The easy uniformity of this sign may well echo the manner in which medieval men and women shared the wearing of the Garter colors and symbols. We will return to this poem soon.

The earliest Garter records made provision for garters and robes for the women of the court, many of whom became Ladies of the Fraternity of St. George, though women were to be denied this degree of participation in later centuries: Henry VII was the last king to make any female appointments. The troubled question of the participation of women in the Order at any given period will be read in Chapter 5 as symptomatic of the potential of medieval tradition to both soothe and disturb the Order's sense of its own modernity.

It would be misleading to suggest a simple process of decline in women's participation from a glorious medieval period of equal participation. The Order was always primarily an association of men, in its military and political orientation, and when its insignia are used in public display, this context is often resolutely masculine. One of the very earliest references to the Garter is found in the Middle English alliterative satire *Wynnere and Wastoure* (dated between 1352 and 1370).[22] In this dream-vision poem, the King appears on a cliff as two armies are preparing to battle. It becomes clear the battle is an allegorical one between the two opposing principles of expenditure and saving, or between the two parts of the royal household, the Wardrobe and the Exchequer. This is a highly masculinized argument, played out between two knights before the King and his son. The narrator names a handful of the plethora of signs and banners, of friars and merchants, "too many to mention," but describes the King's embroidered garments and pavilion in loving detail. The Garter motto appears, translated into alliterative English, on the pavilion:

> Then were th[er] wordes in þe webbe werped of he[u],
> Payntted of plunket, and poyntes bytwene
> Þat were fourmed full fayre appon fresche lettres,
> And alle was it one sawe appon Ynglysse tonge,
> "Hethyng haue the hathell þat any harme thynkes."
> (*Wynnere and Wastoure*, 64–68)

Vance Smith draws attention to the motto's "quite literal materiality," whereby its embroidered texture and the form of the letters seem to take precedence over the words themselves. For Smith, this display is symptomatic of the Edwardian and Ricardian practice of investing signs with "an accretion of obvious material grandeur": "The assertion of royal dominance is clearly imagined in the second half of the fourteenth century in symbolic terms, in the formation and maintenance of signs whose opulence, grandeur, or magnificence legitimates whatever particular institution or occasion they actually refer to."[23] The Garter motto is cited in English, uniquely in the medieval period, and instead of invoking shame, in the more customary "honi," the poet alliterates on the English word for "contempt": *Hethyng haue the hathell that any harme thynkes*. It is as if this celebration of magnificence can have nothing to do with shame: no place is given here to any querulous objection to the royal spectacle.

The pavilion is further decorated with "bezants": these have a dual reference as both heraldic roundels and coins. Each disc is encircled by a blue garter decorated with gold: "gayly vmbygone with garters of inde, / And iche a gartare of golde gerede full riche" (62–63). It is clear that the Garter has been fully integrated into the royal signifying system, part of the court's symbolic splendor.[24] When the poet comes to describe the King—"One of the lovelyeste ledis, whoso loveth hym in hert, / That ever segge under sonn sawe with his eghne"—he lingers on his robes, with his mantle embroidered with golden falcons, each carrying a blue garter, while ducks and drakes fly around his belt, quaking in fear of the royal falcons. It is a very imposing vision.

> Fawkons of fyne golde, flakerande with wynges,
> And ichone bare in ble blewe als me thoghte
> A grete gartare of ynde gerede full riche.
> Full gayly was that grete lorde girde in the myddis:
> A brighte belte of ble broudirde with fewles,
> With drakes and with dukkes— daderande tham semede
> For ferdnes of fawkons fete, lesse fawked thay were.
>   (*Wynnere and Wastoure*, 92–98)

Again, the emphasis falls on royal puissance, amid the gorgeous blues and golds of the Garter colors, firmly established as a dominant theme in the court's self-presentation. There is no hint that the Garter represents any kind of recently inaugurated Order, just as there is little acknowledgment in this poem that the sumptuous display of a tournament or an allegorical debate about the economy of conspicuous consumption might find a female audience, or have a female origin. Nor is there any trace, yet, of mythic medievalism: this early representation of the garter appeals to sartorial fashion, not cultural memory.

The King's robes are in fact strikingly similar to those described in a roll detailing expenses from the Wardrobe accounts of 1351–52. In Kay Staniland's translation:

> A robe of 4 garments of red velvet for the king for the feast of St. George—2 supertunics, 1 tunic with hood, 1 cloak well embroidered with silver clouds and eagles of pearls and gold—that is, under

every alternate cloud an eagle of pearls, and under every other cloud
an eagle having in its beak a garter embroidered with the words of
the King's motto *hony soit qe mal y pense*:

> 1 draughtsman at 12¼*d*. for 10 days.
> 12 workers at 9¼*d*. each for 24 days.
> 5 female workers at 3¼*d*. each for 21 days.
> for thread and making thread of 6 oz of gold (*auri sodat*) at 9*d*.
>   per oz.
> £13 15*s*. ¾*d*.[25]

Such accounts remind us that medieval women were involved to a significant degree in the production of court robes, albeit in smaller numbers and at
much lower rates of pay than men.

The court context here is one of conspicuous, triumphant consumption and heraldic display. The mid-fourteenth-century evidence suggests that
the Order of the Garter very quickly attained a formal institutional home at
Windsor, and began its ritual life, lifted out of the messy circumstances of
fourteenth-century politics, whether these were Edward's claim to the French
throne, his attempt to rise above a sexual scandal, or a combination of both.

Foundational Texts

Many medieval writers were nevertheless fascinated by the problem of the
Order's origins. The evidence of the chroniclers and poets is often ambiguous and sometimes even circular, but it does help us calibrate the transition
from an atmosphere of sexual scandal in the first few decades of its history
to the growing possibilities of mythic resonance, especially in the sixteenth
century.

The central witnesses here are Jean le Bel, writing in the 1350s, and Jean
Froissart, who served at the court of Edward III and Queen Philippa, and who
based the first volume of his chronicles on Le Bel's narrative.[26] Froissart, as
we have seen, conflates the 1344 tournament with the founding of the Order,
while his failure to mention the King's retrieval of a lady's garter was taken by
many early commentators and heralds as a sure indication that the story was a
fabrication of Polydor Virgil in the 1530s. Nor does Le Bel make any allusion
to it. However, he does mention another episode that many scholars argue sits
behind the Order, a dark shadow behind the celebration of courtly esprit and

gallantry in the traditional narrative. In this story, Edward is not gallant but sexually violent, guilty of raping the Countess of Salisbury.

According to Le Bel, Edward was in love with the countess, who virtuously refused his approaches. Finally, he sent the count into Brittany and went to stay with the countess. One night he entered her chamber and barred the door against her attendants. He "then took her and held her mouth so firmly she could only cry out two or three times, and then forced her so grievously and in such a manner than no woman was ever treated so vilely; and left her lying completely unconscious . . . , bleeding from the nose and mouth and elsewhere, which was a great wrong and a great pity. Then he left the next day, without saying a word, and returned to London, deeply angry at what he had done."[27] Froissart makes no mention of this episode in the first version of his chronicle, and in the second version insists he has been unable to corroborate it.

How can a story like this bring us closer to the origins of the Garter? Are we not simply confusing the issue with another difficult-to-prove narrative? Certainly this story generates its own afterlife, particularly in French literature and culture.[28] It gets intertwined with stories of the countess losing her garter, muddling the semiotics and the sexual and national politics of the story even further. Add to this the problem of trying to identify the woman who is meant by the title Countess of Salisbury and we have a veritable tangle of possible referents for the date, occasion, and motive of this story *and* its possible relation to the Order of the Garter.

The most comprehensive recent study of this material is Francis Ingledew's *Sir Gawain and the Green Knight and the Order of the Garter.* Many of its suggestions and conclusions (for example, that *Sir Gawain and the Green Knight* is an Edwardian mid-century poem, not a Ricardian late-century one) are contentious. More successfully than many accounts, however, it brings together the analysis of the archival record with other forms of cultural and textual production in the fourteenth century, arguing for the "logic of the eros of history, that force of mutual attraction by which in the medieval period the erotic and the martial tend to summon each other up as primary modalities in the construction of history."[29]

For Ingledew, the delay between the Round Table tournament at Windsor and the institution of the Order of the Garter is crucial. He argues that the years between 1343 and 1348, well before Edward's affair with Alice Perrers, were "dense with sexual scandal in Edward's court and especially in Edward's person," citing writers such as Thomas Bradwardine, the author of the

Bridlington Prophecy, and romance poems like the French *Vows of the Heron*.[30] Ingledew argues that having already decided to found a chivalric order, Edward's plans started to fall apart because the atmosphere of scandal around his court threatened to derail the project. He quotes Adam Murimuth, who says obliquely that work on the building of the Round Table at Windsor was stopped "for various reasons" (*ex certis causis*).[31] Ingledew develops the suggestion made by Richard Barber that the Order's motto was perhaps Edward's reply to the "shameful stories" in circulation about him, including the story of the rape reported by Le Bel.[32] He argues that Edward "trumps" the sexual scandal surrounding his court—which may or may not have included an incident with a lady's garter—"by making of the very thing that threatened to derail his plan for a self-apotheosizing order that order's fulcrum."[33] Ingledew also suggests that the religious foundation at St. George's Chapel was an important element in this rehabilitation of the King's reputation.

Many of Ingledew's arguments and interpretations are contingent ones, circling around plausibilities and possibilities, as, for example, in his reading of *The Vows of the Heron* (previously discussed as a Garter allusion by Malcolm Vale).[34] In this poem, Edward's knights make various vows to fight in France. The Earl of Salisbury vows not to open the eye he has asked his lover to close with her finger until he has arrived and fought in France; and she in turn promises herself to him then. Edward's queen is pregnant, and vows she will not give birth until Edward has taken her to the place where he will fulfill his own vow. But before she makes her vow, she rebukes Robert of Artois for asking what her vow will be, before the Queen has been given permission by her husband to make a vow: "Honnis soit li corps qu jà si pensera."

Here is another problematic text, then, that seems to circle around the cluster of people associated with the Garter (king, queen, a woman linked to the title Salisbury),[35] and that invokes a version of the Garter motto around the same time Edward starts to use it. The poem is set precisely in 1338, and Whiting dates it between 1340 and 1346. Ingledew constructs an elaborate argument for dating this poem to 1346, very shortly after the battle of Crécy. "The *Vows of the Heron* functions therefore as a witness to Edward's place in an erotic drama at the midpoint of the years in which the Round Table turned into the Order of the Garter, at a time more precisely when he had carried the garter and the motto on his French campaign; and as an illustration of how fitly Edward might make the garter colors those of the French royal house: the garter would function much like Salisbury's closed eye, as the sign of Edward's own love-pledge carried into the wars with France."[36] Much of

Ingledew's book, like this passage, depends on layers and sequences of speculation (for example, that the relationship between Salisbury and his love is more
romantic and courtly than that between king and queen; and that the King is
captivated by Salisbury's mistress). Elsewhere, too, he argues from omissions
and silences, as in his contention about division and dissent at Edward's court,
guessing that the nobles who were *not* named in the first company of the
Order were those who had been critical of the King, "a group who thought
'mal' of whatever the garter referred to."[37]

The difficulties of reading medieval literary texts as a set of topical allusions to historical events are legion. In the absence of definitive dates, such
discussions can easily become circular; and even when the dates all add up,
suggestive allusions often resist the final click of certainty. Ingledew's emphasis
on the imbrication of sexuality, culture, and politics in the Edwardian court
is well taken, however.

Sir Gawain and the Green Knight exemplifies the problems of untangling
knots and allusions. This is the earliest text in any language that even hints at
the story recorded much later about the woman's garter. It offers a suggestive
parallel of an accessory transferred from a female to a male body that is then
also transformed from a sign of personal shame to one of courtly honor, all
with the official sanction of heraldic symbolism. *Sir Gawain and the Green
Knight* is a poem closely concerned with the life of signs: their transmuta-
tion and their interpretation. We are told many times that though the girdle
is elaborately embroidered, it is of no material value in itself, apart from its
magical life-preserving qualities. During the three days Lord Bertilak is out
hunting, his beautiful young wife visits Gawain in his bedroom, engaging
in delicious courtly dalliance that frequently takes as its subject a knight's
courtly duties to a woman. Their flirtation concludes on the third morning
with an elaborate ritual of gift giving and exchange, in which Gawain accepts
the magical girdle on the understanding that he will not hand over the gift
to the lady's husband during their customary evening exchange of "winnings"
during the day. In the final encounter with Bertilak, the elaborately embedded
plot is unknotted, and Gawain's sin of omission is revealed as the major moral
turning point of his quest. This was not, as he had thought, the trial of turning up to receive a mortal axe blow from the gigantic Green Knight. In anger
and shame he flings the girdle to the ground and curses all women as deceitful
daughters of Eve. Setting out for home, he knots the girdle around him as a
baldric signifying his shame, and on arrival in Camelot makes full confession
of his humiliating failure to Arthur and Guenevere. But his personal shame is

instantly transformed to collective honor. The court laughs at Gawain's scruples, and Arthur transforms the girdle into a permanent heraldic sign that all the court will wear as a mark of honor and fellowship.[38]

In contrast to *Wynnere and Wastoure* and its purely honorific, masculine representation of the King's court, *Sir Gawain* makes a strong thematic connection between shame and a feminized court, and it is easy to see the correspondences between the poem and the Garter myth.[39] Someone, possibly the same scribe, appended the Garter motto (in an abbreviated form, as "Hony soit qui mal pense") to the only surviving manuscript of this poem.[40] This seems to be strikingly concrete evidence, no matter when we date the poem, that at least one reader thought the romance referred directly to the Order of the Garter, and wanted to assert or underline that connection. If Edward's Garter was thought to be a revival of a battle sign used by Richard I's (as was suggested in the sixteenth century) the addition of the motto would make much less sense. As it is, the presence of the motto suggests that the story about a woman's garter was in circulation by the time the poem was copied.

However, there are substantial differences between the two stories. The two objects in question—one a green and gold girdle, and the other a blue garter—enjoy very different narrative trajectories. One starts its ritual life as a secret gift invested with magical properties that is the key prop in an elaborate moral test; and the other is a piece of underwear that accrues ritual significance only through a daring act of royal willpower. The final scenes of *Sir Gawain*, which show how a sign of shame can be converted to a sign of honor, offer the strongest connection between the two stories. It is worth recalling, too, that the poem predates any surviving written version of the Garter myth: the addition of the motto to the *Gawain* manuscript makes best sense to modern readers only in the light of later renditions of the story about the lady's garter.

The most detailed is the least well known. Joanot Martorell's epic romance of chivalry, *Tirant Lo Blanc*, was begun in 1460, completed by Martí Joan de Galba, and published in Valencia in 1490. Martorell claims his text was translated first from English into Portuguese, and then into the Valencian vernacular, or Catalan. He excuses himself for any defects, since "the blame lies with the English language, some words of which are impossible to translate."[41] No record survives of this putative English original, which may function here as an untraceable but authorizing fiction. It is equally possible that Polydor Vergil was right to claim in the 1530s that there was a popular oral narrative in circulation. Most early historians of the Order did not know

Martorell's romance, however, and Vergil makes no direct mention of it, so there is no obvious line of transmission to later accounts. Yet it is by far the most comprehensive early version of the Order's foundation.

Martorell's narrative is a heavily embedded one, framed by the distancing fictions of romance, though it is also situated with some precision around the marriage of an English king to a French princess. Martorell did spend some time in England, so if we wish to seek a historical point of reference we may suppose the King represents Henry VI, and the Princess, Margaret of Anjou: they were married in Tours in 1444, and the King held a three-day tournament to celebrate her coronation at Westminster in 1445.[42] (The conclusion to this chapter discusses the beautiful copy of the Garter statutes presented to Margaret on the occasion of her wedding.) In Martorell's romance, the Breton nobleman Tirant recounts the story of the wedding, and then Diaphebus, another knight, takes over the narration to recite the praise of Tirant, who had been the tournament's champion. He then tells of an order of knighthood the King of England established, "similar to King Arthur's Knights of the Round Table in olden days."[43]

The wedding festivities lasted a year and a day, but the King asked everyone to stay on a little longer as he wanted to announce his founding of a new order. "This order's inspiration, as I and all these knights heard it from the king's own lips, came from an incident one day when we were dancing and making merry." This detailed narrative includes most of the central elements in later versions of the story: a dropped garter, an embarrassed woman, a chivalric king, and, significantly, the ease with which the King is able to transform a trivial object into a sign of greatness, a sign of shame into a sign of honor.

> Many knights were dancing with ladies, and by chance one damsel named Honeysuckle [Madresilva] drew near the king. As she whirled, her left garter, which was trimmed with silk, fell off. Those nearest His Majesty beheld it on the floor, and do not imagine, my lord, that she was fairer or more genteel than others. She has a rather flirtatious way of dancing and talking, though she sings reasonably well, yet one might have found three hundred comelier and more gracious damsels present. All the same, there is no accounting for men's tastes and whims. One of the knights near the king said: "Honeysuckle, you have lost your leg armor. You must have a bad page who failed to fasten it well."

She blushed slightly and stooped to pick it up, but another knight rushed over and grabbed it. The king then summoned the knight and said: "Fasten it to my left stocking below the knee."

The King wore this garter on his leg for four months, until finally one of his favorite servants told him how concerned everyone was.

The king replied: "So the queen is disgruntled and my guests are displeased!," and he said in French, "*Puni soit qui mal y pense.* Now I swear before God that I shall found a new knightly order upon this incident: a fraternity that shall be remembered as long as the world endures."
    He had the garter removed and would wear it no longer, though he still pined for it in secret.[44]

Diaphebus then recounts how the King dedicated a chapel at Windsor to St. George and established an order of twenty-four knights, describing their robes, capes, hoods, and garters, and mentioning the rule that they always had to wear the garter below the left knee. He recounts the oaths they swear (emphasizing their obligation to assist ladies in distress), their ceremonial processions, and the rituals for the installation and degradation of a knight (which involve dressing a scarecrow in his armor). He also cites the vows sworn by ladies of the Order: that they will never urge their male relatives to return from war; that they will do all they can to aid any such relative starving under siege; and that if those relatives might be taken prisoner, they will spend up to half their dowry to ransom them (there is no mention anywhere else of such vows in the medieval records of the Order). Finally, he comments that the ladies must always wear their garters on their left sleeves.[45]
    This account is by far the most detailed of all early variants, and commands our attention, even if it frustrates our desire for a precise referent. Its historical context bears little relationship to the court of Edward III, while its list of knights in the Order, including the fictional Tirant, matches neither the original company nor the Order under Henry VI. The King's motto is also different, as he invokes punishment, not shame (*puni*, not *honi*) on any who might think ill of his Order. Most accounts do not foreground the Queen's anger or displeasure, as this one does; and it is also alone in making overt the nature of the garter as fetish, as the King pines for it in secret long after he has had it removed from his clothing. Martorell is further unique

in naming the woman as Madresilva, rather than making her a queen or a countess.

If Edward III drew inspiration for his order from an actual event, the definitive evidence is probably lost to us now. But stories like Martorell's offer strong explanatory power, and if we pair this with the evidence of *Sir Gawain* and other commentators like Mondonus Belvaleti, who wrote in 1463 that "many assert that this order took its beginning from the feminine sex, from a lewd and forbidden affection," [46] we are justified in considering this story as a powerful myth of origins that performs important cultural work in making sense of the Order, especially to fourteenth- and fifteenth-century audiences. I return to Martorell's story below.

There is one final piece of evidence for this story, the one that is quoted most often. Polydor Vergil, around 1512, makes no reference to Martorell, and offers less detail, but he is emphatic in citing popular tradition (*fama vulgi*) as his source.

> But the reason for founding the order is utterly uncertain; popular tradition nowadays declares that Edward at some time picked up from the ground a garter from the stocking of his queen or mistress, which had become unloosed by some chance, and had fallen. As some of the knights began to laugh and jeer on seeing this, he is reputed to have said that in a very little while the same garter would be held by them in the highest honour. And not long after, he is said to have founded this order and given it the title by which he showed those knights who had laughed at him how to judge his actions. Such is popular tradition. English writers have been modestly superstitious, perhaps fearing to commit lèse-majesté, if they made known such unworthy things; and they have preferred to remain silent about them, whereas matters should really be seen otherwise: something that rises from a petty or sordid origin increases all the more in dignity.[47]

Vergil implies that the tactful silence of the English commentators on the matter is further proof of the story's veracity or plausibility, but his central point is the metamorphosis of this very humble object into a sign of honor and dignity. In other works, Vergil had been dismissive of many of the traditional and popular British myths of Trojan settlement and the Arthurian legends.[48] Set against his reputation for skepticism, even irreverence, in the face of some dearly loved mythologies, his apparent support for the popular tradition of the Garter narrative (while admittedly declaring its origins were "utterly uncertain") sparked equal measures of fascination and resistance. For every writer who accepted the story and reveled in its narrative possibilities, there was another who took scholarly delight in its vigorous rebuttal. The most vehement of Vergil's attackers was Peter Heylyn, who in his *Cosmographie* of 1652 dismissed the story as "a vain and idle Romance, derogatory both to the Founder, and the order."[49] Vergil, after all, was a foreigner to English shores, and could hardly be expected to understand the native tradition.

Heylyn was cited approvingly by Elias Ashmole in his influential history of the Garter,[50] and by many other seventeenth-century writers, so that by 1724, John Anstis, Garter King of Arms, was drawing on a long tradition when he confidently described Vergil's and similar stories as "absurd" and "ridiculous," as "romantick Fancies."[51] Since then, many antiquarians, heralds, and historians up to the present day have similarly resisted the idea that Edward could have founded so great an order of knighthood on an item or event so trivial or, we may say, so shameful as a "wardrobe malfunction" of this kind. Accordingly, the Order's recent official historians, Peter Begent and Hubert Chesshyre, quote Anstis with approval, saying it is better such stories be "left in the dark."[52]

My later chapters will return to the question of this story's reception, but even in the critical discussion of its likelihood, among scholars reading back from Martorell and Vergil, there is a persistent fascination with this story, and an equal distrust of it. Poets and other writers are drawn to its powerful etiology—it makes *sense* of the Garter—but they are divided about the identity of the woman at the heart of the story. In fact, the ambiguity of her identity is another symptom of the problem.

Leo Carruthers untangles the confusing marital history of Joan of Kent, who became Lady Holland, then Countess of Salisbury, and finally Princess of Wales, after marrying the Black Prince. "It seems likely that this beautiful woman with whom men fell madly in love, whose disputed marital status more than once provoked a scandal, may have become a peg, one on which a later generation hung a tale invented to explain both the Garter and the motto."[53] Carruthers suggests the story about the garter and the implied affair between king and countess may have been invented, or at least enthusiastically disseminated, by Henry IV and his Lancastrian successors to discredit the mother of Richard II.

The desire to find precise historical referents for various characters in *Sir*

Gawain and the Green Knight is part of the same dynamic. Commentators have found flattering allusions to Edward's son Lionel, the Duke of Clarence; or to Henry of Grosmont and his uncle, Thomas, Earl of Lancaster, and his famous belt, while Ingledew reads the poem as a criticism of Edward's Arthurian aspirations.[54] Mark Ormrod stresses, however, that the Garter's symbolic meaning, like the functions of the Order, evolved gradually over the second half of the fourteenth century; and that its first origins were rather more exclusive, and not designed, initially at least, for a mass audience.[55]

Setting aside the various critiques of Vergil's and Martorell's narratives, there are other ways of approaching the plausibility of the Garter narrative; namely, by drawing on the vexed history of costume, fashion, and ritual dress.

According to J. L. Nevinson, writing in 1948, medieval women used tapes, not garters, to hold up their hose: "So the legend of the Countess of Salisbury dropping her garter at the dance must go on record as the invention of Polydore Vergil."[56] Begent and Chesshyre comment, however, that Nevinson is "too sweeping in his statements which do not appear to reflect the true position."[57] They argue medieval fashions were not uniform, and there is evidence of different kinds of garters: strips of woven cloth, jeweled or not, fastened with a buckle or not. The function of a garter also varied according to the length of the hose: whether it secured shorter hose around the leg or tightened the fit of longer hose, worn by men under the shorter garments fashionable in the earlier fourteenth century. The practicalities of dress are not always reducible to textbook histories of costume, either: we do not have to imagine a modern elastic garter to imagine the ease of tying a decorative strip or ribbon beneath the knee to secure the smooth fit of hose that may have been attached to undergarments, whether this is above a male or a female calf. Certainly the manuscript evidence shows the wearing of male garters in this period. The Luttrell Psalter, dated c. 1325–35, has several examples, and we know that Edward III had a pair of garters sewn with pearl and gold in the 1330s. Ingledew also draws attention to Henry of Lancaster rebuking himself for vanity over his garters in the *Book of Medecynes*.[58] This raises the further question of the semiotic and ideological coding of garters and the notorious difficulty of mounting arguments about historical events from the history of fashion. Jonathan Boulton suggests a garter was chosen for Edward's order "because it was an obsolescent item of male attire that would be distinctive when worn."[59] Richard Barber, on the other hand, argues that "garter" as a word is rare before the foundation of the Order; he cites a late fourteenth-century manuscript, *Femina*, that says: "From those men of the garters comes the use of garters."[60]

This suggests that the Order set a fashion, rather than appropriating either a current or obsolescent fashion, but dating fashion quite as precisely as these texts do is rarely a reliable science. Begent and Chesshyre conclude that "the buckled garter, sometimes highly decorated, probably used to keep the hose in place rather than to hold it up, was to be found throughout the greater part of the fourteenth century."[61] Elisabeth Crowfoot, Frances Pritchard, and Kay Staniland show a photograph of a garter, knotted with the end hanging down, from a late fourteenth-century deposit, and discuss the techniques involved in weaving these "narrow wares."[62]

Martorell, writing in the 1460s, is specific about the similarity between the Garter insignia and fifteenth-century women's garments, as he describes the Garter robes: "The hoods were lined with ermine and embroidered with buckled garters, the kind many noblewomen use to hold up their stockings. Once they have buckled these garters, they loop them over to make a knot and let them hang almost halfway down their legs."[63]

Given the paucity of evidence and the degree of critical investment in interpreting the ephemera of fashionable adornment, it is almost impossible to break out of this vexed hermeneutic circle, especially as garters, girdles, and laces of different kinds often also had a ritual or an erotically charged life in the world of romance.[64] Writhe's Garter Book, compiled in the fifteenth century, records the custom whereby a knight wears a silken lace on his shoulder, which he wears until a reliable witness, such as a herald, can testify to his deeds of arms. At this point, a noble lady may remove it.[65] Other stories resonate here like Gawain's girdle or the belts exchanged by the lovers in Marie de France's *Guigemar*. The courtly and ritual exchange of such garments between men and women at the very least naturalizes the transfer of the garter from woman to man in the Garter myth.

Later evidence and discussions are similarly both suggestive and potentially circular. In 1467 Chester Herald compiled an elaborate account of "a story of staged chivalrous display," in Maurice Keen's words, of a joust between Lord Scales and Anthony, the Great Bastard of Burgundy, at Smithfield in 1467, at the Arthurian-inflected court of Edward IV.[66] Chester's narrative is preserved in British Library Manuscript Lansdowne 285. It quotes Scales's own account of leaving Mass at Easter and making obeisance to the Queen, when he was suddenly surrounded by "all the ladies of hir Court." He then found that they "of theire grace had tied aboute my thye a Coler of goolde garnysshid with precious stones and was made of a letter the which for to say trough whan I perseyvid was more nyghe my harte than my knee and to the same coler was attachide and tiede a noble floure of Souvenaunce ennameled." Scales goes on to tell how, "all abasshede of this adventure," he realized the ladies had dropped a little roll of parchment into the cap he had taken off to make his bow. This bill outlines the terms of the adventure he must now undertake: a two-day encounter with the Bastard. The elaborate process of this chivalric event, and the delicacy and suggestiveness of the challenge—the gold collar or garter tied around the thigh, "nearer the heart than the knee"—may allude to the Garter myth, but at the very least affirms the longevity in court culture of its sexualized resonances.[67]

Isaac Jackson quotes Butler's *Hudibras* and Herrick's *Hesperides*, which both allude to wedding garters being worn as favors, while a pageant for Queen Elizabeth at Kenilworth in 1575 featured "lustie lads and bolld bachelerz of the parish," each with his "blue buchram bridelace upon a braunch of green broom . . . tyed on his left arm."[68] Certainly the left arm, where women wore the Garter, is suggestive, while the term "bride lace" recalls the *Gawain* poet's "luflace." Even though he offers no specific medieval allusions, Jackson guesses that a bride lace, or garter, may have been worn by the Black Prince at his wedding to Joan of Kent. Most of Jackson's speculations are barely sustainable, but there is a hint that bride laces and garters belong to a longer and older tradition (one that is still honored today). Barber also finds that in 1389, prostitutes in Toulouse had to wear a badge of a garter by royal decree, and comments: "Once again, there is a suggestion of political mockery and propaganda."[69] In all these later examples, as in *Sir Gawain and the Green Knight*, a poem much closer to the founding of the Order of the Garter, garters, girdles, and laces are clearly associated with sexual exchanges of one kind or another. A further difficulty resides in the very great differences between the use of this common item of clothing, and the Garter in its formal manifestation. And this is another reason for the popularity of the Garter myth: it serves in large part to bridge that gap between everyday wear and ritual practice.

A number of commentators have found alternative, more highly motivated explanations of the Garter's origins that testify to some complex cultural investments in medievalism. Many of these are marginal cases, without the support of much, if any, historical evidence, but they serve as a powerful reminder of the way the Middle Ages often functions as the site of occluded "knowledge" that seems to confer a kind of authority, or indeed, mythic capital, on those cunning or bold enough to decode it.

Margaret Murray suggested in 1921 that the garter was a symbol of great significance in the "Old Religion," and the lady's embarrassment derived from this accidental proof that she held a high place in that religion.[70] Edward's kind words would have indicated to his guests that he understood the sign and sympathized with its affiliations. Donald Michael Kraig goes even further, commenting: "Many believe that Edward was a Witch and the Order of the Garter (the garter being a Witch symbol) was a Witch order," though he offers no evidence for this supposition.[71] Such views carry no weight with medieval historians, however. For Mark Ormrod, Edward was "utterly conventional and predictable in his personal devotions. . . . [His] personal religion is interesting not because it was unusual, but because it was so typical of his time."[72]

Dan Cruickshank, "an architectural historian with a track record of finding sex in improbable places," according to Maev Kennedy, argued in a BBC2 television program in 2002 that St. George's Chapel contains many carved examples of the *vesica piscis,* the fish-shaped vessel he describes as "a holy symbol representing the vagina of the Virgin Mary."[73] For Cruickshank, the Garter takes its origin from this shape, and the "y" of the Garter motto thus refers to the vagina. His supporting evidence comes from Mondonus Belvaleti's ambiguous remark that the garter "took its beginning from the female sex," an idea that was also taken up by Catherine Blackledge in her *Story of V: Opening Pandora's Box,* as further support for her claims about the long history of venerating the vagina.[74]

Such explanations underline the idea of a secret, encoded meaning to the mysterious combination of garter and motto, an idea that also plays a part in cabbalistic thought; for example, in Hargrave Jennings's 1870 study of Rosicrucian rites in which Edward is thought to have picked up not the lady's garter but an undergarment stained with menstrual blood (though his language and reasoning are coy to the point of opacity).[75] Some of the most sensationalist interpretations gain added mileage by speculating on whether the current knights and Companions "realize" they may be processing in honor of the Virgin's vagina. Kennedy paraphrases Cruickshank, "The knights would be astonished if they realised the origin of their glittering stars and silver and blue silk straps." Jenny Diski, in a very skeptical review of Blackledge's book, nevertheless calls on the same trope, the contrast between formal dignity and the sexual subtext: "We must hope that the likes of Baroness Thatcher, Elizabeth Windsor, the Emperor Akihito and James Callaghan were informed of this when they were inducted into the order."[76] Commentaries like this certainly seem to be accepting the motto's invitation to say or think what cannot or should not be said or thought.

These occluded narratives sit at the margins of the Garter myth, but can still be grouped together with Martorell's and Vergil's stories as a feminized mythic narrative, a story of shameful, trivial origins that has been systematically discounted for almost as long as it has been told.

This feminized story of shame could not be repressed without being displaced by a more honorable account, however, and there arose an alternative explanation with a narrative history almost as long, though it has never seized the popular imagination. In this account, first appearing in Henry VIII's *Liber Niger*, the "garter" is a small military strap or arming buckle that Edward elevated to prominence (following the inspiration of Richard I), to celebrate his great victories in France; and the motto is a defiant challenge to any disputing his claim to the French throne (the Garter's colors are blue and gold, the colors of the fleurs-de-lis on the French coat of arms). The statutes of this period stress that the Garter is tied on the leg of the knights as a sign of their brotherly companionship with one another, and the ties of affection and loyalty between knights and sovereign feature strongly in all the official discourse of the Order. And lest we start thinking any shameful thoughts about homosocial or homosexual bonds, the registrar corrects our suspicions in the "Institutio Ordinis" in the *Black Book*: "It must be a very wicked and unchristian Thought, for any to imagine that the divine Spirit was not with them in his Work."[77] We will return to this question of "brotherhood" in the next chapter.

Most recently, Richard Barber suggests that the Garter resembles a miniature belt, reminiscent of the belt used in the investiture of a knight,[78] and Boulton suggests Edward's choice of the insignia for the Order was far more deliberate than occasional, influenced by his cousin Alfonso XI of Castile's recently formed Order of the Band.[79]

In many of the accounts that privilege these chivalric or military origins over the more popular courtly or feminized ones, from the sixteenth century through to the present, scholars take a distinct pleasure in telling the more romantic and amusing feminine story and then displacing it with the "truer" more historical and masculine one. In these alternative readings of the Garter, the military drive to conquer France is seen as the less shameful act, while this alternative derivation from a tiny and unspecific "strap" is not seen as shameful at all, especially if it can replace the embarrassing female garter. The English are not ashamed of pressing the royal claim to the French crown; but they are ashamed if their king shows a weakness toward women or lets the conventions of courtly chivalry dictate military or heraldic policy.

In all discussions about the Order's origins, it is almost impossible, even now, to disentangle critical and political motivations. These investments are an indication, I think, of the order's signifying power as a form of ritual practice that still has the capacity to contribute to the monarchy's mythic capital.

So, is there a verifiable historical core at the heart of the Order? A narrative or an explanation on which we can all agree? Not really. If there was a particular foundational moment behind Edward's decision, it seems lost to time. This absence at the heart of the Order functions, however, as a perpetual invitation to explain and account for Edward's choice of insignia and motto for his new order of chivalry. The mythic residue of the Garter legend continues to work by generating rather than closing down interpretations. The fact that so many responses to that invitation appeal, one way or another, to the structures of myth and romance is a powerful measure of the Order's medievalism; the way it seems to permit the expression of desire for what the medieval past should have been like.

Honi soit qui mal y pense

The *Honi soit* motto is well documented in association with the Order from its first records, and seems to provide a reassuring core of authoritative textual certainty among the confusion of incomplete Wardrobe accounts and conflicting histories. But if the Garter insignia has become an undecidable emblem, the motto positively celebrates its own ambivalence. This is not unique among heraldic mottoes: such ambiguity is a frequent feature of their syntax, and the signs and badges that often accompanied them. A. C. Fox-Davies comments on the badge: "It generally partook of the nature of what ancient writers would term 'a quaint conceit,' and much ingenuity seems to have been expended in devising badges and mottoes which should at the same time be distinctive and should equally be or convey an index or suggestion of the name and family of the owner."[80] Richard II's white hart is the most famous fourteenth-century example of the badge.

As we saw in the first section of this chapter, mottoes were a crucial part of the rich textual and visual culture of Edward's tournaments. New motifs and colors for painting, textiles, clothes, and embroidery were often designed anew for separate occasions, although the specific allusions are often ephemeral and now lost to us.[81] Like the Garter insignia, another oblique motto, "It is as it is," was distributed liberally on clothes and ceremonial bedcovers in the 1340s.[82] Another—"Hay hay the wythe swan by goddes soule I am thy man"—demonstrates the ease with which the King invoked the feminized world of romance for the purposes of his Christmas games at Otford in 1348.[83] This is the king who appeared incognito as "Monsieur Lyonel" at the tournament at Dunstable in 1344, encoding his favored personal symbol of the leopard.[84] Edward's games and tournaments often involved masquerade and dressing up, and he and his knights appeared as Tartars in 1331, and as the pope and his cardinals in the Smithfield tournament of 1343.

Notwithstanding the undoubted seriousness and lasting impact of Edward's decision in 1340 to quarter the arms of England with those of France, it is helpful to recall, in this context, the medieval court's capacity to *play*. Juliet Vale argues, for example, that Richard I's legendary pilgrim disguise was an important model for Edward's own disguises, which either called up Arthurian traditions such as the Round Table, a feast at Pentecost, and characters like Lionel; or other mythological creatures like the wodwose, or wildman, who appears in *Wynnere and Wastoure*.[85] The appearance at a tournament in 1375 of Edward's mistress, Alice Perrers, dressed as the Lady of the Sun, is another example of the English court's willingness to experiment with alternative mythologies.

Susan Crane also draws attention to the enigmatic nature of many of the personal signs, mottoes and badges that proliferated during the period of the Hundred Years' War: "Some stories may be lost, but the enigmatic quality of most mottos suggests that personal devices were often deliberately occulted. Rather than simply proclaiming the bearer's identity, enigmatic signs work to mystify the aristocratic self by enlarging its signature but at the same time resisting close scrutiny."[86] Like the motto "jamais" of Charles VI (a deeply embedded reference to an Arthurian spiritual allegory)[87] or "in my defens," adopted as late as 1475 by James III of Scotland, Edward's two favorite mottoes ("It is as it is" and "Honi soit qui mal y pense") both invite more questions than they answer.[88] Crane comments, "Even as they assert control, these mottos preserve the empowering enigma characteristic of mottos: . . . what 'it' and 'y' refer to is unspecified. Shame unto him who thinks ill of this garter? of this gesture? of this order? of this claim to France?"[89]

"It is as it is," as Vale suggests, "is the kind of phrase that might have provided the refrain in some forms of contemporary lyric," and the Garter motto shares the same allusive and elusive qualities.[90] It seems likely that Edward may have chosen a phrase that was deliberately vague in its reference, either to mystify his purpose or to initiate a kind of courtly guessing game. The occulted quality of the Garter motto may even be its primary meaning, rather than an oblique reference to an original event of which we have lost all trace. There are other possibilities, too. The popular story may well be true; and Edward may have founded his Order or named it to celebrate an amusing incident, feeling no embarrassment about the association. Alternatively, the motto may already have had some currency, as bon mot or lyrical refrain, when such an event took place: the humor may arise from its perfect application, as *le mot juste*, on such an occasion. This may indeed be the kind of currency the motto enjoys when it is appended to the end of *Sir Gawain and the Green Knight*.

Either way, this provocative motto—*Honi soit qui mal y pense*—becomes a kind of small but powerful textual machine for generating explanations and etiological narratives. Its long history is as complex as that of the garter itself, as that most ephemeral of garments becomes a richly symbolic sign, capable of endless transformation across a series of embodied, sartorial, and heraldic contexts. The garter also comes to function as an unstable supplement, in the deconstructive sense of the word, to normal costume. The garter adorns the knightly body as an additional mark of distinction, but that body then faces constant scrutiny to ensure it is correctly and fully adorned to this last point: a Garter knight's formal dress is not complete if he does not wear the garter in some form or other.

These possibilities allow us to speculate on a more critical level about the various explanatory accounts that circulate around the Garter story and to focus on their competing explanations of Edward's motto as much for what they tell us about how their authors conceptualize "shame" or "evil" as for their plausibility as historical narratives. In the absence of any definitive four-teenth-century explanation, all such accounts are imaginative exercises in his-torical reconstruction, describing the motivations of the King at a distance of at least several generations.

One of the hermeneutic challenges posed by the motto derives from its problematic form. As a subjunctive—"Honi soit qui" (*May he be shamed who*)—the motto's illocutionary effect is conditional.[91] It is only if the terms of the second clause—"mal y pense" (*thinks evil of this*) are accepted, if the observers should indeed think it evil to souvenir a lady's garter, to wage war on France, or some other action, that they are to be shamed. The story of the lady's garter is the only one to generate a social narrative, but in this story it is always assumed the King's motto is successful as a performative act: he does indeed "shame" his courtiers and stop their laughter. As Emily Steiner ob-served to me, it is the King who decides when it is a game and when it is seri-ous, when the laughter must stop.[92] But there is then an important distinction between the way the King's speech is used in Martorell's romance, for example, to silence the courtiers' mockery, and the way it functions in the future, as an injunction against any such laughter or condemnation.

For most writers from the fourteenth century to the sixteenth (from *Sir Gawain and the Green Knight*, to Martorell, Vergil, and many Elizabethan commentators), the equation of "shame" with a story like the Garter myth (or Gawain's girdle) seemed perfectly natural. Medieval and Renaissance court culture naturalizes and facilitates the transformation into chivalric ritual of a contingent encounter between a king and a court lady; the shame of her costume falling apart; female underclothes becoming public property to be exchanged among men; a king falling in love with a woman whose garter might be so "loose"; and finally, the King being so infatuated that he would allow this feminized encounter to influence military and royal policy.[93] Later writers, however, for whom the courtly era belonged emphatically in the medieval past, are certain that *this* would be an "evil" thing indeed, if this were the origin of the Order. In this way, the problem of the motto is symptomatic of one of the problems of medievalism: the ways modernity writes about and *explains* medieval culture.

To compound the difficulties of identifying a single original event, two of the earliest literary references to the Order are not strictly concerned with shame at all. As we saw above, *Wynnere and Wastoure* presents the motto in English, as "Hethyng haue the hathell that any harme thynkes." "Hethying" (from Old Norse) is usually glossed as "contempt," "scorn," or "hatred"; the word may have been chosen for its alliterative effect, but perhaps also as a weak misreading of "shame." Perhaps this author, so loving in his praise of Edward, and so concerned with economic and political theory, was unable to think any shameful evil at all in association with him. Certainly there is no hint here of any courtly or feminine engagement: the context is purely masculine, military, and civic. To the frustration of those wanting to find early evidence of the more bellicose reading, this poem is not really concerned with the King's foreign policy either; the debate that takes place concerns only the national or household economy.

Martorell's variant is even more powerful: his king will have anyone who thinks evil punished (*puni*). Here, the ethical invocation of shame is displaced by the much stronger disciplinary threat. Shame, however, features strongly in much of the discourse around the Order, as we will see in Chapter 4.

One of the most intriguing features of the motto is its potential to make divisions between its hearers or viewers: between those who might find evil and those who do not; between those who might find something evil and those who might find something else evil; between those who are thus shamed and those are not; and finally, most importantly, between those who understand what is going on and those who do not. If the motto is a machine for generating meanings, it is also a powerful instrument for distributing a hierarchy of knowledge and royal favor. This reading brings us back to the social and ritual meaning of the motto, the emblem, and the Order.

Ritual Meanings

Whatever the historical truth of the story about the lady's garter and despite the many doubts cast on its veracity, it circulates around and through six and a half centuries of official and popular discourse of the Order with a vigorous life of its own, a juicy piece of historical gossip. And like gossip, its circulation is increased rather than diminished by the many attempts to discount it, thus raising the mythic capital of the Order even further. The greater the mystery about an institution's origins, the greater its glamour and the more it seems beyond the capacity of curious outsiders to comprehend. No matter how earnestly historians protest its unlikeliness, and no matter how strongly they urge the rival origins of Garter and motto, the story of the lady's garment and Edward's defiant defense of her remains by far the most popular account. Even those most keen to dismiss it seem compelled to repeat it, because it testifies to the Order's popularity in the national imagination, and thus bolsters their own inquiries into its longevity and symbolic resonance—in other words, its mythic capital.

It is no small part of the motto's success that it foregrounds the distinction between those who do comprehend its mysteries and those who cannot. Even if we do not follow the path of the conspiracy theorists or think of the Order as a secret society, its elite and exclusive nature, like the various regulations about the wearing of its symbols, affirms a crucial difference between those inside and those outside its ranks. For most of the Garter's history, that difference has been primarily a difference of class.

However, there is another explanation for the story's persistence, an explanation that speaks more to the cultural and ritual work it performs than the question of its historical veracity or likelihood. It is now time to explore the social and symbolic dynamics of the story, and the insights it simultaneously discloses and conceals. In the most satisfying way imaginable, this story answers to a ritual need to debase or humiliate a king, and to see the king's majesty restored after that humiliation. In this section I am reading the Garter myth, as I will call it, less as a textual artifact than as a kind of composite narrative that gains its force not from any particular retelling or any historical origins but from the features that appear across a number of retellings. One of the chief differences between nearly all early versions, for example, concerns the identity of the woman. This is of interest to the historian but is of little account in the ritual context. Although I will refer to the versions offered by Martorell, Vergil, and others, in this section I am unashamedly reading the story for its mythic function. Most of my readings must be hypothetical; they are presented as a meditation on the social meanings that are embedded in this story, and that account for its vexed reception in the history of the Order. Finally, I will argue that the Garter story's confused status as historical record, popular tradition or myth is a key feature of its reception.

The prime meaning of the Garter myth is its celebration of the King's capacity to make meaning and to generate signs. From a random accident of female embarrassment, and from the slightest of undergarments, the King conceptualizes a great order of chivalry, transforming the humble, eminently unstable and feminine item into a permanent, masculine, heraldic emblem, complete with its own formal motto and blazon. With a single, decisive gesture and a defiant speech, he also anticipates the transformation of the courtiers' mockery of the woman, the item, and his own action, to an attitude of almost sacred veneration.

That this symbolic reading is the dominant one is borne out, ironically, by the counter-narrative. If the "garter" refers to a strap, or part of a horse's trappings, or of a knight's armor, or his belt, these versions rehearse the same dynamic of elevating a small item into an honorific sign, though the degree of transformation from trivial to momentous is slighter. The military reading may be less risky and may seem to redound more to the King's honor than the sexualized one, but the magnitude of the structural shift from low to high is thereby diminished: it is the dramatic and unexpected juxtaposition between the humbleness of the item and the greatness of the subsequent institution that measures the King's power to make symbolic meaning, and to generate a rich symbolic economy.

This is the view of C. Stephen Jaeger, who reads the story of the lady's garter as emphasizing the King's power to translate signs and symbols from one sphere to another, from what is "vulgar, obscene and illicit" into what is "noble, and worthy of veneration." Jaeger writes of the "enchantment," the magic circle that surrounds the body of the King and gives additional force to these "social acts" that reinforce inherent values.[94] In his more developed reading, in *Ennobling Love,* Jaeger describes the King's act as

> a challenging gesture, which places the observing courtiers before two realms of perception—the base and the sublime. They see in doubtle-optic, and are free to interpret the gesture as effeminate, to chuckle knowingly about the implied liaison between the (married) king and his dancing partner. Or they can regard it as an act of chivalry, courtliness in a heroic mode. The one is vulgar and insulting; the other exalting. The one brings down on them the shame and embarrassment of evil thoughts—not to mention the king's anger. The other raises them up to membership in a chivalric elite. Backed by those incentives, the sublime intimidates the base and silences it.[95]

Susan Crane supports Jaeger's reading of the King's transformative abilities, though she also emphasizes the risks the King, like Gawain, takes in "cross-dressing," in transferring the female garment to his own body, in a context where shame is at stake.[96] "In that moment when they can be described as cross-dressing, Edward and Gawain dramatize the risk of submitting to public judgement and the gap where their interiority might be distinguished from their renown." Crane emphasizes the recuperative power of both narratives: "In the garter and girdle narratives the illicit holds an important role as that which is denied in order to establish that which constitutes noble identity: the illicit is the trace of a potential for private identity that the aristocracy actively rejects in favor of a public identity constituted in renown." As Crane comments, it is not the wearing of these female garments as such that poses the risk to knightly dignity. A knight may appear to be feminized by the courtly ritual of accepting a lady's sleeve to wear on his helmet, but this is far from cross-dressing. Again, when Lancelot dresses as a woman in Malory's tournament of Surlouse, the effect is one of hypermasculinity or heteronormativity, because the point of the story is that even while humbled in this way—it is a kind of burlesque effect—he is still able to defeat his opponents and attract feminine approval. There is very little performative or drag effect here, since the context in which these acts take place is so clearly normative, so clearly not transgressive in any way, and since the knight's gendered identity is never questioned: he is never treated or recognized socially as female or as passing, even momentarily, as female. Rather, we may say that wearing a lady's favor *links* or *ties* or *knots* the knight to that lady, like the chains of gold by which twenty-four ladies led the Garter knights from the Tower of London to the Smithfield tournament of 1390,[97] or the belt that Margaret ties around the dragon's neck to subdue it in narratives of St. George. It does not suggest in any way that a knight *becomes* such a woman.

As Crane acknowledges here, any risk is less to the King's sexual identity than to his dignity and his control of the situation. It is less a kind of trans-vestism than a more general abasement that threatens him. Instead of being transfixed by the woman's eyes, the traditional site of amorous infatuation in the courtly sphere, he takes (or is taken by) the mostly lowly, humble, banal aspect of her dress, that which has been discarded, lost from, or symbolically excreted from her body.[98] Martorell's version is explicit, using all but the mod-ern term, about the fetishistic aspect of the King's attachment to Madresilva's garter, as he cherishes the object instead of pursuing any further encounters with the flirtatious dancer. We may even read the "looseness" of the ineffectual garment as a sign of the "looseness" of the woman: Martorell makes a point of telling us that she was far from the most comely or most gracious woman present. A further contrast is implied between the King, who is in such com-mand of signs and symbolic garters, and the woman, who cannot even control a single material example of one. Whatever the official status of the woman (queen, countess, lady, or dancing girl), the King disrupts courtly and social conventions to place an inverted value on the garment. First, he makes it an indirect sign of the women's sexuality; second, he draws attention to its ca-pacity to undo, or unman, his royal dignity; and third, he uses it as a testing ground for his capacity to recuperate a higher meaning.

In all the various identifications of the woman, all draw some kind of sexual link with the king. If the woman is his queen, there is legitimate sexual-ity, and it is the privity of the Queen's body that is claimed by the King. If the woman is his mistress, it is the privity of illegitimate sexuality made public. If the woman is the object of his desire, it is the rehearsal of sexual conquest. If the woman is his rape victim, the taking of the garter signifies the rape itself. In either direction, the end result is the same: a private exchange (like Gawain's encounter with Bertilak's wife) is exposed, only to be translated into a public sign, diminishing its personal effect.

As the King stoops to the ground, to the laughter of his courtiers, it is not simply his masculinity that is in danger but his social supremacy. In rit-ual terms, we might suggest that the symbolic or mythological truth of the story dramatizes a kind of initiation rite, not for the knights who will become honored Companions, but for the King himself. In picking up the garter, the King passes through a liminal state, in Victor Turner's sense, a form of ritual humbling before the laughter and mockery of his court, from which he arises more powerful than before. This is suggested both by the gesture of bending to the ground and by the handling of the trifling object, as if he were the lady's maid. As soon as he ties it to his own leg, however, he has begun the transition out of that liminal state.

Turner's prime case study is the Ndembu installation rites, where the chief-elect and his wife are subject to ritual humiliation and abuse before the mockery of the tribe. The man must suffer all in patience, before emerging triumphantly to be installed as chief with full ceremony. Turner cites similar examples from other traditions, and draws two relevant analogies from European chivalric or royal tradition, to show that "he who is high must experience what it is like to be low."[99] First, he cites the medieval knight who, fasting, keeps vigil on his knees in the church overnight before his elevation to knightly status. Second, he mentions Prince Philip's decision to send Prince Charles to a "bush school" (actually, the rural retreat of an exclusive private school) in Australia in 1966 to prepare him for his future role as king amid the uncourtly Australians in the rugged terrain of western Victoria (figure 5).

The subjection of modern princes to the discipline of the armed services is another example, but the most obvious historical analogy is the ritual of washing the feet of the poor on Holy Thursday, as practiced by the pope, other religious leaders, and English monarchs from Edward II to James II. The archbishop of Canterbury notably revived this practice in 2003. This is another ritual that involves the subjection and lowering of the body, but with no loss to the sum dignity of the monarch or priest. As an act of *imitatio Christi* the humble act of foot washing is immediately consecrated, in Bourdieu's sense; it quickly accrues symbolic capital for the monarch or priest, and is soon surrounded by its own charismatic rituals. The garter story seems even more dramatic, since it makes a feature of the court's laughter. This is a significant aspect of the social work performed by the story. The King is abased before his court, only to rise above them again. As Turner comments, "The chief has to exert self-control in the rites that he may be able to have self-mastery thereafter in face of the temptations of power."[100]

The Order of the Garter continually returns to this contested myth of origins because it stages such a compelling recuperation of royal dignity. At a second-order level, this myth further suggests ways in which heritage culture and royal custom can manage the possibility of ridicule across the growing

Figure 5. Prince Charles at Timbertop, 1966. © National Library of Australia.

gulf between medieval court culture and the postmedieval staging of that culture. As the centuries of Garter tradition rolled on, and as its ritual costumes
diverged further and further from everyday wear, the very act of appearing
in its elaborate regalia sometimes seems, especially since the early twentieth
century, to stage a similar risk of ridicule.

The image of Winston Churchill in an awkward modern accommodation

Figure 6. Sir Winston Churchill, 1954. © Bettmann/CORBIS.

of traditional Garter wear hints at the potential discomfort of its excesses (figure 6).

In a more recent example from Garter history, when Prince William (now the Duke of Cambridge) was invested as a member of the Order in 2009, a widely circulated photograph showed Prince Harry and Kate Middleton, then his brother's girlfriend, laughing at the embarrassed second in line to the throne as he processed past them. Extending his own leg out in jest, the prince seems to draw attention to the Garter, even though neither he nor his brother is wearing it around his leg (figure 7).

Figure 7. Prince Harry, Kate Middleton, and the Duchess of Cornwall,
2009. © Press Association.

In contrast to this merriment, the prince was described as looking "sheepish" by the *Daily Mail* reporter Rebecca English, who wrote:

When looking daft in a hat decorated with a plume of heron and
ostrich feathers, a man might hope for a bit of moral support from
his brother and girlfriend.
      Not so Prince William, who was forced to watch younger

Figure 8. Prince William in his first Garter procession, 2009. © Press Association.

brother Harry and Kate Middleton collapse in giggles as he strode past in ceremonial gown yesterday.[101]

Other papers printed a picture of the embarrassed, "sheepish" William (figure 8).[102]

The younger prince's laughter may look like the juvenile mockery of his elder brother. I think it also functions as a structural or ritual moment, akin to the laughter in the garter myth. As Edward's courtiers laugh at the discomfited lady and at the ridiculous king they enjoy a moment of social, collective supremacy, while also demonstrating exactly why they are not, themselves, the leader, as they are soon shown to be unable to conceptualize the greatness of the King's vision. Indeed, they are instantly shamed into silence by the King's motto, which performs a devastating division between those who are willing to find "evil" in his actions and those who are not. For all of Prince William's embarrassment, *he* has been elevated to the Order, while Harry has not. As "girlfriend," at the time, Kate Middleton stands even further outside the magic circle. Nevertheless, their laughter can also be read as part of the ritual.

We might observe that Prince William was unlucky to be caught with such an expression. We can probably expect him to learn how to accommodate these robes and appear with greater composure as the years go on, for ritual customs carry their own momentum and dignity, as anyone who has ever taken part in a university graduation ceremony will acknowledge. Nevertheless, the media's captivation with this particular image is a powerful instance of the structural desire to mock members of the ruling elite when they appear before us at moments of greatest vulnerability.

Hans Christian Andersen recognized there is something ridiculous about royal pageantry. "The Emperor's New Suit" tells of the dandy emperor seduced by two tricksters into praising and then "wearing" imaginary robes, with the alleged magical power to be visible only to those who are worthy to hold office. Of course, all the courtiers pretend they can see the robes until the emperor parades in front of his people.

> "But he has nothing on at all," said a little child at last. "Good
> heavens! listen to the voice of an innocent child," said the father,
> and one whispered to the other what the child had said. "But he has
> nothing on at all," cried at last the whole people. That made a deep
> impression upon the emperor, for it seemed to him that they were
> right; but he thought to himself, "Now I must bear up to the end."
> And the chamberlains walked with still greater dignity, as if they
> carried the train which did not exist.[103]

The story is usually read as an exemplary narrative about vanity and folly; or the strength of the innocent who has not been seduced by, or who resists the flattering blandishments of, fashion. But the story also demonstrates the powerful dynamics of ritual practice. Faced with the ridicule of his people, and walking along, either naked or in his underwear, the emperor is carried through by force of the ritual. "Now I must bear up to the end," he says to himself. Not only does his own will triumph, it also extends to the members of his court, who maintain the imperial fantasy, walking "with still greater dignity." Amidst the laughter and the ridicule of the people, the procession continues unbroken.

Andersen's story has several analogues, but its focus on the public scene of shame and the sustaining strength of the ritual—so much larger than the individual embarrassment of the emperor—is instructive for the capacity of ritual structure to carry powerful meaning and to sustain individual acts of humility as well as moments of humiliation.

Pursuing the ritual analysis, we might even suggest that the brief moment of courtly laughter in the Garter myth invokes the carnival inversion of social hierarchy or status reversal that is a regular feature of late medieval culture. If we can imagine pausing the progression of our narrative at the point where the courtiers are still laughing, and before the King retrieves the situation, a different kind of moment is exposed. When the story is told as an etiological narrative, in order to explain Edward's otherwise mysterious choice of an emblem, our attention is drawn to the ultimate destiny of the garter. But before the King has effected that transformation, it is worth remembering that the scene is consistently pictured as one of revelry and dancing. Indeed, Martorell's text describes how Madresilva's garter fell off "as she *whirled*" (*al voltar*) in her "rather flirtatious way of dancing and talking" (*un poc desembolta en lo dansar i en lo parlar*).[104] These details remind us that for at least one early redactor the dancing is by no means stately but at the very least lively, and possibly even quite wild.

To take a further lead from Bakhtin's reading of carnival, the moment of the garter's retrieval celebrates the "lower body," especially if we focus on the garter's emergence from beneath the lady's gown. To this extent, it anticipates the ritual of many modern "traditional" wedding receptions, in which the bridegroom kneels before his bride in her voluminous white gown and triumphantly retrieves with his teeth a frilly blue garter, as a public rehearsal of the private sexual encounter to come. In medieval, early modern, and traditional European societies, where the bridal couple is escorted to bed with all the noise and bawdiness of the *charivari*, no such ceremony is needed.

Support for my reading of the Garter narrative's ritual form comes from a surprising source. In 1672, Elias Ashmole argued vehemently against the likelihood of Vergil's story, but he could nevertheless see a structural parallel with another medieval Order:

> It hath thus fared with other Orders of Soveraign Foundation;
> and an Amorous instead of Honorable Account of their Institu-
> tion, hath by some been untruly rendred. . . . Nor hath it hapned
> otherwise with the Order of the Golden Fleece, even that also hath
> met with the same fate; and the Institution reported to have risen
> from an effeminate ground: for it is said, that its Founder entring
> one morning into the Chamber of a most beautiful Lady of Bruges
> (generally esteemed his Mistress) found upon her Toilet, a Fleece of
> low Country Wooll; whence some of his Followers taking occasion
> of sport, as at a thing unusually seen in a Ladies Chamber, he (as is
> reported of King Edward the Third, upon such another occasion)
> vowed that such as made it the subject of their derision, should
> never be honored with a Collar of the Order therof, which he in-
> tended to establish, to express the love he bore that Lady.[105]

Like the Garter narrative, this is a most suggestive story. What did the founder, Philip, Duke of Burgundy, really see in the "fleece of low country wooll?" Does the story embed a proscribed vision of the lady's pubic hair? Or is a narrative of anxiety about the duke's "low" tastes, in the courtiers' easy mockery of the Flemish woman and her reminder of the vibrant trade in wool, other commodities, and international finance in Bruges? Just as Edward elevates the humble garter, whatever its origins, into a formal heraldic sign, so does Philip elevate the natural "country wooll" into the mythical Golden Fleece, founding this order in 1430.[106] Ashmole's story even gives us the am-biguous word "low" with its triple referents (the low country of Flanders; the "natural"; and the humble). Ashmole draws an analogy between two "untrue" stories, but the effect might in fact be to reinforce each one.

Out of disarray, confusion, shame, and laughter, the King constructs a powerful mythology. We may see him as a courtly version of Lévi-Strauss's *bri-coleur*, assembling a mythological structure from a "heterogeneous repertoire which, even if extensive, is nevertheless limited,"[107] using "the remains and debris of events," or in this case, of costume.[108] Edward Muir similarly glosses *bricolage* for a late medieval or early modern context: "The amalgamation of pre-existing elements into playful or ritual assemblies: a simple wafer of bread is utterly transformed in the rite of the mass or the simple gesture of dropping a glove takes on a dire significance when it is a challenge to a dual."[109] So, too, the raising of a garter is the first step in its utter transformation. It also has a powerful emotional and ethical effect, since it emphasizes the King's power over his courtiers' desires and emotions, as well as their social behavior.

However, from the perspective of most royal, military, or heraldic historians, such mythmaking activity is quite incommensurate with the dignity of royal polity. This is one of the main reasons why it has been rejected as an account of the true origin of the Order: the disparity between the lost garter and the greatness of the Order is just too large. As Hugh Collins writes, from the perspective of the historian celebrating Edward's domestic and foreign policy, "It is hardly likely that Edward III, given the serious intent underlying his conception, would have risked trivializing it by selecting such an inappropriate badge."[110] Collins is typical of many commentators who resist the mythological aspect of the story in favor of a narrower historical explanation in terms of Edward's military strategy alone. At the same time, he acknowledges the ideological power of the Order's "enigmatic and consciously romantic associations" to "glamourize" the war with France.[111] In this tradition, the absence of a definitive or contemporaneous account suggests the events never happened, rather than that they might have been in some sense unwritable. Moreover, the opposition between "serious" and "trivial" that structures many early discussions of the garter can be misleading: the laughter at Camelot at the conclusion of *Sir Gawain and the Green Knight* reminds us that fourteenth-century court culture was certainly capable of weaving together several strands of interpretation around that poem's girdle: the penitential and the joyful. In that poem, too, laughter makes a powerful distinction between Gawain and those who are amused by his suffering: both the Green Knight *and* the Arthurian court.

In addition to those who reject the story completely, however, there are many other redactors who offer telling variants on it that substantially modify the elemental aspects of the story. Martorell's account is the most detailed, and includes a more fully imagined setting. In his story, it is not the King but a knight who actually retrieves the garter from the floor. Nor can the King even remove the garter from his body; he commands it be removed. This unwillingness to show the King actually stooping to the ground is reflected in the striking paucity of any visual representation of the story from the fourteenth century through to the present. It is another indication, perhaps, of the story's power to test the dignity of its monarchs and its royal traditions. None of the conventions of official royal portraiture would guide an artist in showing a king kneeling down to pick up a crumpled garter. Medieval and renaissance artists are coy even about representing the ritual of a monarch kneeling to install a knight with his garter, and it seems the task was more often than not delegated to another knight. The few exceptions I have found are telling: one is a line drawing in a pamphlet for children about St. George's Chapel, a context in which the story is disarmed (see Chapter 6); the second is the parodic illustration from *1066 and All That* discussed in Chapter 1.

Indeed, there are not that many illustrations of the Garter myth at all. Howard Davie, in an illustration that was used for King Edward VII's Christmas card in 1908, captures the moment of Edward III's greatest, most dignified triumph, as he turns to address the court. The garter has already been straightened out, already on its way to becoming a heraldic sign, while any embarrassment here is the countess's alone (figure 9).

Vergil's account, by contrast, is much less detailed but more direct about the King's action: from a greater historical distance he reports the popular tradition that the King is said to have gathered the garter from the ground (*è terra collegisse*). Chapter 3 explores the implications of this association of popular tradition with medieval culture in greater detail. For now, we may observe that Vergil's popular story dramatizes a brilliant and strategic reversal from humiliation to courtly triumph, and that for a brief moment it opens up a vision of a king in a liminal state of social reversal and ritual humiliation prior to his initiation, or installation, into his own Order. This transition from abasement to sovereignty is firmly sealed, brought to a decisive end by the King's own authoritative pronouncement. As a formal speech act, in French, in the courtly language of honor and shame, the King's pronouncement provides an unanswerable climax to the story, signaling the resumption of the King's authority. The contrast between reported "low" gesture and documented "high" speech could not be more marked.

This mythic story of the King's passage through this transitional, liminal, or inverted state plays a powerful role in the maintenance of the Order's cultural supremacy, even if the more literal-minded of its historians reject it as a historical narrative. There are other aspects of ritual practice in the Garter's history, too, which I consider in later chapters. When the Order negotiates its own traditions, reviving and reforming them in different ways over the centuries, it both reshapes its own rituals and takes part in the second-order rituals of revival and reformation.

Much of the opprobrium attached to the story of the lady's garter is closely associated with its medieval origins. The medieval can have different

Figure 9. *The Origin of the Order of the Garter*, illustration from *Stories of Royal Children from English History*, by Doris Ashley, published by Raphael Tuck, 1920 (color litho), Howard Davie (fl. 1914–44). Private Collection / The Bridgeman Art Library.

valencies for heritage tradition. When it comes to tracing the Order's origins
in the courtly chivalric culture of Edward III, and the possibility of the King's
weakness, the conventions of medieval courtly society can be either venerable
or downright embarrassing.

Fortunately, there is an alternative set of medieval associations that are
far less problematic, and that lend themselves much more easily to visual representation. From the very earliest moments, the Order's patron saint was
named as St. George of Cappadocia. His most famous deed, killing the dragon
to save the maiden being sacrificed, was a much less problematic subject to
represent than a king holding a woman's garter, and the image of St. George
rapidly became the Order's major figurative or pictorial icon. From the sixteenth century, Companions wore either the Greater George, a large ceramic,
often heavily ornamented model of St. George on horseback vigorously impal-
ing the dragon, suspended from a heavy golden collar, or the Lesser George, a
medallion bearing a similar image, threaded on a blue ribbon. St. George was
the obvious saint of choice, too, to illustrate manuscript copies of the statutes.

One of the most beautiful early examples is British Library Manuscript
Royal 15 EVI, the statutes presented to Margaret of Anjou in 1445. Folio 439
features the King and his Garter knights, wearing long blue Garter mantles,
on either side of an altar showing George as a knight in armor thrusting a red
lance into the mouth of a prone dragon, while the maiden, in fashionable
horned headdress, stands behind, accompanied by a little white lamb standing up on its hind legs (figure 10). Such images of St. George stem from and
are part of a longer iconographic tradition, and they were readily incorporated
into the Garter's own iconography.

It seems, then, that while vernacular fictional and romance texts like *Sir
Gawain and the Green Knight* and Martorell's *Tirant lo Blanc* are comfortable
exploring the momentary abasement of a chivalric knight or a king, the traditions of royal portraiture and deluxe manuscript illumination are rather more
constrained.

In the face of these constraints, the heroic story of St. George is a more
than acceptable alternative, as it embodies what becomes an almost quintes-
sential image of medieval chivalry: in one bold decisive stroke, the knight
rescues the maiden, releases the country from tyranny, and subdues the low
worm with his resolutely phallic lance. Like the Garter story, it features a
knight rescuing a woman and the dragon is a suitably fierce creature, but this
story poses far less risk to the knight's authority. We will have occasion to revisit the history of St. George in later chapters; for now, let us note only that

Figure 10. St. George slaying the dragon in view of the King and Garter Knights. © All Rights Reserved. The British Library Board. BL MS Royal 15.E.vi. fol. 439.

gold thread with which the maiden, a Margaret like the recipient of the manuscript, leads her lamb. In De Voragine's version of the saint's life, and in several
accounts, George subdues the dragon but does not kill it initially. Instead, he
asks Margaret to take her girdle and put it around the dragon's neck, whereupon it follows her meekly back into town "as if it were a little dog." One of
the misericords in St. George's Chapel features this chain around the dragon's
neck. It also "binds" the dragon in Uccello's famous painting of St. George.
Margaret's girdle is the female instrument with which the dragon is subdued,
reminiscent of the virgin's hair that can subdue a unicorn. Even when court
culture attempts to displace the female garter, it reappears.

Chapter 3

Histories

Love, Honor, and Medievalism

Nobilitas sub amore iacet: Nobility falls subject to love.
—Ovid, *Heroides*

When Umberto Eco wrote in the mid-1980s about the different ways we "dream" the Middle Ages, he gave the study of medievalism an important critical vocabulary and an enabling taxonomic structure.[1] At the same time, this vocabulary affirms an epistemological hierarchy between the "real" Middle Ages and the secondary Middle Ages of medievalism, whether they are dreamed, invented, or imagined. Eco's taxonomy—his "ten little Middle Ages"—is in part ironic, and yet it is undoubtedly predicated on the idea of historical difference between the medieval period and modernity's dreams of that past.

As a more or less continuous form of ritual practice enduring from the Middle Ages through to the present, the Order of the Garter allows us to approach the challenge of medievalism studies in a more fluid and open-ended way. Throughout its long history the Order offers a series of different and changing relationships with its medieval past, especially through its mixed attitudes toward its origins. The robes, the procession, the motto, and the insignia of the Order all recall its medieval origins to varying degrees, while a substantial proportion of the Garter's mythic capital depends on the longevity of its history and the idea of a tradition continuing from the medieval past into the present. That continuity is neither unbroken nor conceptually straightforward, however. The Order's links with the medieval past—both tangible and intangible ones—have to be renegotiated anew at different periods in the Order's history.

These negotiations are part of the work of ritual criticism: the discussion and critique of the origins and the performance of the ritual. In the context of the Order of the Garter, ritual criticism becomes a form of medievalism, meditating on the ways medieval practices are carried forward into the present. These two discourses offer mutually informing ways of moving backward and forward in time, destabilising the customary oppositions between past and present, medieval and modern.

While the dominant discourses associated with modernity continue to construct the Middle Ages as a distant past, the "dark" era against which the new age of the modern defines itself, we recognize now that this story of modernity's modernity, as it were, had specific origins in the Renaissance. In England, for example, across a range of cultural forms, political and religious practices, historiography and literary style, Tudor writers established a number of distinctive boundaries between the medieval past and their own present. This did not imply anything so simple as a rejection of medieval style—the medieval remained quite fashionable in court contexts—but it did involve two central ideas: first, that the medieval was a stylistic choice, rather than a necessary inheritance; and second, the resolute opposition, so successful it now seems banal, between the medieval as old and the modern as new. This has had wide-ranging implications for our ideas of historical progression, and indeed for the way in which historians and historical critics see themselves in relation to the medieval past. Sylvia Federico and Elizabeth Scala write: "It is of course the necessity of the Middle Ages, of the idea of the medieval, that makes a very discourse of modernity possible. In this sense, then, the concept of an outmoded "other" Middle Ages is one that other literary periods and the idea of periodicity and modernity themselves cannot do without."[2]

In a similar vein, Bruce Holsinger argues that the idea of the emergence of interiority and inwardness, conventionally associated with the Renaissance, actually *served* the early modern period and its historians "as perhaps the most effective ideological instrument for the construction of a medieval past that (read: the abjection of medieval selves who) lacked the capacity to exist in this same condition."[3]

Important historical work around the period of the fourteenth to sixteenth centuries is helping to rewrite, often quite radically, the history of this transition out from the Middle Ages.[4] Recent critical discussions in the field of medievalism are also helping us to conceive this historical problem less as an opposition between past and present and more as a series of multiple, layered temporalities.[5] In such a model, cultural practices and textual traditions inherited from the Middle Ages are interleaved and interwoven, often in contradictory ways, with the successive stages of modernity.

The Order of the Garter is a restricted and atypical example of the slow and gradual transformation of medieval culture into the present. As a form of ritual practice its claims to represent the course of European, even English, history are indeed limited. Yet the long history of its ritual criticism, the ways people have thought, painted, written, and dreamed about the Order, is an intriguing resource for medievalism, and for understanding its odd temporalities. Through much of the Order's history, the medieval is simultaneously called up into the present, as the authorizing foundation of traditions that can be practised *now*, and sent back into the past, as a history that explains the distant origins of current practice, and that can simply be superseded by newer traditions.

Over the course of its six-hundred-and-fifty-year history, the Order has oscillated between two impulses. As an institution, it wants to preserve traditional forms, but it also wants the freedom to renovate or reform them whenever they threaten to become unpleasantly obsolete, whenever, that is, the impulse to modernize takes precedence over the impulse to preserve or revive the medieval. At various points in the Order's history, the medieval aspects of its foundation are easily converted into mythic capital. At other times, they threaten to diminish the Order's symbolic capital in the fragile balance the monarchy needs to strike between affirming its traditional authority and its relevance to any given moment of modernity. Chapter 5 considers some of the changes to the Order's ritual practice in its period of greatest turbulence in the sixteenth and seventeenth centuries. The present chapter examines the critical and historical discourse—the ritual criticism—of the Order in this period, especially in the competing accounts and histories of the Order's origins in poetic, dramatic, and narrative form, and in the transition to the historiographical tradition that still structures our response to the Order today.

The first section explores the division between the official and popular histories that originated in the sixteenth century and that remains a structuring force in Garter history. The second section continues to examine the story of the lady's garter, tracking the persistent popularity of this story in a range of poetic, fictional, and dramatic texts, as well as its appeal for the romantic medievalism of the nineteenth century. The third section examines the history of alternative explanations and traces the uneasy interplay between the discourse of male friendship and homosociality that haunts many of the most severe critiques of the foundational Garter myth. The final section tracks the origins of a more disinterested academic discourse in the seventeenth century, distinguished by its desire to register a significant cultural shift between Edward's court and later periods. In this strategy of distance, historians become very willing to dismiss the Garter story as a symptomatic "romance" from a medieval period now lost.

Gossip and History

The persistence of the popular story about the origins of the Garter is a thorn in the side of the Garter's more sober historians, especially those writing from the seventeenth century onward, who reject any suggestion that a sexualized court intrigue might have generated a royal chivalric order. In other contexts, however, the story exemplified the kind of glamour and intrigue that made court life the object of such fascination in both the medieval and the early modern periods, and even within the contemporary era. Indeed, one of the striking features of the Garter story's favorable reception is its appeal in both courtly and popular contexts: it seems to be accepted equally by those living and writing *within* the court and those beyond its privileged circle.

For nearly one hundred and twenty years, between the 1530s and the 1650s, Polydor Vergil's account was the most widely quoted source for the Order's foundation. Its narrative account is compelling, but Vergil also frames his story in a way that generates its own interpretative and historiographical tradition. After telling the story, Vergil comments on the nature of this "popular tradition": "Such is popular tradition [*fama vulgi*]. English writers have been modestly superstitious, perhaps fearing to commit lèse-majesté, if they made known such unworthy things; and they have preferred to remain silent about them, whereas matters should really be seen otherwise: something that rises from a petty or sordid origin increases all the more in dignity."[6]

Vergil readily makes a distinction between the modest and sober discretion of the written tradition and the more widespread rumor among the people. This distinction will come to typify later understandings of the hierarchy between official and popular culture. We may go one step further and remark that in Vergil's reading, the story has all the hallmarks of royal gossip. It is undeniable that over the centuries it has generated the narrative and social pleasures we associate with that genre and that activity. Like other rumors, the story permits us to speculate about the private life of members of the royal family, to wonder at their strange customs, to take delight in their sentimental weaknesses, and even to air a knowing skepticism about the status of the rumor. Gossip is usually written about as the activity of sharing information about contemporary events, but stories like the Garter myth, by enabling gossip about the Middle Ages, introduce a diachronic dimension to the pleasure. In this way, we affirm two kinds of distance from medieval royalty: we are emphatically modern subjects and proud commoners.

Vergil's commentary anticipates the discursive hierarchies that distinguish gossip. There is the first-order pleasure in the content of gossip, and then the second-order pleasure of analyzing gossip, much like the pleasure of ritual criticism. For gossip is often accompanied by its own elaborate critical, if informal, discourse that examines the status, sources, and likeliness of gossip, which draws analogies and comparisons with other stories, and which identifies deeper psychological or institutional structures at work. A third stage, facilitated by contemporary global media, is often a reflective stage, where the gossipers reflect comfortably on the horrors of life in the goldfish bowl of celebrity culture or membership in a royal family, underlining their own immunity from such gossip and affirming a position of comfortable moral superiority over the subjects of their gossip.

One of the particular pleasures of royal gossip is its opposition to the official discourse of the royal family: the possibility that we may share informal "real" and popular knowledge of their secrets. *They* may be wealthy and powerful and attract the eyes of the world's media, but *we* are able to say and know things about them that they cannot say themselves. This is the pleasure of denouncing the emperor's new clothes. There is also the even more straightforward pleasure of undermining their authority: *they* may be of noble birth, but *we* are clever enough to identify and diagnose their folly. We saw in Chapter 2 that the Garter motto seems to draw a distinction between those who can comprehend the King's design and those who cannot. The pleasures of gossip and historical speculation about the medieval period offer a kind of secondary, or compensatory, knowledge and power over the story, over the medieval past, and over the privileged participants in the ritual.

Vergil's knowing distinction between popular and written tradition generates a further division, however: one that would have a serious and deleterious effect on the status of his version of the Order's founding. In accounting for the silence among the English commentators, the Italian scholar adopts an outsider's position in seeing things "otherwise." This would be used to discredit his explanation as that of "a stranger to the affairs of England," in Peter Heylyn's words (see below).

Most critical accounts of the Garter story end with this passage, but Vergil's discussion is even more expansive. By way of support for his generalization about the increase of dignity, he offers several examples of institutions that found their origins in humble circumstances, concluding with an ambiguous quotation from Ovid: *Nobilitas sub amore iacet.*

I quote here the Elizabethan translation of Vergil, entitled *Cronicle of Polydore Virgil*:

> What I pray you is now in more estimation then divers thinges which heere to fore have beenn lothed and abhorred. [*from margin:* . . . was there in tymes past any thinge accompted in many contreys more deformed or to be more despised then a shaven croune which now is the onlie difference of the holie and profunde heade.] Weare the ii brothers called Arvales fratres, whome Romulus created Sacrificiarios in suche highe estate at the beeginninge as they in conclusion aspiered unto, as was storified in our booke *de Rerum Inventoribus*? [*from margin:* Arvales fratres weare supposed to bee the fostre brothren of Romulus to whom hee gave the dignitie of priesthood, to make sacrifice for the increase of corne.] What as touchinge the office of Censore, was it not a function as Livie wittnesseth at the firste contemned among the Romanies, and yet not longe after was not all the good orderinge of the cittie under the Jurisdition thereof? Then, the troue originall of the ordre of the Gartier, shoulde not bee passed over in sylence not with standinge that the first Institution therof sprange peradventure of Loove then the which nothinge is more noble as testifiethe Ovide sayeng, Nobilitee dothe Lie in Loove and Noble is her Lord. Whearfore undoubtedlie I will not say that this Rumor of the common people is alltogether Vayne.[7]

Vergil's citations of classical authorities and examples are his best means of shoring up support for his report. The quotation from Ovid is particularly fortunate, as it is even more ambiguous than the Garter motto it purportedly explains, as the rather loose English translation shows. This longer passage from Vergil's *History*, never cited in any of the Garter commentaries, can be read as a meditation on *fama vulgi*, or popular tradition. The phrase implies a hierarchy between official culture—reticent about the true origin (*origo vera*) of the

Garter—and popular culture, which comes to seem the more candid bearer of truth that can be authenticated by analogy with older historical traditions. Vergil's concession that he was reporting the version current in popular tradition would count strongly against him, however, among those concerned to protect the specialist and privileged discourse of heraldry and the apparent dignity of the Order. Indeed, there is a discernible transference of "vulgarity" between the story's transmission in popular culture and the sexualized, or "sordid," content (Vergil's *sordida*) of the story.

William Segar, for example, in his *Booke of Honour and Armes* (1590), gives a brief version of the story: "Thus haue I heard it vulgarlie reported."[8] In 1672, Ashmole similarly dismisses the story as "the vulgar and more general" view: "And yet hath it so fallen out, that many learned men, for want of reflection, have incautelously [*sic*] swallowed and run away with this vulgar error; whereupon it hath come by degrees to the vogue it is in now."[9]

Vergil's commentary is a classicizing rather than a medievalizing one. His analogies have the effect of setting the fourteenth-century court back further in the past, another example of the shifting temporalities of medievalism. From the triumphant perspective of the sixteenth century, when the Garter was firmly established as the preeminent chivalric order, Edward can be likened to Romulus as a national founder. It will be a common theme in this and the next chapter that the relation between medieval and Renaissance, especially in the context of the royal court, often bears witness less to epistemic rupture than to continuity.

As we saw in the discussion of mythic capital in Chapter 2, this "popular" account of the Garter's origins is a persistent source of narrative pleasure, even amid the tremendous force of institutional skepticism about its veracity or even its likelihood. It answers to the need to find a secret or hidden message behind the formality of ritual practice, as well as the need (or desire) to find sex (or desire) behind official conduct. It also generates the secondary pleasures of learned commentary, and of distributing a hierarchy of knowledge about the medieval past.

"There Can Not Be a More Excellent Devise"

It is important to stress that for many decades Vergil's reception was a happy one. Raymond Waddington argues that the Elizabethan court seems even to have encouraged the propagation of Vergil's romantic story, as it harmonized with the Petrarchan sexual politics of the court mistress: "Rejection of the probably more genuine origination of the garter as a symbol of battlefield bonding among fighting knights and the substitution of an exemplary anecdote of courtly gallantry in defense of a lady's reputation encodes the mythic truth of what the Order had become under Elizabeth."[10] Many Elizabethan writers accepted Vergil's account of the Order's foundations, even if they presented variations in the story or altered his emphases. So reasons Holinshed, in 1577. He accepts the tale's popular origin ("there goeth a tale amongst the people"), and moves quickly, echoing Vergil's citation of Ovid, to counter any suggestion that this might denigrate the Order:

> Though some may thinke, that so noble an order had but a meane
> beginning, if this tale be true, yet manie honorable degrees of estates
> have had their beginnings of more base and meane things, than of
> love, which being orderlie used, is most noble and commendable, sith
> nobilitie it selfe is covered under love, as the poet Ovid aptlie saith,
> Nobilitas sub amore iacet.[11]

The quotation from Ovid appears in his *Heroides*, from Phaedra's letter to Hippolytus. It also appears in the emblem book of Otto Vaenius, under *Nescit amor magnis cedere divitiis* (Love will not yield to all the might of wealth), in the following quatrain:

> Nobilium gazas Amor, atque insignia calcat;
> Nescit enim priscis cedere imaginibus.
> Nobilitas sub Amore iacet; nam rustica Regi,
> Regia rurali saepè puella placet.

The English version, by Richard Rowlands Verstegen, is entitled "Love excelleth all":

> With Cupid is no birth esteem or welth preferd,
> A King a shepheards lasse to love hee maketh seen,
> And that a shepheards love may light upon a Queen,
> Equalitie of state love litle doth regard.[12]

The accompanying illustration shows Cupid ignoring a walled city in the background, and a chest overflowing with treasure in the foreground; he tramples on an elaborate coat of arms, its helmet with mantling and a heavy chain of office, as he appears to beckon the lover on.

Whether nobility *succumbs to, is submitted to*, or is *covered under* love, the citation of the epithet in accounts of the Garter story has the effect of normalizing and generalizing its insights, minimizing the medieval context of the Order's founding and bringing the King's speech act into the area of classical, Latin rhetoric. In the *Anatomy of Melancholy*, Burton makes the same generalization: "All our tilts and tournaments, orders of the garter, golden fleece, &c.—*Nobilitas sub amore jacet*—owe their beginnings to love, and many of our histories."[13]

George Puttenham, writing in 1589, foregrounds this connection: the Order's motto is an exemplary instance of "the device, or embleme . . . the Posie transposed."

> There can not be a more excellent devise, nor that could containe larger intendment, nor greater subtilitie, nor (as a man may say) more vertue or Princely generosite. For first he did by it mildly and gravely reprove the pervers construction of such noble men in his court, as imputed the kings wearing about his neck the garter of the lady with whom he danced, to some amorous alliance betwixt them, which was not true. He also justly defended his owne integritie, saved the noble woman's good renowme, which by licentious speeches might have been empaired, and liberally recompenced her injurie with an honor, such as none could have bin devised greater nor more glorious or permanent upon her and all the posteritie of her house. It inureth also as a worthy lesson and discipline for all Princely personages, whose actions, imaginations, countenances and speeches, should evermore correspond in all trueth and honorable simplicitie.[14]

Puttenham has the King tying the garter around his neck: a unique variant that may allude to the Tudor fashion for wearing the great gold collar of the Order around the neck and shoulders, rather than, or in addition to, wearing the garter on the leg. But his chief concern is with rhetorical figure, and so he characterizes the King's pronouncement as mild and grave, and commends the favor it grants to the lady and "all the posteritie of her house." Such is the power of rhetoric, in Puttenham's treatise, that it can immediately foreclose any unwarranted speculation and sexual gossip.

In contrast to Vergil's account, which can comfortably accommodate the transition from what is "petty or sordid" to what is rich in dignity, Puttenham barely countenances the King's transformation of the object and is quick to dismiss the idea of an "amorous alliance . . . which was not true." Puttenham retrojects, as it were, the dignified conclusion of the story back onto its entirety, so that the whole story becomes a mirror for princes, "whose actions, imaginations, countenances and speeches, should evermore correspond in all trueth and honorable simplicitie." Perceived as a model of ritual grace, this is the purest courtly reception of the story. There is no risk here to the King, who is in perfect control of the situation, rhetorically, ethically, and dynastically.

In such accounts there is little apology for the story or any sense of embarrassment. If anything, we find evidence of a cultural continuity from the Edwardian to the Elizabethan court in the sphere of poetry and romance narrative, underpinned by a common familiarity with classical tradition. In this dynamic, the medieval is comfortably and easily modernized, with little sense of epistemic rupture.

Vergil's anonymous, rather expansive sixteenth-century English translator similarly endorses the story of the woman's garter, while also attributing it to "the ruder sorte." Once more, our attention is drawn to the disparity between courtly play and the "Vulgare opinion" of outsiders. This translator offers a remarkable dramatization of the King's courtiers making sport with the retrieved garter:

> Among the ruder sorte, the sayenge is as yet that the Kinge on a
> time tooke upp from the grounde the gartere of the queene or som
> paramoure which she beefore hadd loste, and that divers of his
> Lordes standinge bie did pulle it in sonder in jeste and strove for
> the peaces therof as men are wonte somtime for a jeuill of small
> importance insomutche that the Kinge sayde unto them, Sirs the
> time shall shortlie comme when you shall attribute muche honor
> unto suche a Garteir, whearuppon he didd institute this order and
> so intituled it. That his Nobles might understond that they hadd
> caste them selves in their owne Judgement. This is the Vulgare opin-
> ion, but the Englishe Croniclers beinge somwhat shamefaced, and
> fearing leaste they shoulde disbast the Kinges royall Maiestie if they
> shoulde seeme to make minde of enie suche obskeuer matter, rather
> thoughte goode to leave it cleane Untouched as thoughe it hadd
> never earste beenne seene, that a thinge which sprange of a vile and
> small principle, shoulde arise to great encrease and highe dignitee.[15]

The translator's addition conjures up an extraordinary image of courtly play, with the bored knights tossing the garter to and fro, pulling it apart for sport, to tease the woman who had lost it. The garter has been thoroughly debased by this homosocial jesting at the expense of the woman. There is no easy transition from the woman's body to the King's; rather, the garter is exchanged and torn apart at the hands of several courtiers, before the King gallantly rescues it, taking the garter "up from the ground" and claiming it at his own, as the inspiration of his new order. This translator is more interested in these lordly games with expensive trifles (the oxymoronic "jeuill of small importance") than in the identity of the woman ("the queene or som paramoure"), and deeply concerned with what their levity reveals about the courtiers' ungallant attitude. Expounding on the nature of the shame that the King invokes, he emphasizes the ethical nature of the King's lesson to his court, but willingly countenances his bodily stooping. This translation offers a powerfully naturalistic dramatization and expansion of the scene that takes for granted a strong degree of cultural continuity and similarity between the medieval and the Elizabethan court.

This version of the story nevertheless underlines the differences between historical courts and the fictional courts of Arthurian romance. In the latter, a woman is most likely to need rescue from a giant, a demon, or a ravishing knight, while in the historical court, her greatest danger is homosocial mockery. When an external threat appears, men compete to save women; in the absence of such threat, the court itself can become a threatening place.

George Peele's romantic vision poem, *The Honour of the Garter,* from 1593, introduces the Order of the Garter in a way that also actively celebrates the continuities in greatness between King Edward and Queen Elizabeth. Spenser-like, Peele includes several touches of archaic expression: "a goodly king in robes most richly dighte"; "the order of the Garter so ycleepd." The poet has a vision of Windsor and sees a procession of great kings and queens, concluding with a celebration of Elizabeth as its presiding queen, in which King Edward speaks to congratulate the knights newly admitted into the order. There is no embarrassment here about the Order's humble origins:

A great effect, grown of a slender cause,
Graced by a King, and favoured of his feeres,
Famed by his followers, worthy Kings and Queenes,
That to this day are Soveraignes of the same.

Peele describes the origin of the Garter:

> The King disposed on a time
> To revell, after he had shaken Fraunce,
> (O had he bravely helde it to the last)
> And deckt his Lyons with their flowre de Lyce,
> Disposed to revell: Some say otherwise,
> Found on the ground by Fortune as he went
> A Ladies Garter: And the Queenes I troe
> Lost in a daunce, and tooke it up himselfe.
> It was a silken Ribban weaved of blewe.
> His Lords and standers by, seeing the King
> Stoope for this Garter, smiled: as who would say,
> Our office that had beene, or somwhat els.
> King Edward wistlie looking on them all,
> With Princely hands having that Garter ceazd,
> From harmelesse hart where honour was engraved,
> Bespake in French (a could the language well)
> And rife was French those dayes with Englishmen;
> They went to schoole to put together Townes,
> And spell in Fraunce with Feskues made of Pikes.
> Honi Soit Qui mal y pense, quoth he,
> Wherewith upon advizement, though the cause
> Were small, his pleasure and his purpose was
> T'advance that Garter, and to institute
> A noble order sacred to S. George:
> And Knights to make, whom he would have be tearmed
> Knights of the Garter. This beginning had
> This honourable order of our time.[16]

Peele offers two rival versions ("Some say otherwise"), but the more detailed, loving account also shows the King "stoope" for the garter to take it up
himself. His courtiers respond not so much by impugning a sexual motivation to the King as by expressing amusement that he should stoop to perform
this menial task. Peele's version, then, evokes what I have diagnosed as the
initiatory aspects of the story, as the King is seemingly humbled, if only for a
moment. Like many of these Garter narratives, and especially those that deploy the oneiric tropes of vision and dream, *The Honour of the Garter* relishes

the play of multiple temporalities. Even in these short extracts, we see Peele invoking the idea of continuity (the Kings—and Queens—who followed Edward III as Sovereigns of the Order); the alterity of the past (when the French language was "rife" among Englishmen); nostalgia for that past (in the wish that Edward had been able to hold on to France); and the reclamation of the medieval Order for the sixteenth-century present ("this honourable order of our time").

We saw in the previous chapter that some medieval French chroniclers seized on this story to impute worse motives to the English king. By the seventeenth century, the story had become a great romance worthy of novelistic treatment, wherein Edward's infatuation with the Countess of Salisbury becomes the motivating emotional force behind his chivalric gesture. In these versions, many of them French, the emphasis shifts away from the King's masterful courtly improvisation and stresses his feminization, his falling subject to love.

In 1620, André Favyn offered a version that is startling in its concrete detail and willingness to expose, as it were, the secret source of shame. Favyn's king is infatuated with the countess, who comes bidden to the tournament and feasts dressed as simply as possible, in an unsuccessful attempt to deflect the King's attention. While most accounts stress the King's action of transferring the garter to his own leg, Favyn has the King, besotted with the countess's beauty, attempting to replace the blue silk garter as high as possible around the countess's leg as he sits conversing (*devisant*) with her: "Il leva quant & quant la Chemise si haut, que les Courtisans l'ayans veuë, ne se peurent tenir de rire."[17] This unique variant firmly sets aside any possibility of cross-dressing. By contrast, the King's attempt to replace the garter around the countess's leg, pushing her dress higher and higher as he does so, exposing more and more of her body, makes him appear both clumsy and sexually crude. Again, this version is unusual in that it reports, if indirectly, the lady's reproach and reprimand. The woman at the heart of the Garter myth is usually embarrassed into silence, an awkward gap that is filled by the King's gallant bon mot.

The English translation of 1623 expands Favyn's narrative even further, with its irresistible desire to spell out exactly what the courtiers see:

> Forasmuch as King Edward being wounded with love of faire Alix,
> the Countesse of Salisbury, one day as hee was devising with her,
> the left Garter (of Blew Silke) of this Lady, hung loosely down upon
> her shooe. King Edward, ready at the Ladies Service, and to take

up the Garter; by little and little lifted her cloathes so high, that the
Courtiers had some sight of her white Smock, & could not refraine
from smiling. The Lady reprehended the King for this publick fault
before his own people (who carried good lookes, but bad thoughts,
and pleased their owne opinion so much, that they made an Idoll
of their vaine conceits:) King Edward therefore, to cover his owne
honour, stopt all their mouthes with these few French words;
Honny Soit Qui Mal y Pense.[18]

This retelling foregrounds the secret of women's privity which underlines
all versions of this story, but which is rarely exposed as dramatically as it is
here, with the shock of the glimpse of white underwear (like the erotically
charged flash of skin between two garments of which Roland Barthes writes
in *The Pleasure of the Text*) and the countess's own unusual words of reproach.

Richard Johnson, in his "Gallant Song of the Garter of England," from
1620, actually attributes the *Honi soit* motto to the queen of France. When her
garter falls during a feast, the snickering courtiers seem to accuse her of dropping it deliberately to attract the King's attention, so it is actually the Queen
who coins the motto in their reproof:

> But when she heard these ill conceits
> And speeches that they made,
> Hony soyt qui mal y pens,
>   the noble Princes said.
> Ill hap to them that evill thinke,
> In English it is thus
> Which words so wise (quoth Englands King)
>   shall surely goe with us.[19]

Edward says England's peers will wear this Garter, with its motto, so all will
know "Our garter came from France."

These narrative variants on and experiments with Vergil's story are all
generated by a range of possibilities around the heterosexual encounter and
subtexts suggested by his account. To return to the argument of Chapter 2,
the motto and insignia seem capable of generating an almost endless array
of interpretations, and we may suspect that the very medievalness of the Order's foundations, their very distance from modernity, plays an important role
in the freedom of invention at play here. At the same time, we must also

acknowledge the force of the narrative drive: the story about the lady's garter is simply a more engaging narrative—after all, it dramatizes love, desire, and shame—than any other explanation of the Order's origins. As we have seen, it maintains the status of foundational myth, even in the face of many attempts to discount it.

The repressed eroticism of the story was particularly conducive to expansion in the romantic medievalism of the nineteenth century. One of Alexandre Dumas' earliest historical novels was *La Comtesse de Salisbury*. It was published in 1839, and an English translation by "E.R.M." appeared in the following year, although the translator "corrects" Dumas' conflation of the Round Table with the rebuilding of Windsor Castle (p. 224). In the main narrative, Edward has performed well at a tournament, and in the height of his success and his love for the countess, at the dance afterward, he

> availed himself of this confidence to press occasionally, as if by chance, the hand which she held forth to him, sometimes to touch her floating locks with his lips, and to luxuriate in all the intoxicating pleasure that surround [*sic*] women in the atmosphere of a ball room.
>
> During one of the labyrinthine figures which composed the tissue of the dance, the Countess's garter, which was of sky-blue satin embroidered with gold, fell off without her knowledge. Edward sprang forward to obtain possession of it; but the movement was not so rapid as to prevent other eyes than his own from guessing at the larceny which the King intended committing. The dance was immediately broken up, amid the smiles of the party. Edward understood, from this courtierly retreat, that his designs were not unsuspected, and putting the ribbon round his own knee, he said aloud: "*Honi soit qui mal y pense.*" This incident gave birth to the order of the garter.[20]

A more romantic atmosphere of flirtation—without the intended larceny of rape, and featuring a uniquely chaste garter (part of the countess's shoe)—pervades John Mackay Wilson's version from 1869. It is part of a collection with the intriguing title *Tales of the Borders and of Scotland: Historical, Traditional and Imaginative*. This suggests the easy blurring of those categories in the heyday of medievalism. Wilson takes obvious pleasure in filling out the bare bones of the received story with novelistic detail:

He had provided a royal banquet for the nobles and the knights
who had distinguished themselves during the French wars. A
thousand lights blazed in the noble hall—martial music pealed
around—and hundreds of the brightest eyes in England looked love
and delight. The fairest and the noblest in the land thronged the
assembly. Jewels sparkled and studded the gorgeous apparel of the
crowd. In the midst of the hall walked the gay and courtly monarch, with the fair Joan of Salisbury resting on his arm. They spoke
of their first meeting at Wark, of the siege and the tournament, and
again they whispered, and hands were pressed, and looks exchanged;
and, while they walked together, a blue garter, decked with gold,
pearls, and precious stones, and which, with a golden buckle, had
fastened the sandal of the fair Joan round the best-turned ankle in
the hall, became loose and entangled among her feet.[21]

Wilson's account offers a rare redistribution of the garter—not upward,
onto sash, collar, and badge but downward, reading the garter back from
its later jeweled state, fit for external display, and displacing its status from
underwear to footwear. The proliferation of detail here, around an entirely
original interpretation of the garter as a shoe strap, exemplifies the mythic
force of the story of chivalric rescue. It is a story ripe for redevelopment and
retelling, like any myth or fairy story, according to prevailing narrative styles
and fashions.

Such elaborate and romanticized versions, however, represent a kind
of conceptual limit to the story's postmedieval development as heterosexual
romance narrative. In contrast, modern narratives develop more distanced
modes of parody and irony, as we saw in the case of Sellar and Yeatman in
Chapter 1, or approach the foundational myth and the rituals of the Order
more obliquely, as we will see in the final chapter.

Friendship, Love, History

The heterosexual romance trajectory is not uncontested: the dominant reception of the Garter myth is in perpetual counterpoint with alternative accounts that contest the story by proposing a different narrative of origins. This
fugal aspect of Garter history—the rival stories chase each other down the
centuries—is facilitated by the series of silences, elisions, and ellipses in the

earliest records discussed in Chapter 2. The 1415 statutes, for example, explain
only that Edward dedicated his Order to the Virgin Mary and to St. George,
while the exegesis in the *Black Book* labors hard to emphasize the way the tying
on of the garter represents the bonds between the Companions and their king.
It says:

> Huic etiam ad aversandam in omni Re non male facta malam
> Interpretationem, & in Significationem integri pectoris honestique
> amoris, Apothegma *Gallice* constituit inscribi, scilicet aureis vel
> preciosis alioqui Literis . . .
>   . . . sic huic ordini cum nominibus, vestes et ornamenta coapta-
> vit, ut omnia hæc ad amicitiam, concordiam, et reliquam virtutem
> tendere, nemo non intelligat.

> Unto this also, to prevent any bad Construction being put upon
> any Thing not done with an ill Design, and for a Signal of their
> Sincerity and Loyalty he ordered a Motto in French Words to be
> wrought round the Garter, in Letters of Gold, or some other costly
> Manner . . .
>   . . . he suited Vests and Ornaments with Names proper for the
> Order, that everyone might know, that all these Things tended to
> Virtue, Friendship and Concord.[22]

This reading makes perfect sense in the military context of a chivalric company modeled on Arthur's Round Table, though its defensiveness is also
noteworthy.

John Ferne's commentary, from *The Blazon of Gentrie*, of 1586, is typical of
this emphasis on the Order as a chivalric company of brothers-in-arms: "The
King, after that he had made knowne his intention unto the Earles Barons,
and Knights of thys Realme, they all with a generall consent applauded hys
Maiesties good pleasure, bycause they saw this thing both in it selfe honorable,
and a secondary cause to increase fame towards their nation, & also to nourish
up love and amity amongst them."[23]

Throughout the centuries, the problem for commentators who seek to
explain away the story about the lady and her underwear is that the Garter
remains a motivated sign, tied closely, both literally and metaphorically, to a
specific part of the male body. The Garter myth celebrates the transition of the
lady's garter from woman's leg to man's leg to heraldic blazon, but this transition

can never be fully perfected. For all its abstracted and neutralized representations on shields, coats of arms, and thousands of decorative objects and textiles,
the heraldic Garter always trails its myth of feminine origins along behind it.

To counter these associations, the Garter is often represented in a form
that has nothing to do with its primary position around the leg. While there
are many full-length Garter portraits that proudly display the Garter tied
above a well-turned calf, there is also a tradition of showing the Garter as the
chain or medallion around the neck and shoulders, or displaced into a coat of
arms in the corner. As an abstract design, too, the Garter is scattered across the
fabric of a medieval king's mantle, embroidered on the shoulder of a robe or
surrounded by a starburst of diamonds on a badge and pinned on a diagonal
sash. The Garter appears even more frequently in a completely disembodied
form. It makes countless appearances as a two-dimensional illustration, usually encircling a coat of arms. It appears on chapel stalls, manuscripts, and
tapestries; on furniture and on the interior and exterior of buildings, dispersed
and displaced from the human body, completely abstracted to architectural
or decorative form.[24] This is the fate of many heraldic charges and insignia,
to be sure, although the Garter's instantiation is peculiarly intense, since it
also forms part of the royal coat of arms: Britons still take it abroad on their
passports, for example.

After the Restoration, the Garter became a fashionable decoration on eat-
ing and drinking utensils. These were the subject of complaint by Francis
Sandford, Lancaster Herald in 1686.[25] The contemporary monarchy has no
such reservations, making Garter memorabilia affordable to all as tourist souvenirs, as we will see in Chapter 7. Over the past few years, my friends and relatives have been seeing the Garter everywhere. Here are three manifestations
they have brought to my attention. The Duke of Windsor and Wallis Simpson
had a Garter tapestry hanging over their bed in their Paris apartment; a piano
in a Melbourne pub is decorated with a coat of arms encircled by the Garter;
and a brass trivet (9 cm high and 15 cm square) of indeterminate vintage features the Garter motto buckled around a shield with two crossed swords and
three crosses, in a design that seems to be merely decorative, or fanciful, not
signifying any historical coat of arms or even conforming to normal heraldic
conventions.[26] Signs of the Garter also regularly appear in commemorative
art and textiles: in stained-glass windows; in the embroidered velvet cover
(colored silks, gold thread, and seed pearls) of Martin de Brion's description of
the Holy Land, presented to Henry VIII;[27] in the tapestry that was woven for
Lord Dynham when he became a member of the Order in 1487 (now hanging

in the Cloisters in New York); and set into the wooden intarsia of the walls of the studiolo built for Duke Federico of Urbino, in the main Metropolitan Museum of Art.

Even when it is worn as an item of clothing or ornamentation, there is a distinct trend for the Garter insignia to be worn on the upper body: as a chain around the neck, an embroidered panel on the shoulder, a sash across the body, a brooch on the sash, even around the thumb.[28] However, the Garter can never become a completely disembodied sign. Even if it is no longer, or only rarely, ever worn around the leg, its visual history and its ritual discourse still affirm its "proper" place is around the leg (or in rare cases, around the arm of a woman).

In the early modern period, commentators who wished to downplay the significance of Vergil's story had to develop an exegetical account of the Garter that took its embodied nature into consideration, expanding on the rival explanations and etiologies discussed in the previous chapter. Over the course of the early modern period, a growing historiographical discourse moved to distance itself from the medieval romance of the lady's underwear. But as we have seen, there is little that is straightforward about the Order's insignia, and its enigmatic motto offers no more concrete alternative. On the contrary, the pairing of the Garter with the motto's problematic invocation of shame compounds the difficulties for all but those most fixated on Edward's military ambitions. Even when commentators dismiss any association with women, the invocation to shame still proves problematic, endlessly capable of generating alternative explanations. Despite the best intentions of this tradition, then, it is almost impossible to maintain a purely "straight" reading of the Garter's origins.

Most particularly, any gloss on companionship or brotherhood leads easily to the ambiguous liminal territory between military masculinity and a loving companionship that finds its easiest metaphorical expression in homosociality.

The easy rhetorical slippage from heterosexuality to homosociality can be seen most dramatically in William Fennor's poem, recited before James I in 1616.[29] Fennor's narrative emphasizes the King's chivalry to the countess, and her own blamelessness: Edward "Catcht up the ribbon had a leg imbract / That never capor'd with a step unchast." Fennor also emphasizes Edward's capacity to turn from courtly dalliance to military endeavor in France to the greater glory of the Order, and rehearses the kind of flattering comparison with other orders that is common in many accounts.

Saint Patrick's Crosse did to the Garter vayle,
　　Saint Jaques' Order was with anger pale;
Saint David's leeke began to droupe i'th'tale,
　　Saint Dennys he sate mourning in a dale;
Saint Andrew lookt with cheereful appetite,
As though to th'Garter he had future right.

Fennor then tracks a chivalric analogy between the heterosexual transfer of woman's garment to male body and the presentation of a similar token from king to his knights.

Say that a man long languishing in love,
　　Whose heart with hope and feare grows cold and warme;
Admit some pitty should his sweethearte move,
　　To knit a favour on his feeble arme;
All parts would joyne to make that one joint strong,
To oppose any that his love should wrong.

The Garter is the favour of a King,
　　Clasping the leg on which man's best part stands;
A poesye in't, as in a nuptiall ring,
　　Binding the heart to their liege Lord in bands;
That whilst the leg hath strength, or the arme power,
To kill that serpent would their King devoure.

Fennor's analogy is only partly successful, of course, in defending the chivalric masculinity of the Order: the Garter, "clasping" the knight's leg "as a 'nuptiall ring," inevitably invokes the erotic imagery of marriage and sexuality. Perversely, too, the idea of the knights killing the serpent that would devour their king conjures up the Order's associations with St. George, but here it has the slightly odd effect of identifying the king as defenseless and feminine, like the maiden George rescued.

John Selden, in his *Titles of Honour*, attempts to weigh the evidence but does not mind admitting defeat in the face of contradictory evidence: "In this uncertainty of the Occasion, our common stories give us but little light. Nor know I whence wholy to cleere it."[30] In blithely reporting the story of the countess's Garter, however, Selden compares the Order's motto to the words Philip uttered upon sight of the Regiment of Lovers slain at the battle of

Charonea, as reported in Plutarch's *Pelopida*: "Ill betide them that thinke any ill of these men." This is clearly a story of homosocial love and affection, as these were soldiers who fought all the more valiantly to impress the men they loved in the same division of the army. Selden's final solution to the dilemma is to propose instead that the Order arose at the same time as Edward III's institution of the Round Table at Windsor, suggesting that the story of the Garter may have arisen at a later date after some event at the festivities. Significantly, his easy invocation of homosocial love as an analogy for heterosexual desire and courtly play (both defying condemnation) indicates how closely the Garter and the Round Table are linked in the minds of some commentators.

Even the historian and geographer Peter Heylyn, most vehement in his refutation of Vergil, in his history of St. George (1633), invokes the *Black Book* to show how the motto and the garter symbolize the knights' loyalty to their king, and to each other:

> as by their order, they were ioyned together as in a fast tye of amitie and concord: so by their Garter, as a bond of love and unitie, they might bee kept in minde to effect each other. *Sic huic ordini cum nominibus, vestes et ornamenta coaptavit, ut omnia hæc ad amicitiam, concordiam, et reliquam virtutem tendere, nemo non intelligat.* Which combination of mindes, and association of affections, lest possibly it might be thought to have some other end in it, then what was just and honourable, *ad adversandum in omni re non male facta malam interpretationem*, as the booke hath it: hee caused that French Motto or Impresse to be wrought in with it, which is still observed: that *viz* of *Honisoit, qui mal y pense*, Shame bee to him that evill thinketh.[31]

In raising the possibility of an unjust or dishonorable reading of the "combination of minds, and conjoyning affections," Heylyn at least countenances a homosexual connotation. It is an intriguing instance of the motto's extraordinary capacity to generate interpretation: in defying shame, the motto invokes shame, generating a whole series of shameful possibilities. In this rare instance, the idea of brotherhood *precedes* the institution of the motto, which is formulated to defy the suggestion of anything improper in the Order's "association of affections."

Rival stories about the Order's founding had enough currency to lead to an established discourse of skepticism, or at least indecision, in both imaginative and historiographical accounts.

William Camden, in 1586, weighs up the evidence and offers three seemingly equally plausible accounts. Some report that Edward gave the Garter
as a sign or a word in battle; others attribute the garter to the Queen or the
countess, and Camden follows Vergil in quoting Ovid to show how this need
not be a "base originall therof" (other translations say "mean" here). Some, he
says, would attribute it to Richard I, and he tells how William Dethicke, Garter King of Armes, had shown him the "verie booke of the first Institution'"
(the *Liber Niger*), which includes this version. Camden is undecided about
the origins: "But upon what occasion soever it beganne, the mightiest Princes
of Christendome, reputed it amongst their greatest honour to be chosen and
admitted into this companie."[32]

Many writers share his indecision, or his discretion. In *The Blazon of Gentrie*, also from 1586, John Ferne makes no mention of the Order's founding,
except to say it celebrated Edward's victories over the Scots and the French. He
mentions the attendance of three hundred ladies and damsels but immediately
comments, "But what shoulde a poore antiquarie, intermedle of so honourable a matter?"[33]

Seventeenth-century writers are equally willing to express uncertainty
over the historical origins of the Order, although this uncertainty is nearly
always subordinated to an emphasis on the King's power to transform something small and insignificant into a matter of great honor. In 1602, William
Segar expanded on his brief discussion twelve years earlier in *The Booke of
Honor and Armes*, in which he mentions both the Countess of Salisbury, "of
whom the King was then enamored," and the Queen's displeasure. In the more
expansive discussion offered in his *Honor Military and Civill*, he dutifully reports an alternative explanation: "Some rather thinke it was made to remuner-
ate those Noble men and Knights, that had best endeuoured and deserued in
his most Royall and Martiall affaires of France, Scotland and Spaine, with all
which Nations he then had warre and triumphed."[34] Segar does not choose
between these accounts, but as the traditional story expands in its scandalous
detail, the more it seems to require the counterweight of scholarly discourse
and an alternative account, no matter how little direct evidence can be mus-
tered in support.

Of all writers on the Garter's origins, Michael Drayton is the most insouciant. In the "Illustrations" to the fifteenth book of his *Poly-Olbion*, first
published in 1613, which describes the area around Windsor, he comments
on the Order: "Whether the cause were upon the word of Garter given in
the French wars among the English, or upon the Queens, or Countes of

Salisburies Garter fallen from her leg, or upon different & more ancient
Original whatsoever, know cleerly (without unlimited affectation of your
Countries glorie) that it exceeds in Majestie, honor, and fame, all Chivalrous
Orders in the world."[35] Like Puttenham and Peele, Drayton is writing under
the signs of poetry and rhetoric, where it seems natural to extol the power
of the spoken or written word, in the form of the motto, to make meaning,
and to exercise its capacity to transform the trivial into the magnificent. Any
skepticism about the historical origins of the Garter takes second place to
these more rhetorical concerns, and the transfer of royal authority from Edward III to Prince Henry.[36]

In 1631, Charles Allen throws the whole question open into an issue of
careless choice. He gives a brief account of the story about the countess, then
summarizes the rival account:

> Some the beginning from first Richard bring,
> (Counting too meanelie of this pedigree)
> When he at Acon tyde a leather string
> About his Soldiars legges, whose memorie
> > Might stir their vallour up, yet choose you whether
> > You'll Edwards silke prefer, or Richards leather.[37]

In offering us a choice of explanations, displaced onto a consumer choice
of luxury fabric or utilitarian animal skin, Allen suggests the insignificance of
that choice, and a division, perhaps, between two rival models of masculinity.

John Denham, in *Cooper's Hill*, similarly downplays the question of origins, in favor of the glory still accruing to the Garter:

> Then didst thou found that Order: whether love
> Or victory thy Royall thoughts did move,
> Each was a Noble cause, nor was it lesse
> I'th institution, then the great successe,
> Whilst every part conspires to give it grace,
> The King, the Cause, the Patron, and the place.[38]

Denham goes on, as many poets have done, to transcend the question
of origins by turning the discussion to a comparison between the greatness
of Edward III, as the founder, and the current Sovereign. In this case it is
Charles I.

When thou that Saint thy Patron didst designe,
In whom the Martyr, and the Souldier ioyne;
And when thou didst within the Azure round,
(Who evill thinks may evill him confound)
The English Armes encircle, thou didst seeme
But to foretell, and Prophecie of him,
Who has within that Azure round confin'd
These Realmes, which Nature for their bound design'd.
(ll. 125–31)[39]

When in doubt about origins, the most regular solution adopted by Garter encomiasts is to praise the longevity and greatness of Edward's foundation. In doing so, they accept and affirm those accounts of the Garter that commend the King's vision, as well as his capacity to make an enduring sign out of a small and transient item. Slowly, and incrementally, mythic capital accrues from the indecisiveness of the historical record.

Vain and Idle Romances

The struggle over the meaning of the Order of the Garter persists throughout its long history, but the early modern period saw the inauguration of a distinctive discourse that attempted to resolve the matter. In addition to the tradition of panegyric, dramatic pageant, or celebratory poem, a more academic tradition of historiography exercised its judgment over the kinds of stories that circled around the Garter. In the transition from antiquarian accounts to an emergent scholarly discourse in the seventeenth century, we can identify the gradual development of a self-consciously modern scholarly method, one that takes active pleasure in sifting and sorting various medieval accounts. It is a historiographical method far removed from Polydore Virgil's, replete with marginal annotations, full of respect for historical (that is, written) authority and medieval and classical analogue, and deeply self-conscious about scholarly decorum. One of the most influential, and most severe, accounts of Garter history comes from Peter Heylyn, in his *History of St. George* (1613) and his *Cosmographie*, first published in 1652. Heylyn dismisses Vergil's account as mere "popular tradition," in emphatic terms that would be echoed by many later writers.

Of S. George, called commonly the Garter, instituted by King
Edward the Third, to increase vertue and valour in the heart of his
Nobility; or, as some will, in honour of the Countess of Salisburies Garter, of which Lady, the King formerly had been enamoured.
But this I take to be a vain and idle Romance, derogatory both to
the Founder, and the order; first published by Polydore Virgil, a
stranger to the affairs of England, & by him taken upon no better
ground than *fama vulgi*, the tradition of the common people; too
trifling a Foundation for so great a building; Common bruit, being
so infamous an Historian, that wise men neither report after it, or
give credit to any thing they receive from it. But for this fame or
common bruit, the vanity and improbabilities thereof have been
elsewhere canvassed.[40]

Heylyn offers an influential revisionary reading of the Order as an emphatically masculine and chivalric brotherhood, in which the King and the
knights are all bound to each other. "So saith the Register of the Order, (in
which occurreth not one word of the Ladies Garter)." Heylyn's critique is
cited in almost identical terms by J[ohn?] N[icholls?] and Thomas Dawson,
for example.[41]

In 1670, Elias Ashmole summarizes Heylyn's view with approval, con-
solidating the pattern of dismissing the Garter myth as "the vulgar and more
general" view. He dutifully reports a number of variants on the story that appeal to the everyday routine of court life: that the King picked up the Queen's
garter as he followed her to her room, or that the motto was the Queen's own
response to the King when he asked her what men would say about her losing
her Garter in such a manner. He also notes the theory that Edward modeled
his Order on an action of Richard I's at Cyprus, when that king sought to
inspire his troops during a long siege by inventing a new device, "a Leathern
Thong or Garter (for such had he then at hand)."[42]

In Ashmole we witness a dramatic shift in historiographical method. He
makes a conspicuous show of comparing and weighing sources for their accuracy and plausibility, and takes particular delight in adopting a second-order
analytical position. He observes that Froissart makes no mention of the lady's
garter and remarks that the French, "who were so forward to jeer at our King
Henry the Fifth's design of invading them, with a return of Tennis Balls,"
could be expected to mock the Garter for such origins if the story had had any

medieval currency.[43] When he relates the comparable story surrounding the Order of the Golden Fleece (see Chapter 2), he observes: "But both these Relations are remote from truth, and of little credit; nevertheless, they give us opportunity to note here, that it hath thus fared with other Orders of Soveraign Foundation; and an Amorous instead of Honorable Account of their Institution, hath by some been untruly rendred."[44]

Ashmole is emphatic in his dismissal, however, of the "groundless imagination" that could suppose King Edward might have "founded this most famous Order . . . to give reputation to, or perpetuate an effeminate occasion."[45] Historical discourse here shores up its own neutral authority by dismissing as "imagination" the idea that Edward had anything other than official military concerns in mind, while simultaneously giving voice to the anxiety that haunts conservative histories, the fear of effeminacy.

Ashmole's final conclusion is a tactful synthesis of kingly deliberation, courtesy, and mythmaking. Edward did not found the Order to honor a lady's garter, he set out to restore Arthur's Round Table, taking as its insignia his own garter, which had been "the signal of a Battel that sped fortunately." At the many festivities held to celebrate its inauguration, perhaps a garter did slip, and thus may have inspired the conjecture that the Order was founded in honor of the occasion. Ashmole is adamant, however: "But that any such accident became the principal cause of erecting the Order, and that the Founder's particular design therein was to advance the honor of that Garter so accidentally taken up, is only a groundless imagination, and hath been already disproved."[46]

Other writers dismiss Vergil's account in terms borrowed from Heylyn and others, only to clear the way for more speculative accounts. Joshua Barnes, for example, in his 1688 history of Edward III "explodes" the paired stories of the King's infatuation with the Countess of Salisbury and the "Original" of the Garter "as vulgarly given."[47] Barnes cites Froissart's silence on the matter of the countess and the growing dispute about her identity. Instead, he proposes an alternative, "more Antient and Mystical" explanation:

> Polydor Virgil, a Man of indifferent Reputation, being the First
> that ever mention'd such a thing, brings it yet but as founded upon
> *Fama Vulgi*, Publique Rumor only. Besides, of all those that hold
> this Opinion, there are different judgements as to the Name, and
> person of the Lady; some calling her Joan, some Alice, some Katherine; others making her Countess of Salisbury, and others again

saying, twas Queen Philippa her self, who once departing from
the Kings presence to her own Apartment, he soon after following,
happen'd to espy a Blew-Garter on the ground, which his Attendants slightly passing by, the King, who knew the Owner, commanded it to be taken up and given to him; at the Recept whereof
he said, "You make but small account of this Garter, but within a
little while the very best of You shal be glad to Reverence the like:
And that the Motto of the Garter, HONI SOIT, QUI MAL Y PENSE, was
the Queens Answer, when the King asked what she thought, Men
would conjecture of her, upon dropping her Garter in such a Manner. This Mr Ashmole quotes (thro lapse of Memory) as from Du
Chesne, who yet in the place alledged has no such matter; but only
speaks of the Countess of Salisbury, whose Garter he says, when the
Lords seeing the King take up, smiled, he said in French, as aforesaid, which signifies, Let him be ashamed, that thinks any Evil.[48]

I quote this passage at length because it is typical of many such passages
in the historical literature of the sixteenth and seventeenth centuries, comfortable in the citation of rival historians and willing to make judgments about
them, and ready, also, to explain how stories and accounts can be "exploded"
as untrue. The ad hominem dismissal of Vergil has by now become a standard
trope. Thomas Dawson says of Vergil that he "does so often decieve his Reader
in other Matters," for example.[49] Barnes also cites the *Black Book* with its
rival account of the Garter as originating with Richard I at the siege of Acre,
but his history is unusual in its offering of a third theory, demonstrating that
skepticism about received accounts is no barrier to the invention of other
explanations.

Barnes links the Garter to the Samothracians: "It was a Custom to initiate certain Great and Honourable Personages, whether Natives or Strangers,
into the Ceremonies of the Cabiri or Potent Gods, whose Names were Ax-
ierus Axiocersa, and Axiocersus. . . . The manner of the Initiation was to tie
a Blew or Purple Fillet, or Bordure about the Body underneath the Paps: The
profit and Effect of these Ceremonies, was to be perpetually secur'd against the
most turbulent Tempests of the Sea; and therefore Casmilus, that is Mercury,
was added to those other Gods; because the skill of Astonomy, over which
Mercury presides, is necessary for Sailers."[50] Barnes finds that among the Ar-
gonauts, Orpheus was initiated in this way, as were Agamemnon, Achilles,
and Ulysses, among other heroes. He then asserts that the Phoenicians had

colonized Britain, and thus that Edward may have inherited this symbol from King Arthur: "the Blew-Garter, Heavenly Mindedness or Unity of Faith, and Concord or Amity, because it is but one, and knit close together with a Buckle of pure Gold about the Leg."[51]

Barnes's theory about the Samothracian origins of the Garter gained little acceptance, but it deserves our attention as an example of classicizing exegesis, and willingness to countenance these broader comparisons in cultural practice. Barnes also draws out the symbolism of the garter or fillet bound around the breast as a device signaling the "initiation" of king or warrior.

But in 1724, John Anstis, Garter King of Arms, dismissed Barnes's "whimsical Dream" along with Vergil's and other similar stories as "absurd" and "ridiculous," as "romantick Fancies."[52] Anstis's expressions are similar to those used by Bishop Hurd in his *Letters on Chivalry and Romance* (1762). As Louise Fradenburg has shown, this opposition between a world of fantasy, romance, and femininity and a modern world of reason has been fundamental to the development of the opposition between the medieval and the modern.[53] It remains a powerful technique for the Garter's modern historians, who express a consistent preference for the more austere view. Accordingly, the Order's recent official historians, Peter Begent and Hubert Chesshyre, quote Anstis with approval, saying it is better that such romantic stories as the lady's garter be "left in the dark."[54] They also comment that "it is most unlikely that Edward, concerned with his public image, would have adopted an item of a lady's underclothing as a device to be displayed firstly upon a major military expedition and later as a symbol of heroic chivalry."[55] Hugh Collins, too, in the most recent study of the Garter's early history, seems relieved to be able to dismiss this account in terms perfectly reminiscent of Heylyn and Ashmole: "Although popular in the fifteenth century, this elaborate version of events lacks credibility. It is hardly likely that Edward III, given the serious intent underlying his conception, would have risked trivializing it by selecting such an inappropriate badge."[56] There is virtually an unbroken thread from the early antiquarian, heraldic, and historical discourse to the late twentieth century, following the same pattern of citing the feminized story only to displace it with the voice of masculine common sense and reason.

As we have seen, however, in addition to this sceptical tradition that links the early modern antiquarians to contemporary historians, there is also a counterpoint sequence of alternative narratives that seem compelled to dramatize the central scene, giving it perpetual life through narrative elaboration of its mythic force. These versions have received little or no discussion in the history of the Order, since they are considered imagined variations on a theme, and thus are not seen to offer any authority as verifiable records of fourteenth-century events. I suggest, however, that in their fascination with the motto, and with visualising or dramatizing the scene of the woman's garter, they represent a fuller, even a truer response to the King's enigmatic pronouncement. At the very least, they give expression to the cultural desire that wishes the story *were* true. This is the desire that drives many of the impulses of medievalism.

In 1908, A. De Burgh was sensible of the sheer pleasure such stories can give, especially when contrasted with the "prosaic" imperatives of modernity and reason:

> In inverse ratio to our artistic education, which becomes complete in proportion to our sensitiveness to beauty, do we become sceptical of romance as our common sense modifies our credulity, or, to put the same sentiment in Carlyle's words, "the graceful minuet dance of Fancy must give place to the toilsome, thorny pilgrimage of understanding."
>
> Woven into the real matters of honours, tinged with sentiment and with humour which not infrequently borders on burlesque, there are threads of romance which by their gorgeous hues of improbability give a touch of vivid colour to what would otherwise be prosaic. Thus in the prime honour of the Order of the Garter . . . is the harvest of romance bound into one sheaf with a woman's garter.[57]

This tradition of associating the Garter myth with medieval romance is an ambivalent inheritance for the Order. Early Garter historians are drawn to the idea of continuity with a national tradition, and relish an excuse to tap into the lovely alterity of medieval romance, but they are equally determined to enact their own critical judgements on that past and its mythologies, attempting to sift truth from rumor, or *fama vulgi*. In doing so they are producing the medieval period as a historical object worthy of study and dispute while affirming their own role as modern historians or antiquarians, distinguishing themselves from the poets who are less anxious about the romantic narrative. But there is no reason why they should thereby deny themselves the narrative pleasure of repeating the story about the countess and her garter. Indeed, there is every reason, with Vergil, Heylyn, and Ashmole, to articulate a hierarchy of knowledge. There is popular (or vulgar) tradition, and there is the academic discussion of that tradition, which permits the repeated recitation of the most dramatic and salacious narratives in the interest of scholarly objectivity. Conversely, Garter poets and novelists tend to dramatize only one foundational story each, but they often also draw on the work of historians to foreground the question of disputed origins, bolstering both the mystery and the mythic capital of their subject.

At the same time, however, the desire to signal their own historical and cultural difference from the medieval period leads many later writers to express a kind of shame at the medieval inheritance of current heraldic practices. At these moments, we find some of the most complex exchanges between shame, history, and writing. The history of the Order thus discloses some paradigmatic strategies in the early modern construction of the "medieval."

Noah Guynn defines "proud historical fictions" as "those that attempt to exclude shame by placing it at a temporal or ontological remove . . . [and] enact through the very gesture of repression an inexorable return to shame."[58] This idea of a "proud" fiction seems to answer very precisely to much of the historical discourse surrounding the Order of the Garter, discourse that systematically builds a proud history and bolsters the value of the honor the Order bestows. From Peter Heylyn in the seventeenth century to all the sympathetic and interested histories that quote the story of the lady's garter only to dismiss it as unworthy of the Order's greatness—all can be seen as "proud" fictions. They offer us a glimpse of the lady's underwear only to relegate it firmly to the margins of the official tradition, or as a medieval romantic fantasy. The reluctance of many official documents to articulate the regulations or the practices of degradation is another symptom of such proud histories. Even an academic historian like Hugh Collins makes almost no mention of the five degradations that took place in the period of his study (1348–1461), since his principal concern is with the meaning of the honor bestowed on admission to the Garter.

The Garter motto calls down shame on any who "think evil," in a pronouncement that is easily comprehensible as a forceful act of the royal sovereignty at the heart of court culture. Yet as this chapter has shown, historians tend to find the most popular account of the Order's founding not so much evil as itself shameful. The easiest solution to the popularity of this embarrassing story is to "medievalize" it as a romance, to historicize it and expel or abject it as belonging to an earlier era. So long as the Order and its apologists seek to minimize the shame that accrues to its origins, they are destined to repeat this kind of historical explanation over and over. For historians and cultural critics alike, the temptation to apportion shame on the past is almost irresistible. So long as the medieval is understood as the dark side of the Renaissance, the history of shame and other emotions will be read according to traditional notions of cultural progression.

The fate of the Garter myth and the problem of the Order's origins encapsulate the mixed inheritance of the medieval past for early modernity, establishing the patterns and structures of medievalism that persist in contemporary historical and popular discourse about the Order. These disputes about the meaning of motto and emblem are powerful examples of the potential of medieval tradition to confer shame and honor, in the regulation and reform of ritual practice and in the exercise of historical skepticism and explanation. The more its commentators strive to explain and analyze, to master the past, the further the Garter and its origins recede into uncertainty, into a middle ages that becomes increasingly untouchable. In contrast, the easy nobility of the King in the Garter myth and the elegance of his courtly gesture take on the romantic lustre of a fairy tale, answering to a very particular desire within medievalism to find in the Middle Ages an era radically different from our own.

For most of the Garter's commentators, the problem of origins takes a dual form. The first problem is the uncertainty and ambiguity of the motto, and the second is the triviality of the Garter as emblem, whatever its original form. If the motto raises the specter of shame, then sexuality of one form or another is the most persistent scenario to be overcome, but even the other explanations (brotherly companionship, a king's claim to a foreign throne) all seem to invoke more shame. However, the most shameful, the most problematic scenario of all seems to be that Edward could indeed have established such a great Order out of such a small item. Not all the earnest arguments of Vergil and others can write away the oddness of this feature of the Order. And that, after all, is the point of the story. Not being kings, we cannot conceive a sign of such mobility. We are indeed *honi*, shamed, or condemned through the verbosity of our own explanations and rationalizations, in contrast to the King's elegant pronouncement.

PART II

Ritual Practices

Chapter 4

Honor, Shame, and Degradation

Gareth has spent a year incognito at King Arthur's court, working in the kitchens under the governance of Sir Kay, who has given him the mocking name Bewmaynes (Beautiful Hands). And so he has endured, says Malory, in "The Tale of Sir Gareth," never displeasing anyone and being always "meke and mylde." When he is finally given his chance to rescue a lady being held prisoner, he is first knighted by Sir Launcelot and then kills a sequence of tyrannical knights wearing different colored armor. The first is Sir Perard, the Black Knight. When his brother, the Green Knight, hears of this, he calls Gareth a low-born traitor and promises to kill him. " 'I defye the,' seyde sir Bewmaynes, 'for I lette the wete [*know*], I slew hym knyghtly and nat shamfully.' "[1]

Sir Gareth insists on a distinction that sits at the heart of the medieval honor system: to be victorious in a rightful battle (to "slay" in a knightly fashion) is to accrue honor; while to be cowardly or unjust in one's victories, or to flee from battle altogether, is to accrue shame. Gareth's innate knowledge of knightly conduct indicates his true nobility: he is not a "real" kitchen hand but the younger brother of Sir Gawain.

The political and social meanings of the "honors" that are bestowed by the Order of the Garter have changed since medieval times, but the medieval opposition between shame and honor shapes a fundamental structure in the symbolism and the ritual life of the institution. The Order's mysterious motto—*Honi soit qui mal y pense*—performs two related functions in this regard: a thematic one and a historiographic one. The motto perpetuates the Order's defiant threat of shame on its detractors but also reminds us of its origins in a French-speaking medieval court, increasingly distant from contemporary concerns. A distinctive and oblique textual form, the motto is thus a switching point between the different temporalities that characterize the Order's history, between the medieval and any number of postmedieval moments. The motto functions as a reminder of the past, and of this continuous tradition. It also seems to address the present with reference to the past: "Shamed be the one who thinks badly of . . . the medieval past."

In structural terms, too, the Order's capacity to distribute honor is always shadowed by its alternatives: the possibility of *not* honoring a hopeful contender with admission,[2] or of shaming a Companion by expelling him from its ranks. Formal ceremonies of degradation are no longer performed, but the Order reserves the capacity to "dispense" with a knight to make a political point, as it did with Emperor Hirohito of Japan in 1941, restoring him to full honors only in 1971.

Even if the medieval ideas of courtly and chivalric shame invoked by the motto are now radically diluted, the long citational history of this tiny text constitutes a powerful example of the different ways an emotion or an affect like courtly public shame can be invoked and represented, from the medieval period through modernity and into postmodernity. In all its thousands of appearances on garters and coats of arms, in buildings, on furniture and clothes, the motto's subjunctive speech act—"shamed be the one who"—defiantly invokes shame on any who challenge the honor it proclaims. The motto is also sometimes used in a vaguely proverbial way. Yet this "shame" can always be interpreted historically, can always be pushed back into a medieval or a mythic past, and made to seem distant from present concerns. The invocation of shame is thus a fault line in the long and proud history of the Order along which it is possible to open up a number of inquiries into the dynamics between shame and honor in the textual traditions, and in the uneven survival of medieval chivalry in postmedieval culture.

Distributing Medieval Shame and Honor

I have suggested that the early discourses of the Order of the Garter are deliberately vague about the occasion of its first founding, and about the referents of its motto and insignia. The official refusal to explain these signs both mystifies and enhances the kingly authority that inaugurates the Order. This mystery becomes a condition of possibility for mythic capital and serves as an open invitation for narrative invention. As Chapter 3 showed, many poets and novelists have risen to the challenge. Late medieval and early modern works of fiction, whether directly concerned with the Order of the Garter or not, offer powerful insights into the workings of shame in a courtly context, helping us unpack the resonances of the motto. It soon becomes clear that in the world of chivalric honor, shame is distributed and apportioned in ways that confirm and maintain social and gendered hierarchies.

In the English romance text that is most closely linked with the Order of the Garter, *Sir Gawain and the Green Knight*, shame is strongly associated with its bodily affects. Blood "shoots" into the face of Arthur for shame when the Green Knight laughs at his court's confusion (l. 317); into Gawain's when the Knight reveals the nature of the deception he has practiced against him (l. 2372); and again when Gawain returns to Arthur's court and shows him the green girdle he is determined to wear as a sign of shame (ll. 2503–4). These are dramatic bodily performances of shame, but they also participate in a carefully organized social hierarchy. Arthur is initially shamed by the seemingly more powerful Green Knight when he appears at Camelot to challenge the King's court, and the poem works hard to demonstrate Arthur's willingness to accept the terms of the beheading game. It is only through Gawain's display of courage, humility and courtesy that the Arthurian court can answer the Green Knight's physical challenge by affirming its cultural authority. When Bertilak reveals himself to Gawain as the Green Knight at the end of the poem, he has also revealed himself as the controller of Gawain's whole adventure, under the direction of Morgan le Fay. Gawain's best chance of recovering equilibrium is to remove himself from that context and return to the more stable environment of Camelot. When he returns home, however, his king refuses to recognize his shame and transforms the girdle or "lace" into a sign of social unity. All three examples indicate that the experience and bodily performance of shame are closely associated with social authority. In each case the distribution of shame is instrumental in the struggle for social and cultural mastery, and is registered powerfully on the body.

By contrast, on the second morning at Hautdesert, the young mistress of the castle attempts to shame Gawain for his failure to speak words of love to her:

> "Why! are ȝe lewed, þat alle þe los weldez?
> Oþer elles ȝe demen me to dille your dalyaunce to herken?
> For schame!
>
> [Why, are you uncouth, you who enjoys so much renown? Or do
>   you judge me too dull to hear your courtly words? For shame!]
>   (*Sir Gawain and the Green Knight*, 1528–30)[3]

Her invocation of shame is powerless to affect the knight, since he enjoys the greater cultural authority and is the acknowledged master of the courtly discourse in question. There is no hint that her words produce the bodily affect of shame Gawain experiences in the presence of the Green Knight or Arthur; on the contrary, her attempt to shame Gawain here is an unsuccessful speech act (it is clear she is inexperienced) because it is not supported by a matching cultural authority.

The richest sources for the study of late medieval courtly shame are the works of Sir Thomas Malory. Malory's world is relentlessly nostalgic, rather than intensely fashionable, looking back to the mythical Arthurian past with a special interest in its representations and modeling of courtly behavior and discourse. Malory is not particularly interested in visual description: there are far more detailed images of color and texture in Edward III's Wardrobe accounts than in Malory's grandest scenes. His world has the advantage for the present discussion, however, of being highly conversational, giving us a forceful picture of the way knights invoke shame on each other in contexts that range from the most profound to the most ephemeral. Malory takes every opportunity to define and rank the hierarchies of knightly behavior. The rhetorical performances of his knights distribute honor carefully while also maintaining the narrative tension necessary to the courtly contest and the chivalric rankings of the Arthurian court. A similar struggle characterizes the court's engagements with those outside its circle. These rhetorical strategies of shame are not always successful performative speech acts, or without contradiction, but they provide an important context for the Garter motto and its distribution of social authority.

When Malory's characters call down shame, it often takes a very intense form, targeted directly at a knight's "name," or courtly reputation. Indeed, shame often takes priority over other considerations. When Balin kills the Lady of the Lake, Arthur's response suggests that the injustice of the action and the loss of the woman's life are less significant than the reputation of the court and the relationship between Arthur and his knights. "'Alas, for shame!' seyde the kynge. 'Why have ye do so? Ye have shamed me and all my courte, for thys lady was a lady that I was much beholdynge to, and hyder she com under my sauffconduyghte. Therefore I shall never forgyff you that trespasse'" (Malory, *Works*, 1.66).

Shame is regularly invoked as an important threat to chivalric identity and a knight's obligations to his oath, his kin, his king, and to women. Facing four knights, Sir Bleoberys "stoode in a dwere [*dilemma*] whethir he wolde turne other [*or*] holde his way." "Than he seyde to himselff, 'I am a knyght of the Table Rounde, and rathir than I sholde shame myne othe and my bloode, I woll holde my way, whatsomever falle thereoff' " (2.685).

In his illuminating discussion of shame and guilt in Malory, Mark Lambert comments: "The important thing is not one's own knowledge of what one has done (the inner life is not very significant in Malory), but public recognition of one's actions."[4] The act of "shaming" someone is usually a speech act. Launcelot comes across Sir Pedyvere pursuing his wife and calls out, "Knyght, fye for shame, why wolte thou sle this lady? Shame unto the and all knyghtes!" (1.284). When Pedyvere tricks Launcelot and kills his wife anyway, Launcelot says "Traytoure, thou haste shamed me for evir!" (1.285). As Andrew Lynch remarks, this last expression "turns out to be a great exaggeration. Very few events in Malory have permanent consequences, though many predictions of the kind are made."[5] These predictions sometimes appear in aphoristic form— "knyghtes ons shamed recoverys hit never" (1.218)—while the knights often visit shame on each other "unto the worldys ende" (1.107; 2.913; 3.1171). Malory summarizes the distinction between the "inner life" and public reputation in his pithy pronouncement on Sir Segwardys, "He that hath a prevy hurte is loth to have a shame outewarde" (1.396).

On other occasions, shame is more lasting, or is visited more gravely or physically on a knight, though this often indicates uncourtly behavior on the part of the victor. The Red Knight in "The Tale of Sir Gareth," for example, has defeated forty knights who have come to rescue Dame Lyonesse; and has shamed them by having their bodies hung up on trees with their shields about their necks. "Truly," says Sir Gareth, still disguised as Sir Bewmaynes, "he may be well a good knyght, but he usyth shamefull customys, and hit is mervayle that he enduryth so longe, that none of the noble knyghtes of my lorde Arthurs have nat dalte with hym" (1.320). There is an implicit hierarchy here: the "good" knight's verbal act of shaming is more authoritative than the shameful knight's uncourtly treatment of his victims. Gareth is also building honor for himself: he will soon succeed where no other knight has ventured, both in defeating the Red Knight and in distributing justice.

When Gawain has refused mercy on a knight but killed his lady instead by accident, four of Arthur's knights address him severely before delivering swift justice: "Thou new made knyght, thou haste shamed thy knyghthode, for a knyght withoute mercy ys dishonoured. Also thou haste slayne a fayre lady to thy grete shame unto the worldys ende, and doute the nat thou shalt have grete nede of mercy or thou departe from us" (1.107).

This example, however, indicates how transient these rhetorical performances of shaming can be, since in spite of the knights' threat, this episode leaves no lasting stain on Gawain's character.

The Garter motto seems to share in the somewhat routinized aspect of these verbal acts of shaming. Conversely, it is also possible, though unprovable, that Malory's regular declamations borrow a little of their force from the authority structure of the Order of Garter. But there is a crucial difference between these fictional accounts and the formal heraldic play of the Garter motto. These examples from Malory and *Sir Gawain and the Green Knight* are explicit about the reason for shame: characters instruct each other and the readers when to feel shame and why. By contrast, Edward's motto appears startlingly oblique and the reason for shame deliberately occluded: *thinking badly of what?* How much more powerful a speech act it is when the court can only guess what he may have in mind. *Honi soit qui mal y pense*: the elliptic and playful motto has invited etiological speculation for more than six centuries, while also measuring its own success by the comprehensiveness of its prohibition against "thinking badly."

Whatever its referent, as a courtly speech act spoken by the King it affirms his power to apportion shame and honor. As Elspeth Probyn remarks, "The body's expressions—including that classic one of shame, the hanging of the head—act as a metonym for the wider structures of social domination."[6] It is easy to think of shame as an individual, ethical emotion or affect, but it is also closely bound up with religious, social, and political hierarchies.

Benjamin Kilborne compares Kierkegaard and Sartre on shame, emphasizing the powerful relationship between shame and surveillance:

> For Kierkegaard, self-consciousness and despair depend upon the notion that God is looking. For Sartre, they depend upon what one can know, imagine and feel of others, who are also looking. For Sartre, shame has three correlates: I am ashamed of myself in front of others. In order to be ashamed, I must feel (and be self-conscious about my feelings of) myself, the other, and myself as I view myself through what I imagine (and experience) to be the eyes of the other. In the final analysis, then, it may not make much difference who is looking on, whether God or Society. What matters is that there is a presence looking on in whose eyes one is being judged and before whom one can never fully be oneself.[7]

This understanding of shame answers closely to the Garter myth, a story that is less concerned with the courtiers' psychological feelings of shame, and more with the King's social and political power to induce the shame effect. As soon as the King has opened his mouth to speak, he is clearly the one who is looking on, who is "fully himself," but who appears to deprive his courtiers of that capacity, in a single powerful speech act. The motto has the last word in the story, too, since none of the various retellings dwells on the shamed responses of the courtiers. They are not only shamed into silence; they are also shamed into narrative absence, or nothingness.

Many modern accounts of shame emphasize its capacity to divide the self from itself, to make one observe oneself from a distance, or to look forward to a reformed self.[8] In the specialized context of court culture, however, whether in literary fictions or in medieval and early modern life, the subjectivity of the courtier, who must always be playing a part, is an uncertain quantity. In what sense could a courtier ever truly be himself or herself?[9] Unlike psychological shame, courtly shame is structured predominantly by performativity, though I do not mean to suggest that medieval and Renaissance courtiers did not experience shame as a powerful emotion. Like all public life, court life is fraught with the constant possibility of shame. However, accounts of shame in the context of the Garter emphasize its performative, ritual, and social aspect over its emotional or psychological affect. In contrast to shaming in a spiritual or religious context, chivalric shaming is primarily an activity of the shamer, not the shamed. Despite the strong performative and social imperatives here, as Susan Crane has argued, late medieval forms of public behavior are still powerful means of establishing and maintaining personal identity.[10] Performances of shame and honor in court culture establish identity that is personal and ethical, but also deeply social.

Shameful Practices: Flying Like a Bat

Once the Order of the Garter was established as an institution, with a pattern of annual meetings and feasts, and protocols of election and appointment to membership, its ritual life underwent only gradual modulation in the fourteenth and fifteenth centuries. Its rules and statutes settled into comfortable written form, and its practices stabilized. The regulatory and disciplinary discourse of the earliest records puts a firm distance between the problem of

origins and the more immediate concerns of feasting, prayers, and the commemoration of the dead. Similarly, the rites of entry into the Order (election,
admission, and installation) or dismissal from its ranks are specified in ways
that make no reference to origins. Membership in the Order is a reward for
honorable and courageous conduct or loyal service, and constitutes an expectation of continued courage, loyalty, and service. As we might expect, the
regulations are vague when it comes to articulating the reasons for appointment to the Order and dismissal from it. This allows the Sovereign much
greater latitude to offer, withhold, or rescind the honor on political grounds.

A chivalric honors system is nevertheless faced with a dilemma when articulating the possibility of punishment or dismissal from its ranks. It must
affirm its capacity to expel a member who no longer meets the standards of
behavior and loyalty that qualified him or her for entry in the first place. On
the other hand, to dwell on the possibilities of such a fall from grace threatens
to diminish the symbolic capital accumulated with the Garter. Yet the Order
needs to regulate itself in order to retain its own meaningful form of elite
social harmony, and to affirm that it is an active collective body, not just a
vestigial ritual from the past. Accordingly, the members and sovereigns of the
Order expend considerable energy tinkering with and adjusting the various
fines for minor infringements: for example, being absent from meetings without leave; not wearing the insignia correctly; passing within a certain distance
of Windsor Castle without coming in to hear Mass (and make donations).

The earliest surviving version of the statutes, dating from 1415, is somewhat vague about the punishments for the chief offence they name: that is,
taking up arms against a fellow knight of the Order. "Que nul dudit ordre soit
arme l'un contre l'autre, s'il ne soit en la guerre de son souverain seigneur ou
en son droit et juste querelle" (that none of the said order should be armed
against another, unless he is in the war of his liege lord, or in his own right and
just cause). These exceptions seem designed to accommodate foreign princes
among the membership, but the language of one's "droit et juste querelle" certainly echoes the distinction Sir Gareth makes, when he answers, "I slew hym
knyghtly and nat shamfully."

It was not until Henry VIII revised the statutes (in several stages, between 1516 and 1519) that we find specific mention of the punitive measures
for degradation. Dismissal would be occasioned by heresy, treason, or flight
from battle. Some manuscript copies include an additional provision, or point
of reproach: that of prodigality, or the inability to maintain oneself and one's
estate, though no knight seems ever to have been degraded on this count.[11]

The Register of 1516 also included provision for the removal of "any knights who be living in a disgraceful manner, if, having been properly warned, they do not amend their way of life."[12]

The fact that no earlier rule about degradation survives does not mean there were no impeachments, however. There seem to have been two degradations in the fourteenth century: of Robert de Vere, Earl of Oxford, once a favorite of Richard II but found guilty of treason by Parliament in 1388; and of Thomas Beauchamp, Earl of Warwick, one of the Lords Appellant who sought to impeach Richard's favorites in 1386. Beauchamp was charged with high treason in 1397 and apparently degraded from the Order of the Garter at that time, though he was restored to full honors in 1400, after the accession of Henry IV. The third degradation was probably that of Henry Percy, Earl of Northumberland, in 1407, after his abortive rebellion against Henry IV with his son Henry "Hotspur." The vast majority of degradations from the Order (twenty-four out of a total of thirty listed by Begent and Chesshyre) were carried out in the fifteenth and sixteenth centuries. There were only three in the seventeenth and one in the early eighteenth century. In addition to these formal degradations, in 1915 eight German princes were "removed by dispensation," followed by the removal of Victor Emmanuel III, king of Italy, in 1940 and the annulment of the orders awarding the Garter to Emperor Hirohito in 1941.

The removal of these foreign princes, or Stranger Knights, indicates that the Order of the Garter was still coded in the twentieth century as a national body, willing to bestow honors on members of allied nations but unwilling or unable to maintain such ties of personal affinity when England is at war with the country in question. By far the majority of degraded knights in the history of the Garter were English, however, when, in an era of dynastic and civil war, and religious reformation and counter-reformation, the charge of treason was readily invoked to attaint knights who for whatever reason no longer offered unconditional support to king or queen.

The dismissals and degradations of the fifteenth and sixteenth centuries were usually motivated by contemporary politics, but the material and ritual practices of those ceremonies were marked by their origins in older, medieval forms. The ritual of the ceremony of dismissal or degradation is not spelled out in the earliest version of the statutes or the Register of the Order of the Garter; and the fullest account from within the institution does not appear until the publication of Elias Ashmole's *Institution, Laws and Ceremonies of the Most Noble Order of the Garter* in 1672. Medieval treatises and discourses on chivalry are often somewhat coy about the punishment for dishonorable or miscreant knights, but some specify a form of degradation or stripping the knight of his chivalric accoutrements, and the Garter annals regularly cite the same historical precedents.

In 1286, Osbert Giffard, having abducted two nuns from the nunnery at Wilton, was sentenced to be deprived of his *insigniis militaribus:* his spurs, saddle, bridle, and sword;[13] and in 1323, Andrew Harclay's sword was broken over his head, for his treasonous alliance with Scotland. The Lancastrian Sir Ralph Grey was court-martialed in 1464 for his resistance to Edward IV at Bamborough Castle, and was sentenced to have his spurs struck from his heels by the cook and his coat of arms torn from his body. In addition, he was sentenced to wear another version of his coat of arms, "reversed," on his way to his execution. This was a humiliation often exacted by a knight's captors, but Edward eventually excused Sir Ralph from undergoing this insult.[14] Maurice Keen discusses the specific charge of "breach of faith," for which a knight could be stripped of his spurs, having "defaulted upon his chivalrous promise to pay a ransom (the fact that it was common practice to set prisoners free on parole to return home and raise ransom money made default relatively easy)."[15] Presumably, in such cases the feelings of personal shame were conditioned to some degree by financial expediency and the conventions of medieval warfare.

The role of the cook in these rituals is intriguing. When the newly dubbed knight emerges from the church (as shown in Writhe's *Garter Book*),[16] the Master Cook cuts off the knight's new spurs as a fee, and promises to do the same again should the knight be untrue to his sovereign lord.

> And in the goynge oute of the Chapell, the Maister Cooke shalbe redy, and doo of his spores, And shall take hem to hym for his fee, And the reason is this, that in case be, that the Knght do aftyr ony thynge that be defawte and repreef unto the Ordre of Knyghthod; The Maister Cooke thanne with a grete knyif, with which he dresseth his Messes, shall smyte of his spores from his heles, And therfore in Remembrance of this thyng, the spores of a new Knyght in order takynge, shalbe fee unto the Maister Cooke, perteynynge dewly unto his Offyce.[17]

This admonitory act, carried out by a senior household officer, is a powerful symbolic reminder of the intimate relationship between shame and honor in the medieval chivalric system. At the inaugural moment of the knight's career in honor, this shame is proleptically enacted on his lower body, so this memory might stay with the knight and prevent giving the cook a reason to repeat the outrage in a more punitive ritual in the future. The force of the opposition between knight and cook echoes Gareth's initial humiliation in being sent to work in the kitchens at Camelot before eventually earning the honor of a seat at the Round Table.

In *Tirant lo Blanc* (1460) Martorell offers an expansive account of the Garter rituals. He suggests that if a knight is ever degraded from the Order of the Garter, for turning his back on his enemies, "a scarecrow is dressed in his armour and christened with his name as part of the ceremony." In another place, he suggests that a wooden effigy of the disgraced knight will be hung "in public view."[18] These strictures bear no relation to any surviving Garter records; like many aspects of Martorell's romance, they are freely inventive. They are similar in spirit, however, to William Segar's discussion of medieval convention in *The Booke of Honour and Armes* (1590). According to Segar, the medieval practice was to bring the knight to judgment fully armed, and have prayers for the dead said over him.

> At the end of euerie Psalme, they tooke from him one peece of his
> Armour. First, they tooke off his Helmet as that which defended
> his traiterous eyes, then his Gauntlet on the right side as that which
> covered a corrupt hand: then the Gauntlet of the left hand, as from
> a member consenting. And so by peecemeale dispoyled him of all
> his Armes, as well offensive as defensive, which one after another
> were throwne to the ground: and at the instant when every part of
> Armour was cast downe, the King of Armes first, and after him all
> the other Herehaults cried aloud, saying This is the Helmet of a
> disloyall and miscreant Knight.[19]

As each item of armor was removed, it was denounced, along with the knight who was repeatedly and insistently renamed as "disloyall and miscreant," emphasizing the ruin of his reputation or "name." Warm water was then thrown over the knight's face, "as though he were anew baptized," and he was renamed "Traitor." These verbal acts of naming and renaming share close affinities with the "shame on you" speech acts of the Garter motto and Malory's verbal articulations of shame.

Formal degradation is rare in Malory's works, because ethical or political differences or the threat of treason are usually resolved through combat, but the case of Mellyagaunce is instructive. Having first abducted Guenevere and then immediately and embarrassingly surrendered himself to her when Launcelot appears, he later discovers the bloody sheets in her chamber after Launcelot's wounded hand had stained them. The knights first agree to fight, so that Launcelot may defend the Queen's honor, but Mellyagaunce (having already tried to imprison Launcelot so he will not have to fight him) yields to him with embarrassing haste.

> Than sir Launcelot bade hym, "Aryse, for shame, and perfourme
> thys batayle with me to the utteraunce!"
>   "Nay," seyde sir Mellyagaunce, "I woll never aryse untyll that ye
> take me as yolden and recreaunte."
>
> (Malory, *Works*, 3.1139)

Launcelot insists on fighting, but Mellyagaunce will agree only so long the knights "disarm" his opponent (first his head, then left arm and left side), and then tie his left arm to his left side behind his back, so he cannot even carry a shield. Mellyagaunce runs toward him with his sword, but Launcelot instantly "smote hym on the helmet such a buffett that the stroke carved the hed in two partyes" (3.1140).

Then, Malory says, "there was no more to do," but Mellyagaunce's body is taken away and buried. It is a most abject and shameful death, that requires "no more" in the way of ceremony. The shame of Mellyagaunce's death is written on his tombstone, but is not enacted on the knight or his body with any ritual while he is alive. However, it offers a curious mirroring of the ritual of shame. On the other hand, Launcelot's courageous disarming is a risky rewriting of the ritual of degradation, when a knight's sword and spurs are removed from him, itself a reversal of the knighting ceremony. Mellyagaunce's shame is further magnified by Launcelot's appropriation of the ritual.

Malory's sympathetic investment in Launcelot's superiority is apparent when it is time for him to be humbled before the Grail and be despoiled of his knightly accoutrements. There is no human knight who can be the agent of his humiliation. It is a sign of divine intervention that returning to the cross outside the chapel, Launcelot simply "founde hys helme, hys swerde, and hys horse away" (2.895).

The earliest Garter statutes make only veiled reference to any ceremony of dismissal, though Begent and Chesshyre take a lead from Ashmole's account and suggest that the specific Garter ritual—the formal removal of the knight's achievements from St. George's Chapel—was likely to date from the early fifteenth century.[20] According to Ashmole, writing in 1672, the Sovereign sends the Garter King of Arms to accompany those Knight Companions appointed to go to the "convict Knight" and solemnly take from him "his George and Ribband, and then his Garter."[21] So, in 1601, after the failure of the Earl of Essex's rebellion against Elizabeth, the Usher of the Black Rod was commissioned to proceed to the Tower of London, "to disgrade and deprise the late Earle of Essex, being attainted of High Treason, of that honnorable Order in pullinge of the George and Garter."[22] Sometimes the Black Rod is used to touch and identify the offending knight.[23] Then at the next Feast of St. George, or sooner if the King commands it, the ceremony in the chapel is held.

First the Garter King of Arms reads out the reasons for the degradation, the "Instrument for Publication of the Knights Degradation."

> This being read, one of the Heralds deputed thereunto (a Ladder being raised to the backside of the convict Knights Stall, and he, in his Coat of Arms, placed there before hand) when Garter pronounceth the words, *Expelled and put from among the Arms*, etc. takes his Crest, and violently casts it down into the Choire, and after that his Banner and Sword, and when the Publication is read out, all the Officers of Arms spurn the Atchievements out of the Choire into the Body of the Church, first the Sword, then the Banner, and last of all the Crest, so out of the West-Door, thence to the Bridge, and over into the Ditch, and thus was it done at the degradation of Edward Duke of Buckingham the 8 of June, an. 13 H.8.[24]

The stall plate of the degraded knight was also removed from its place in the choir, and broken in two.

Among the knights who were degraded from the Order in this early period are Thomas Howard, Duke of Norfolk, 1547; William, Lord Paget and William Parr, Marquess of Northampton in 1552; the Earl of Northumberland in 1569; the Earl of Essex, in 1601 (his achievements were only thrown down, not spurned out of the door); and Lord Cobham, in 1604 (his achievements were spurned out of the door, but not into the ditch, "by the Kings Clemency").[25] The last formal degradation from the Order—the hurling down of the knight's achievements from St. George's Chapel—was that of James Butler, Duke of Ormonde, in 1716, after his participation in the Jacobite rebellion of 1715.

Not infrequently, a degraded knight was restored to the Order at a later date (and his achievements and stall plate replaced in the chapel), under a different political climate, usually on the accession of a new sovereign, as was the case with Lord Paget and the Duke of Norfolk, on Mary's accession in 1553. Ashmole gives the text of the Queen's edict. It makes no mention of the question of political and religious affiliation but attributes the duke's degradation to a mistaken slander: "Through wrong information and accusation cleerly expelled and removed, and his Hatchments to his no small slaunder and dishoncolor openly cast down, and taken from the Stall appointed for him in our Chappel at Windsor."[26]

The ceremony of rebaptizing and renaming the disgraced knight as "Traitor" suggests, as do Malory's works, that the question of naming is paramount, and that chivalric honor is a question of public identity, a means of measuring one's place inside, at the head of, or expelled from, the ranks of honor.

The heraldic proclamation of a knight as a traitor could also represent a direct political intervention. On February 8, 1601, for example, as the Earl of Essex entered London attempting to raise support for his rebellion against the Queen, the Privy Council instructed the heralds to proclaim him a traitor. This was done in several parts of the city. Nevertheless, like most speech acts, this had the potential to go astray or misfire in a number of ways. On examination after their arrest, several of his supporters claimed not to have heard the proclamation, while another, William Masham, said that on seeing the heralds, he tried to persuade Essex to stop, but that the Earl said "for two shillings he might have a harold to do any thing & that it was a cosening tricke of his enemyes."[27]

This example hints at the potential disjunction between the social, political world and the world of the heraldic archives. Dishonorable or treasonous knights may be expelled from the ranks of honor, but the desire to expunge the name of the knight, to take him *out* of the lists of honor, strains against the archival and textual compulsion to record the names and the procedures of degradation. This means that the archives are sometimes a little hard to untangle, because the Order wants to record its actions and affirm its authority to expel members while also protecting both its glorious record *and* the glory of its records. Begent and Chesshyre, for example, list thirty knights who were degraded between 1407 and 1716, but many aspects of this list are provisional, and they concede that the records are incomplete and often contradictory.

Henry VIII's *Black Book* is frank about the dilemma: "blotting out" the names of traitors would made the books "look ugly." The register of the feast at Windsor on May 9, 1540, records this debate:

Where they began to advise, what they should do about the Names of Traytors, viz. Whether they should continue wrote down with the rest or be blotted out as they deserved; as to which Point they agreed together, first to consult the Sovereign, That something might be done thereon according to his Determination. For they well saw on one Hand that their Demerits required, That those who are accused, and convicted of High Treason, and duly degraded and divested of the Badges of so sacred an Order, should have their Actions as well as Names abolished and extinguished; and on the other, that the Books out of which they should be erased, would look ugly; and therefore his Majesty was consulted, who keeping a Medium between these two, adjudg'd that wherever the Actions and Names of such Persons were express'd, there should be wrote in the Margin, Oh! Traytor [*vah! Proditor*].[28]

Some of the armorial records in the College of Arms—beautiful drawings and paintings of the knights' coats of arms—have a single line, or two lines, crossed through the illustration. Records of honor are canceled, made into records of disgrace by being put quite literally *sous rature*, under erasure, though in a minimalist way that preserves the overall beauty of the page. The vocative exclamation, "vah! Proditor," recalls the exclamations of Malory's knights and is echoed in the heralds' proclamations against Essex, as the shamed, traitor knights are addressed and renamed directly in the records.

There was no easy way to cancel such a cancelation, however. On the restoration of the Duke of Norfolk in 1553, Queen Mary ordered the Register of the Order, the Dean of St. George's Chapel, to "cancel and utterly to put out of your Register all Writings, Records, or other mynyments making mention of the said deviation."[29] Anstis surmises that the entire record of the duke's degradation by Edward VI (see above) was torn out of the Register, as an entire leaf of the book is missing at this point: "The Duke of Norfolk had been removed from this Order by Edw. VI, who being attainted in the End of the Reign of Hen. VIII, his Degradation was without Doubt in this first Chapter held after it. Now Queen Mary not only restored him, but commanded all Writings and Records that mentioned his Removal to be cancelled out of this Register, and probably the easiest Method of doing it was practiced, which might be taking out the entire Leafe."[30]

Even if a treacherous knight was not degraded, a code of silent discretion was sometimes observed. At least, Matikkala remarks on the rarity of seventeenth-century commentary on those knights of the Garter who turned against Charles I and took up arms against him. "In the spirit of reconciliation, and in the face of political realities, none of the rebellious KGs was ever formally degraded from the Order, either during the Interregnum or at the Restoration."[31]

The vast majority of degradations are the result of political and religious disagreement (named formally as "treason") rather than the result of charges of cowardice or desertion. We have just seen how the Duke of Norfolk was dismissed from the Order by Edward VI but restored to favor, along with William, Lord Paget, on Mary's accession. In turn, Mary then degraded John Dudley, Duke of Northumberland; William Parr, Marquess of Northampton; and Andrew Dudley. Parr was restored in 1559. The dismissal and eventual restoration of Mary's Catholic sympathizers mirrors the fate of Edward VI's protestant reforms of the Garter statutes to expunge its more overtly Catholic elements, reforms that were reversed by Mary as soon as she ascended the throne (see Chapter 5).

During the civil wars of the fifteenth century, especially the deposition of Henry VI in 1460, his "readeption" in 1470, which interrupted the reign of Edward IV (d. 1483), and then the quick succession of Edward V (1483), Richard III (1483), and Henry VII (1485), there were dramatic reversals of fortunes of those most closely associated with the two sides, Lancastrians and Yorkists.[32] Jasper Tudor, Earl of Pembroke, was "attainted, and deprived from the Garter" in 1461 by Edward IV, for his "espousing the Lancastrian Interest" but was restored to the Order in 1485.[33] In periods of civil war, even the King can be declared "Traitor and Usurper" by Parliament, as Edward IV was in 1470. Earlier, on his accession in 1461, the swords and helmets of the deposed king, Henry VI, and those of the Earl of Wiltshire and Lord Welles were taken down from their stalls in dishonor and moved to the vestry. Then the swords, helmets, and crests of the Duke of York, the Duke of Buckingham, the Earl of Salisbury, the Earl of Shrewsbury, Viscount Beaumont, and Lord Scales "were honourably offered up at the altar."[34] Anstis's convoluted prose articulates the difficulty of keeping track of these irregular movements:

> But though Hen. VI continued not in the Title of the Readeption
> of the Crown, till St George's Feast in the annual Return, yet as
> Edw. IV was during that Time, by Parliament declared a Traitor and
> Usurper, and several of his Adherents likewise attainted, so it is very
> probable some Knights of this Order, were in Consequence therof

degraded from it, and that their Stalls might be filled by an Election
at least; and it cannot be doubted, but that Jasper of Hatfield Earl
of Pembroke, a Companion in the 37th of Hen VI, being attainted,
and deprived from the Garter by Ed. IV, for his espousing the Lancastrian Interest, was upon this Re-adeption of the Crown, restored
as well to this Honour, as to his Earldom; though it may be difficult
to guess, whether he might have a Restitution to the Stall wherein
he was first seated, because upon his Degradation in 1. Ed. IV, the
Duke of Clarence was placed therein, who at this Time was in the
Interest of Hen. VI, but there were Vacancies, by the Deaths of William Lord Herbert Earl of Pembroke, and of the Earl Rivers.[35]

Anstis's remarks about Jasper of Hatfield's stall now being occupied by the
Duke of Clarence are a reminder that the question of honor is not simply a
binary one: knights are not just either "in" or "out" of the Order but carefully
ranked according to rules of precedence and seniority. Many of the Order's
deliberations are concerned to set out the rules and principles of the allocation
of stalls.[36]

Each stall carries its own history, with a separate plate for most if not all
the knights who have held that place. When a knight is degraded, his stall
plate is broken in two. As with the armorial records, the witness of the stall
plates is sometimes imperfect and inconsistent. Thomas Howard, fourth Duke
of Norfolk, was convicted of treason and degraded from the Order in 1572
by Elizabeth I for his plan to marry Mary, Queen of Scots. His plate was removed, and was missing until 1955, when it was found and restored to a place
in the south quire aisle with support from the Friends of St. George's. An
earlier Thomas Howard escaped execution when Henry VIII died the night
before the death penalty was to be enacted. On his restoration in 1553 a new
plate was made, naming him as Duke of Norfolk, though he did not succeed
to that title until 1524, fourteen years after he was first elected to the Order.[37]
Again, there are several restored plates in the choir that still show the break.
The Order thus lovingly archives its own history, even if that is a history of
reversals of political favor.

These political examples underline the extent to which appointment
to the Order's honors could be firmly contingent on bonds of affinity and
loyalty, in addition to military achievement, which predominated only in its
early years. In the case of foreign knights, the question of loyalty to the Sovereign of the Order presented an even greater challenge, and many ended

up renouncing the Order, or simply ceasing to wear the Garter. Successive monarchs have used the Order as an important diplomatic strategy, such as Elizabeth I's investiture of Charles IX to mark the end of hostilities between England and France in 1564, but there were strict limits to the spirit of international cooperation when the foreign country was at war with the Crown, or when any test of loyalty was made. A number of knights withdrew from the Order and surrendered their English lands at moments of particular tension between England and France: Enguerrand de Courcy (1377), who also left his English wife, Edward III's eldest daughter, Isabella; François de Surrienne (1450); and Jean de Grailly "de Foix" (1462). Boulton suggests these last two might have resigned to avoid the fate of Galhard de Durefort, who was expelled from the Order for changing his allegiance.[38]

Durefort's case is most instructive. Begent and Chesshyre include him in their list of degraded knights, with the note "possibly deg. 1476"; and the *Black Book* records the events thus: "After this Nomination the King having fully and duly considered all Things, and degraded the Lord Duras, for that he having deserted him, flying like a Bat over to the Side of the King of France [*vespertilio transfugiens in partes Regis Francorum*], had sworn Obedience to him, decreed that Sir Thomas Mongomery, a singular good Knight should be chose out of Hand in his Stead; Which was immediately agreed to by a general Consent, and was afterwards done with no unbecoming Solemnity."[39]

Anstis, however, records a different note in his introduction, suggesting that Lord Duras had scrupulously resigned from the Order "pour cause, qu'il est juré homme feal & subject du Roy de France" (because he was a man sworn faithful and subject to the King of France).[40] The *Black Book*'s expression, describing Lord Duras as "flying like a Bat over to the Side of the King of France," is unequivocal in its condemnation, while the insult is heightened when we compare the early fifteenth-century bestiary and fable tradition, in which the bat is described as "a lowly animal" (*animal ignobile*).[41] If anything, the bat is a boundary crosser who in several stories fights first with the birds and then with the quadrupeds. In some versions, the birds eventually win the battle, in others no battle takes place; but in each case, the bat is reviled as a shifting creature of unstable identity. Chivalric discourses of shame and honor have little patience with such flexible allegiances.

The exegetical tradition goes one step further. Edward Wheatley describes the allegorical exegesis of the traitor bat in a late fourteenth- or early fifteenth-century commentary on the fable, "De Quadrupedibus et Avibus." After the birds win the battle, the bat is denuded and forced to fly only at night. In this manuscript, the birds are allegorized as Christians and the quadrupeds as gentiles or Jews. The bat is Judas, the ultimate traitor, who in being "stripped of his pelt" is "deserted by the clothing of innocence."[42] Galhard did not stay in England to be stripped of his Garter regalia. Anstis finds, indeed, that he took his leave of Edward IV at Calis [*sic*] "where he caused a Mass of St. George to be celebrated, and then offered up his Garter, upon his Intention of embracing the interest of France."[43] Nevertheless, the embedded tradition of the shamed, denuded, and disinvested bat, so reminiscent of the stripped and degraded knight, may well have suggested the *Black Book*'s vituperative imagery.

The most famous degradation from the Order of the Garter is a contested one. There is dispute among scholars and heralds whether Sir John Falstaff was officially or fully degraded from the Order in 1429, for having fled from the battle of Patay. In any case, he seems to have been restored the same year.

Shakespeare dramatizes this scene in *Henry VI, Part One*, though he makes the English champion, Lord Talbot, the agent of Falstaff's shame, not the Duke of Bedford. Falstaff comes on stage announcing a letter from the Duke of Burgundy, and Talbot responds angrily:

> *Tal.* Shame to the Duke of Burgundy and thee!
>   I vow'd, base knight, when I did meet thee next,
>   To tear the Garter from thy craven's leg, [*Plucks it off.*]
>   Which I have done, because unworthily
>   Thou was installed in that high degree.[44]

The stage direction ("plucks") echoes the account of Essex's garter being "pulled" from him in the Tower. Like the slamming of the door in the Victorian Parliament (Chapter 1), this is a premeditated ritual action that is still carried out with considerable violence.

Talbot explains to Prince Henry and others how Falstaff left the field of battle, resulting in the loss of twelve hundred men. He continues with an appeal to the first founding of the Order, and goes on to equate cowardice with profanity of the Order's honors. Degradation is fitting, since it will reduce the knight's status to that of a "hedge-born swain":

> *Tal.* When first this Order was ordain'd, my lords,
>   Knights of the Garter were of noble birth,
>   Valiant and virtuous, full of haughty courage,
>   Such as were grown to credit by the wars;

Not fearing death nor shrinking for distress,
But always resolute in most extremes.
He then that is not furnish'd in this sort
Doth but usurp the sacred name of knight,
Profaning this most honourable Order,
And should, if I were worthy to be judge,
Be quite degraded, like a hedge-born swain
That doth presume to boast of gentle blood.
K. Hen. Stain to thy countrymen, thou hear'st thy doom!
Be packing, therefore, thou that was a knight;
Henceforth we banish thee on pain of death.   (4.1.33–47)

The ritual of degradation takes place in four stages. First, the invocation of shame: "Shame to the Duke of Burgundy and thee!"; then the stripping of the Garter from Falstaff's leg; the account of his shameful behavior; and finally, the King's accession to this judgment, as he banishes Falstaff, "thou that was a knight." Falstaff simply exits at this point. Having been degraded and shamed, and having lost his identity as knight, there is simply no more to be said. Heraldic shaming does not allow for any response, whether in narrative, dramatic, or ritual form.

The degradation involves the removal of the Garter, just as the ceremony of installation involved tying it on, as a sign of the brotherly companionship represented by membership of the Order. Shakespeare's substitution of Talbot for Bedford both increases the dramatic tension in this scene and highlights the rhetorical and social structure of shame, remarkably similar to what we find in Malory. The drama is heightened because Talbot is not only the greatest English fighter in this play but also the one who most exemplifies the quality of chivalric honor, as we see in act 4, scenes 5 and 6, where Talbot and his son each try to persuade the other to flee from what will be certain defeat and death at the battle of Bordeaux. Shakespeare uses the rhymes on "shame," "fame," and "name" (and "blame") to reinforce the honor of the family.

Tal. Shall all thy mother's hopes lie in one tomb?
John. Ay, rather than I'll *shame* my mother's womb.
Tal. Upon my blessing, I command thee go.
John. To fight I will, but not to fly the foe.
Tal. Part of thy father may be sav'd in thee.
John. No part of him but will be *sham'd* in me.

Tal. Thou never hadst renown, nor canst not lose it.
John. Yes, your renowned *name*: shall flight abuse it?
Tal. Thy father's charge shall clear thee from that stain.
John. You cannot witness for me, being slain.
      If death be so apparent, then both fly.
Tal. And leave my followers here to fight and die?
      My age was never tainted with such *shame*.
John. And shall my youth be guilty of such *blame*?   (4.5.34–47)

This scene provides a stark contrast with the earlier account of Falstaff's desertion (1.4.38ff.). But the terms in which shame and reputation are debated here are very similar to Malory's understanding of the relation between shame, reputation, and "name."[45] Talbot eschews the shame of desertion for himself, and his son has clearly internalized the same principle.

In act 1, scene 4, Talbot describes his capture by the French, and the shaming ritual of public humiliation, but his spirited defiance and aggressive resistance signify clearly that he himself is not shamed, in any personal sense, by the French. These are merely the misfortunes of war; they have no effect on the reputation (the "name," line 49) of the truly honorable knight. Just prior to this speech Talbot has been expressing his anger with the "treacherous Falstaff," so that when he finally encounters the "craven" knight in act 4, Talbot has been clearly identified as the moral exemplar of honor, fully authorized both to pronounce shame on Falstaff and to remove his Garter.

This is the most sustained literary analysis of degradation from the Order of the Garter: it offers lively testimony to the imaginary force of the Order's rituals in the late sixteenth century, two and a half centuries after its first founding.

The afterlife of the degradation ceremony in military court-martials is less obviously coded as medieval than the Garter or knightly ceremonies, but nevertheless draws much of its force from the same symbolism of stripping. One of the most famous degradations in modern history is that in 1895 of the falsely accused Captain Alfred Dreyfus, who, protesting his innocence against the charge of leaking French military documents to Germany, underwent the ceremony in calm defiance, a little like Talbot himself. Léon Daudet's account for *Le Figaro* is filled with hatred, but is all the more compelling for its unwilling testimony to the composure of Dreyfus, the "wretched" Jew, in the face of this ritual humiliation. "Without an instant of hesitation, the executioner goes for the military cap; he tears off the insignia, the fine gold braids, the ornaments of the jacket and sleeves. The dumb puppet prepares himself for the atrocious work; he even lifts his arms. He shouts a few words—'Innocent! . . . Innocent! . . . Long live France! . . .'"—which hardly carry through the heavy, anguish-filled atmosphere. . . . I catch a glimpse of the condemned man's wan and weasel-like face, raised up in final defiance. But I am engrossed by his body, that run-down body of a liar, from which is skinned away, piece by piece, everything that gave it social value."[46] In many ways this is an exceptional instance. Nineteenth-century French anti-Semitism played a crucial role in the Dreyfus affair; and in any case, this is a military ceremony, albeit underpinned by political and national concern, carried out under a dispensation and disciplinary regime very different from that of a chivalric honors system. Daudet's exegesis, however, is remarkably similar to the medieval allegory of the treacherous bat (or in this case, the weasel), stripped of "everything that gave it social value"; it demonstrates how this medieval practice could be seamlessly absorbed into and adapted for the military system.

Rudyard Kipling's 1890 poem "Danny Deever" also registers the disciplinary effect of military cashiering (in this case, followed by execution), as the entire battalion must line up to witness the degradation and hanging of the soldier found guilty of murdering his colleague: "They've taken of his buttons off an' cut his stripes away, / An' they're hangin' Danny Deever in the mornin'." The poem is structured as question-and-answer between the young private and the more experienced sergeant, and registers the fearsome effect of the spectacle, the "solemn sadism," in Maurice Keen's words, on the troops.[47]

> "What makes the rear-rank breathe so 'ard?" said Files-on-Parade.
> "It's bitter cold, it's bitter cold," the Colour-Sergeant said.
> "What makes that front-rank man fall down?" said Files-on-Parade.
> "A touch o' sun, a touch o' sun," the Colour-Sergeant said.

As these two nineteenth-century examples indicate, the medieval ceremony of degradation persisted as a powerful instrument of official military discipline. Neither of these instances depends on any visual form of medievalism, yet the terror of the spectacle draws in part on the rarity of the event, a rarity that makes sense only as an inherited tradition from the past.

In contrast, the Order of the Garter makes constant appeal to its medieval origins, presenting itself through its costume and its motto as a survival of medieval tradition, although over the course of the fifteenth to the seventeenth centuries, the Garter gradually became more political than military in orientation, more about loyalty than obedience, slowly evolving to become the predominantly symbolic honor it is today. These changes were gradual, uneven, and layered, as we would expect of a ritual practice with a long history, and as is common with many medievalist traditions.

The Garter examples I have discussed in this section, from Edward's playfully ambiguous motto through to Talbot's proud defiance, suggest that within the restricted field of medieval and early modern courtly and chivalric practice there is a substantial degree of continuity in the understanding of shame and the practice of chivalric degradation. Chivalric and courtly shame is often ritualized and performative, embedded in anxieties about social and political hierarchy and public reputation rather than psychological inwardness as such. If there is a cultural shift in the reception of the Garter motto and its invocation of shame in the early modern period, it coincides not with the traditional epistemic shift from a medieval to a Renaissance or early modern sensibility and sense of self but with a historicizing, antiquarian move away from chivalric culture and its easy slippages between the domains of sexuality and politics, toward a modern historical sense that medievalizes court culture as belonging to a romantic past, as we saw in Chapter 3.

In spite of many modern studies that problematize the traditional easy opposition between medieval and Renaissance culture, the popularity of such generalizations continues to cloud the study of historical emotions and affects. A recent book by Ewan Fernie, *Shame in Shakespeare*, is problematic in this regard. Fernie traces what has become a very familiar history of the self. "[Shame] has been part of experience for as long as societies have had a concept of identity and individuals have had selves. . . . But, as the cultural configuration and value of the self changes through history, shame alters too, so that what is shameful in one epoch is not always so in the next, and the severity, depth and issue of the experience varies also. Less shame is found in cultures with *a debased view of the self*; it is in societies where individual integrity and dignity is prized most highly that corruption and disgrace are most lamented [my emphasis] . . . there is thus a marked increase of shame between the medieval and Renaissance periods."[48]

Medievalists will not be surprised by Fernie's next move in this chapter, "Shame Before Shakespeare," which is to contrast the classical and the Christian, medieval senses of shame as an important but contradictory inheritance for Shakespeare and his contemporaries. Whereas classical literature affords many "impressive and memorable" or "outstanding" instances of shame (Menelaus and Achilles in *The Iliad*, Sophocles' *Ajax* and *Oedipus Tyrannus*, and Euripides' *Heracles*), these examples show shame as the product of external circumstances rather than any internal fault. In contrast, "with the advent of Christianity shame is absorbed within, to the extent that human flesh itself becomes intrinsically shameful."[49] Fernie thus draws a very typical and simple equation between medieval culture and Christianity: most of his discussion of medieval shame focuses on the Crucifixion, the Expulsion from the Garden, St. Augustine, and St. Aquinas. Brief mention is made of Gawain's shame before the Green Knight as his confessor (though he does not discuss Gawain's return to Arthur's court and his problematic reintegration into courtly society), and Launcelot's dismissal from the Grail, but Fernie's central point is to contrast the two concepts of shame (worldly, classical shame and internalized Christian shame) inherited by Shakespeare.

Fernie does not really discuss medieval chivalric culture, although he does suggest that "the public aspect of shame has been exaggerated," defining shame as "paramountly shame in one's own eyes."[50] Malory's preoccupation with shame as the obverse of courtly honor is not registered here because Fernie is looking only for instances of internalized shame that would match those of an Othello or a Hamlet. Fernie characterizes Arthur's "generous indifference to shame" in the matter of Guenevere and Launcelot as unthinkable to a Renaissance nobleman: "Othello murders his wife at the mere suggestion of adultery," he marvels.[51]

When Fernie implies that medieval culture has "a debased view of the self," it is almost as if the language of degradation has affected his view of medieval culture, in comparison with the Renaissance. The historiography of shame shares an intimate relationship with the ideology of periodization and the common perception of cultural difference between the medieval and the modern. Fernie insists that shame in Shakespeare's plays invariably opens the way to personal reform: shame is "ultimately also a liberation from the illusions of pride into truth. Shakespearean shame turns out to be the way to relationship with the world outside the self."[52] Unlike classical shame, which ends in tragic death, or medieval shame, which is a condition of Christian humanity, Renaissance shame for Fernie is frequently a motive or starting point for radical and dramatic rethinking in the "enhanced self-awareness" he says is a salient feature of the early modern period.[53] This reductive cultural teleology and the equation of medieval shame with religious shame alone shares several affinities with those historical accounts of the Order of the Garter's founding that are embarrassed, or shamed, by the risky sexuality of the Garter myth. Both share the desire to abject the medieval, by pushing it further back into the past, and marking a firm boundary between medieval and postmedieval social and cultural forms.

The opposition between shame and honor appears in its most dramatic form when it is played out in public, in the cases of individuals who are cast down from the state of honorable elevation to that of shameful degradation. Just as the ritual king in the foundation myth passes from honor to shame and back to honor, so do these individual knights mirror these transitions as they are elevated into the Order, then "disgradid" and dismissed from its heights. Whether these falls are the result of individual behaviour or changes in the political climate, there is an undeniable schadenfreude in witnessing or contemplating the degradation and the humiliation of another person. The ritualized nature of the degradation sanctions that thrill and gives it a formal shape as a structured, ordered process, affirming the solidarity of the group that ejects one of its own. Even now, when this ritual is no longer an element of Garter practice, it is still remarkably pleasant for modern subjects to wonder at the fall of the proud, to imagine the clattering sound of the heralds kicking the disgraced knight's helmet, sword, and crest down the aisle of St. George's Chapel and out into the ditch; and to imagine a world where one's political opponents could be subjected to such ritualized personal and public disgrace.

Like the Garter motto, then, the idea of ritual degradation functions as another temporal switching point, permitting modern subjects to thrill at its drama while distancing themselves from this medieval practice, which is often seen as an affront to a modern, or Enlightenment, sense of self. Greg Walker, for example, describes Thomas Cromwell's degradation at the hands of the Dukes of Norfolk and Southampton as "a grotesque pantomime of social humiliation": "The Duke of Norfolk stepped forward and reproached Cromwell with his 'villainies' (the word was carefully chosen, redolent of aristocratic contempt for the churlish behaviour of a 'villein' or social inferior), and then tore the insignia of the Order of the Garter from around his neck. Then William Fitzwilliam, the Earl of Southhampton untied the garter itself and pulled that off. Cromwell was literally stripped of his honour and dignity before men, many of whom he had assisted to their present positions. He was then led through a postern gate to a boat waiting to convey him to the Tower."[54]

Walker's account condemns the practice ("a grotesque pantomime") while pausing over its semantic niceties and the performance of its rituals, and offering a hermeneutic gloss. His narrative relish over the details is not unusual, and taps into a similar vein of horror, abjection and melodrama as Kipling's poem.

As Ashmole's dramatic account of the "hurling down" of the degraded knight's achievements from St. George's Chapel shows, the body of the knight does not need to be present to satisfy the need to expel unworthy members, or to rehearse the possibility of such an expulsion. Indeed, his recitation of the practice, even if it were never enacted, would still be productive of its own distinctive pleasure: the intersection of ritual criticism and medievalism. Several discourses and practices are clustered together here: a ritual practice layered with medieval origins; a seventeenth-century recitation of what has become a customary practice; and the citational history of his account, which is repeated in every comprehensive historical study of the Garter. Such layered histories allow modern readers to move back and forward with ease, imagining social worlds where medieval practices are more familiar, closer at hand than they are today. Earlier medievalisms than our own give us the additional, second-order pleasure of contemplating the way other postmedieval societies mediate and represent the middle ages and their discourses and practices of shame.

Feathers Wagging, Velvet Dragging

We may also marvel at the discourses of honor, though the nature of that pleasure will depend to a greater degree on the nature of our sympathy with or distance from the Order of the Garter. There are many Garter records testifying to the grandeur of its formal ceremonials, from the fourteenth century through to the early nineteenth, in a range of textual and visual media, though these ceremonial traditions are not unbroken, as we will see in Chapter 5. Most of these pictures and histories continue the tradition of "proud histories" concerned with the origins of the Order. They give a strong sense of the theatrical nature of many of these earlier forms, especially before these practices fell into abeyance amid the less polished productions of the nineteenth century.

Where there is honor, though, there is often also shame or the danger of shame, especially in the risky business of public and proud display. Many Garter practices suggest that shame and honor are closely and subtly bound up with each other, not just as a career sequence or as the occasion of high drama but at an ontological level. Later chapters will consider moments in the history of ridiculing or critiquing the Garter from the perspective of an outsider. At this stage, by way of supplementing the Order's official management of its shame culture, it is intriguing to look a little behind and beyond its own formal processes. At the margins of the Order, much closer to the limits of the discourses and ordered practices of honor, lies the threat of shame, or simply disorder: the opposite of the carefully controlled rituals that are designed to reflect the Order's elite hierarchies. Processions in the reign of Elizabeth I, for example, were so popular they often produced a problem of crowd control.[55] Supported by the political machinery of the court and the governance of the heralds, this threat is normally kept at bay, some distance from the Garter's stately processions and formal rituals, but there are occasional glimpses of the possibility of shame and disorder that sit behind the ordered rituals of honor. Similarly, the *Honi soit* motto—invoking shame on those who prove themselves unworthy of the Garter's honors by mocking them—works hard to disable the risk of shame, but can never do so completely. Nor can the motto control the uses to which it is put; and this chapter concludes with several particularly decadent examples of the motto being lifted out of the Garter context and being made to refer, with much less ambiguity, to sex.

It is not always easy to modulate the proud display of Garter honors. In addition to the Order's official occasions, Begent and Chesshyre remark that "from Tudor times it became the custom for the Knight Elect to travel to Windsor in a magnificent procession," often commencing with a grand display in London.[56] Such ostentatious occasions threatened to embarrass the Order, however, which started to place restrictions on the numbers of liveried attendants. The Duke of Norfolk was nevertheless attended by two hundred followers on his journey to Windsor in 1563. In 1597 the newly elected knights agreed to take only fifty men each, though Sir Henry Lee and the Lord Chamberlain are recorded as planning to take two hundred and three hundred, respectively.[57]

James I tried again to restrict such processions, but under Charles I the mood had changed again, and in 1629 the Earl of Northampton rode "with such splendour and gallantry and exhibited so brilliant a cortege, being attended by nearly a hundred persons, that a vote of thanks was decreed to him by the Chapter of the Order."[58] These individual processions to Windsor became increasingly rare in the seventeenth century, however, in the years leading up to the execution of Charles I. After the Restoration they seem to have been regarded as excessive displays risking public opprobrium instead of admiration. This is an example of the ease with which the display of honor can quickly turn to the shame of excess, or inappropriate pomp.

In 1667, Samuel Pepys described "a most scandalous thing": "our King and Knights of the Garter the other day; who, whereas heretofore their Robes were only to be worn during their ceremonies and service, these, as proud of their coats, did wear them all day till night, and then rode into the Park with

them on. Nay . . . my lord Oxford and Duke of Monmouth [in] a hackney
coach with two footmen in the park, with their robes on; . . . so as all gravity
may be said to be lost among us."[59] Pepys' comments remind us that ritual
costumes rapidly lose their dignity when worn out of context, even in the relative novelty of the Restoration. Very little license is allowed these Garter lords:
there are clear and finite limits to the practice of honor and its rituals, and to
public tolerance of such grand display.

A milder example of the allure of the Garter's robes and jewels are the
many examples of the families of Garter knights being unwilling to return
the insignia, the beautiful jeweled stars, garters, collars, and "Georges" on
the death of the knight. During the reign of Elizabeth I, Companions were
required to stipulate in their wills that their Garter "ornaments" should be
returned to the Sovereign, and their robes should be delivered to the dean and
canons at Windsor.[60] And in the early seventeenth century it became customary for the chancellor of the Order to receive the collars of deceased Companions, though this was soon commuted into a financial payment, and the
privilege was abolished in 1838.[61]

Kenneth Rose recounts a modern instance of the difficulties of returning
the regalia: "On the death of the fourth Marquess of Salisbury in 1947, his
elder son, himself a recently installed Knight of the Order, dutifully assembled
his father's gold collar and George, his star and his lesser George. But the garter itself, of dark blue velvet embroidered with gold, could not be found. So,
at the prompting of Buckingham Palace, the new Lord Salisbury had every
corner of Hatfield House searched for the missing object. And no fewer than
three garters came to light."[62]

The knights' reluctance to return their regalia is further witnessed by the
numbers of garters and Georges that regularly turn up for auction among
heraldic collectors. A modern attempt to solve the problem of returning the
regalia is the convention of inviting the family to a memorial service in St.
George's Chapel in honor of the deceased knight, with the expectation that
the family will return the regalia on that occasion. When Sir Edmund Hillary
died in 2008, there was a general feeling reported in the New Zealand press
that the royal family should send a representative to his funeral in Auckland.[63]
Instead, however, a private memorial service was held for members of his family in St. George's Chapel: we may suppose his regalia were returned on that
occasion.[64] Like the many rules and regulations that seek to enforce various
fines, dues, and obligations, these practices hint at the disorder, or the dishon-
oring of customs, that threatens to undermine the process of ritual honors.

When the Order of the Garter goes on public display, a different kind of risk appears. In the eighteenth century, the Garter became a popular subject for theatrical performances in drama that borrowed many of the forms of the court masque, forms that themselves shared close affinities with the Garter's ceremonials. Deeply embedded within one particularly complex dramatic tradition, however, is a carnivalesque note of potential critique that threatens to turn a "proud history" to a moment of shame.

In 1742 Gilbert West wrote a long poem, *The Institution of the Order of the Garter*. In the form of a lavish rhetorical pageant, it celebrates Edward III's institution of the Order by showing him considering and then rejecting various princes in favor of his own son, the Black Prince, as the most worthy second member after himself. In the tradition of George Peele's poem, *The Honour of the Garter* of 1593, which I discussed briefly in Chapter 3, West's poem is written from a perspective that glorifies the Garter, the honors it bestows, and the ceremonies attendant on its celebrations. But this does not necessarily make it engrossing to read.

Samuel Johnson wrote of West: "His *Institution of the Garter* (1742) is written with sufficient knowledge of the manners that prevailed in the age to which it is referred, and with great elegance of diction; but, for want of a process of events, neither knowledge nor elegance preserve the reader from weariness."[65] Johnson's comments cut to the heart of the problem with proud histories and proud ceremonials. Too much reiteration of uncritical honor, without the interest of "events," leads quickly to tedium.

Nearly thirty years later, interest in the Garter was revived, inspired by the investiture of nine knights of the Garter at Windsor Castle in July of 1771. West's poem was adapted and restaged by David Garrick as *The Institution of the Garter, or Arthur's Roundtable Restored*, at Drury Lane in 1771.

In the same year, at the rival theater of Covent Garden, George Colman staged *The Fairy-Prince*, itself an adaptation of Ben Jonson's *Oberon*, and similarly including visionary scenes of Edward III and his knights at St. George's Chapel. Martin Butler and Roger Savage describe it as "a spectacular and varied pageant, mixing Jonsonian pastoral with robust political celebration of the kind favoured by eighteenth century audiences."[66] This play included various nymphs, satyrs, and faeries, and also drew in part on Shakespeare's *Merry Wives of Windsor*, and Mistress Quickley's instructions on how to decorate the chapel for the Garter service. *The Fairy-Prince* also borrowed from the praise of Windsor in West's work.

This is a moment, then, of extraordinary enthusiasm for the Garter and

its fantastic theatrics, and an instance of the extent to which its textual traditions are embedded. It is not difficult to see the generic affinities between the
official feasts, speeches, processions, and presentations of the Order, and the
elaborate conventions of the dramatic masque. Both deploy the discourses of
honor, but it is Garrick's additions to *The Institution of the Garter* that command my interest here. They include various "comic characters," who are introduced singing the following song.

I.
O the glorious Installation!
    Happy nation!
You shall see the King and Queen,
    Such a scene!
    Valour he Sir,
    Virtue she Sir,
Which our hearts will ever win;
    Sweet her face is,
    With such graces,
Shew what goodness dwells within.

II.
O the glorious Installation!
    Happy nation!
You shall see the noble Knights!
    Charming sights!
    Feathers wagging,
    Velvet dragging,
Trailing, sailing on the ground;
    Loud in talking,
    Proud in walking,
Nodding, ogling, smirking round——
    O the glorious &c.[67]

Garrick's interpellated verses testify to the often irresistible urge, when confronted with the sight of the elaborate processions and clothes of office, and
especially the ostrich feather and velvet robes of the Garter, to laugh and
mock, to find a hint of shame in the greatest heights of honor. Garrick puts
the mocking words in the voices of lower-class comic characters, giving his

audience grounds to distance themselves from this uncomprehending response by affirming the distinctions of class. Like Andersen's little child, these characters offer to speak on our behalf, without committing us to full identity with them.

Garrick's second stanza in particular strikes an unusually sardonic note, which seems to tap into a long tradition of sartorial satire, mocking the pretensions of elaborate clothing and proud behavior. Its expression is also strikingly reminiscent of the Middle English *Ubi Sunt* poem "Were beþ þey biforen us weren?" with its sweet nostalgia for the glory and beauty of aristocratic life:

> Eten and drounken and maden hem glad,
> Hoere life was al wiþ gamen ilad;
> Men keneleden hem bifore.
> Þey beren hem wel swiþe heye,
> And, in a twincling of on eye,
> Hoere soules weren forloren.
>
> Were is þat lawing and þat song,
> Þat trayling and þat proude 3ong,
> Þo hauekes and þo houndes?
> Al þat ioye is went away,
> Þat wele is comen te weylaway,
> To manie harde stoundes.[68]

The poem answers these gorgeous visions with the answer that these worldly folk are now dead. They took their paradise while they were alive and now they burn in hell ("Hoere paradis hy nomen here, / And now þey lien in helle ifere"). This poem insists that all such worldly glory, no matter how elegant, is transient. Even if there is no direct link between this poem and Garrick's verses, together they remind us, again like Andersen's story, that the proudest, most honored forms of public display are always shadowed by the possibility of mockery, of seeming ridiculous and vainglorious.

Dignity is also at threat at the margins of the celebrations. After the great installation of 1805, an anonymous author penned this account of the feast provided for the inhabitants of Windsor:

> About a quarter past eight, the 18 tables which had been previously placed in the Castle-yard, and set out in a triangular form, were

covered with provisions of all kinds, and 9 hogheads of ale were
placed on three large tables or benches. During the time the dinner
was getting ready for the populace, all the gates leading into the
Castle-yard were closed, and sentinels, both horse as well as foot,
were stationed without to keep the unruly in awe, and prevent them
from approaching too near the entrances. From the strict discipline
kept up, the crowd, which was very great, were prevented from
making a general rush into the yard before the order was given
to admit them, which would infallibly have been the case, had it
not been for the Bow-Street Officers, who were very active on the
occasion. The impatience of the multitude was at last appeased by
the gates being thrown open by a detachment of the Coldstream
Guards, about twenty minutes past eight o'clock, when they poured
in like an overwheming torrent, and bore down every thing before
them. The scene of confusion which ensued exceeds all description,
every one being more anxious to plunder than to eat; they carried
off that which came soonest to hand, while the less robust were
frequently robbed of their prey in retreating to a place of safety.
From the windows of the Queen's apartments the Kings and Princes
of the blood surveyed the scene. From what we could learn no accidents happened. This may be accounted for from the circumstance
of very few knives being placed upon the tables.[69]

This is a lovely reversal of royal theatrics. Here the royal family is the audience, looking down on this chaotic scene of largesse. However, it appears to
have been carefully programmed to produce the spectacle of the "overwhelm-
ing torrent," in order to contrast with the ordered procession of the nobility
earlier in the day. This scene is a powerful confirmation of the social exclusivity
of the Order of the Garter and the deliberate ritual of the Garter feast, borne
out by the contrast with the unruly rush for food in the courtyard. This does
not mean, of course, that all Garter feasts were conducted with due decorum:
Matikkala cites several accounts of the Garter mission to the Prince of Orange
in 1733, when the heralds, including Anstis and his son, were drunk for most
of the mission, while the feast itself seems to have been particularly riotous.[70]
The installation dinner of 1750 also degenerated into chaos, when "the mob"
broke into the hall, and the Duke of Bedford's breeches "came down in the
scuffle."[71]

At the margins, then, or at the limits of the discourses and practices of honor, lies the possibility of shame and chaos. Supported by the disciplinary machinery of the court, this threat is normally kept at bay, some distance from the stately processions and formal rituals. Even on contemporary royal occasions the ordered passing of the royal family, whether on foot, on horseback, in carriages, or in cars, is contrasted with the casual masses of fans, families, and tourists held back by barriers, police, and security guards, and subjected to the now familiar regimes of counterterrorism. The order and decorum of ritual practice are shown to best advantage in contrast with crowds of unruly and potentially suspicious observers.

Shame and Sex

Just as royal processions model social order while constraining unruly crowds, the Garter motto works by daring observers to think badly, while at the same time inviting speculation that something bad is there to be found. Over the course of Garter history, the motto works ostensibly to deflect the threat of shame away from the Order and its official practices, but it is doomed to a kind of happy failure, since it can never control the motto's dissemination into other contexts. Thus its fame continues to grow; and its application widens. Edward III may have capitalized on the popularity of the *Honi soit* phrase as a kind of refrain, but its deployment as the Garter motto seems to invite its use on many other occasions. In particular, while the motto attempts to cast shame away, its grammatical niceties tend to be obscured, and the idea of shame clusters around the French words like iron filings to a magnet. Most of the examples I have found are ephemeral and date from the twentieth century, to be discussed in the final chapter, but this section offers four intriguing examples from a period when the sexuality and shame implicit in the Garter motto and its associations struck a peculiar balance between titillation and coyness.

My first example is an etching published in 1830 by Thomas McLean. It features two views of three elegantly dressed, tightly corseted, and elaborately coiffeured young women, all wearing off-the-shoulder gowns with long sleeves (figure 11).

On the left side of the etching is an interior scene. The women are shown from the back as they look outside through a window. On the right, we see them from the street as they look out. The shutters or blinds in the bottom half of the window come up as far as the tops of the women's dresses, so that it

Figure 11. Thomas McLean, *Honi Soit Qui Mal Y Pense*. © Author's collection.

looks as if they are completely naked beneath their elaborately dressed heads; perhaps, indeed, as if they are soliciting custom from the street (indicated by the railing in front of the window). At the top of the picture appears the Garter motto—*Honi soit qui mal y pense*—and at the bottom, the legend: "A gentle hint to the Ladies." Reference to the Order of the Garter is only oblique, but this cautionary, mocking image taps into the persistent association of the Order with an improper glimpse of women's bodies beneath their formal attire. The dual image shames these proud and elegant women by suggesting that they look like prostitutes; and by implication, that all women do, or are. Perhaps it also encourages the observer to look for the naked truth of women's bodies in other contexts, too. Its diptych structure affirms the twofold relationship of shame and honor.

The invocation of the motto also accords with its suggestiveness as a sung refrain, easily applied to a number of possible situations, usually concerned with women's sexuality. In 1789–80 Jean Dauberval's new ballet, *La Fille Mal Gardée*, was presented at the Theatre Royal in London with the alternative title, *Honi Soit Qui Mal Y Pense*, presumably referring to the scene in which

Lise and Colas emerge from Lise's room when she is about to be married to Alain.[72] Both these examples extend the Garter motto's open invitation to find shame with the Order by inviting us to apply the motto in other contexts.

Two more examples reinforce the persistent association of shame with women's sexuality, and its availability to the gaze of men. I quote them both in full, since they are not readily accessible texts. The first, "Honi Soit Qui Mal Y Pense," is a song by Richard Carle and Alfred E. Aarons, published in 1899, to be performed in a "tempo di polka":

Perhaps you'd like to hear,
The start of my career,
From when my income was quite microscopic,
When I was in my teens,
I met a man of means,
Whose interest was purely philanthropic.
Despite the fact that he,
Bought jewels rare for me,
His attitude toward me was most platonic,
Tho' when to friends he'd state
This fact so delicate,
They'd aggravate him with their smiles sardonic.

"Honi Soit qui mal y pense," My patron made reply,
But ev'ry one looked wise and answered "Maybe,"
Yet it looks a trifle queer,
When we chance to overhear,
Her call you "Popper" while you call her "Baby."

My patron elderly,
Suggested once to me,
That we should go away for a vacation,
We left the continent,
For dear old England went,
Upon a search for rest and recreation,
He chose a lovely suite,
With furnishings complete,
And then to make the whole affair provoking,

The clerk suspected fraud,
When popper said, "My ward,"
For he winked his eye and said: "Stop your joking.

"Honi Soit qui mal y pense," My patron said to him,
Yet, still the clerk looked doubtful and said "Maybe,"
But that tale's an old one here,
For many times a year,
It's worked by some old popper and his baby.

One very cloudy day,
My popper went away,
And consequently I felt very lonely,
That such a handsome clerk,
Should be compell'd to work,
I thought a shame and sent him one word only,
He came up speedily,
I sat upon his knee,
Ne'er thinking that there might be an eavesdropper,
When to our great dismay,
The door was torn away,
I jumped up and I quickly said to popper.

"Honi Soit qui mal y pense,"
He answer'd with a rage,
"With my own eyes I saw you["] said I "Maybe
But if you are quite sincere,
In loving me my dear,
You'd not believe your eyes before your baby."[73]

The reply from "Baby" is reminiscent of the fast-talking May in Chaucer's *Merchant's Tale*. That the wealthy "popper" is elderly, that he gives jewels to "baby," and that the clerk recognizes his citation of the Garter motto as an old "tale," suggests the old world of Garter privilege being debased, confronted with the new linguistic world of "popper" and "baby." Sexuality does not change, we are invited to agree, though the terms of abuse and endearment we use may do so.

The poem by "Pagan", the pseudonym of Adam Cairns McKay, in Australia's *Bulletin* magazine in 1901 declares its affinities with the Garter more directly, but is predicated on similar assumptions about women's sexual desire and its capacity to make fools of men.[74] Freed from the constraints of the formal discourses of honor, and perhaps even fired by colonial cynicism, "To Mollie—A Flirt" is similarly structured around the motto as a refrain: "Sing '*Honi soit qui mal y pense.*'" It opens with a knowing view of the Order's founding that is based on women's flirtation and the persistence of "that naughty spirit" that still "wakes":

Once, when our first King Edward sat
    An hour apart with some fair lady,
And no one knew what they were at,
    Well hidden in an arbour shady,
When they appeared, the courtiers skipped
    All ways at once to hide their laughter,
For down her knees her hose had slipped
    And Ned himself had donned her garter.

      The gallant monarch saw at once
        The reason of their titillation,
      And "*Honi soit qui mal y pense!*"
        He cried, and saved the situation.

I know a girl who's not a prude,
    And hardly takes her life sedately,
But who is willing to be wooed,
    And finds her fun commensurately;
So when upon a verse I start,
    To drive away my melancholy,
'Tis natural that the rhymer's art
    Should seek a sound to echo—"*Mollie.*"

      What power hav'e all of Slander's tongues
        To wound you, Mollie, or to hurt you?
      Sing "*Honi soit qui mal y pense,*"
        And show your dainty heels to Virtue.

Though such as she no chances give
    To even the wittiest Faith's Defenders,
(For modern girls, as I believe,
    Secure their hose with silk "suspenders")—
Still does that naughty spirit wake
    Which spurred a king to sport so shocking;
And should a silken ribbon break,
    You may find Cupid in the stocking.

      Here let me mention sans offense
          A fact empirically shown, dear;
      (Sing *"Honi soit qui mal y pense"*)
          My chaussure fits you like your own, dear.

Dear Mollie! when you settle down,
    The moon of some suburban heaven,
And twice a week go into town
    Instead of every day in seven;
When Something in a pinafore
    Has taught you what it is to marry,
Yet strangers think the darling more
    Like neighbor Ned than husband Harry;

      And, once outside your gate, commence
          To hint untruths about your figure
      (Oh, *Honi soit qui mal y pense!*) —
          I'll hide behind my hedge and snigger.

These two fin de siècle songs or poems recall the prevailing climate of decadent culture, titillated by the potential of sexualized women to mock a venerable institution like the Garter. They testify to the failure of the Order's official historians to control its mythical associations with women and sex, and also to the irreverent ease with which its discourse can be lifted out of the aristocratic context and applied to suburban sexual mores, as when "our first King Edward" becomes first "Ned himself," and then "neighbor Ned." Like McLean's drawing, these poems invoke the Garter indirectly, from an outsider's perspective, mocking its attempts to regulate the distribution of shame and honor. Ritual practice works hard to shape and formalize social hierarchies and the particular values encoded in a given institution, but sometimes its success can be a two-edged sword: the price of the Garter's fame is its dissemination in contexts it cannot control.

Chapter 5

Ritual, Change, and Tradition

If the opposition between honor and shame is structural to the ritual origins and traditions of the Garter, the movement between these two poles is observed most dramatically in the careers of individuals when they are elevated into, or shamefully dismissed from, its ranks. At an institutional level, the Order projects an image of stability and unchanging ideals, as it performs its customary rituals and exercises its discretionary judgment over who might or might not be worthy to join its ranks. It is also mutable, however, subject to change and reform at irregular intervals over the centuries. Modifications to the Order of the Garter can be calibrated on two levels: on the small scale of variations to its statutes and the year by year modulation of customary practice; and on a much larger political canvas. The fate of the Order is linked closely to the political fortunes, the personal style, and the popularity of the monarch and the royal family at any given time. Accordingly, the Order of the Garter underwent several revivals in the fifteenth century, under Henry V and then again under Edward IV, who saw himself as the second founder of the Order.[1] There was also a sequence of dramatic religious reversals in the sixteenth century; and periods of exile and the suspension of most of its activities in the seventeenth. Even when the monarchy has been more stable in political terms, interest in its ceremonial activities has often lapsed or faded, necessitating various acts of renewal and reform when the ritual impulse reawakens.

Such changes and periods of decline represent a major challenge to the ideology of continuous medievalist tradition. Modifications to its ritual practice are standard fare in histories of the Garter, but this chapter takes a special interest in moments when the Order reflects on, or conducts debate about, those practices. It is time to analyze the Garter's discourses on change and tradition as the performance of Ronald Grimes's "ritual criticism," considering the extensive cycles of debates and discussions *about* the rites and ceremonies, as well as practical changes in those practices.

Writing the History of Change

Most histories of the Order are commemorative or "proud" histories. When they write about change, they rehearse a consistent and subtle line of argument about evolution and tradition. No one ever claims the Order's rituals are unchanging, although the constant appeals to ancient tradition and mythic origins certainly imply great stability and continuity. The Order's heralds and most of its historians praise its great adaptability, its successful "blending of the old and the new,"[2] and the survival of its "continuing tradition and ideals" into modernity.[3] A typical expression of this view is offered by Peter Begent and Hubert Chesshyre, who wrote in 1999 that when "in due course of time" it becomes necessary to update the printed collection of the Order's statutes that is presented to all new members, only a few additions will need to be made: "The main text will no doubt remain unchanged, for it is one that has survived now for centuries and which, although many of its provisions are obsolete, bears within it the traditional force and knowledge of how this great Order was founded, how it has been run, what ceremonial has been associated with it. Edward III's founding statutes may be lost, but today's book of Statutes contains the record and memory of that founding and of the consequent evolution of the Order as a living body whose vitality within traditional values seems ever to be renewed."[4]

These remarks follow the discussion of one of the most recent additions to the statutes, the declaration made by Queen Elizabeth II in 1987 that women might now be appointed to full membership of the Order, as Lady Companions. The changing status of women in the Order constitutes a substantial challenge to the Order's abiding conception of itself as an enduring company of chivalric brothers. Begent and Chesshyre's comments, however, encapsulate the insiders' sympathetic view of the capacity of Western ritual traditions and institutions (a monarchy, a church, a parliament) to "evolve," always in the direction of positive improvement, to reflect social change and answer the insistent imperatives of modernity for constant renewal. Despite the very great uncertainty about the origins of the Order, for example, Begent and Chesshyre affirm that the statutes celebrate the "traditional force and knowledge of how this great Order was founded."

Yet the statutes present only a formulaic record of the Order's founding and its reason for being, rather than a historical account of its origin: as we have seen, this "knowledge" of its foundations is actually the subject of considerable dispute. And so our authors have recourse to vaguer terms such as the "force" and the "memory" of the foundation and origins of the Order. The statutes do not "remember" the original founding in any straightforward way at all. If anything, they confound the need to recall any details, keeping the popular memory of that foundational myth always on the margins, beyond the bounds of official discourse. As a numbered list of rules that can easily accommodate the addition of new ones, the statutes naturalize the way in which the Order changes over time as an "evolution" rather than as the result of any dramatic or deliberate reform or revolution. With a remarkable degree of candor, Begent and Chesshyre even track the process by which various statutes become "obsolete," and their endless reiteration in manuscript or printed form "absurd," or even "verbiage." Their summary nevertheless has the rhetorical effect of smoothing the rough edges of change and innovation.[5] Like the remark in the same paragraph about "traditional values," the word "traditional" says both everything and nothing: it clearly aligns the Order of the Garter with the past, though that past is vague to the point of obscuring the medieval; and it appeals candidly to "traditional values" without specifying or naming a single one. As in so many aspects of the Order, there is a degree of veiled or cryptic understanding here, a sense that initiates will be able to identify these traditions, and acknowledge a stable, timeless core of meaning and significance at the heart of the ritual.

Rituals can change in different ways, however, and it is a central premise of this book that the Order can no longer claim this kind of deep cultural continuity. "Evolution" implies a gradual strengthening and growth, but many changes to the Order's practices are the result of gradual, or even severe, entropic decay and dilution, to say nothing of revolutionary rupture and substantial challenges to the social hierarchies at its heart. Even within the Order's history, change has been vigorously contested, through radical movements of reformation, counter-reformation, revival, and invention.

In 1983, the essays collected by Eric Hobsbawm and Terence Ranger in *The Invention of Tradition* studied the nineteenth- and twentieth-century phenomenon of "invented traditions," revised or newly formulated ritual or ceremonial practices of public display that "normally attempt to establish continuity with a suitable historic past."[6] The collection offers many examples of the "traditions" we associate with royal, national, and sporting culture that were deliberately framed and established in relatively recent times. In particular, David Cannadine demonstrated that much of the precisely efficient pageantry we currently associate with the British royal family is not the natural expression of a national characteristic but the product of nineteenth-century invented forms. Cannadine isolates the years between 1877 (when Queen Victoria was made Empress of India) to the beginning of the First World War as the period during which "ineptly managed ritual, performed in what was still preponderantly a localized, provincial, pre-industrial society," was transformed into expertly managed ceremonials, many of them newly designed.[7]

Royal and parliamentary rituals were made both more public and more polished in their performance, deliberately to foster a stronger sense of national pride and accomplishment, and to counter the impression of shambolic incompetence that had come to dominate the public image of an unpopular royal family. Cannadine describes the years between 1918 and the coronation of Queen Elizabeth II in 1953 as "the period in which the British persuaded themselves that they were good at ceremonial because they always had been." Over the course of the current queen's reign, during Britain's decline as a world power, these spectacles capitalized on the public media of radio, photographic print journalism, and television, and became an intrinsic component of heritage and national tourism in Britain. In more recent years, global media outlets and Internet sites dedicated to or produced by the monarchy freely circulate photographs, videos, and news stories about the royal family in ways that feed that tourist industry, supplemented by the close-ups made possible by contemporary technology.

The modern history of the Order of the Garter accords with many of these developments. Garter ceremonials had lapsed during the nineteenth century, while the procession at Windsor has taken place there in its current form only since 1948. Similarly, the recent appointment of Prince William to the Order as its one thousandth member received instantaneous, worldwide coverage, bringing the Garter festivities to an even larger audience.

Cannadine sketches out the longer historical context that precedes the period of his study. He comments on the forcefulness of the "coherent ceremonial language" developed by the Tudor and Stuart dynasties, which itself built closely on the magnificent displays of the late medieval court. Henry VII, Henry VIII, James I, and Charles I all presided over a number of magnificent Garter occasions. On his restoration to the throne, Charles II paid careful attention to the Garter ceremonies, and his reign was, as Antti Matikkala says, "the high point of the ceremonial life of the Order."[8] Similarly, under the

Hanoverians, many of the customs associated with the Order of the Garter fell into disuse in accordance with the pattern Cannadine notes, while the execution of its ceremonies was sometimes marked by delays, or "neglicence & Indiference."[9] In 1805, seven knights were installed by King George III with great celebrations. This occasion also brought together the two parts of the admission process, investiture and installation; but there would be no further formal installations in St. George's Chapel until 1948. In Queen Victoria's reign, 133 new knights entered the Order, but their investitures were mostly private ones at Windsor, rather than public occasions. New appointments came through recommendations from the prime minister, sometimes with the advice of Parliament, and there is no record of any electoral meetings of the Garter chapter after 1860.

When the Order comes to write its own history, it rarely feels it has to apologize for any innovations or disruptions to its traditions. Indeed, the long, varied, and uneven history of the Order of the Garter contributes to its symbolic and mythic capital. Garter historians and commentators adopt a number of different perspectives on the question of the continuity or discontinuity of its rituals, however. Change, variation, and interruption are welcomed by modern writers and apologists as further testimony to the idea of tradition, even if they choose a different vocabulary. In this context, traditions are not "invented" but "living." Here is A. K. B. Evans, describing St. George's Chapel: "St. George's Chapel is no anachronism. It is more than an ancient and beautiful building and the burial place of Kings. Like so much that is typical of English life, it combines respect for the heritage of the past with a ready response to the needs of the present."[10]

Evans naturalizes change as the response to present needs, an argument that is constantly rehearsed over the twentieth century and into the twenty-first. Here is Peter Begent again, this time in an illustrated colour pamphlet, *The Most Noble Order of the Garter: Its History and Ceremonial.*

> The high point of Garter ceremonial is the Feast Day. In early times this was usually held upon St. George's Day and was celebrated by magnificent processions, solemn services and splendid banquets. Few Feast Days were observed in this grand style after the Restoration and although the Hanoverians not infrequently gave Garter Dinners, no Garter Services were held from 1805 until the reign of George V when four were held in the years preceding the Great War. One was held by George VI in 1937 and it is to the latter

Sovereign that, following the celebration of the six hundredth anniversary of the Foundation, we owe the great revival of Garter Day; a magnificent and moving blend of ceremony, medieval and modern, sacred and secular which annually reminds us of the continuing tradition and ideals of the Most Noble Order of the Garter.

Remarkably, an abeyance of more than a hundred years, over most of the nineteenth century and into the twentieth, is no impediment to the idea of "continuing tradition." Here, the invention of tradition is coded as "the great revival" of 1948. But this is just one in a long sequence of revivals and reinventions.

Silence and Sorrow: Histories of Decay and Corruption

The Garter histories I have cited so far in this chapter are good examples of "proud histories." But it would be possible to write an alternative history of the Order: a history of the neglect and dishonor into which it has fallen at various stages. Such a history would be an easy way of redressing the often uncritical histories written by the Order's officials. It would also bring the medieval and early modern periods into dialogue with the modern "invention" of tradition. It would draw attention, for example, to the irony that Ashmole's great study of the Order took its origin from one of these periods of neglect. Poring over the manuscripts and records of the Order with Christopher Wren during the Interregnum, when the Order had gone into exile with Charles I, Ashmole had the idea of compiling his *Institution, Laws and Ceremonies of the Most Noble Order of the Garter*. "As I ever had a great veneration for the most Noble Order of the Garter, so must it needs be imagined, that I was accordingly much concerned, in the late unhappy times, to see the honor of it trampled on, and it self sunk into a very low esteem among us."[11] His work is itself an act of restoration as he seeks to "inform the world of the Nobleness of its Institution, and the Glory which in process of time it acquired," and to produce, as it were, a kind of formulary for future use, "in case the Eclipse, it then waded under in our Horizon, should prove of so long continuance, as that many occurrences, worthy of knowledge, might come to be in a manner forgotten."

Writing the Order's history as a history of forgetting—of eclipses—complements Cannadine's insights with a longer historical perspective,

revealing patterns of discontinuity and dramatic reversals and changes in the
Order's practices, costumes, and rituals; in its underlying expressions of religious affiliation; in the similarities and differences it shares with the history
of the monarchy; and the contradictory nature of its appeals to its medieval
origins.

We might start with the rapid disintegration of the College of St. George
after its first founding in 1348. When Richard II asked Adam, bishop of St.
Asaph, to visit the college in 1378, the bishop found the warden was "remiss,
simple and negligent," and that he had appropriated the poor knights' absence
fines for himself. There were only three such knights at this time (a far cry
from the twenty-four initially ordained by Edward, a number increased to
twenty-six in 1352), and two were found to be irregular, at best, in behavior
and attendance. The third was "given to insolence, attended Chapel but rarely,
and when he did come immediately went to sleep."[12] The canons came in for
severe criticism too, for their irregular attendance. One was "formerly of evil
fame for wenching and is wanton and buxom, and associates with laymen
in the time of Mass and other hours scandalously," while another, Edmund
Clovell, "did not celebrate as he might, but was a huntsman and a hawker."
The bishop recommended that the chapel's charters and other documents be
locked up immediately for safekeeping. The final article gives a vivid sense of
the neglect into which the chapel had fallen: the cloister should be properly
maintained, and be "at once cleansed of nettles and noxious weeds."[13] This was
only thirty years after the Order's founding.

The inventories of the chapel, detailing its holdings of silver and gold
plate, its vestments and ornaments, are full of such vicissitudes, especially in
the sixteenth century. The conduct of divine service at St. George's, as a royal
chapel, fluctuated between traditional religious practices on a grand scale and
the simplicity of the reformed Protestant Church, in which most of the altar
ornaments were not used. Many such items were sold in the late 1540s, although the profits often found their way into the private purses of members of
the Chapter. After 1552 when the second Book of Common Prayer prevented
the use of Mass vestments, a new inventory revealed many items were missing.
The dean and chapter were impenitent, claiming that the ornaments belonged
to them and had been sold to cover additional expenses.[14] Commenting on
a particularly insouciant remark about some "little Emeralds" that were un-
accounted for, Maurice Bond remarks, "There had been plenty of loot; the
distribution of it had been careless, and the Chapter were not particularly
anxious to conceal the fact."[15] In October 1552 the commissioners identified

twenty-three items of plate and jewels that were considered "superfluous" to the ritual needs of St. George's Chapel: they were melted down and turned into coin, to the weight of 685¾ oz. of gold and precious stones, and 3,549¼ oz. of gilt and silver.

When Mary restored the divine office and Mass in 1553, many such ornaments had to be bought back or replaced and installed in St. George's; but they then "disappeared" again during the first decades of Elizabeth's reign, presumably sold off much as they were in the 1540s.

In any case, St. George's became less of a focal point for the Order under Elizabeth, who rarely attended the Order's services at Windsor and preferred to observe the feast days in London or elsewhere. A magnificent festival was held at Windsor in 1561, but according to Ashmole, the "greatest and almost fatal blow" fell on the castle's traditions in 1567, when the Queen decided that the Feast of St. George need not be held there but could be celebrated wherever the Sovereign should happen to be.[16]

Charles I had begun restoring the chapel to its former glory as part of an extensive program of redefining Elizabethan and Jacobean chivalric traditions,[17] but the Puritans held Windsor during the civil wars, and in 1642 most of the chapel's plate was seized by the parliamentary governor of the castle, Colonel John Venn.[18] The priceless robes and Garter jewels of King Gustav Adolph of Sweden, initially hung in honor above the tomb of Edward IV in 1638, were also pillaged (the King's Garter and George being dug up from their hiding place under the floor of the Treasury in 1645), a matter of considerable regret to the impoverished royalists (Gustav's Garter was decorated with 411 diamonds spelling out the *Honi soit* motto).[19] The chapel had fallen into disuse when the body of Charles I was brought there for burial seven years later: "no one remained who belonged to St, George's, and the Chapel was 'so altered and transformed' by the pulling down of all its familiar landmarks that it was impossible to find the royal vault until an aged poor knight appeared to point it out. 'In silence and sorrow,' the King's body was laid down."[20] Ashmole remarks that Charles, "of ever blessed and glorious memory," had planned to develop a grand burial place for himself and his descendants in the east end of St. George's Chapel, "had not bad times drawn on, and such, as with much ado, afforded him but an obscure Grave, neer the first haut-pace in the Choire of this Chappel, his Head lying over against the eleventh Stall on the Soveraigns side, and in the same Vault, where the Bodies of King Henry the Eighth, and his last Queen yet remain."[21]

During this period the three great Registers, or collections of statutes

—the *Black, Red* and *Blue Books*—also disappeared from the chapel (see below). As Lord Protector, however, Cromwell won Council approval in 1654 for an Ordinance that maintained the Poor Knights, though he replaced the obligatory prayers for the monarchy and the knights of the Order of the Garter with daily Bible readings.[22]

These stories of disruption to the Garter's ritual practices are compelling to read: interruptions and breaks to custom, tradition, and ritual command are simply more interesting to read than identical accounts of perfect ritual performances. This is one of the lessons of Kafka's parable of the leopards: the story helps us contemplate the pleasure we take in the warps in ritual practice, when formal ritual is disrupted by accident, irregularity, and bricolage. Many instances from the archives of the Garter offer comparable narratives in the cathexis of past, present, and future, whenever its rituals are repeated, changed, forgotten, revived, and reformed.

The fascination with things going wrong is one reason why the foundational myth of the Garter—the dropped item of clothing and its recuperation into public honor—has enjoyed such longevity, since it dramatizes the moment when a social accident begins its magical transformation into deliberate and sleek ceremonial.

Despite the detailed prescriptions for personal behavior at every level of the Garter regulations, it is moments of individual variation to those prescriptions that generate the richest narratives. Rupture, discontinuity, and decline in traditional practice are surprisingly memorable. For example, Edward VI wrote in his diary of the death and burial of his father, King Henry VIII: "Also in this time the late king was buried at Windsor with much solemmte and th'officers broke al thear staues, hurling them into the grave. But thei were restored to them again when they come to the towre."[23]

The grand image of Black Rod and the other officers breaking their staves and burying them with the King to signal the end of his reign suggests a powerful ritual with a strong sacrificial component, but the young King cannot help but remark this telling detail of their return when the officers came back to the Round Tower. Were the staves still broken? Were they ever really broken in the first place? Even the Garter's Sovereign is drawn to this intriguing but unsustainable rite, one that characteristically poses more questions than it can answer.

On the day before his execution, Charles I called his two youngest children to him: Princess Elizabeth, aged thirteen, and Henry, Duke of Gloucester, aged nine. He took young Henry on his knee and suggested he never let them make him king, as they would then cut off his head. The child replied, "I will be torn to pieces first." Charles then shared with the children his last remaining wealth: "diamonds and jewels, most part broken Georges and Garters" that he had secreted "in a little cabinet . . . closed with three seals." The pathos of these fragments shored against the King's ruin is immense.[24]

This often-told story is both ordinary (many households will have a store of broken jewelry that can be neither repaired nor discarded) and emblematic of the greater breaks, both in the King's body—horribly anticipated in the child's brave defiance—and in the traditions of the monarchy that would follow the next day. At the height of his powers, the Sovereign would "give" the Garter to his chosen knights and foreign allies in ceremonies that would cement his own royal authority: on the eve of his execution, he is still giving garter jewels, but in a fragmented, diminished form. Charles kept his own garter, which spelt out the motto in 412 diamonds, to wear on the final day.[25]

The Restoration of the monarchy in 1660 witnessed the most dramatic revival, or renewal, of the Order's rituals in its history. While in exile, Charles II had continued to make new appointments to the Order (as indeed had Charles I after 1642), and continued to appeal to its chivalric values of honor in his conduct of the war,[26] but on his return to the throne, he set about restoring the Order to its former glory, and, indeed, inquiring into the loyalty of the Garter knights to the Crown.[27] It was the dean of Windsor's son, Christopher Wren, later to become the architect, who returned St. George's Chapel's three great books of Garter records to the King, a "highly symbolic moment in the process of rebuilding the dignity and authority of the Crown."[28] But Charles had to work hard to fill the chapel's depleted ranks: seven new knights were nominated between 1660 and the coronation in 1661; and considerable attention was also paid to aspects of ritual dress. Chapter 6 examines Charles's reforms to the "underhabits" of the Order, which he says have come to resemble too closely the modern fashion. His proposal that the members should all wear the "old trunk hose" beneath their robes actually reintroduces a Tudor rather than a medieval fashion, but its outmoded style is designed to signal the play of tradition across the bodies of the many new knights. The Order of the Garter cannot appear entirely new, any more than it can appear entirely old.

Even periods of relative stability in the Order of the Garter are shadowed by absence and loss: many of its regulations work hard to fill this sense of loss, or falling away, from the plenitude of an ideally performed medieval ritual. For example, the earliest symbol of his office carried by the Register was a scroll, but by Elizabeth I's time, he carried a book. James II ordered the dean of Windsor, Dr. Christopher Wren, to cover the book in crimson velvet, and to have the borders decorated with gold and silver. Wren was also ordered to carry the book on all Garter occasions when he wore his mantle; and he used a belt and harness to secure its weight. Perhaps because it became heavier and heavier with more additions, or perhaps as the Register himself aged, from at least 1677 the book seems to have been replaced by a box, decorated to look like the Register, and then at some time in the eighteenth century, by a board, similarly decorated.[29] In 1968 or 1969, the Register at Windsor had one of these boards in his possession, but none is known to exist now.[30] This is just one small example of the perpetual management and revision of tradition, and the odd careers of signs, symbols, and texts in ritual practice.

Other examples of ritual commentary similarly cluster around the play of presence and absence. The early statutes insisted that if a knight could not join the feast at Windsor, he should nevertheless wear his mantle from the first Vespers on St. George's Eve until the second Vespers on the Feast Day, and in 1552, Henry VIII revised the statutes to say he must erect a stall with the Sovereign's arms, and one with his own, in whatever church or chapel he was to hear divine service.[31] Moreover, he must measure the same distance between his own stall and that of the Sovereign as would separate them in St. George's Chapel. Precedence and hierarchy are of fundamental importance here. Even in the absence of the other knights, and the Sovereign himself, the due distance and order must be observed. Similarly, Ashmole reports that if a knight is too ill to attend service, a stall should be set up in his room, with his Garter mantle laid over his bed for the feast period "according to the ancient Custom and Statutes; and upon this account, Ambrose Earl of Warwick falling ill at Greenwich, when St. George's Day was there celebrated *an. 30. Eliz.* retired to his Chamber, and there sat in his Robes."[32]

Discussions of ritual change often refer back to the medieval past. Begent and Chesshyre study the role of the secretary of the Order, an office instituted in the first years of the twentieth century. They begin their account by acknowledging the oddity, "that an Order which had been administered by five officers since the Middle Ages should suddenly feel the need for a sixth in the early twentieth century."[33] They resolve this mystery with a pithy explanation, in "the ending of two long reigns, Queen Victoria's in 1901 and that of Sir Albert Woods, Garter King of Arms, in 1904." In their discussion of Woods, ritual criticism becomes distinctly more pointed, because they perceive him as standing in the way of the Order's evolution.

On his accession in 1901, Edward VII was keen to revive many of the splendors of royal ceremonial that had lapsed under Victoria, but "for as long as Sir Albert Woods remained alive, this revival of chivalric activity was hampered. It was not the 'done thing' for heralds to retire in those days but to soldier on until they dropped."[34] Then follows a rather sad account of accusations of avarice and neglect. Woods was meticulous in his correspondence and had an unrivaled knowledge of ceremonial and precedent, but his "declining faculties" and his insistence on "clinging to office instead of training up and making way for a successor" led to substantial tension between herald and king, particularly over the question of the fees payable to Garter King of Arms on the installation of Field Marshal Lord Roberts, in 1901. The King had ordered that the fees should be remitted, but Woods seems also to have clung to the letter of the statutes (formulated in 1669–70), refusing to erect the knight's banner, crest, and stall plate unless the fees had been paid. "Poor Sir Albert seemed to forget that every warrant dispensing with formal installation not only produced fees for Garter but demonstrated the Sovereign's power to override the Statutes."[35] Woods was unable to go to the College of Arms for six or seven years, and his agorophobic assistant, Kirby, was equally disabled from carrying out many of his duties. Begent and Chesshyre quote Sir Arthur Ellis describing Woods as "quite a fly in amber—and entirely ungetatable for good or for evil."[36]

These tensions within the Order are at one level minuscule, and have little effect overall on the way the Order is perceived. They are also typical of any ritual practice or institutional history: the tale of the old official refusing to retire is hardly unique to the Order, and heraldic history is full of such tensions and dramas.[37] Nevertheless, the somewhat irreverent tone in the analysis of Sir Albert's career allows us to contemplate personalities other than the Sovereign's within the Order: those of the heralds and household servants who ensure the smooth performance of the ritual. The anecdote also underlines the capacity for individual desires and aspirations to impede or disrupt even the most august institutions. It may also be easier for heraldic historians to criticize heraldic officials, rather than monarchs.

In 1937, Russell Thorndike published his *Children of the Garter, Being the Memoirs of a Windsor Castle Choir-boy, during the last years of Queen Victoria*, in which he discusses the custom of "spur money." If a knight wore his spurs into St. George's Chapel, they were confiscated, and he had to pay a fine to the choir boys before the spurs could be redeemed. Thorndike constructs a mystery about the origins of this custom to rival that of the Garter: it has been attributed to both Edward III and Henry VIII, to punish a knight whose spur got caught in the dress of "a favoured lady of the Court," possibly Anne Boleyn. Or perhaps the custom originated in St. Paul's Cathedral, where the noise of spurs on the stone pavement was disrupting the services.

When Thorndike was writing his memoirs, the fine had recently been abandoned.

> Alas for the St. George's Boys of to-day! Such a bitter attack was re-cently launched against the practice by a certain officer that the fine is no longer to be imposed. This officer will no doubt go down to history as a friend of impecunious officers, but he must also remain the arch enemy of the Children of the Garter. As a boy said to me in St. George's the other day when discussing it:
> "A bit rotten of him, wasn't it, sir?"
> I agreed, from the standpoint of the Choristers. Even in these democratic days one likes to cling to ancient privileges, and it seems a pity to put an end to queer customs. It is as bad as giving the lie to a good old legend. Yes, surely, Guy Fawkes himself would not deny the children their squibs on the Fifth?[38]

Thorndike dramatizes the sense of loss felt when outmoded components of ritual practice give way and collapse under the pressure of modernity. The multiple explanations of the spurs fee parallel the structure of the Garter myth, even down to the disputed origins of the custom in damage to women's clothing.

I suggested above that despite its apparently accidental quality, the story of the dropped garter tells a broader story about how ritual histories can be built around such accidents, once they are worked on by social imperatives of order and performance. These histories of decay and decline similarly offer a kind of mirror to another aspect of this medieval story: the fact that it is lost to our direct contemplation. The idea of loss haunts the Garter story and its rituals in equal measure: the lost Garter is taken up and transformed accord-ing to a medieval sensibility and ritual practices that constantly threaten to become lost or outdated themselves, needing rescue by a benevolent, reform-ing monarch.

Reforming the Order

In contrast to these stories of decline and resistance, there is a vigorous discourse of reform throughout the history of the Garter, a discourse that grapples earnestly with the *need* for reform, even as it embraces the pleasure of articulating change and the renewal of the rite.

The earliest set of substantial reforms of which we have much evidence are the statutes of Henry VIII, which put a number of procedural changes in place, and which revised the overall format of the text. One of the most significant changes in cultural terms was Henry's decision in 1519 to produce the statutes in English, though it was not until 1538 that complete English versions were sent to the English Companions.[39] However, during his reign, the statutes were in a "constant state of revision," so that very few copies surviving from his reign are identical to others. Only some, for example, include the new ordinance that knights "who be living in a disgraceful manner" (*ignominiose viventibus*) should be removed from the Order if they do not amend their ways after a warning.[40]

Looking at the dizzying array of the statutes' variants, and the multiple attempts by successive sovereigns to reform, streamline and make them consistent, it is hard to escape the conclusion that the Order has often struggled to codify its own practices in any permanent and comprehensive way. There is a degree of institutional obsessiveness discernible in the many commissions established to peruse the statutes and identify any inconsistencies, although most such commissions foundered through lack of interest. In the same way, it is surprisingly difficult to make an accurate list of the entire membership of the Order. Many publications include such lists, expressing a passion for containing and ordering its history of inclusions and exclusions. These lists strike particular difficulties when a knight is degraded and then restored to full honors, when courtly and heraldic discretion often impedes the accuracy of the historical record.

Living under modern bureaucratic regimes, we may regard it as the nature of paperwork and juridical reform to lag behind changes in ritual and institutional practice, though this might be a symptom of modernity, rather than reflecting the Order's ritual practice right back to its medieval origins. The earliest surviving statutes date only from 1415, and Lisa Jefferson has shown that they are not, as previously thought, a variant of Edward's originals. In fact, while later texts like Henry VIII's statutes describe Edward as forming

"divers honorable estatutes and laudable ordinances,"[41] there is no textual trace
of these initial ordinances, and it may well be that the Order's practices were
not codified in written form at the moment of its founding; that Edward was
chiefly concerned with the performance of the ceremonial procession, and
the articulation of the appropriate relationship between the Order's spiritual,
chivalric, and military interests. The allusions to the earlier statutes may themselves be an act of medievalism, making the rhetorical case for the authenticity
of the sixteenth-century version.

In any case, the statutes give us only a limited picture of the Order's ritual
criticism: it is often the discourse *around* the statutes that tell the clearest story
of the Order's life and the ways it regulates and reforms itself.

For example, although Henry VIII made a number of changes to the
rules and statutes, the great political turmoil of his reign barely appears in
these changes, which are registered principally in the variations to his title as
supreme head of the Church of England, then in 1542 from "Lord of Ireland"
to "King of Ireland."[42] It was not until the accession of his son, Edward VI,
that there was a full commission to examine the statutes in 1549, to make them
reflect England's changed religious dispensation.[43] Most commentators agree
that the new king was passionate in his efforts to detach the Order from what
has been described as "the cult of St George." Diarmaid McCulloch comments: "In a kingdom where the royal supremacy was the central principle
of the reformed Church, one could regard a reformed chivalric Order as the
highest expression of what this reformation was about."[44] The symbolic resonance of the Order was substantial, and its inheritance of medieval religious
traditions incited considerable scrutiny. Edward seems to have regarded the
Order as a kind of test case for the new church, but the history of his short-
lived reforms is one of the most instructive cases of the challenge and difficulties of carrying out ritual criticism, even from the position of royal supremacy.

Edward himself redrafted the "somewhat mangled text" of the statutes
several times, aiming to restore their original purity, but primarily laboring to
strip them of any sign of religious symbolism that too closely resembled pre-
Reformation iconography and religious practice.[45] There are five manuscripts
connected with these revisions: three in the King's handwriting; and the Latin
and English versions of the statutes as passed by the chapter in 1552, with
alterations to these two in the hands of the King and Sir William Cecil, chancellor of the Order.[46] The drafts are the most virulently antipapal; the final
statutes are more moderate in their language and the changes they propose.
However, a consistent thread is the progressive detachment of the Order from

any association with St. George. It is to be known no longer as the Order of St. George, only as the Order of the Garter; and the knights shall wear garters on their legs. In one draft, Edward specifies that about their necks, instead of the figure of George slaying the dragon, they shall wear "a horsman graven, holding in one hand a sweard pearsing a boke on wich shal be written verbum dei, and on the sweard Protectio, and in thother hand a shild on wich shal be written Fides, wich devise shal have a garter about it on wich shal be written *Assumite universam armaturam dei* [this motto crossed out and replaced with] *Honi soit qui mal y pense.*"[47] This anxious proliferation of signs and mottoes represents a raw attempt to invest the Order with a completely new symbolic regime.

The preamble to the statutes of 1552 reveals the King's concerns: the Order was founded "to advance to honor and glory good, godly, valiant, well cour-aged, wise and noble men for their notable desertes, and to nourishe a cer-taine amytie, fellowship, and agrement in all honest thinges among all men."[48] Previous kings of England "devysed" such men "in a token of concord and unitie, to tie abowte their legges a certaine gartier." But then Satan, resentful of these men's inspirations to virtue, "stuffed the statutes of this fellowship with many doubtefull, superstitious, and repugnant opinions. But We, being greately moved with thantiquitie, with the Maiestie, and with the godlines of this ordre, have studyed, with all our travaile, to reduce it to the pristine and auncyent fundation."[49] This is very strong language indeed; it introduces the extraordinary thesis that the surviving statutes have not just fallen out of date but are in fact corrupted through the work of Satan. It is a remarkable disown-ing of inherited tradition. So vehement is the King's association of St. George with Catholicism, he prefers to suppose there is a prior, more ancient founda-tion than his father's statutes testified to, and that the great Order has become corrupted, "stuffed . . . with many doubtefull, superstitious, and repugnant opinions." Here the idea of the lost medieval statutes is used less to bolster the current ones and rather to argue for their corruption.

The word "ancient" plays a key role here, as it often does in the sixteenth century, to praise those aspects of medieval culture it regards as worthy of preservation or restoration. Thomas Speght, in 1598, published *The Workes of our Antient and Learned English Poet, Geffrey Chaucer.* "Ancient" is used to encode what would later be described as "medieval": this is well before the first uses of that word in the nineteenth century. There is very little sense here that "ancient" carries any precise historical reference. Indeed, it has the effect of stretching out the time (only just more than two hundred years) between the current debates and the original foundations. The further the origins are pushed back into the past, the more venerable the Order appears, and perhaps perversely, the freer the hand that seeks to "reduce" it back to its original form. Edward confesses himself "greatly moved" with the "antiquity, majesty and the godliness" of the Order. As early as the mid-sixteenth century, then, the Order's age exercises a substantial attraction and authority. This is the magical appeal and the mythic capital of medieval or "ancient" tradition: conveniently, the original statutes are not available to disprove the King's thesis about the corruption of the current ones. Edward's strategies in reading the Order accord with many other aspects of mid-century ecclesiastical and political reform, but they are unusual in the Garter history for their emphasis on the corruption of the ancient form of the statutes.

No mention is made in these drafts and revisions of the Order's uncertain myth of origins. Polydore Vergil's *Anglica Historia* had been published just ten years previously, but Edward steers clear of its murky waters, emphasizing the fellowship shared by the knights as "equalles of degre." This fellowship, composed of "those that had very well borne themselfes at home in matters of peace, and had tryed themselves valiant and wise abrode in martiall feates," agreed to tie the Garter around their legs "as though therby they shulde witnes that for their contrey, religion, and Goddes cause they wolde spende their lief and goodes, and for this cause they called it thordre of the garter." This beautifully circular argument neatly displaces the question of Edward III's choice of insignia, which has become a completely arbitrary sign betokening the decision to form the Order of the Garter, and the fidelity and companionship of its members. Any salacious associations are secondary, compared to the taint of superstition and "poperie."

Edward is unable to identify the works of Satan directly in his revisions. One of his earlier drafts spells out the dangers even more clearly than the "doubtefull, superstitious, and repugnant opinions": "that serpentes craft wich hath deceived Adam, and continually like a roaring lion gapeth for his pray, and so studieth to pervert good order into evill custome and superstitiousnes hath darkened with doutfulnes and contrarietes, hath perverted with superstitiousnes and idolatrie and finally almost destroyed with bringing of poperie and abusion."[50]

This last phrase was changed from the initial draft, where Edward wrote of "poperi and naughtines."[51] Both expressions pathologize "poperie," and somehow render it a novel intrusion into the antiquity of the Garter, dramatically severing the relationship between English medieval religious tradition and

Catholicism. MacCulloch describes the language of the first draft as "over-excited"; and indeed it is toned down in later versions, and in the statutes themselves, perhaps under Cecil's influence.[52]

Nevertheless, it is interesting to see how Edward invokes, but cannot sustain, the principle of distinguishing the Order's original features from the ones he regards as popish, satanic abuses of a once Edenic purity. The principle is impossible to enforce; for at no point in the history of the revisions to the Garter do any of the reformers concern themselves with the material or chronological history of the thing they want to change, correct, or restore. Such documents tend to focus only on present custom and the anticipated reform. Their deep concern with discursive formulae dooms them to clumsiness from the beginning. There is a world of difference between the successive scratched-out and corrected versions of Edward VI and the elegant *sprezzatura* of Edward III in founding the Order. Nor can any amount of rewriting bring back the immediacy or the impulsive drama of that medieval moment.

One symptom of Edward's difficulty is his desire to remove any reference to St. George. The saint was one of the original patrons and spiritual sponsors of the Order (Thomas Hoccleve even invoked George when exhorting Henry V and the Garter knights to stamp out the Lollard heresy),[53] but by the middle of the sixteenth century, the practices associated with the worship and honor of the saints had become highly contentious. Edward's drafts anticipate the abolition of the saint's day by Parliament in 1552, though the various reasons given for doing so reveal no small degree of ideological uncertainty. It was not simply a question of bringing the Order into line with a reformed church: it was also the particular nature of the Order's association with St. George, or rather the particular nature of the saint's associations, that was problematic.

George was a saint "of decidedly legendary character,"[54] but even had his credentials been unimpeachable, he would still have been at risk. From the very first draft Edward is clear that the Order should be known no longer as the Order of St. George, "whereby the th'onour due to god was gevin to a creature" but as the Order of the Gartier.[55] On investiture, a knight would be invested with the collar of roses, with the image of "a horsman," with no mention of the dragon. It also suggests that the Feast of St. George is too near to summer "and a feast not meet to be kept bicause the dedication of th'ordre is holly taken from that as before it apperreth," and so the general assembly is moved to the end of November, making an important calendrical and seasonal separation from St. George's Day, "because of dedicating to him shall come both idolatry and also superstitiousness and hypocrisy, mother of all vice."[56]

The context is crucial. At various times in the English Reformation, the observation of saints' days was raised as a contentious issue, and St. George is often taken as an example in these debates. He is mentioned by Erasmus in *The Praise of Folly*, first printed in 1511. After criticizing those who are seduced by wondrous tales of "ghosts, spectres, phantoms and the dead," Erasmus puts in the same company those who put special credence in painted or wooden images of the saints. "They've already got a second Hippolytus, but in George they've found another Hercules too. They piously deck out his horse with trappings and amulets and practically worship it. Its favours are sought with some new small offering, and an oath sworn by the saint's bronze helmet is fit for a king."[57] Later he singles out George in company with Christopher and Barbara as examples of the more legendary saints who receive "far more devout attention than Peter or Paul or even Christ himself."

In the 1540s the wearing of the George had also been taken up as an example in the discussion of images and idols. In 1547 Bishop Gardiner had heard Bishop Ridley of London preach a sermon at court on Ash Wednesday, denouncing the use of images and holy water. Gardiner wrote a letter in response, using the image of St. George as an example in his defense of the righteous use of images. Ridley had denounced images along with the use of the King's cramp rings to cure sickness, but Gardiner makes the distinction between the making of images and the worshipping of them. "For it is one kind of worship to place them worshipfully, so as if a man place an image in the churche or hang it about his neck, as al use to do thimage of the cross, and the knight of thOrder, S. George, this is som peace of worship."[58]

Elsewhere in Gardiner's letter it appears that St. George was regularly taken as a point of argument in the debate about images and idols, like the King's rings. Gardiner cites objections that have been made that he uses the King in his arguments, "as when I reasoned thus: . . . If images be forbidden, why doothe the King weare S. Georg on his brest? But he weareth S. Georg on his brest; ergo, images be not forbidden. If saincts be not to bee worshipped, why kepe we S. Georges feast? But we kepe Saint Georges feast; ergo, etc."[59] If this is a debate taking place at court, it suggests that the Garter observances may have been a particularly contentious issue for the young king.[60] In fact, Gardiner was arrested soon after preaching a sermon in which he was invited to clarify his position and bring it in line with Ridley's, but refused to do so.

There was considerable anxiety around the use of St. George, then; and it seems that the eyes of the court and various figures were on the King to assess what he would do. If the Order was known as the Order of St. George, it is little wonder that Edward addressed himself to the question of the Order's saintly patronage.

The King is remembered for making a joke at the saint's expense during the Garter ceremonies of 1550. Foxe tells the story:

> That King Edward the Sixth, the fourth year of his reign, being then but thirteen years old and upward, at Greenwich, upon St. George's day, when he was come from the sermon into the presence-chamber, there being his uncle the duke of Somerset, the duke of Northumberland, with other lords and knights of that order called the Order of the Garter, he said to them, "My Lords, I pray you, what saint is St. George, that we here so honour him?" At which question the other lords being all astonied, the lord treasurer that then was, perceiving this, gave answer, and said, "If it please your Majesty, I did never read in any history of St. George, but only in *Legenda Aurea*, where it is thus set down: That St. George out with his sword, and ran the dragon through with his spear." The king, when he could not a great while speak for laughing, at length said, "I pray you, my Lord, and what did he with his sword the while?" "That I cannot tell your Majesty," said he. And so an end of that question of good St. George.[61]

It is also possible that other associations came into play. St. George was the focus for many civic rituals and processions in early modern England, especially around the alleged date of his martyrdom, 23 April. This was declared a holy day in 1222, and given official status as a feast of the church in 1415.[62] George's defeat of the dragon was commemorated with elaborate plays and processions during the fifteenth and sixteenth centuries, and the cult was sustained by the literary tradition, especially Voragine's *Legenda Aurea*, mentioned by Edward's treasurer, which had been translated by Caxton in the mid-fifteenth century. At Windsor, the medieval knights of the Garter had staged processions in the saint's honor, and held a banquet to which the Queen and other women were invited. But the saint was also associated with rituals of resurrection and seasonal renewal, while the dragon he slays is sometimes associated with winter. The timing of his feast day so close to Easter may reflect these traditions.[63] As Muriel McClendon comments, "This timing may also help to explain the popularity of his feast in many late medieval agricultural communities, during the season when the ground was beginning to thaw, new growth beginning to appear on the trees, and the task of planting was once more being undertaken."[64]

Henry VII and Henry VIII both had strong allegiances to the saint,[65] and St. George's Day had escaped Henry VIII's first injunctions against the observance of many of the church's holy days in 1536. This was a severe attack on the saints' days, in particular, for their great number was declared to be "prejudicial to the common weal, by reason that it is occasion as well of much sloth and idleness, the very nurse of thieves, vagabonds, and divers other unthriftiness and inconveniences." Moreover, many of them fell in the "good and serene weather" of summer and autumn, when the harvest needed to be gathered in, so they were seen as a threat to a productive economy.[66] In 1552, Edward VI's Parliament modified Henry's strict rules but included St. George's Day in the list of prohibited observances, with a special exception made for the knights of the Garter to observe the day as the feast of their order.[67]

Many parishes abandoned their St. George's Day processions and plays in the Reformation, but sometimes reluctantly. In Norwich, the pageant figures of St. George and the Lady Margaret were eliminated in 1559, but "for pastime" the mayor permitted "the dragon to come in and show himself as in other years."[68]

Like many other ceremonial aspects of the Order, the St. George's Day festivities were revived by James I, with a series of tournaments and jousts; the feast at Windsor was an important part of Charles I's Garter observances; and Charles II signaled the Restoration of monarchy and the old order by being crowned on April 23, St. George's Day.

In 1894, Edward Thompson edited and analyzed Edward VI's drafts. He expressed surprise at the King's reasoning in wanting to move the Garter festival from April to the end of November, "because (a strange reason) 'the feast of St. George is too near the summer.'"[69] But if the Garter procession had come to be associated with some of the more riotous festivals of seasonal renewal, this would be an obvious reason for the King to wish to detach the Garter feast from the saint's day, especially if rumours of Edward's Wiccan sympathies persisted in popular memory. The feasting and ceremonial thought proper to the saint and his day might have threatened to be taken to an extreme, to bubble over into "licentious" or "superstitious" revelry, to become carnivalesque, as it did in some of the feasts discussed in the previous chapter. No wonder the procession became as formal as it did.

Throughout the Order's associations with St. George there is a curious interplay between these elevated court rituals, Reformation and Restoration politics, and the practices of popular and parish culture on the other. Once more we find traces of this movement back and forward between the proper and the improper, between the formal and informal, as well as between the present and the past; and in ways that help to define the medieval *as* the past. As James Simpson has recently argued, the image is usually associated with the past, as the receptacle or container of the past: "As in every revolutionary period, the new order's aggressive repulsion of the previous cultural and political dispensation involves the demolition of images as one of its first and most spectacular tasks. Images are metonymically identified with the *ancien régime* itself; to inflict suffering on the images is to wound the *régime* and to imply that the *régime* ruled by mesmerising the imaginations of its subjects. The most effective way of making a break in history is to break the images and to repudiate the past dispensation as the period of idolatrous imagination."[70] Certainly, in Edward's revisionary history of St. George his image is associated with an idolatrous past in this fashion.

Six months after revising the Garter statutes, Edward was dead. When Mary came to the throne in September 1553, one of her first acts was to rescind his changes. In contrast, her language is not that of religious polemic; rather, she invokes the discourses of reform, modernity, and conservative ritual criticism. The new statutes were said to be "in no sort convenient to be used, and so impertinent and tending to novelty" that they should be abolished immediately,[71] and the Order reverted to the forms it used during the reign of Henry VIII. Clearly, "novelty" is only a relative term. This preeminently ideological battle was played out using the weapons of temporal continuity, and appeals to antiquity and novelty, rather than religious debate or appeals to content.

When Elizabeth ascended the throne in 1558, few changes had to be made. In 1560, four knights were "impowered to read over and consider those Statutes, and being so read over and viewed, to consider with a watchful care and diligence, if any of them were disagreeable to the Religion, Laws, and Statutes of this Realm."[72] But because Mary had simply reverted to the form of the statutes as they had been revised under Henry VIII—they "were no other than Transcripts of her Father's Body of Statutes"[73]—Elizabeth's commission found little it needed to change. Certainly she seems to have been far less concerned about the Order's association with St. George.

This did not mean that the forms of ritual practice followed the statutes precisely, or that minor changes were not made to the feast and services. Elizabeth, for example, did not attend the requiem Mass in the chapel in 1559, and we have seen she preferred to celebrate St. George's Day wherever she was

holding court, rather than making the trip to Windsor. Words such as "Mass"
were gradually replaced by "divine service"; and "altar" by "table." The English
litany was used in the procession, the Epistle and Gospel read in English, and
the priest no longer elevated the host.[74] But in general, as Roy Strong remarks,
the "Catholic statutes and along with them St George, so detested by the reformers, survived into a Protestant England."[75]

William Fennor in 1616 closes his poem in honor of the Garter with a
defense of "the George," the image of the saint slaying the dragon, worn on
the golden chain of the Order since the reign of Henry VII:

> For which the George is as a trophy worne,
>> And may it long, and long remaine with those,
> Which to that excellent dignitie are borne,
>> As opposites unto their country's foes.
> God keepe our King and them from Rome's black pen,
> Let all that love the Garter say, Amen![76]

James I similarly tried to reform the statutes, but with no real will for
change. In the ninth year of his reign, he commanded the Earls of Notting-
ham, Worcester, Pembroke, and Northampton "to examine the Registers, and
other Monuments, which pertained to the Order; and where any thing should
be found obscure, to make it cleer, where contrariety appeared, fitly to reconcile it, *yet with no endeavour of innovating any thing, but an intention of renew-
ing all things*, as neer as might be to the first and most ancient Institution of
the Order" (my emphasis).[77]

All these monarchs—Edward, Mary, Elizabeth, and James—wanted the
Order both to accord with current religious feeling *and* to represent the Order's first forms. Its first medieval institution was thus a deeply mixed inheritance for the sixteenth and early seventeenth centuries. These dynamics of loss
in religious terms dominate changes in cultural ones at this time, but this is
the last period where religious affiliations are a major point of contention.
Gradually, these questions become layered beneath questions of politics, society, and modernity.

As a counterpoint to these impulses toward reform, moreover, we also
need to set a high degree of institutional apathy. In contrast to the young
Edward's enthusiasm, Ashmole reports that in the sixteenth year of his reign,
James I asked six knights to go through the statutes once more, looking for
inconsistencies and ambiguities, and for ways of making the Order "more

famous and illustrious." But the work went forward very slowly, and the first recommendation to be passed suggested that each year the Sovereign should propose such a commission to report back the following year. Only minor changes were made under James, principally concerned with the Alms Knights.

In Ashmole's view, it was Charles I in 1631 who designed "the most compleat and absolute Reformation of any of his Predecessors."[78] The dean of Windsor, Christopher Wren the elder, labored hard to bring the Garter's records up to date, and was later to expend considerable time and money on recovering the *Black*, *Blue*, and *Red Books* of the Order after their loss during the Commonwealth.[79] Charles's commission was designed to consider whether any "Doubt or Ambiguity" appeared in the statutes and ordinances, but in spite of the commission being reissued three months later, nothing was done for another seven years, when it was issued once more, in 1637. But even then, the chancellor of the Order, Sir Thomas Rowe, wrote that he was having difficulty getting the knights even to read the commission: "That he found such difficulty to procure meetings, and a certain non-chalance in every one, as if it were but a ceremonious Affair, and so few hearty in it, that he feared, he and the Officers should wait to little purpose."[80]

Garter knights are often less than enthusiastic about monitoring the statutes to ensure their consistency. Clearly there was greater urgency when a king wanted to change the Order to reflect religious and ideological changes, but even the chapter meeting before Charles II's coronation in 1661 was unable to bring about much change. Ashmole concludes this section on these "Several Endeavours for Reforming the Statutes" by commenting that the late King's design has since "slept in silence and neglect." It is ironic that Ashmole himself should have unsuccessfully sought official recognition of his own contributions and labors, in the new office of Historiographer and Remembrancer of the Order, an idea that came to nothing.[81]

This period of reform and counterreform shows a sequence of more and less dramatic attempts to reformulate the Order's rules to reflect current interests and practices. Successive sovereigns seem driven by the desire of ensuring the Order's uniformity. Throughout these reforms, and the variously unfulfilled plans for further ones, it is possible to hear a strong tinge of melancholy and mourning for the lost medieval originals, and for the promise of "uniformity" to the founder's intentions they seem to hold out. This projected, idealized text haunts the statutes, but it always lies beyond recovery; the scribes and heralds can only copy out the new improved versions, endlessly updated by successive generations, in a ritual quest for the plenitude of medieval origins.

"Ladies of Eminence Known to Us"

The religious vicissitudes of the sixteenth century and the political disruption of the seventeenth gradually gave way to a more stable and less spectacular period in the monarchy's history and the ritual history of the Order. Successive monarchs and chapters continued to make revisions and reforms to the statutes, to the manner of appointing Companions, and to the ritual practices of feasts and processions. There was even a period of revised interest in chivalric orders, as evidenced by the foundation (1687) and revival (1703–4) of the Order of the Thistle, and of the Order of the Bath in 1725, in what Matikkala characterizes as the Chivalric Enlightenment.[82] There were no such deeply ideological reforms, though, that might challenge the very foundation and nature of the Order, and its association with St. George in the manner of Edward VI, or that reflected the trauma of an executed king and an Order in exile in the Interregnum.

However, just as it was possible above to sketch out a negative history of the interruptions, the decay, and the corruption of the Order's much vaunted continuity in its first few centuries, there are other kinds of alternative histories to be written. This section considers ritual criticism of the changing role of women in the Order of the Garter. The conventional, honorific way of writing their history should be easy to imagine: a list of women's names; and a celebration of the progressive "updating" of the Order to take account of changing roles for women. However, this history can also be read as a series of interruptions and moments of resistance. To summarize: women played an important role in the fourteenth and fifteenth centuries, but the survival of this medieval courtly tradition did not persist beyond the reign of Henry VII; and there was a substantial gap in the history of women's formal association with the Order between the end of the fifteenth century and the beginning of the twentieth. The struggle against this aspect of the Order's medieval inheritance troubles its narratives of continuity, disclosing an important rupture both in the Order's implicit claims of survival or revival of medieval custom and in its claims to gradual and progressive reform in line with a developing modernity.

The historiography of women in the Order is actually quite a slender tradition. The first thorough study did not appear until 1985, when James Gillespie's "Ladies of the Fraternity of Saint George and of the Society of the Garter" summarized the surviving evidence of their involvement.[83] There are many records of women being given Garter robes in the Wardrobe accounts of the fourteenth and fifteenth centuries, although the records between 1348 and 1361 have been lost, and the surviving records are also incomplete.[84] Many of the lists of women who are to receive Garter robes in the Wardrobe accounts end with the throwaway phrase "and divers other Ladies." Later lists compiled by historians and archivists also offer substantial variation. If there is sometimes doubt about the status or identity of the Knight Companions at different points in the Garter's history, the problem is compounded in the case of women, whose names and titles vary even more widely with marriage and remarriage. As we saw in Chapter 2, there is substantial disagreement about the identity of the woman at the heart of the Garter myth, even if we accept the title "Countess of Salisbury" as our starting point. There is a further mystery around the figure of the "Countess of Tancarville" (or Tankervile), whose effigy, now lost, reputedly showed the countess wearing the garter on her arm.[85] She is thought to have been either Joan, daughter of Edward Cherleton, KG, or Antigona (or Antigone), the natural daughter of Humphrey, Duke of Gloucester. Both were married to Sir John Grey, KG, Earl of Tancarville.[86] In 1999 Hugh Collins compiled the most thorough list of women who were given robes between 1348 and 1461,[87] but the exact status of their association with the Order remains uncertain. Begent and Chesshyre discuss the early granting of robes to women, but their list of the "Ladies of the Garter" mentions only the nine queens, queens consort, or princesses included in the Order between Queen Alexandra in 1901 and Princess Anne in 1994 (since the publication of their study, Princess Alexandra became a Lady of the Garter in 2003).[88]

Occasionally there are glimpses, too, of unofficial contributions to Garter history by women, who sometimes play an influential role in Garter rituals and elections. Matikkala draws attention to the efforts some queens and royal mistresses exerted in procuring the Garter for various courtiers and favourites, a role that is sometimes alluded to in fiction.[89] Similarly, Herbert Norris reports that Charles II's decision to change the color of the ribbon for the lesser George from sky blue to a deeper shade was "in compliment, it is said, to the beautiful Hortensia Mancini, Duchesse de Mazarin, who came to live in England in 1672; this shade was her favourite colour, and is still known as 'Mazarin blue.'"[90]

In some of its less official and formal customs, too, the Order sometimes exercises a kind of courtliness toward women. Samuel Pepys describes being shown around St. George's Chapel, in 1666: "So took coach and to Windsor to the quarter, and thither sent for Dr Childe,—who came to us, and carried us to St. Georges Chapel and there placed us among the Knights' Stalls (and pretty the observation, that no man, but a woman, may sit in a Knight's place where any brasse-plates are set). . . . And so to other discourses, very pretty, about that Order."[91] Pepys is responding here to the charm of antique custom, although the convention that women may sit where men may not simply underlines the absolute exclusion of women from the Order at this time: female bodies offer no challenge to the hierarchy of the male knights.

The nature of the precedent for modern appointments provided by medieval models is thus inconsistent, or at least open to variable interpretation. This aspect of the Garter's history offers a powerful lesson in the extremely selective ways medieval "tradition" is used and invoked by the Order.

Some commentators write as if medieval women's membership were analogous to the men's and comparable in seriousness of intent; and it is true that the women members are sometimes known as the "Dames de la Fraternité de St Georges" or "Dominae de Secta et Liberature Garteriis." Collins offers the strongest reading of the women's role, describing the "Fraternité" as the Order's "sister association" or as a "sorority," though he offers no evidence of how such an association might have functioned.[92] Nicola McDonald also suggests that a Garter sorority might constitute evidence of a kind of ad hoc community of women readers for a poem such as Chaucer's *Legend of Good Women*.[93] It seems likely that such a fraternity was rather more nominal and ceremonial than social: there is no evidence, for example, that the women constituted an association who met independently, and the surviving records do not mention any other form of participation than the award of robes. Certainly no woman ever endured the humiliation of degradation or dismissal from the Garter.

In the first flush of enthusiasm for the Order as it emerged from chivalric and courtly society, the granting of Garter robes to the wives and daughters of the knights, or in the fifteenth century to the Queen's ladies-in-waiting, was a customary part of court life, akin to the giving of robes for Christmas, coronations, or christenings. This practice was especially prevalent under Edward III and Richard II. It is clear from the Wardrobe accounts that the ladies did not wear the Order's mantle. Their colored robes would have complemented the knights as part of court spectacle, processions, or feasting, or when they led them to the tournament lists, as they did in 1390.[94]

The fifteenth-century dream-vision poem, *The Floure and the Leafe*, describes the matching white velvet clothes worn by the ladies and knights of the Flower, and the green ones of those of the Leaf, where the jousting and the processing take place before an audience of ladies. The dreamer's interlocutor explains that he is watching the Nine Worthies, the knights of the Round Table, the French Douseperis, and the "knights old of the Garter" (line 519), who all did honor to the green laurel. This sounds very similar to the account of the 1488 Garter feast at Windsor:

> And at after noone the king accumpanyd with his brethren of the garter in their mantells, and in the gownes of the lyvery of the last yer, roode from the quadraunt on hakneyes to the college, And went to ther Chapiter, and helde ther Chapiter a great tract of tyme, and from thens went to evensonge; the Quene, and my lady the kings moder being in like gowne of the lyvery riding in a riche chare coverede with riche cloth of golde, xi coursers in that sune chare, harnest with that same cloth of golde, Also xii ladyes and gentilwomen following the quene, cledde al in Cremsesyne velvett gownes, and riding apon white palfereys, ther sadells of cloth of golde, the harnesse of golde smythes work with white roses demy trapper wise.[95]

As this account demonstrates, Garter robes for women played an important role in the conspicuous consumption that was such an important feature of the ritual magnificence of the medieval court, a magnificence that was often mirrored in courtly poetry.

Of all the sovereigns of the Order, Richard II was the most enthusiastic about involving women: he granted robes to approximately thirty-six women, more than half the total number of women appointed in the fourteenth and fifteenth centuries.[96] These women were for the most part wives or daughters of the knights or of court favorites, or the Queen's ladies-in-waiting, or in the case of Katherine Swynford—who was appointed by Richard in 1387—the mistress of one of the founder knights, John of Gaunt. The membership of women has always been completely at the will of the Sovereign: there are no records of any elections or formal installations of women in this early period, and for Collins this is an indication that their appointments were primarily strategic or political in nature.

It is thus a mixed inheritance for the Order. While there is evidence of a strong tradition of women's participation in the Garter festivities, there is little evidence of any textual tradition or even customary practice, with the possible exception of the English queens who were appointed. If the women's role was primarily occasional and ceremonial, and totally subject to the royal whim, it

is not surprising that it failed to generate any of its own conventions or traditions. After Henry VII showed little interest in appointing women as Ladies of
the Garter—he made only one appointment, his daughter Elizabeth, in 1495,
the year she died—the custom lapsed.

Accordingly, there is a huge gap in this aspect of the Order's traditions,
between 1495 and 1901, when Queen Alexandra, wife of Edward VII, was declared a Lady of the Order by special statute. This is a space of four hundred
years between the appointment of women to the Order, so it is impossible to
make a prima facie argument here about a continuous, living tradition.

There were several unsuccessful attempts to reintroduce Garter honors for
women in the intervening centuries. A motion was put to the Garter chapter
in 1638, and was referred to Queen Anne for consultation, but the Civil War
intervened with this development. John Anstis made a similar proposal in
1724, and various other suggestions appeared in 1731 (in the *Monthly Intel-
ligencer*, with respect to Queen Caroline) and in 1842, by Sir Harris Nicolas,
but nothing came of the proposals.[97] While the Order may have depended on
an audience of women for its first great feasts and processions, it had clearly
become more resolutely masculine in its identity.

Begent and Chesshyre offer a fascinating account of the resistance shown
by Sir Albert Woods, Garter King of Arms, whom we met in the second
section of this chapter, when King Edward VII commanded in 1901 that a
special statute be promulgated giving Queen Alexandra the title "Lady of the
Order of the Garter." Woods seems to have ignored the King's request to raise
the Queen's Garter banner in the chapel, and in subsequent correspondence
over a two-year period there was considerable discussion between Woods and
Henry Knollys, the King's private secretary. In a campaign of resistance to
this idea, Woods argued for the lack of precedents for such a procedure and
the difficulties involved. Knollys wrote back firmly, saying the King "has already made the Queen a Knight of the Garter and he is afraid therefore that
he must ask you to give directions to have her banner put up in St George's
Chapel."[98]

After further correspondence, Woods finally conceded that a stall should
be allocated to the Queen on the right of the Sovereign's. He reserved a final
barb, pointing out this would put pressure on the other places and inquiring
which of the knights should be left out.[99] This is an example of ritual criticism as resistance to change, as Woods's deep-seated reluctance to elevate the
Queen's banner indicates his devotion to his sense of continuous practice—
and also, we may guess, his sense of his heraldic authority as Garter King of

Arms—over even the King's wish and statute. In this case it was the herald who clung to the old rules in defiance of the reigning monarch, who was seen as a thoughtless modernizer, reminding us that ritual change can easily be coded as either progressive or regressive.

When the current Queen decided women could enter the Order as full Companions, with the same rights as the knights, in 1987, she ran no risk of such resistance, and promulgated a formal statute. This acknowledged that her predecessors as sovereigns of the Order "have been pleased to admit Ladies of exalted rank or eminent Station into association with the Knights Companions of the said Most Noble Order," permitting them to wear the robes and ensigns of the Order, "and to participate in the celebrations and other solemnities of the Order." Elizabeth appeals to tradition and precedent, but the statute is completely vague about which precedents she may have had in mind. In this instance, the medieval practice of a "fraternitie" and any suggestion of a separate society or association of women is collapsed into the ceremonial appointment of individual queens such as Alexandra, or the Queen's own mother, sister, and daughter; or, indeed, her own appointment as Princess Elizabeth in 1947, five years before her accession.

The statute continues: "And whereas We the Sovereign of the Most Noble Order of the Garter are desirous of evincing in a fitting manner Our abiding sense of the virtues and worth of Ladies of eminence known to Us by making such of them as We are pleased to choose and select to be Companions of Our said Most Noble Order." The document goes on to affirm that the Ladies will enjoy "the like rights and privileges . . . as have been enjoyed hitherto by Knights Companions of Our said Order," "any Statute, Decree, Rule or Usage to the contrary notwithstanding." The emphasis on the "Ladies of eminence known to Us" is a clear reminder that membership of the Order of the Garter remains tightly restricted to the Sovereign's prerogative. Begent and Chesshyre comment, "This development was of course occasioned by changes in society and the equal status of women in (almost) all areas of life."[100] At the time, a Buckingham Palace spokesman commented, "She amended the statutes . . . to do away with sex discrimination."[101]

We see here the tremendous will of the Order's insiders and apologists to see it as *responsive* to social change. When I attended the Garter procession at Windsor in 2001, the loudest cheers among the royalist crowd, apart from those for members of the royal family, were for Baroness Thatcher, by far the most recognizable public figure, and apart from the members of the royal family, the only woman in the procession.

In the case of the Ladies of the Order, the medieval inheritance is richly ambiguous. The custom of granting robes to medieval women can be disregarded as superrogatory to the Order, and its one thousand male companions; or it can be invoked to bolster the formal inclusion of women to its full honors. Alternatively, this inheritance can be deployed with all the selectivity of royal prerogative. Victoria reinstigated the medieval style for women of wearing the Garter around her arm, but without for a moment considering reviving the medieval custom of welcoming other women into the Order (see Chapter 6). The history of the Order's queens is another story, of course, and we will consider the difference made by a female body at the head of the Order in the next chapter.

Perhaps because of this uncertainty at the heart of the Order, the problem of women's roles in the Order has been particularly telling. Whatever we believe about the historical facts of Edward III's intentions in founding the Order of the Garter, there is a central dispute among the Order's historians that can be read as a disagreement about the nature of the courtly and chivalric heart of the Order. For the serious and literal-minded historian, the worst-case scenario is that the Order takes its origins from a great military king's romantic (or foolish, or violent) attachment to a woman; that centuries of tradition and ritual observance are founded on a light-hearted moment at a party. More liberal commentators from the sixteenth through to the twenty-first century argue there is something "ennobling" about this commemoration. Just as the King elevates the garter to heraldic symbol, so too do the years of practice elevate the order into a tradition.

Every time the Sovereign or a chapter of the Garter considers making changes to its practices or traditions, he or she must confront or displace its problematic medieval origins. Although these origins enhance the Order's mythic and symbolic capital, they do not always stand up to close scrutiny as a model for postmedieval ritual behavior. If the Order begins as a heterosexually oriented game of court culture, it calls up a medieval world where knights are led by women and golden chains to tournaments and where kings pick up women's underclothes and wear them as part of their own costume. The modernizing impulse is often deeply embarrassed by these medieval associations. While the discourses of continuity emphasize the intertwined spiritual and chivalric impulses of the order, its original religious expressions have not always accorded with the dominant religious forms of the postmedieval English monarchy. And finally, if the medieval Order is regarded as inaugurating a tradition that commemorates homosocial chivalric and military culture, this becomes problematic when the Order is led by a queen—as has been the case for three of the most stable periods of the Order's history: a good 150 out of 650 years. The next chapter turns attention to the material, embodied expression of the problem of medievalism: how men and women should wear the Garter.

Chapter 6

Bodies, Clothes, and Medievalism

It was only in those too rarely required robes that he had the sense of being fully dressed.

—Max Beerbohm, *Zuleika Dobson*

In the centerpiece of the Garter's rituals of investiture two bodies and two moments in time both touch. Tying the Garter around the leg of the new Companion, the Sovereign commemorates the medieval inauguration of the Order and affirms a long and powerful continuity with previous Sovereigns and Companions. Less officially, but equally firmly, the act also recalls the foundation myth of the lady's garter. At the same time, the fellowship shared by the contemporary members is reinforced, as their bonds of allegiance are recalled. The act is accompanied by a formal admonition. This is its current form: "To the honour of God Omnipotent, and in Memorial of the Blessed Martyr, St. George, tie about thy leg, for thy renown, this Most Noble Garter; wear it as the symbol of the Most Illustrious Order never to be forgotten or laid aside, that hereby thou mayest be admonished to be courageous, and having undertaken a just war, into which thou shalt be engaged, thou mayest stand firm, valiantly fight, courageously and successfully conquer."[1] These ritual words look back to the past (they have not changed much since the investiture of the future Charles II in 1638) while also invoking the future of the new Companion. As we might expect, they show clear signs of strain, as the old words are repeated in a modern context. The words "never to be forgotten or laid aside" technically refer to the Garter itself, recalling a much earlier insistence that it should always be worn, when infringement was punishable by a fine of half a mark payable to the warden and the College of St. George.[2] Yet it

is easy to hear these words as referring to the Order itself, "never to be forgotten," as if shoring up the Order's own future against the risk of oblivion. The
military admonition to courage and valor in a just war similarly now asks to be
read metaphorically. The embodied language of "standing firm" in battle bears
little relationship to the actual conduct of modern warfare, while in any case,
Companions of the Garter tend to receive the honor in their later years, *after*
a long period of military, diplomatic, or political service. Any vestigial trace
of the Order as an incitement to greater valor or chivalry on the battlefield is
long gone, replaced by a more generalized sense of the honor and the symbolic
capital now accruing to the new member of the "Most Illustrious Order."

In practice the scene rarely takes place in this way. The Garter has not
been tied on since early Victorian times; instead it is "made up" with the knot
and pendant end fixed, and the two ends of the Garter being joined with
a clip. Nor is the Garter actually fastened on the body during investiture.
It is simply held briefly around or against the left leg of the man or the left
arm of the woman; and sometimes simply presented as an object to the new
Companion.

Over the course of the Garter's history, there has been a steady movement
away from the very intimate act of tying on the Garter: the Sovereign has
rarely performed this act in person. Some of these changes and modifications
to the Garter's practices are related to changes in costume and fashion, particularly once the male leg was less often enclosed in armor or in tight-fitting
hose. This chapter will repeatedly have cause to remark the gradual movement
of the Garter's signifying function upward on the body, onto the chains, medallions, ribbons, sashes, and brooches that all draw attention to the upper
rather than the lower body. It is not difficult to read this generalized movement away from the leg as a movement of double embarrassment both with
this more intimate part of the body *and* with the Order's curious medieval
origins. The difficulty of tying a garter tightly around a part of the body now
ordinarily draped in loose-fitting trousers is an acute reminder of how fashions
and social customs have changed. The act would be anachronistic on several
levels, registering the historical distance between present and past practices
of the Order; and between medieval chivalric regimes and their postmedieval
continuation or re-creation. The Garter now bears no relation to everyday
costume, and its primary sense as a marker of royal favor and membership of a
social elite is shadowed by its secondary significance as a marker of traditional
ritual practice.

There is another layer of radical difference that sits behind this ritual act.

While the scene of investiture recalls the Order's first foundation, as the new Companion joins the fellowship of knights first conceived by Edward III, there is a significant difference in the relationships of bodily touch evoked by the two moments. This difference arises from the contested origins of the Order. According to the popular story the King takes up the lady's garter and ties it, still warm from her body, around his own leg (or in at least one version, as we saw in Chapter 3, back around her leg). It is easy to read the King's appropriation of the garter as a relationship akin to that of the fetish: the garter stands in for the unattainable woman's body, and inaugurates its own rituals of possession and desire. The idea of intimate or sexualized "touch" between man and woman is thus heavily mediated or displaced onto the touch of the garter as it encircles the male limb.

We have seen that many early historians were quick to disconnect the Garter from such a scene, to disentangle it from the world of the boudoir, ballroom, or dance hall, and to fix it firmly in the heraldic or military sphere, either as a formal version of a personal badge or as the strategic elevation of a tiny item of clothing or armor into a richly symbolic sign. But even these apologists have to concede that the Order's insignia is an item of clothing, not just a badge or medal. Whatever the origins of the Garter, its proper place is inescapably an embodied one: not just *on* the body, but in a constrictive form *around* the leg. Perhaps for this reason, the Garter itself does not persist for very long as the sole indicator of membership in the Order; its signifying force is soon dispersed among the mantle and robes, the great chain of office, and other insignia, such as the diagonal blue sash and the radiant Garter star.

Over the centuries, as fashions and costumes change, the nature of the ritual body's relationship to the Garter and the relationship between ritual and everyday costume undergo subtle modification. The Garter is an eloquent supplement to a knight's clothing, but its relationship to the rest of his outfit varies according to whether he is wearing medieval armor, traditional court costume (breeches, hose, and dress coat), or modern everyday wear. When female bodies are involved, either as recipients or bestowers of the Garter, another series of difficulties is put into play. This differently sexed body transforms the relationship of exchange as the Garter is given and worn, and as the act of exchange draws attention to the bodies participating in the ritual.

All these changes put substantial pressure on the way the Order of the Garter creates social meaning and mythic capital, especially since fashion in clothing is such a profound register of temporality and modernity. This chapter explores these difficulties, tracing the various movements toward and away from embodiment in the Order's ritual transformations of its foundational moment, the changing dispositions of bodies, the clothes they wear, the gestures they use. We will avoid a "straight" historical narrative of changing fashions and conventions, and seek to uncover some less familiar dynamics in this aspect of Garter tradition, some of which can be seen as downright queer.

Two Bodies Touching: Kings, Queens, and Their Garters

We begin with an intriguing pattern of negativity. For all the times the Order's foundational myth is told and retold, it is hardly ever portrayed. The moment when Edward III, the founder, ties a garter round his own leg, or when a later sovereign ties a Garter around someone else's at the moment of induction into the Order, is very rarely the subject of visual representation. I have found only a few illustrations, for example, of the often-quoted story about the King retrieving the lady's garter, and none before the very end of the nineteenth century. One from an illustrated pamphlet for children shows the King about to tie the garter around his leg (figure 12).[3]

Other illustrations prefer to show the King in the moment of declaring the motto, like Howard Davie's, chosen by Edward VII for the King's Christmas card in 1908 (see figure 9, above). In Davie's picture the Queen remains on her throne in the background while the countess looks down abashed, holding her hand to her breast. By contrast the King holds his head up high and looks around at the staring courtiers, holding the Garter at full length between his two hands, and pointing his own well-turned foot forward, out from under his long robes. There is no question of his bending down to put the garter on himself at this point. His own robe is held in by a loose belt that is knotted in Garter form, with a short pendant end, a neat prolepsis that suggests the easy alignment of the Garter with masculine clothing.

A similar gesture appears in *An Island Story: A History of England for Boys and Girls* by H. E. Marshall, illustrated by A. S. Forrest, from 1920, as Edward is shown about to invest his son, the Black Prince, with the Order (figure 13).[4] Here the young Prince is portrayed as a military hero receiving his reward, with his leg safely encased in its carapace of armor. Even so the illustrator shows the moment before the King must bend his head below his son's and touch his leg to tie on the Garter.

It is easy to discern a failure of nerve about these representations, a

Figure 12. King Edward III picks up the garter. Rena Gardiner, 1981. © The Dean and Canons of Windsor.

Figure 13. Edward III invests the Black Prince with the Garter, A. S. Forrest, 1907. From H. E. Marshall, *An Island Story: A History of England for Boys and Girls*, with pictures by A. S. Forrest (1907; rpt. New York: Frederick A. Stokes, 1920), 280.

respectful unwillingness to show a monarch on his knees. Unsurprisingly, the most direct illustration of the king's subjection comes from the parody of English history by Sellar and Yeatman in *1066 and All That*, which we considered earlier. But in general terms, while the myth of the Garter has not diminished in popularity, it has proved resistant to visual representation. This reluctance extends to the idea of illustrating the moment when monarchs invest new knights with the Order, and must similarly lower their bodies. In this resistance to portraying the Sovereign on his or her knees, or attending to the lower part of someone else's body, we can diagnose the prevalent sense of risk in the Order's foundational myth and its awkward, embarrassing aftermath. As we saw in Chapter 2, the Garter myth dramatizes the ritual abasement of the King, but even independently of that myth, the Garter's position on the lower leg risks the monarch's dignity.

The visual resistance to portraying the King on his knees began quite early. One of the earliest illustrations of a knight receiving the Garter shows Henry IV standing with hands resolutely on hips while another knight actually ties the garter around the knee of Richard Beauchamp, Earl of Warwick, after the battle of Shrewsbury in 1403 (figure 14).[5]

When the current Queen bestows chivalric and courtly honors, the happy recipients kneel, bow, or curtsey before her, and must then back away for several steps before they can turn around. In the 2006 televised documentary *The Queen at Eighty*, the Garter is presented to John Major, not in the large public chamber room with the hundred or so others, but in a private audience with Her Majesty at Buckingham Palace, in which she pins the Garter star to his suit, and simply places the Garter into his hands. (The formal ceremony of installation in which the new knight is escorted to his stall in St. George's Chapel takes place later, during the annual service in the chapel at Windsor.)

From a longer historical perspective, the reluctance to represent the moment of bodies touching is a symptom of the anxiety the Garter generates about the monarch's body, or more precisely, about the monarch's two bodies. According to this theory, famously outlined by Ernst Kantorowicz, medieval political theory distinguished between the monarch's natural body and the body politic.[6] One of the reasons the Garter myth appears so disturbing to many of its early historians is that it threatens to confuse these two things. Martorell's fifteenth-century *Tirant lo Blanc* rehearses these anxieties most comprehensively. Most later versions of the Garter's origins emphasize the King's elevation of the humble item almost immediately to the status of public sign: the quickness of his riposte and his coining of the motto signify his

Figure 14. Henry IV observes the Earl of Warwick's investiture with the Garter, BL MS Cotton Julius E.iv. © All Rights Reserved. The British Library Board.

command of the moment. In contrast, Martorell stresses the delay. His king wears the Garter for *two weeks* before he is encouraged by a concerned courtier to remove it from his body, whereupon he transforms it from a personal to a public sign. Martorell's version is intrigued by the Garter's capacity to confound the theoretical separation between the monarch's natural body and his/her body politic. The Garter is a slippery boundary crosser from one to the other, from a single, personal item of clothing into the formality and endless reiteration of heraldic discourse and display.

Moreover, the Garter's transition from natural to formal sign, from body natural to body politic, is never complete because the irresistible workings of history and cultural memory obsessively return us to the contested medieval origins of the Order. Ritual memory insists we constantly switch backward and forward among the multiple temporalities of medievalism, testing the past against the present. We have seen how many historians and heralds want to dismiss or disprove the foundational myth of the Garter but cannot resist keeping that story before us, recalling it constantly and further enhancing its mythic capital. And whenever that story is told, it reminds us of the Garter's first and true place, around the leg. Even in its most contemporary, most abstracted form, the Order cannnot be detached from its history as an embodied sign.

This history becomes problematic in a different way when the Order's Sovereign is a Queen. These are not just marginal cases: for nearly a third of the Order's history, it has been led by a woman.

When Edward III conceived of his great military and chivalric Order, with his son the Black Prince as his second-in-command, he did not envisage a time when a woman might occupy the Sovereign's position alone. Two hundred and five years later, Queen Mary could not envisage it either. She exercised her sovereignty jointly with Philip of Spain from 1553, sending his Garter to him at Southampton on his arrival in England before she had even met him.[7] On her death in 1558, Philip took up his place as an ordinary knight of the Order. William and Mary similarly presided together as joint sovereigns, but Elizabeth I, Anne, Victoria, and Elizabeth II, the thirtieth sovereign, all led the Order in their own right, though with varying degrees of involvement and engagement. Each time a queen ascends the throne, the Order needs to make a careful accommodation of its original military and chivalric orientation, and each of these queens effected subtle or major changes in the practices, if not the statutes of the Order.

Elizabeth I was the second female Garter Sovereign, and her long unmarried reign meant that the Order underwent a significant shift in its orientation, rituals, and politics. We have already read of Ashmole's distress at the Queen's abandonment of the feast at Windsor; and indeed, for Mary E. Hazard, Elizabeth's relationship with the Order as a whole was characterized by her "abrogation of the formalities of presence."[8] Where her younger half brother had labored over successive drafts of the revisions to statutes that would be overturned by Mary, Elizabeth accomplished her own form of ritual criticism simply by staying away, or by retreating into her private closet during Mass. These changes were often motivated by religious politics. But Elizabeth also avoided some of the more secular Garter functions, or "delayed or evaded making relevant decisions," and neglected to fill Garter vacancies.[9] Commenting on the Queen's reluctance to wear the full habit and to partake fully in its rituals, Ashmole speculates: "But this may admit of some excuse; first as a Woman, she thought her self not so strictly tyed, to the exact observation of the Rules of so martial an *Order*."[10] Second, he speculates that the robes may have been "a little too heavy and cumbersom."

Hazard reads these developments as the Queen "resisting assimilation into the masculine model of princedom": "On these Garter occasions, she was asserting her own feminine style by defining the terms of her own presence, withholding it as a sharp reminder of her prerogatives and of the dependent nature of the Knights' Garter, bestowing her presence when it pleased her and how it pleased her, with all of the splendor decorously and legally appropriate only to the monarch."[11] However, Elizabeth's father, Henry VIII, had similarly often avoided the Garter feasts and "consistently . . . declined to exploit the pageantry of the Garter ceremonies,"[12] so we may need to read this as part of a more general, less gendered pattern of Tudor monarchy: the careful manipulation and withholding of royal presence.

The Queen's sovereignty also strengthened the political role played by the Order of the Garter. Whereas Henry VIII had moved away from the tradition of making Garter appointments to the same family groups, and had used membership in the Order as a reward for his Privy Chamber, under Elizabeth the members of the Privy Chamber were women, so the power of connection with the monarch's body could no longer be translated into such direct political advantage. In Raymond Waddington's account, "With a power vacuum created by the obvious incapacity of the Privy Chamber, the need arose for another institutional elite within the court, an inner circle of nobility that could be graced by intimacy with the sovereign, yet not intimacy of a kind that might violate the decorum of fealty to a noble lady, bringing discredit to a female monarch. Just such an institution was available in the Order of the Garter."[13] Waddington demonstrates that Elizabeth I used the Order as her father had used the Privy Chamber. Appointments to the Queen's Privy Chamber were women, so the Queen elevated an inner circle of advisers and favorites to Garter honors.[14]

The tying or buckling on of the Garter was usually delegated to a Knight Companion, although foreign princes often received it in person from the monarch. As a mark of "special grace and favour," in Ashmole's words, the Queen herself "adorned" Lord Burghley and Henry, Earl of Sussex, with the Garter.[15] Sometimes she would place the collar of the Order around the neck of the new Companion, while another knight would buckle on the Garter, as occurred in the case of the Earl of Shrewsbury. In 1593, at the age of sixty, she invested Sir Francis Knowles, in his late seventies, not only with the collar, but also with the Garter, "an act which moved bystanders to tears."[16]

The ceremony of creeping to the cross on Good Friday (making one's way on one's knees to a cross and kissing it) had been abolished by the Protestant Church. Nevertheless, Elizabeth maintained those ceremonies that demonstrated the complex mixture of royal humility and power: washing the feet of the poor in imitation of Christ (though these were all women); and touching for the King's evil, in accordance with the traditional belief that the anointed monarch could cure scrofula. Carole Levin notes that the women's feet were all carefully washed by the Yeomen of the Laundry, before the Queen's ritual washing.[17] Levin quotes William Tooker's account of the first ceremony: "How often have I seen her most serene Majesty, prostrate on her knees, body and soul rapt in prayer."[18] Again, there are no surviving visual records of the Queen in this position, though Lavinia Teerlinc's miniature (figure 15) gives some sense of the occasion, showing how the occasion combines the twinned registers of royal stateliness (the Queen's lady-in-waiting holds her train) with humble service (the Queen's long white apron). Humbling herself at the leg of the new Garter appointments, acting as their servant or page,[19] was a ritualized reversal, but this was still clearly reserved only as a mark of special favor: the conventions of Elizabethan, Tudor, or royal iconography certainly do not lend themselves to the visual representation of the scene.

We will return to this question of the Queen's body in later periods elsewhere in this chapter, but I interrupt this trajectory now to consider the problem from a less historical point of view. As I have suggested elsewhere in this book, it is often in medievalist fiction, poetry, and parody that we can tap into the imaginative force of a myth like the Garter, even if the official discourse about

Figure 15. *Elizabethan Maundy*, Lavinia Teerlinc. © Beauchamp Collection, U.K. / The Bridgeman Art Library.

the Order flattens this dimension. If that official discourse is reluctant to show the Sovereign subjecting himself or herself, artists and writers are much freer to explore the Order's mythic and poetic force. For a fully realized image of a personal installation, then, we may turn to the fictional and cinematic imagination.

The Queer Garter

In a short scene early in her 1992 film of Virginia Woolf's *Orlando*, Sally Potter works from a position *outside* the Garter's rituals to offer a fearless, sympathetic account of the intimacies of the Garter. The film is a lavish production, full of richly imagined historical detail in its costumes and settings, even as it explores the idea of one body magically extending over five centuries. It lovingly re-creates Elizabethan, seventeenth-, eighteenth-, nineteenth-, and twentieth-century settings, as it follows the movement of Woolf's novel, and her hero/heroine across these successive periods and a mysterious change of sex from male to female. In the scene in question, the aged Queen Elizabeth is seated outdoors, surrounded by five male courtiers, a lady-in-waiting, and two enormous wolfhounds. One of the men holds the dogs while Orlando goes down on one knee, kneeling on a red cushion. He is magnificently dressed in red hose and a gold and red doublet and cape. The Queen is robed in a gown similar to that worn in her Rainbow portrait. She leans forward in her chair and ties the Garter below Orlando's left knee as he looks down. All the colors and textiles are sumptuous and layered, thrown into greater relief by contrast with the horizontal and vertical planes of the walled garden: green grass beneath their feet, and the darker green wall of hedge behind them. The sheer lavishness of the Queen's and Orlando's costumes seems excessive and ornate, making movement difficult, even for the young Orlando.

These people are groomed and dressed in every part, encrusted with jewels, bound and draped with layers and layers of embroidered and stitched fabric. It seems nothing can be missing. But there is more to come: the Garter is added to Orlando's costume as the supplement to his dress that has the odd effect of making his leg seem curiously *unadorned* prior to the bestowal. It is, then, a Derridean *supplément*. To appear before the monarch the subject is fully and ornately dressed, but the addition of the Garter immediately makes that clothed, courtly body seem undressed, or incompletely dressed. Thereafter, too, that body will be examined to see if it is in fact dressed completely, wearing its Garter.[20] And indeed, the statutes of the Garter regularly insist that the Garter must always be worn (whether the fully buckled item, or a blue ribbon, or a medallion on a blue ribbon around the neck, or under the arm); if not, a fine must be paid. This implies a culture of regular surveillance, as the bodies of the Garter Companions are inspected to see if they are correctly, fully, adorned.

Woolf describes the scene of investiture thus:

"Come!" she said. She was sitting bolt upright beside the fire. And she held him a foot's pace from her and looked him up and down. Was she matching her speculations the other night with the truth now visible? Did she find her guesses justified? Eyes, mouth, nose, breast, hips, hands—she ran them over; her lips twitched visibly as she looked; but when she saw his legs she laughed out loud. He was the very image of a noble gentleman. But inwardly? She flashed her yellow hawk's eyes upon him as if she would pierce his soul. The young man withstood her gaze blushing only a damask rose as became him. Strength, grace, romance, folly, poetry, youth—she read him like a page. Instantly she plucked a ring from her finger (the joint was swollen rather) and as she fitted it to his, named him her Treasurer and Steward; next hung about him chains of office; and bidding him bend his knee, tied round it at the slenderest part the jewelled order of the Garter. Nothing after that was denied him. . . . At the height of her triumph when the guns were booming at the Tower and the air was thick enough with gunpowder to make one sneeze and the huzzas of the people rang beneath the windows, she pulled him down among the cushions where her women had laid her (she was so worn and old) and made him bury his face in that astonishing composition—she had not changed her dress for a month—which smelt for all the world, he thought, recalling his boyish memory, like some old cabinet at home where his mother's furs were stored. He rose, half suffocated from the embrace. "This," she breathed, "is my victory!"—even as a rocket roared up and dyed her cheeks scarlet.[21]

Potter shows a variant of this second scene, too: the old Queen's dress is removed by her attendants, and still wearing a stiff bodice and petticoat, she is carefully hoisted into her bed, where she summons Orlando. He approaches hesitantly and only slowly reaches the position the Queen demands, with his head resting on her bodice. At this point she breathes, "This is my victory!" and tucks the deeds to Orlando's mansion into the Garter on his leg, giving it to him in perpetuity "*on condition you remain young.*" This does not appear in Woolf's novel, but in its echo of the waitress receiving a tip of notes tucked into her bra or her bodice, it makes manifest the sexual politics behind

Orlando's elevation and his/her longevity. Woolf's own version sympatheti-cally recalls the foundation myth: an act of intimacy between monarch and subject generates centuries of tradition.

Potter follows Woolf's lead to explore this scene for what it may reveal about the Queen's fondness for a youthful male leg, though Woolf also hints that the Queen may guess something of Orlando's sexual ambiguity: "Was she matching her speculations the other night with the truth now visible? Did she find her guesses justified? Eyes, mouth, nose, breast, hips, hands—she ran them over; her lips twitched visibly as she looked; but when she saw his legs she laughed out loud. He was the very image of a noble gentleman. But inwardly?"

But *Orlando* is even more richly layered, because both the Queen and her knight are in drag. Elizabeth is played by Quentin Crisp, while Orlando is played by Tilda Swinton. So a man dressed as a queen ties the Garter on the leg of a woman dressed as a boy who will later become a woman and live for several hundred years. We might see this, then, as the queer Garter: a sign that inaugurates shifting sexualities and multiple temporalities, and one that is also intricately linked with the complex rituals of clothing, performance, and dressing up.

Before we dismiss this as an aberration—a highly contingent combina-tion of Woolf's modernist, androgynous imagination with Potter's inventive, postmodernist casting—let us ask whether this moment of queer touch can teach or show us anything new about the conjunction of bodies, clothes, and traditions that constellate around the moment of investiture. For one thing, the dizzying layers of reference here license us to speculate on the physical, material realities of receiving the Garter. Most representations are painfully re-spectful, steering attention away from the moment when the two bodies meet, and focusing our gaze on the newly adorned body or the moment just prior to the presentation. Through the privileged eye of the camera, Potter shows us how unnatural this action is, what an odd vestige of tradition it embodies; and how, when the monarch's body is that of an old queen, it appears awkwardly remote, already an archaic act of medievalism.

As an exercise in medievalism, this cinematic invention also reaches both backward and forward. In its visual splendor and the representation of this ritual, it recalls, first, the medieval origins of the Order; second, their Tudor embodiment in the Queen; and third, the writing of Woolf, who towers over so much of twentieth-century literature. Yet it also looks forward to the con-temporary period, and the current Garter traditions. Taking inspiration from

Carolyn Dinshaw's idea of the queer touch of medievalism,[22] we may stretch this elastic movement backward and forward even more, to suggest that the queerness of Potter's Garter moment might also move backward and forward beyond the scene presented here. In the dynamics of bodily touch, there might also be desire, and that desire might sometimes be queer.

There is another historical dimension to the queer Garter. In 1743, Sir Cyril Wich was the British ambassador to Russia. He wrote to Lord Carteret: 426/238/6159/9,8/9176/515113/236/543/226/6159/19316/237/19451/9314/804/639 /737/5168/8817/12,14/9016/378/1353/31123/1320/2015/11167171. . . ." Luckily, someone transcribed his diplomatic cipher into elegant handwriting so that we may read of the Czarina, Empress Elizabeth, being presented with the King of Poland's Order. Sir Cyril goes on: "Your Lordship cannot conceive how much the Czarina is pleased with these Distinctions; and I am sure, that nothing in the world would be more agreeable to Her than if the King would send Her the Order of the Garter. I do not know whether it be practicable, but if it can be done, I am persuaded it would have a very good effect. The Czarina frequently appears in Man's Clothes, and the new Ornament of the Garter would, I am sure, please Her above all things."[23] There are many instances of male and female names being proposed for membership in the Order, many more than are elevated to its honors. At this time there were no women members of the Order, but Sir Cyril's letter implies that the rules might well have been bent for foreign princes or czarinas. Certainly the bestowal of the Order on the Russian empress would be a diplomatic coup, but the ambassador makes no bones about saying it would be a wonderful ornament to the Czarina's cross-dressing (she sometimes dressed in the military uniform of her regiments): the "great effect" it would have is both diplomatic and sartorial.

Such an effect would go one step further as an official act of transvestism than the dancer "La Bacelli," Giovanna Zanerini, the mistress of the Duke of Dorset, who was reported by Horace Walpole to have worn the duke's Garter around her forehead in Paris while he was ambassador there.[24] Tom Taylor commented in 1863, "The '*honi soit qui mal y pense*' has never been put to such a test before or since."[25] Zanerini's appropriation of the Garter as a sign of conquest and mockery uncannily returns us to the foundational myth and its scene of dancing and revelry, threatening to undo centuries of sacralization. If the Garter myth celebrates Edward's translation of a humble sexualized sign into the dignity of royal ritual, Zanerini demonstrates the ease with which this masculine sign can return to the female body, and move out beyond the world of aristocratic and class privilege. As the fin de siècle poems examined in

Chapter 4 testify, the Garter myth trails a persistent association with sexual desire as a threat to aristocratic dignity, and there are further examples to come.

Cross-dressing itself shares long associations with medieval and medievalist entertainment. Henry Knighton complained in the second half of the fourteenth century about the women who attended tournaments, "dressed in various and amazing men's clothes." "They wore parti-coloured tunics, half one colour and half another colour, with short hoods whose long points were wound round their heads like ropes, belts studded with silver and gold, and they also have knives called 'daggers' in pouches slung over their stomachs."[26] In the next century Malory describes the tournament of Surluse, in which Sir Lancelot wears a woman's dress over his armor when jousting, and then mocks Sir Dinadan by having him dressed in women's clothes and parading before the Queen. This is the carnivalesque aspect of the medieval tournament.

In Sir Cyril's discreet ambassadorial discourse there is a powerful and suggestive cathexis between the ideas of cross-dressing and dressing up, deepening the idea that the Garter both supplements and completes one's outfit. Moreover, in its naturalization of the idea of cross-dressing, and the idea of the Garter as "ornament," Sir Cyril's letter would be curiously—queerly—at home in the world of *Orlando*. Fiction and history are inescapably intertwined in the history of the Garter, and sometimes these twists and turns are queer ones.

The ultimate queer Garter, however, comes from the life of the intersexual Dr. James Barry (d. 1865), who took the Garter motto—*Honi soit qui mal y pense*—as his own personal motto for a most irregular life. Christened sometime in the 1790s as Margaret Ann Bulkley, he was brought up as a girl but lived as a man throughout his adult life, enrolling as a medical student in Edinburgh, becoming a surgeon in the British Army and inspector general of hospitals. Reticent about revealing his body, he was identified as female only after his death by the woman who prepared his body for burial. Many accounts written after his death claimed to share this knowledge. His recent biographer, Rachel Holmes, argues that it was at the onset of puberty that Barry took on a masculine identity in an attempt to resolve the intersexual nature of his body, and to allow him to undertake medical studies. Barry's thesis was a study of femoral hernias in women (which are often the result of recently descended testicles in intersexual bodies), and Holmes speculates that Barry may have been his own "unnamed subject of this startling document to the problems of sexual differentiation."[27] Throughout her study, Holmes insists on the difficulties of "knowing" or observing sexual identity.

The performance of gender in Barry's case is equally complex. He was a dandy who arrived in London in 1812, around the time when "dandyism" was entering the English lexicon. Like other dandies of the "Adonis" type, Barry employed a stay to shape his upper body in a manner that approximated the female form: a narrow waist, wide trousers, and quilted stomacher. Holmes writes:

> The chest and upper sleeves of Barry's dress and frock coats were stuffed with malleable wadding that enabled reshaping of the upper body. His day boots and evening shoes were worn with stacked heels, and his favourite were "dandified top boots with red heels," dyed to match the colour of his hair. Stays held up his sharply tailored jackets, and like every self-respecting dandy he employed the services of a stay-maker to shape his corsetry. He strove to realign the shape of his body through the artifice of his clothes. And in doing so he was conforming to the most avant-garde male fashion. He was an unusual, feminized "monstrosity." And thus typical of the very apotheosis of male fashion of the time.[28]

At the same time, Barry prided himself on his chivalry and fought in at least one duel during his time in Cape Town. He was also accused of sodomy with his protector, Lord Somerset.

This intriguing character appropriated the Garter motto as his own.[29] Unlike most of the uses of the Garter considered so far, this is a forceful appropriation into a radically different social and personal context. During Barry's lifetime, the motto functioned as an invocation of the Order's royal grandeur and its long traditions, and as a defiant challenge to anyone scorning his dandified masculinity. After his death and the subsequent revelation of his "female" body, the motto offers a dramatic retrospective on the capacity of women to excel in the field of medicine from which they were still banned, on a lifetime of performed masculinity, and perhaps even, given Barry's medical interests, on the long but hidden history of intersexuality.

This is an extreme case of the queer Garter, facilitated by the motto's missing referent. Once more we observe the motto's irresistible, infinite capacity to suggest and signify. In the case of James Barry, it unravels completely the normative masculinity and heterosexuality of the chivalric ethos on which its origins depend.

Bodies, Clothes, and Garters

My discussion of the queer Garter deliberately interrupted my straight historical narrative of the ways the Order's queens wear their Garters. These extreme
examples—a speculative queer film that shows us the historical gesture the
Garter records prescribe but do not show; a genuinely historical hypothesis
of a cross-dressing Garter; and an intersexual appropriation of the motto—
suggest some alternative possibilities for wearing and talking about the Garter.
Conventional histories of costume, dress, and fashion tend to be written along
linear and chronological models, and the history of the Garter regalia is no
exception here. In this section, however, I concentrate less on the changing
form of the Garter and its robes, and more on the expression of ritual criticism *about* those robes and the multiple temporalities of ritual costume as it is
layered over fashionable or conventional wear. By considering the way people
talk and write about the sartorial history of the Garter, we may learn more
about the way it recalls, reforms, and modernizes its medieval inheritance. The
material history remains fundamental to my inquiries, however, as powerful
testament to the different ways male and female bodies are clothed, represented, and transformed by the touch of medievalism in the Garter.

In conventional histories the discussion of women and the Garter tends
to take place as a kind of appendage or decorative accessory to the main narrative. The lists of female members always follow the lists of men, and their
regalia is similarly studied as a special case. This is as we would expect in a
preeminently masculine order. Nevertheless, we may write this history somewhat differently by approaching the topic from a point of difference, rather
than continuity or similarity. This section investigates the effects of the female
body on the Garter traditions. Only then will we turn to the male body and
the way it wears the Garter.

In the late fourteenth and fifteenth centuries, Les Dames de la Fraternité
de St. Georges or the Ladies of the Garter were granted robes for feast days and
probably attended Garter feasts and tournaments. When the Garter knights
entered the lists at Smithfield in 1390 they were led by ladies with golden
chains, presumably the women of the Garter. From the evidence of two fifteenth-century effigies in Oxfordshire, we also know that Garter women wore
their Garters around their left arm. These are the tombs of Alice, Duchess of
Suffolk (and granddaughter of Geoffrey Chaucer), at Ewelme; and Margaret
Harcourt, given Garter robes in 1448, who is buried next to her husband at

Stanton Harcourt. Alice wears the Garter about her forearm; Margaret around her upper arm. Ashmole tells us a third tomb, that of the Countess of Tankerville, was similarly adorned, but no one knows where her tomb is, whether it survives, or even which of the earl's two wives this was (see Chapter 5). In Lincoln Cathedral, the double tomb of Katherine Swynford, who died in 1403, and her daughter Joan Beaufort, who died in 1440, featured heraldic panels in brass on the sides, with the two Garter women's coats of arms surrounded by the Garter and motto.

Of these early examples, the tomb of Alice is the most semiotically rich. It is formed of three levels or tiers. On the top of the tomb, an alabaster effigy presents a serene image, dressed in a wimple and mantle: she is described as "clothed in the habit of a vowess," though her robe is a fashionably close-fitting cote hardie.[30] The effigy is adorned with a ducal coronet and a ring; and draped around her left forearm is the Garter. The second tier is the chest enclosing her body. The third tier, on the bottom, is an open space framed by arches through which one can see another carving: an emaciated, stretched body, its head tilted back, the tip of the nose missing and the mouth open. The triple tomb functions as a momento mori: the decaying body beneath reminds us of the transitory nature of the body in its secular glory. The duchess's coronet and Garter, then, are significant distinguishing features, the only signs on her clothing of her worldly magnificence (figure 16).

At Stanton Harcourt, Margaret lies next to her husband. His effigy is wearing full armor with the Garter below his knee; hers shows the Garter above her left elbow (figure 17). Both were painted, though the colors have now faded.[31]

Apart from these effigies there are no records of any queen or woman wearing the Garter before Queen Anne in 1702. Elizabeth I is sometimes shown wearing the collar, the great chain of office instituted by Henry VII, seemingly in imitation of the Order of the Golden Fleece, which included a collar as part of its regalia from its first foundation in 1430.[32] The collar has not changed much since its introduction: it is fashioned of alternating golden knots and medallions of red roses encircled with the Garter. The "Great George," the gold and enameled ceramic figure of St. George killing the dragon, is suspended from the chain. There are also several portraits that show the Queen wearing "the lesser George," a medallion of St. George strung on a ribbon. Here, the Queen holds the medallion up for the viewer to see (figure 18).

There is no record of the Queen wearing the Garter on her arm, according to the fifteenth-century precedents, or of her showing any interest in this

Figure 16. Alice, Duchess of Suffolk, Ewelme. Photograph by the author.

Figure 17. Lady Margaret Harcourt. Photograph by the author.

Figure 18. Elizabeth I by unknown artist. © Government Art Collection, U.K.

aspect of the Garter history. It is possible she did not want to imitate this practice if it threatened to appear too secondary, too unkingly, or if it reminded people of the custom of appointing ladies to the Order.

Various accommodations were possible, however. William Teshe's "Verses on the Order of the Garter" describe Elizabeth holding court with her Garter knights, surrounded by other lords and ladies. All the Garter knights are wearing a "bend" about their arm, each with his own personal motto. Each in turn comes to stand before the Queen, declaiming his motto and presenting his embroidered bend into the hands of the Queen. This ceremony appears to resolve the problem of the Queen's wearing the Garter, since the Garter men wear their personal mottoes in the place where medieval women wore their garters. Teshe puts an English version of the motto into the Queen's mouth: "'Shame to the mynde that meanes' (quod shee) 'amisse'."[33]

But the problem of the Queen's Garter was not lost on her contemporaries and near-contemporaries. Sir William Segar, Garter King of Arms (1607–33), wrote an account of his embassy to Frederick Henry, Prince of Orange, to present him with the Order in 1627. During the festivities he dines with the prince, who is curious about the Queen's manner of wearing the Garter: "During dinner his E asked me sundry questions, Namely whether Q. Elizabeth did weare the Garter of the order about her legg, as the knights did. I awnswered I thought not for it was not proper for her sex so apparently to shew her legg." The prince also asks about the origins of the Order and Edward's reasons for choosing a Garter, but Segar finds these questions barely worth his notice: "So with divers other tryviall questions the dinner was spent and ended and I with due thankes and humble salutations tooke my leave."[34] The prince's questions, only one generation after the death of the Queen, show that the female Garter was a still a lively issue for outsiders, while Segar was representing the heralds as unconcerned with such "tryviall" curiosity.

In 1702 Queen Anne is said to have consulted with several members of the Order prior to her coronation as to how she should wear her Garter. They advised her that the Garter should be worn upon the left arm, and this is how all women since that time have worn it, although no surviving portraits show the Queen wearing the Garter thus.[35]

Queen Victoria is said to have been similarly perplexed as to how to honor the Garter's customary position around her leg. Prior to her coronation a "special embassy" was sent to Ewelme. "To the relief of all," writes Herbert Norris, "it was discovered that the duchess, a Lady of the Garter, was wearing the insignia buckled round her left forearm. For some reason or other it was decided that Queen Victoria should wear her Garter high on the upper arm."[36] But when I visited the church at Stanton Harcourt in 2002, I was told that the Queen had taken *that* church, where the effigy of Margaret Harcourt wears the Garter around the upper arm, as her model. Norris offers another account of the problem, according to which Queen Victoria asked the Duke of Norfolk "in simple naïveté," "My Lord Duke, where am I to wear the Garter?" Apparently a print of Queen Anne was found, showing the Garter worn on the left arm, but Norris could not identify that print. Norris's tone of coy relief ("To the relief of all") captures the perennial salacious speculations about making the Queen's leg visible, though Norris's anxiety expresses the dynamics of Victorianism as well as medievalism. If popular mythology thinks the Victorians put drapes around the legs of their pianos, the prospect of Victorian hysteria about a garter around a queen's leg promises an even more thrilling affirmation of Foucault's "repressive hypothesis."[37]

There is an anonymous lithograph in the British Museum, dated 1837, that shows the Queen sitting on a couch with the Duke of Norfolk bowing before her, holding out a Garter. The Queen coyly holds one hand to her chin and looks sideways at the duke, saying, "How am I to wear it, my Lord Duke?" The caption is "Honi Soit Qui Mal Y Pense." Whether Norris's account derives from this cartoon or whether they have a common source is not clear, but the caption amusingly deflects the problem from the Queen onto the salacious readers and viewers of the cartoon. The image also addresses the gendered anxiety about a female Sovereign by reversing the presentation of the Garter: the Queen receives it *from* the Duke, rather than bestowing it upon her own Companions.[38]

I tried to find out more about the story about Victoria and wrote to the Royal Archives at Windsor, wondering if any of their records might be able to shed any light on this development. They replied politely in the negative and referred me to the College of Arms, speculating that if any commission had been sent to Oxfordshire it would have come from the heralds: to the best of their knowledge there were no documents that would warrant my coming to Windsor to search their archives in person. But when I put this to the college's archivist, he wondered if they had been "fobbing you off." Mr. Yorke kindly carried out a search of the college's records from 1836 but was not able to find any confirmation of the story. When we spoke on the phone before my visit he wondered politely if I had been confusing the story about Victoria with the account of Anne's problem about the Garter, since this is the story recorded in Begent and Chesshyre. I mentioned the footnote Norris adds, saying he had heard the story about Ewelme from "the late Earl of Oxford and Asquith in 1926." Mr. Yorke commented, "Ah, but how old was the Earl of Oxford at that time?" The earl was born in 1852, so would have been around seventy-four, but he had been made a knight of the Garter in the previous year, 1925. Perhaps he had recently been initiated into one of the Order's oral traditions.

In these fragments of Garter history—Queen Anne's and Queen Victoria's confusion about how to wear the Garter—we may discern a subtext of critique, implying these queens' inability fully to inherit the Garter tradition. This vignette into the history of a rumor about women wearing the Garter is typical of the way knowledge of its inner mysteries is contested; and also of the very real limits in the surviving material. Many of the Garter archives are not readily accessible or searchable; and this was not the only time during the course of my research on this project that in spite of the great courtesy shown me, I felt that definitive answers to some of my questions would remain elusive.

These examples show the Order reinventing itself, but taking example from the medieval precedents rather than from Elizabeth I. Victoria was painted several times for formal portraits wearing the Garter, adopting Margaret Harcourt's rather more practical position for the Garter, around the upper arm. Her Garter itself was made of dark blue velvet, the motto being spelled out in diamonds (figure 19). Begent and Chesshyre comment that it was probably a remodeled Garter that had previously belonged to George IV.[39]

Victoria was certainly interested in medieval revivalism, famously appearing with Prince Albert dressed as Queen Philippa and Edward III, though sans garter, at their costume ball in May 1842. The reinauguration of the medieval custom of the Garter on women's arms sat comfortably with the prevailing fashion for medievalism.

Other artists came up with different solutions. Richard Lane's steel engraving, produced early in Victoria's reign, in 1838, similarly struggles with the Queen's gendered body and the Garter regalia but resolves the problem by reorienting it as evening dress. The Queen is shown seated, with the Garter mantle low around her shoulders in the manner of a stole, so that the embroidered scutcheon that is designed to sit over the left shoulder is draped over her upper arm. In John Plunkett's description: "An expressionless face combines with an exaggerated neck, heaving bosom, and impossibly hourglass waist."[40] It is a remarkably sexualized portrait that somehow renders the Garter mantle as a seductive, off-the-shoulder gown (figure 20).

On less formal occasions, Queen Victoria, like Queen Elizabeth II and Queen Elizabeth the Queen Mother, also took full advantage of the custom of wearing the Garter in the form of the star, a brooch pinned on a ribbon. The current queen wore the Garter star at her coronation but not the Garter itself. Since the statute opening up the possibility for women becoming full Companions of the Order, the Queen and other Garter ladies seem to wear their Garters in this way more often. The Queen and Princess Alexandra, for example, were seen wearing their Garters above the elbow at a reception in the documentary *The Queen at Eighty.*

The Queen has also worn her Garter above her elbow, over the Victorian

Figure 19. *Queen Victoria*, Alexander Melville. © Schloßmuseum Schloß
Friedenstein.

long black dress (and black lace mantilla) worn by female royalty for her several audiences with the pope at Rome (figure 21).

    In the light of the practical difficulties about wearing the Garter that are
repeatedly put in their way, it is ironic that when postmedieval women *do*
wear the Garter, they embody the medieval women's convention in a manner
that is much more stable than the masculine tradition. Conventional wisdom
and sartorial satire tells us that women's fashions are highly changeable, but
when women wear the Garter (as opposed to the star or chain) they have always worn it in the same way: adding a garter to one's arm is much easier to

Fig. 20. *Queen Victoria,* Richard Lane, 1838. © National Portrait Gallery,
London.

accommodate to changing fashions in dress than adding it to one's leg. Even
though styles of women's clothes vary, the length or shape of a sleeve does not
affect the temporal coding of the Garter—its accommodation to contemporary dress—as much as does the difference between armor, tight-fitting hose,
or loose-fitting trousers.

We turn now to the changing disposition of the Garter on the male leg,
a tradition that is both more continuous, and more variable. Scholars and

Figure 21. Queen Elizabeth II at the Vatican. © Press Association.

historians of costume have sometimes sought to explain (or explain away) Edward's adoption of the Garter with reference to mid-fourteenth-century fashion. The evidence is mixed and potentially confusing, however, when we look at medieval pictures of the royal court. The King is often pictured wearing a long robe, while his courtiers appear in the short, tight-fitting clothes that became fashionable again in the mid-1330s. Sometimes a garter appears below the left (and sometimes, the right) knee of such courtiers, though it is not always clear that this is the Order's insignia. For example, in the presentation manuscript of Philippe de Mézière's *Epistre au roi Richart*, Richard II is dressed in a long robe, while his courtiers wear a range of clothing. The man on the right has what looks like a garter on his left leg, colored in blue, but of an unusual form, with a long decorative pendant. He is wearing particolored hose, and his right leg, covered in white, seems to have a garter with a pendant of some kind too (figure 22).[41]

This garter resembles the Garters worn by some of the knights kneeling to the right of the altar featuring St. George slaying the dragon in the copy of the statutes of the Order given to Margaret of Anjou on her marriage to Henry VI in 1445 (see figure 10). The King and the Garter knights all wear long blue mantles with large Garters embroidered on them, but the two knights kneeling at the front on the right are wearing shorter, knee-length belted garments, with Garters buckled or tied below their left knee, with a long pendant hanging down.

The earliest Wardrobe accounts for the Garter mention robes for men and for women as often as they mention Garters. Nicolas argues that the twelve Garters made for the King "de blu broudat de auro et sico qult hnte dictamen–Hony soyt q mal y pense" and the twenty-four Garters made for the prince, mentioned in the accounts for November 18, 1348, which mentions "de Societate Garter," were worn by two teams of knights, one under the King, and one under his son, at a joust or tournament, "each having a Garter round his left knee in the Lists, and wearing Robes covered with Garters during the festivities on the occasion."[42] These robes are reminiscent of those worn by the King in *Wynnere and Wastoure*.

There are a number of different registers, then, for wearing the Garter, depending on whether the occasion is festive, courtly, or military, and whether the body in question is old or young (and thus more likely to be wearing short garments); royal or in service to royalty; alive or made of stone or glass. As with the Garter women, the evidence of effigies and stained glass helps confirm both the identity of early Garter knights and also the varying fashions

Figure 22. Richard II. © All Rights Reserved. The British Library Board. BL MS Royal 20B.vi, fol. 2.

in which their Garter affiliations are recorded in death. We should distinguish, too, between illustrations of formal Garter occasions and scenes like the Mézière manuscript where the appearance of the Garter (if indeed it *is* the Garter) is simply incidental.

When the Garter knight or the King is shown in his long and opulent robes, however, the Garter can be worn by someone else: St. George. In the miniature of John of Lancaster, Duke of Bedford, in the Bedford Hours, the duke is wearing a beautiful long-sleeved houpelande, kneeling before the saint, who is wearing an ermine-lined Garter robe with insignia on the left shoulder and the characteristic long ties, over a suit of armor, with a surcote with the red cross on it; and with a blue Garter just below his knee (figure 23).[43] George also wears the Garter in a number of illustrations of his own story.

Even in contexts that celebrate the Garter directly, like William Bruges's fifteenth-century book of Garter knights, the Garter is not always worn. Bruges's knights wear heraldic tunics over their armor and the long robes of the Order but not the garter itself.

Sixteenth- and seventeenth-century fashion was kinder to the Garter, since civilian costume for men once more favored the close-fitting hose, a style of dress that helped naturalize the wearing of the Garter around the leg. Changes in methods of textile manufacture had also seen the introduction of the Spanish fashion for silk knitted stockings in the early sixteenth century. According to John Stow, Henry VIII wore cloth hose (made from woven material cut on the cross with a seam down the back of the leg), except when "by great chance there came a pair of Spanish silk stockings from Spain." These knitted stockings, made from a much finer textile than wool, would have shown the Garter to great effect, while the fact that they were a luxury item would further have encoded Henry's gartered leg as an elite leg.[44]

Holbein's sketch[45] for Henry VIII's famous portrait in Whitehall with legs astride and hands on hips (figure 24) certainly features his Garter, but also shows a similar band (without motto) on the other leg, and this is not uncommon in Garter portraits, until as late as the early twentieth century. Sometimes the ungartered leg band is adorned with a large rosette.

In a portrait of George Villiers, Duke of Buckingham, the Garter and its robes can play a powerful role in the construction of a very different model of male beauty (figure 25). Here the resonance is emphatically courtly and elegant, rather than powerful and stately. Villiers's Garter appears much more elaborate than Henry's band; it is held with quite a large buckle and long pendant.

Figure 23. John of Lancaster, Duke of Bedford, with St. George. © All Rights Reserved. The British Library Board. BL MS Add. 18850, fol. 256v.

Figure 24. Hans Holbein, sketch for portrait of Henry VIII. © National Portrait Gallery, London.

Figure 25. George Villiers, Duke of Buckingham, attributed to William Larkin. © National Portrait Gallery, London.

But the Garter is not always worn so formally. The great chain and robes can signify a knight's allegiance to the Order, and the towering ostrich plumes can appear in the portrait, as it does in Buckingham's case, without actually being worn on the head. Sometimes the Order appears only in a corner of the portrait, encircling the subject's coat of arms, and not worn on his clothes at all.

If the Garter is the ultimate accessory, it is not the only one. During Charles I's reign, the robes and appurtenances of the Order became more and more elaborate. It was Charles who added the diamond starburst or "Glory," the beams of silver radiating out from the Garter in the form of a cross, in the form regularly worn by the current Queen as a badge. In her study of Edmund Harrison, "the King's embroiderer," Patricia Wardle provides details from Ashmole and the Wardrobe accounts about Harrison's work, embroidering scutcheons for the shoulders of Garter robes, and Garters decorated with pearls and "twists" of Venetian gold thread, reminding us that it was not only medieval robes that featured this elaborate embroidery.[46] From April 1626, all the Knights also had to wear an embroidered escutcheon of the cross of St. George on their coats and cloaks at all times, whether wearing the full regalia or not.[47]

The Order's rituals involved the further dissemination of Garter jewels and adornments. When the Garter regalia of Gustavus Adolphus of Sweden were returned to Windsor, the various parts (his surcoat, the book of statutes, robe, Garter, two Georges and the collar) were brought along in a procession, on embroidered cushions of velvet.[48] Harrison also embroidered a purse for the new seal of the Order, using gold and silver, silk and pearls, at a cost of £13l.6s.10d.[49] Robes and gowns became regular objects of exchange, both as gifts from the sovereign to the knights, and from the knights to the heralds.[50]

The Garter could also be worn more practically as the lesser George, a medallion with an image of St. George and the dragon strung on a blue ribbon. For ease of riding, too, it was permissible to sling this under one arm. It was this version of the George—cut in onyx, set with forty-two diamonds, and enclosing a portrait of Henrietta Maria—that was the last thing Charles I removed at his execution, handing it to Bishop Juxon with the single word: "remember."[51]

Certainly Charles's son remembered. On his return from exile in 1660, no detail of costume or ceremony was too small for the restored honor of the monarchy and the Order of the Garter. One intriguing detail concerns us here. Until 1661, none of the early statutes prescribed the wearing of any particular clothes under the Order's surcoat. But Charles was of the view that "constancy and immutability" added greatly to the "luster and dignity of our most noble order" and commissioned an inquiry "to see if possible length of time, and change of customes might have introduced any thinge in them which might make them swerve from the ancient rules so farr as they were not unconsistent with the present usance. Wee have thought it not unworthy our care to descend unto the particulars off its clothing. And therupon having found that in what concerns the underhabits usd by the companions att the solemnizing of enstalments or the celebration of St Georges feast they followed too much the modern fashion, never constant and less comporting with the decency gravity and stateliness of the upper roabes of the order." Instead the Companions "shall be obliged to a certain and immutable form and fashion for their underhabits," viz., "the old trunke hose or round breeches," to be made of cloth of silver. This statute was passed on May 10, 1661.[52]

The fascination with getting the right underhabits resonates suggestively, though unconsciously, with the myth of the Order's founding and its own repressed fascination with the movement of garments and items of clothing between unofficial and official usage. If Edward had the capacity to transform a woman's garter into a heraldic insignia, so too did Charles exercise the capacity to render everyday fashion unacceptable for the Garter rituals, and to introduce an outmoded fashion into official costume. This example betrays the Order's contradictory desires in a most instructive way. Seeing the current Companions following modern fashion, and identifying the absence of a tradition, Charles seeks to find an "immutable . . . fashion," a delightful contradiction in terms. We may speculate that the use of everyday fashion is too much of a reminder of the modernity of the Restoration; that Charles sought to make the Order look as old as possible, hence the appeal to "the old trunk hose." This is rather a Tudor than a medieval fashion, with less medieval precedent than the revival of the women's convention of wearing the Garter around the arm. Its deliberately outmoded style is designed to signal the play of tradition across the bodies of the many new knights. In a restored monarchy, the Order of the Garter cannot appear entirely new, any more than it can appear entirely old.

Charles's wax effigy is preserved in Westminster Abbey. In Begent and Chesshyre's description, "The breeches are of cloth of silver and are decorated with lace, ornamental buttons and bunches of silk and silver ribbons. They hang low upon the hips and button from top to bottom on the back with a single button in front. The material is set in very full pleats which pouch and hang over the lower edge. There are no divisions for the legs and the impression is given of a very short skirt. . . . Under the breeches are white silk drawers to which the long white silk stockings are sewn, rather like modern ladies' tights" (figure 26).[53]

After this period Garter wear remained relatively stable, in harmony with the conventions of court dress in the eighteenth and nineteenth centuries. The white silk hose and silver pants were still worn on the most formal Garter occasions into the early twentieth century, though various accommodations to modern dress were increasingly made as the contrast between Garter (and

Figure 26. Portrait of King Charles II (1630–85), c. 1675 (oil on canvas), Sir Peter Lely (1618–80) (studio of). Private Collection / Photo © Philip Mould Ltd., London / The Bridgeman Art Library.

court) robes and everyday wear became more and more stark. It is easy to
mock the Garter on account of its unfashionability: its outdated clothes and
costumes were read as a direct sign that it was an institution that had passed
its prime. In 2008 it was rumored that Australia's former prime minister John
Howard was to be offered a place in the Order. Melbourne's local ABC morning presenter, Red Symons, laughingly speculated about the idea of Howard
(whose most distinctive fashion innovation was the patriotic green and gold
tracksuit in which he conducted his morning power walk) appearing in his
"pantaloons and tights," "a picture," said Symons, "no artist would paint."
Because we are so attuned to changing fashions in clothes as powerful indicators of social class, gender, and the cultural performance of subjectivity, ritual
costumes are an obvious and visible marker of what is "old" fashioned.

In the next chapter we will track the twentieth century's various attempts
to modernize the Garter costume, along with its other rituals, but this chapter
concludes with an account of the most extreme form of dressing up: the Garter knight as dandy.

"The Most Grandiose of All Costumes"

Like film, fiction has the capacity to heighten the forms of representation in
ways that can deepen our understanding of socially symbolic acts. My central
example in this section comes from the extremes of literary representation:
social satire and literary parody.

Max Beerbohm's novella *Zuleika Dobson* (1911) tells the story of the young
Duke of Dorset, an Oxford undergraduate who is also a knight of the Garter,
who falls in love with Zuleika, the niece of the warden of Judas College. After
a desultory career as an impoverished governess, moving from family to family as the young men in each household invariably fall wildly and unsuitably
in love with her, Zuleika steals one such young man's box of magic tricks and
establishes herself as a star of the music hall. She has never felt love for any of
her many conquests until the Duke of Dorset ignores her on her triumphant
entry into Oxford. Over the course of the next day it becomes clear that he
does in fact love her, but she is repelled and dismisses him, refusing his vast
estates and spectacular wealth.

In despair, the duke says he will drown himself for love of her, at which
news she is delighted, wanting only to ensure that he will call out her name as
he plunges into the river after the intercollege boat race. Hundreds of equally

besotted youths make the same pledge, and the duke attempts unsuccessfully to dissuade them. On the morning of the fateful day the duke tries on his Garter robes one last time and is so captivated by his magnificent appearance in the mirror that he decides to make his grand gesture of love thus adorned. Once the boat race is finished it starts to rain and, fearing becoming a soggy lump of bedraggled ostrich feathers, the duke plunges into the river. His Garter mantle floats a while on the surface before finally sinking along with its wearer. Hundreds of other young men similarly drown themselves; and we last see Zuleika, entranced by the possibility of repeating this mass conquest, asking her maid to commission a special train to Cambridge.

The Garter robes play an important role in the characterization of the duke as a dandy, while there is a further subtheme reminiscent of the exchange of clothes that is such a feature of the Garter myth. Zuleika wears one pink and one black pearl earring, but by a form of transcendental or sympathetic magic, two of the duke's white pearl buttons on his dress shirt spontaneously change color—one to pink, one to black—over the course of their first evening together. There are several exchanges of this nature, affirming the similarities between Zuleika and the duke both as highly and elaborately dressed beings (and perhaps also recalling Walpole's story about an earlier Duke of Dorset and his ballet-dancing mistress). At another point, too, the duke contemplates making Zuleika a gift of the "octoradiant star": "Why had he not asked her to take the star and keep it as a gift? Too late now! Why could he not throw himself at her feet?"[54]

We learn the duke becomes a knight of the Garter after making an impassioned impromptu speech in the House of Lords that results in a bill being deferred for six months. A nervous prime minister "procured for him, a month later, the Sovereign's offer of a Garter which had just fallen vacant. . . . But you must not imagine that he cared for [the insignia] as symbols of achievement and power. The dark blue riband, and the star scintillating to eight points, the heavy mantle of blue velvet, with its lining of taffeta and shoulder-knots of white satin, the crimson surcoat, the great embullioned tassels, and the chain of linked gold, and the plumes of ostrich and heron uprising from the black velvet hat—these things had for him little significance save as a fine setting, a finer setting than the most elaborate smoking-suit, for that perfection of respect which the gods had given him."[55]

The narrator explains, "It was only in those too rarely required robes that he had the sense of being fully dressed."[56] This is the paradox of the supplement we saw earlier. Once the Garter is added to a knight's body, that body

seems underdressed without it. But Beerbohm's parody goes further, suggesting that it is only on the body of the dandy that the Order's robes and insignia
appear in their full glory. The ultimate destiny of the duke is to wear his Garter
robes to his death; but by the same token, the Garter robes only attain their
full glory when worn by someone of the duke's perfection. "It was as a Knight
of the Garter that he had set the perfect seal on his dandyism. Yes, he reflected,
it was on the day when first he donned the most grandiose of all costumes, and
wore it grandlier than ever yet in history had it been worn, than ever would
it be worn hereafter, flaunting the robes with a grace unparalleled and inimi-
table, and lending, as it were, to the very insignia a glory beyond their own,
that he once and for all fulfilled himself, doer of that which he had been sent
into the world to do."[57] Beerbohm adds: "He cared for his wardrobe and his
toilet-table not as a means to making others admire him the more, but merely
as a means through which he could intensify, a ritual in which to express and
realize, his own idolatry."

On the fateful morning of his death, the duke reflects. He is not afraid of
dying, and compares himself to Shelley and Byron, whose middle age would
have been appalling in its mediocrity. And then he is seized by the idea of seeing himself in his Garter robes once more. I quote this passage of his enrobing
at length, because it explores the idea of the duke's dressing up as a kind of
technology of the self, a kind of reverse striptease that progressively encases his
body in the intricacies of court dress. His pleasure is both childish and vaguely
sexual. Beerbohm insists on the singularity of this Garter knight, in contrast
to our general sense that such a knight, much older, might have "doddered
hopeless in that labyrinth of hooks and buckles."

> His eyes dilated, somewhat as might those of a child about to "dress
> up" for a charade; and already, in his impatience, he had undone his
> necktie.
>   One after another, he unlocked and threw open the black tin
> boxes, snatching out greedily their great good splendours of crimson
> and white and royal blue and gold. You wonder he was not appalled
> by the task of essaying unaided a toilet so extensive and so intricate?
> You wondered even when you heard that he was wont at Oxford to
> make without help his toilet of every day. Well, the true dandy is
> always capable of such high independence. He is craftsman as well
> as artist. And, though any unaided Knight but he with whom we
> are here concerned would belike have doddered hopeless in that

labyrinth of hooks and buckles which underlies the visible glory of a Knight "arraied full and proper," Dorset threaded his way featly and without pause. He had mastered his first excitement. In his swiftness was no haste. His procedure had the ease and inevitability of a natural phenomenon, and was most like to the coming of a rainbow.

Crimson-doubleted, blue-ribanded, white-trunk-hosed, he stooped to understrap his left knee with that strap of velvet round which sparkles the proud gay motto of the Order. He affixed to his breast the octoradiant star, so much larger and more lustrous than any actual star in heaven. Round his neck he slung that long daedal chain wherefrom St. George, slaying the Dragon, dangles. He bowed his shoulders to assume that vast mantle of blue velvet, so voluminous, so enveloping, that, despite the Cross of St. George blazing on it, and the shoulder-knots like two great white tropical flowers planted on it, we seem to know from it in what manner of mantle Elijah prophesied. Across his breast he knotted this mantle's two cords of gleaming bullion, one tassel a due trifle higher than its fellow. All these things being done, he moved away from the mirror, and drew on a pair of white kid gloves. Both of these being buttoned, he plucked up certain folds of his mantle into the hollow of his left arm, and with his right hand gave to his left hand that ostrich-plumed and heron-plumed hat of black velvet in which a Knight of the Garter is entitled to take his walks abroad. Then, with head erect, and measured tread, he returned to the mirror.[58]

The duke stands before the mirror, disturbed by the thought that he must "presently put off from him all his splendour, and be his normal self," until the thought comes to him that he would wear his robes to his death. "The shadow passed from his brow. He would go forth as he was. He would be true to the motto he wore, and true to himself. A dandy he had lived. In the full pomp and radiance of his dandyism he would die . . . what he loved best he could carry with him to the very end; and in death they would not be divided."

In one sense, Beerbohm's parody represents a comprehensive corruption of the Garter honors, as the entire system of courtly, chivalric, and military honors is reduced merely to the appearance of its admittedly magnificent robes, themselves seen here, somewhat perversely, as the perfect expression of dandyism. On the other hand, like other invocations of the Garter in fiction and poetry, *Zuleika Dobson* captures some of the unofficial force and strength of the Order's capacity to seize the imagination. In the most forceful way imaginable, the novel dramatizes the idea of the Garter as that which invests the ordinary man with extraordinary charisma. Similarly, the duke's decision to walk to a watery death for unrequited love, wearing his robes, is presented here as perfectly characteristic of the Order and what it stands for. "He would be true to the motto he wore, and true to himself." The invocation of the Garter motto—*Honi soit qui mal y pense*—reminds us that the Order is founded on a history of men doing foolish things for love. Whether it is picking up a dropped garter or throwing oneself in the river, the Garter motto distinguishes those who wear it with this heightened capacity for greatness, for transcending the ordinary.

The moment of the duke's death is worth pausing over, too. He is surprised to find, "standing as he did on the peak of dandyism, on the brink of eternity," that his attention is distracted by the question of which college would win the boat race: Judas or Magdalen? But it starts to rain, and he is impelled to action.

> His very mantle was aspersed. In another minute he would stand sodden, inglorious, a mock. He didn't hesitate.
>
> "Zuleika!" he cried in a loud voice. Then he took a deep breath, and, burying his face in his mantle, plunged.
>
> Full on the river lay the mantle outspread. Then it, too, went under. A great roll of water marked the spot. The plumed hat floated.

But before he dies, the duke's face appears beside the Magdalen boat; his eyes meet those of the Magdalen cox, an apparition that disrupts his rhythm. As a consequence of this, one of the Magdalen rowers misses his stroke, and the duke's college, Judas, win the race. "A white smiling face, anon it was gone" (figure 27).

I have discussed *Zuleika Dobson* at such length because in the decadence of its writing, and the decadence of its Garter knight, it represents a kind of *n*th degree of Garter excess. Beerbohm's parody of romanticism, dandyism, and medievalism is truly gothic: the dying duke's face is a ghostly vision of excess that nevertheless propels his college to victory.

Ellen Moers describes *Zuleika Dobson* as "the very last of the dandy novels," and its hero as "fabulously wealthy, miraculously gifted, consummately dandified"—and "wholly insufferable. Like Disraeli, Beerbohm saw in the

Figure 27. Dust jacket of Max Beerbohm, *Zuleika Dobson*, 1961. Artist George Him. © Penguin.

dandy hero a natural subject for romance; unlike Disraeli, whose lasting respect for the English aristocracy approached adoration, Beerbohm used the gilding of fantasy primarily to evoke laughter. *Zuleika Dobson* was written both as a devoted return to the tradition of full-fledged dandy fiction, and as an outrageous farce with a noodle of a dandy for its hero."[59]

Beerbohm's own writings on the dandy emphasize the importance of contemporary costume, but he does also open up a space for the costume, and the rituals of the past. "Of course, the dandy, like any other artist, has moments when his own period, palling, inclines him to ancient modes."[60] In despair of his life Beerbohm's duke evokes this ancient mode in the form of his medieval robes.

Beerbohm's fantasy, however, may also draw on a set of subliminal associations between the Garter, dandyism, and queer beauty. Rather earlier, in 1753, in *The Analysis of Beauty*, William Hogarth used the Garter to exemplify his "line of beauty," the serpentine curve of a perfect set of stays: "Every whalebone of a good stay must be made to bend in this manner: for the whole stay, when put close together behind, is truly a shell of well-varied contents, and its surface of course a fine form; so that if a line, or the lace were to be drawn, or brought from the top of the lacing of the stay behind, round the body, and down to the bottom peak of the stomacher; it would form such a perfect, precise, serpentine-line, as has been shewn, round the cone, figure 26 in plate 1.— For this reason all ornaments obliquely contrasting the body in this manner, as the ribbons worn by the knights of the garter, are both genteel and graceful."[61]

Hogarth does not specify whether these perfect stays are for a male or female body, and the passage goes on to discuss a range of curves he numbers from one to seven. Of these number four is the most perfect, and would best fit "a well-form'd woman," while number two (less serpentine) would best fit "a well-shaped man." Hogarth concludes from the preeminent beauty of the fourth curve that a woman's body surpasses a man's in beauty, but his range of abstracted curves suggests that there is a continuum of body types and shapes, rather than a straightforward opposition between male and female. It is hard not to recall James Barry's intersexual, corseted, and dandified body, and the ease with which the corset modulates the shape of the body and facilitates the performance of gender. Hogarth's example of the Garter winding around the male body as "both genteel and graceful" also suggests the ease with which male beauty and the aristocratic knights of the Garter are aligned.

Beerbohm's parody is extreme, but his class-based drama is in close accord with a dominant strain in Garter reception that rehearses a series of anxieties and resentments about the English class system, without shying away from mocking its trappings. When the Garter appears in fiction, it is usually as an unambiguous signifier of class and social prestige. In Wilde's *Picture of Dorian Gray*, for example, the painter Basil Hallward describes his first meeting with Dorian, but complains first about Lady Brandon: "She brought me up to Royalties, and people with Stars and Garters, and elderly ladies with gigantic tiaras and parrot noses." Shortly after he also describes "a truculent and red-faced old gentleman covered all over with orders and ribbons."[62] This is a typical example of mockery of the Order of the Garter as pomp, circumstance, and excessive ornamentation (we will examine Virginia Woolf's diatribe on the subject in the next chapter).

The Garter is given greater prominence in B. C. Stephenson's libretto for Arthur Sullivan's one-act opera *The Zoo*. The Lord of Islington has disguised himself in humble dress in search of virtue. He finds it in Eliza Smith, who is charge of the refreshment stall at the zoo. Having eaten too many of her refreshments, "Thomas" collapses, and as his clothes are loosened, the Garter is discovered on his body. It is the phrase in which he summons his "minions" that gives him away:

> *Thomas. (rousing himself.)* Ho—guards! Minions!
> *Laetitia.* What did he say?
>   His exclamation shows that he's of noble birth.
>   CARBOY undoes BROWN's coat.
> *Carboy.* Great powers! the Garter!
>   He's a peer!
>   He's a peer,
>   A peer in disguise,
> *Laetitia & Carboy.* Oh yes he's a peer in disguise,
>   We can tell by the look of his eyes.
> *Chorus.* Oh yes he's a peer in disguise,
>   We can tell by the look of his eyes.
>   He's a peer, a beautiful peer.
>   He's a peer, a beautiful peer.
>   A beautiful, beautiful, beautiful, beautiful peer.[63]

The repetitive mockery of "a beautiful peer" and the crowd's retrospective and shallow recognition of the duke's aristocracy ("we can tell by the look of his eyes") should not distract us from the observation that this brief invocation of the Garter neatly channels the occluded class anxieties of the Garter myth. If a humble piece of woman's underclothing captures a king's imagination, it is a reminder that love and sexual desire are not bound by the class system (as the sixteenth-century invocations of the *Nobilitas sub amore iacet* motto attest). We may here recall Martorell's humble dancing girl, Madresilva, who attracts the King's attention when her Garter falls to the floor. There are a number of Garter women, then—Madresilva, Zuleika, La Bacelli, and Eliza—who signify the threatening capacity for sexual desire to undermine aristocratic dignity. Even a Garter knight like this duke, who is in search of virtue, can be led to folly. Eliza is reluctant to leave the zoo to become the Duchess of Islington, but the duke has arranged simply to buy all the animals:

> And every morn,
> At early dawn,
> The gentle armadillo,
> Or rattlesnake,
> When you awake,
> You'll find upon your pillow.[64]

The primary function of the clothing and the rituals of the Order of the Garter is to symbolize election to this most elite company, but their secondary functions are more complex and more intriguing, and shared by much greater numbers. After all, it is easy to emulate and appropriate the Garter, as when the Minnesota Renaissance Festival instituted its own "Most Noble Order of the Garter," "as an award for characters who demonstrate the quality of chivalry and who have been of service to the crown." The numbers are limited to twenty-six, and the male and female members wear a blue garter with the *Honi soit* motto around leg or arm, as well as the star.[65] The term "characters" refers to the assumed personae in these elaborate role-playing games.

Other appropriations, like James Barry's, are more quizzical and parodic. John Elliott, the midshipman on James Cook's second circumnavigation, writes about the tattoos observed on the warriors of Bora Bora, tattoos that seemed to signify a fellowship of some kind. "We therefore called them the Knights of Bora Bora, and all our mess conceived the idea of having some mark put on ourselves, as connecting us together, as well as to commemorate our having been at Otaheite." Calling themselves the "Knights of Otaheite," they had a star tattooed on the left breast. Several of these were among the mutineers on the *Bounty*. At least one of them added to his star by having the tattooed mark of "a Garter around his Left Leg with the Motto *Honi Soit Qui Mal Y Pense.*"[66]

As a parodic performance, this tattoo nevertheless inscribes in the most literal way possible the association of Garter regalia with the male body. Even if this man was the only one of the group to link his star with the iconography of the Garter, it still resonates with the idea of shared fellowship, a secret band of brothers. Ironically, too, a permanent mark like this ensures his Garter is "never to be forgotten or laid aside."

Dick Swiveller in Dickens's *Old Curiosity Shop* invokes the garter as an ironic figure for a convict's irons: "'So I'm Brass's clerk, am I?' said Dick. 'Brass's clerk, eh? And the clerk of Brass's sister—clerk to a female Dragon. Very good, *very* good! What shall I be next? Shall I be a convict in a felt hat and a grey suit, trotting about a dockyard with my number neatly embroidered on my uniform, and the order of the garter on my leg, restrained from chafing my ancle by a twisted belcher handkerchief? Shall I be that? Will that do, or is it too genteel? Whatever you please, have it your own way, of course.'"[67]

When we observe the Companions in their robes, when we speculate about their attitudes to wearing their robes, when we mock them for wearing them at the wrong time and place, and even when we research their cultural history, we give ourselves license to play with the idea of medievalist exhibitionism from the safety of our own modernity. One of the most dramatic features of contemporary medievalist practice and reenactment societies is dressing up in medieval or premodern "garb." Among members and nonmembers alike, the Garter's ritual costume provides the stuff of historicism, fantasy, imagination, and parody. Its long sartorial history models a six-hundred-and-sixty-year history of royal medievalism, but in ways that confound a simple distinction between the synchronicity of any historical moment and the diachronicity of medievalist revival. The uneven history of clothing and fashion across the centuries and across a range of social contexts provides an elegant visual template for the layering of multiple temporalities in the traditions of ritual practice.

PART III

Ritual Modernities

Chapter 7

Royalty and Medievalism, Medieval to Postmodern

Sex and Royalty

In April 2005, after Charles, Prince of Wales, had married Camilla Parker Bowles in a civil ceremony, a religious service was held to bless their union at St. George's Chapel, the home of the Order of the Garter in Windsor Castle. It was another gripping installment in the long-running saga of the prince's romantic and sexual life. It is now common knowledge that Charles and Camilla were lovers well before the prince's wedding with the virginal Diana in 1981, and throughout much of the tumultuous public misery of their marriage. As Diana, Princess of Wales, famously commented in her *Panorama* interview with Martin Bashir in 1995, "Well, there were three of us in that marriage, so it was a bit crowded." Charles's wedding with the divorced Camilla, eight years after the death of Diana, with the apparently grudging approval of the Queen, and amid constitutional concerns about the status of Camilla after her marriage, represented a triumph of royal and princely will over public scandal.

People were not particularly shocked or surprised to hear that the Prince of Wales had had a lover before and during his marriage. There were familiar historical precedents, after all; and once the extraordinary public mourning for Diana had subsided there was more than a hint of public sympathy with the lovers and the prince's final union with his mistress. However, we knew much more about Camilla Parker Bowles than previous generations had known about Alice Perrers, Nell Gwyn, or Wallis Simpson. Technological developments in surveillance, combined with the modern global media's insatiable appetite for celebrity gossip, had offered an international public a new kind of relationship with the intimate transactions of the lovers. Much of the scandal around Charles clustered around the release of the "Camillagate" tapes in 1992. These were transcripts of an illegally tapped late-night telephone conversation between the two, which was undoubtedly tender, deeply sexual, and endearingly familiar, right down to their reluctance to be the first to hang up at the end of the conversation. Infamously, in the shared fantasy that Charles could live in permanent intimate relationship with Camilla's body, and with her underwear (even, indeed, as a tampon), the conversation gave us what seemed to be an unprecedented glimpse into the personal life of the royals.[1] In this respect, the continuity was less with the past than with the present, as their private life was shown to be just as personal as our own lives, and their lovers' discourse just as silly and sentimental and self-mythologizing as anyone else's.

The details of this tape circulated around the world at lightning speed, and I even played my own small part in the story. At this time my sister was working for an Italian news agency in London. The transcripts had not been printed in England, but Australia's *New Idea* magazine had not shown such restraint, and at Jocelyne's request I dutifully faxed the appropriate pages to London so they could be translated into Italian for Rizzoli. I think that by the time I sent the fax (moving only at normal academic speed, not the speed required by international journalism), the documents were already available in London, but no matter. I certainly read the transcripts with hypocritical fascination, priggishly appalled to be part of their public dissemination yet unable to resist this glimpse into the private life of the famous couple.

As the wedding of 2005 demonstrated, however, these embarrassing revelations could be smoothed over and forcefully displaced by the perfections of English ritual and protocol. The messy, desiring bodies of Charles and Camilla were firmly contained in sleek layers of silk, embroidery, feathers, and discreet gray tailoring, while footage of the pair emerging from St. George's Chapel closed *The Queen's Castle* television documentary's cycle of the royal year in formal and elegant triumph. The home of the Order of the Garter and the force of ritual, framed by medieval and Tudor architectural authority, played a major part in helping the couple live down the scandal and rise above the violation of their privacy. Through these formalities, the embarrassing but touching absurdity of Charles and Camilla's conversation was brought into the fold of royal protocol, and their wedding was commemorated like other royal occasions in photographs, medallions, mugs, and tea towels.

This royal wedding resonates with Garter history on several levels. The

Garter myth demonstrates how royal fiat and determination can transform something small or embarrassing—someone's underwear—into the highest honor of state and courtly prestige. Ritual practice and proud display like the Garter processions or carefully orchestrated royal appearances can also heal the perpetual tension between private bodies and public symbols that drives the very concept of a royal family. Even if we resist the truth claims of the story about the lady's garter and dismiss it as a fanciful invention, we may still appreciate the institution's capacity to rise above this persistent myth of origins. Indeed, as we saw in Chapter 3, the compulsion to tell the story while dismissing its frivolity *as* a myth is a tacit recognition of the story's appeal and an indirect affirmation of the Order's capacity to transcend mockery. We might even suggest that the royal family occasionally *needs* a scandal of this kind to affirm its relevance to the world outside its charmed and privileged circle. Certainly in the recent history of the British monarchy—a series of unhappy marriages and financial scandals—there have been well-documented vicissitudes in its popularity as public opinion ricochets wildly between contempt, apathy, national hysteria, and national pride.

This royal wedding draws our attention to the dialectic of unlikely similarities and dissimilarities between the royal family and our own families. We too wear underwear, have ridiculous conversations with the ones we love, and have family disagreements. However, we are forcibly reminded that our own weddings can never compete with royal ones in luxury, formal ceremony, and public attention. Tom Nairn articulates the monarchy's brilliant manipulation of the concept of the royal family in the twentieth century, a concept that is structured around an intriguing and productive tension between tradition and modernity, between formality and informality, and between the unfamiliar and the familiar. A royal family ensures the Crown's succession while naturalizing "normal" relations between the various members of that family.

We might even go so far as to suggest that the monarchy's long history of overcoming shame, scandal, and political challenges, from sexual peccadilloes to depositions, beheadings, civil war, and abdications, can be read as a long, continuous gloss on the Garter motto. Certainly by holding the royal blessing of Charles and Camilla in St. George's Chapel, the home of the Order, the prince seemed to make a silent appeal to the *Honi soit* motto to continue its defiant magic.

But while we may take delight in such parallels and veiled allusions, it is an interpretative pleasure shared only by those with an interest in royal, heraldic, or ritual history, or the traces of medievalism in modern culture. There is also a kind of myopia that a project such as this can induce, whereby every-thing becomes an allusion to its subject matter, and where the subject matter is called to account for every related phenomenon. My appeal to what is oblique, secretive, and deliciously obscure about the Garter is not unproblematic in this context. The temptation to find Garter allusions everywhere, and to read them as direct or indirect invocations of medievalism in the various forms of the Order's ritual practice and cultural history is immense.

So it is now time to approach the topic of the Garter's modern history from a different angle. The question that guides this chapter, then, is one that strikes at the heart of the medievalism project: how medieval, now, is the Order of the Garter?

How Medieval Is It?

This is not a question that troubles the medieval or heraldic historian, for whom the facts provide a clear answer. The Garter, founded in 1348, is ir-reducibly a medieval institution. Whatever its current forms, or its historical variations in styling and costumes, or its changing political meaning in post-medieval times, the Order's medieval origins are the primary starting point for the student of historical traditions. Subsequent centuries of ritual and politi-cal practice might make more or less direct acknowledgment of the Garter's medieval foundation, but for scholars of those later periods, that foundation becomes simply an uncontested background fact. It is of far less interest than the Order's role in the changing relationships between monarch, Parliament, and aristocracy, for example, or the monarchy's deployment of ceremonial at any given time.

It is rather more difficult to define the medievalness of the Garter's rituals as they extend into the postmedieval era. At times the Order makes direct ap-peal to its medieval origins; at other times its honors are fully absorbed within the synchronic system of other chivalric orders: this was particularly the case around the founding of the Order of the Bath in 1725. Similarly, the medieval origins of the Order can be a source of historical pride but also of ideological confusion—as we saw in Edward VI's tortured explanations of its Romish customs. Those medieval origins are regularly flattened out in the vagaries of popular history, where the specificity of the medieval is subsumed into the im-precise category of "tradition." The Garter's own propensity for describing it-self as "ancient" does little to discourage such disregard for historical precision.

As this final chapter turns to consider the Order in the twentieth and twenty-first centuries more closely, it is worth remembering that a phenomenon does not have to *look* medieval, does not need to be framed by a medieval mise-en-scène, still to serve as a trace or reminder of the medieval, to do the work of medievalism, or to carry forward ideas about the medieval past into the future. The current form of the Garter procession at Windsor has its origins in medieval custom, and the full-length robes of the Companions similarly echo the medieval mantle, but to the casual observer, the procession may not signify the medieval so much as it appeals to the category of royal spectacle, or heritage tourism or tradition. Compared to the familiar medieval iconography of William Wallace (long hair, blue face paint, rough-spun kilt) or Robin Hood (bow and arrow, feathered cap, forest-dyed clothes), the Queen, her family, the foreign princes, former politicians, the military leaders, and the civil servants in the procession do not *look* medieval. They are recognizable principally as figures of contemporary politics, diplomacy, and celebrity culture. Yet without its medieval origins, and without its traces of medieval forms and rituals, the procession could not appeal to tradition the way it does.

As we have seen, much of the official discourse of the Order stresses its modernity, its capacity to adapt and change in response to contemporary needs. Such a discourse necessarily pushes the medieval origins of the Order into the background in a process we may describe as "demedievalization." Other forms of this process involve the insistent modernization of the Garter's more obviously medieval visual coding: the blue Garter that is worn almost anywhere but below the knee. Similarly, Garter conventions, practices, and discourses characteristically blur the distinction between "tradition" and "the medieval." This conflation is certainly visible in many of the honorific accounts of the Order, where commentators and apologists often run the two together in a seamless appeal to the virtues of long-standing custom.

The genre of royal satire and ridicule is even more cavalier about historical accuracy or the contexts of medieval history. Such satire and criticism dates back at least as far as medieval chroniclers' complaints about the conspicuous consumption and immorality of tournaments. It ranges through Oliver Cromwell's dismissal of Parliament's royal mace ("Remove that fool's bauble!"), to critiques of the class system and the persistence of medieval ceremonial forms in modern political practice, but it begins to take a distinct form in the twentieth century, when the adjective "medieval" starts to assume a decidedly negative valency.

Nor do we need to see the words "medieval" and "Garter" to observe how easily the trappings of ritual practice are envisaged as medieval: the plumage, glittering objects, and ceremonies of the Garter are regularly glimpsed in such contexts. In 1938, for example, in *Three Guineas*, Virginia Woolf characterized the "clothes worn by the educated man in his public capacity":

Now you dress in violet; a jewelled crucifix swings on your breast; now your shoulders are covered with lace; now furred with ermine; now slung with many linked chains set with precious stones. Now you wear wigs on your heads; rows of graduated curls descend to your necks. Now your hats are boat-shaped, or cocked; now they mount in cones of black fur; now they are made of brass and scuttle shaped; now plumes of red, now of blue hair surmount them. Sometimes gowns cover your legs; sometimes gaiters. Tabards embroidered with lions and unicorns swing from your shoulders; metal objects cut in star shapes or in circles glitter and twinkle upon your breasts. Ribbons of all colours—blue, purple, crimson—cross from shoulder to shoulder. After the comparative simplicity of your dress at home, the splendour of your public attire is dazzling.[2]

In this collective blazon of ceremonial adornments Woolf refuses to identify or name any of the institutions to which these regalia belong. She abstracts the adornments from their cosmological and signifying frame, but has refused their easy entry into the modern, except as pastiche and fragment. It is a powerful act of defamiliarization, one that deliberately resists the heraldic point and purpose of these symbols: namely, to signify hierarchical distinctions among the wearers and recipients of honors. Woolf argues that while the elaborate and fashionable dress of women is an easy satirical target, men in public office regularly indulge in similar, or greater, excesses. *Three Guineas* is illustrated at this point with photographs of judges in wigs, academics in procession, and highly decorated members of the military and the church. There are no pictures of Garter costume, but they would not be out of place here. Woolf goes on to mock the ceremonies and ritual practices associated with the institutions of public office: "Here you kneel; here you bow; here you advance in procession behind a man carrying a silver poker; here you mount a carved chair; here you appear to do homage to a piece of painted wood; here you abase yourselves before tables covered with richly worked tapestry. And whatever these ceremonies may mean you perform them always together, always in step, always in the uniform proper to the man and the occasion."[3] There is nothing that is specifically named as medieval in any of Woolf's examples, though the associations of gaiters, ermine, tabards, unicorns, and tapestry are clearly medieval. The "rows of graduated curls," on the other hand, suggest the judicial wigs that represent a survival of seventeenth-century court dress. Again, an important component of Woolf's satire is to blur the historical distinctions that specific groups hold so dear. Amid the pleasures of mocking the pretensions of public office, the archaic rituals and excesses of its costumes, and its performances of embodied public display, there is little interest in isolating the fourteenth-, eighteenth-, or nineteenth-century origins of a particular costume or gesture. Woolf's scorn is unusual in being oriented along gendered lines, though her critique of patriarchy's propensity to decorate itself certainly echoes Beerbohm's satire of the Garter dandy in *Zuleika Dobson*.

Such critique is even easier when these public performances are themselves flawed by incompetence, or in periods when the monarchy is undergoing one of its phases of widespread unpopularity. In his influential essay on the "invented traditions" of English royal ritual, David Cannadine shows how the first three-quarters of the nineteenth century witnessed the deep unpopularity of the royal family and the monarchy, while most of its royal pageants "oscillated between farce and fiasco."[4] Cannadine offers numerous examples of the shambolic performances of parliamentary and royal ritual, even as the rites and trappings of such rituals were being generously distributed throughout the British Empire. In *Ornamentalism,* he comments: "The most successful British proconsuls and imperial soldiers were knights and peers several times over, veritable walking Christmas trees of stars and collars, medals and sashes, ermine robes and coronets, who personified the honorific imperial hierarchy at its most elaborate."[5] There is something irresistible about the accumulation of these decorations, both for the ambitious recipients of these honors and for the rhetorical impulse of the satirist.

However, the critique or satire of ritual does not depend on the ritual's incompetent execution. Bumbling incompetence is easy to mock, but so is military precision. Over the final decades of the nineteenth century and the opening of the twentieth, as Cannadine demonstrates, the performance of English ritual was reformed and renovated, and its privatized, inward-looking rituals were replaced by polished public displays. The proliferation of honors and the very professionalism of royal rituals could also be seen as a "circus," the empty performance of customary ritual that has been emptied of any meaningful symbolic import. As Woolf says, "*whatever these ceremonies may mean* you perform them always together, always in step, always in the uniform proper to the man and the occasion."

Such criticism of the symbolic emptiness and meaningless of the monarchy gathered strength over the course of the twentieth century, as its rituals became more and more polished. John Osborne, the most famous of the "angry young men," wrote in 1957 an impassioned defense of working-class socialism and an impatient critique of the English adulation of the royal family, of its "protocol of ancient fatuity," and the "political and literal horseplay of a meaningless symbol."[6] "I can't go on laughing at the idiocies of the people who rule our lives," he writes. "My objection to the royal symbol is that it is dead; it is the gold filling in a mouthful of decay. . . . When the mobs rush forward in the Mall they are taking part in the last circus of a civilization that has lost faith in itself, and sold itself for a splendid triviality, for the 'beauty of the ceremonial' and the 'essential spirituality of the rite.' We may not create any beauty or exercise much spirituality, but by God! we've got the finest ceremonial and rites in the world! Even the Americans haven't got that."[7]

A more recent and influential exponent of this critique, Tom Nairn, writes in *The Enchanted Glass* of "the sociology of grovelling" that characterizes the British cult of celebrity, and the seductive enchantments of the royal family, its pageants and processions: "These emblems are guaranteed harmless and merely 'colourful': not badges of inward shame and hopelessness, but the insouciant symbols of a society so confident of its modernity that it can afford to play charades with the imagery of the past."[8] Nairn draws attention to the play of the archaic and the modern in contemporary royal ritual, the historical backdrop to this insouciant modernity, and its invocation of tradition and heritage culture as something that can be quite deliberately manipulated, or "played" with. Ritual costumes, here, are little more than childish dress-ups.

Even in this limited sample, it is possible to identify something of a shift in the way these symbols are talked about over the twentieth century. Where Woolf abstracts the signs and symbols of office from their context, and attempts to empty them of signifying power, Osborne and Nairn both draw attention to the way modernity "plays" with these symbolic forms, celebrating their emptiness and displacing their symbolic meanings with the confident charades of ceremonial beauty. In such a progression, we see the same absorption of the historical origins of these ritual forms into the much looser concept of "tradition." In Nairn's reading, whereby modern society "can afford to play charades with the imagery of the past," the meaning and origins of these symbols are almost completely attenuated, displaced by public display of "tradition" for its own sake. We might say, then, that royal *processions* risk becoming examples of Jean Baudrillard's *"precessions* of simulacra," in which signs no longer refer to a material or conceptual "real" but refer only to themselves in an endless displacement of symbolic meaning.[9] The medieval may give initial form to a series of symbolic practices, but postmodern skepticism about the symbol has the effect of flattening the medieval as a historical category into the paradoxically timeless category of a national "tradition." "It's a shame this has to be for her death, but it's what she deserves. We put the P in pageantry," said Tim Aston, an electrician working on a building site overlooking the parade held on the occasion of the death of Elizabeth, the Queen Mother, in 2002.[10]

Several years ago, there was an extraordinary and well-documented encounter between two women: a clash between modern skepticism about the symbolic rituals of the Garter and the contemporary embodiment of those rituals. It should not surprise us to realize it was an argument about clothes.

In 2007 Annie Leibovitz was filmed as part of the documentary *Monarchy: The Royal Family at Work* (2007) as she was preparing to photograph the Queen. Leibovitz was willing to embrace the traditional aspects of the task, though her example showed she was thinking back only several generations, and only within the modern genre of portrait photography. "I like tradition. Cecil Beaton's pictures—they're very important to me," she said at a reception at Buckingham Palace. When it came to the photo shoot, however, she found the full complement of Garter robes and tiara excessive. Leibovitz starts to suggest the Queen might remove the tiara, but the Queen interrupts her request with a bemused and not altogether friendly expression, saying, "Less . . . dressy? What do you think this is?" and pointing to what she is wearing. The Queen's response is spoken from a position firmly inside the ritual, a position in which the perfection and the completion of the robes is self-evident. Leibovitz, the American outsider, in her desire to break this perfection, is given no concessions.

Yet in the same documentary we also see the Queen's own impatience with dressing up in the elaborate robes. The voice-over commentary describes Leibovitz and her assistants waiting for the Queen: "But the Queen's elaborate costume has taken longer than expected to put on. . . . She will be wearing the full regalia of the ancient Order of the Garter, complete with tiara. Few royal outfits could be more complicated, or cumbersome." The Queen then appears walking down the corridor wearing the Garter robes, saying impatiently, "I'm not changing anything. I've done enough, dressing like this, thank you very much."[11]

These scenes were spliced out of sequence in the promotional trailer for the documentary in a way that suggested the Queen had walked out on Leibovitz. The BBC was later to apologize for the implication, and at least one employee lost his job over the incident.[12] Clearly, the wearing of the robes, and the touchiness of the Queen on the subject, is a very sensitive issue.

Leibovitz was later to express admiration for the Queen's impatience: "She entered the room at a surprisingly fast pace . . . and muttered: 'Why am I wearing these heavy robes in the middle of the day?' She doesn't really want to get dressed up any more. She just couldn't be bothered and I admired her for that."[13] The opposition in style between the Queen—in her heavy, formal Garter robes, with the crown that cannot be removed without disrupting her elaborate white coiffure—and Leibovitz in her loose-fitting pants and shirt, with long flowing hair, could not be greater. Leibovitz's comments seem to embrace the modernity of the Queen: "She just couldn't be bothered and I admired her for that." If Leibovitz was unsuccessful in her bid to produce a less formal Garter portrait, she nevertheless still desired to project her own original "reading" of the Queen from the perspective of her own modernity, as someone who was tired of the rituals, the clothes, and the traditional encumbrances of office.

The modern photographer speaks from the cynical position of the observer outside, or, more tellingly, beyond, the magic of traditional ritual, though the loyal English subject might simply accuse Leibovitz of ignorance or disrespect. Either way, her voice is in direct opposition to the official voice that comments on royal rituals from within, or the television commentaries on royal processions by Richard Dimbleby, for example, who was so crucial in mediating the world of royal ritual to a new television audience, on the occasion of the Queen's coronation in 1953. In this instance, the new medium was the vehicle for the most traditional and conservative commentary, spoken from a position inside the ritual magic.

The 2007 documentary is framed to show Leibovitz entering the Queen's world, but the photographer's remarks attempt to domesticate the Queen, to draw her into Leibovitz's world, to make her recognizably one of us, and to efface the distinction between the royal and the nonroyal body. Certainly the photographer makes a perfunctory remark about honoring tradition, and brings her daughter to present the Queen with a conventional bouquet of flowers, but her comments portray the monarch as a stern woman who may never retire, who is almost never off duty, and who will never allow herself to lay aside the heavy Garter jewels and mantle.

Leibovitz's remarks are characteristically modernist in that they seem to present a new, outsider's perspective on the world of traditional ritual. But the tradition of such demystifications is also of long standing, as we have seen elsewhere in this book. It extends back at least as far as the sixteenth-century skepticism about the Order's foundational myth, and is the presiding trope of much satire and analysis, such as Woolf's and Osborne's. Moreover, documentary footage about a photographic portrait might well be expected to highlight an opposition between modernity and tradition. But again, the opposition is hardly a new one. In 1957, Antony Armstrong-Jones (later to marry Princess Margaret and become Lord Snowdon) took a number of photographs of the Queen, the duke, and their two eldest children, Charles and Anne. In one frame the two children were photographed standing on either side of a huge globe of the world, against a stark white background, devoid of any other props or setting. The press received the pictures with delight. As Snowdon writes: "The relatively informal pictures were received by the press as 'off-beat' and 'unconventional studies.' 'The end of the old stuffy era in princely portraiture,' said the *Express*."[14] Thus, fifty years before Leibovitz's encounter with the Queen, the press was already declaring the end of the "old stuffy era" Leibovitz clearly also saw herself as extinguishing.

In such encounters, we see how easy and appealing it is to simplify this opposition between tradition and modernity, rendering them as a pair of stark alternatives. But the history of the Order of the Garter has shown us that this tension between tradition and modernity, or between what is "stuffy" and what is new, is never resolved. Modernity never achieves the clear victory over tradition it appears to claim, and the opposition is restaged, reinvented, and repeated by subsequent generations of the royal family and their marriage partners throughout the modern era.

As Snowdon's photographs suggests, the concept of the royal family, with its emphasis on dynastic succession and generational change, is a perfect vehicle for holding these traditional and modern elements in suspension. In 1971, for example, J. G. Blumler and a group of researchers published the results of their qualitative research into English attitudes to the monarchy around the Investiture of the Prince of Wales on July 1, 1969. They concluded, as others have done before, that "Englishmen . . . would like the Queen to be at one and the same time grand and common, extraordinary and ordinary, grave and informal, mysterious and accessible, royal and democratic."[15]

And not just the English. The poet David Campbell wrote in "The Australian Dream" (1968) of a surprise visit from the royal family. In this fantasy, the Duke of Edinburgh willingly goes off to sleep in the boiler room, while the Queen and Queen Mother share the poet's bed. The Queen brushes out her hair, and folds her newspaper—*The Garter*—up on a pouf. The ladies undress:

> They tucked away
> Their state robes in the lowboy; gold crowns lay
> Upon the bedside tables; ropes of pearls
> Lassoed the plastic lampshade; their soft curls
> Were spread out on the pillows and they smiled.
> "Hop in," said the Queen Mother. In I piled
> Between them to lie like a stick of wood.[16]

In its juxtaposition of regal glamour (crowns, pearls, curls) with the suburban everyday world of bedside tables and plastic lampshades, Campbell's poem simultaneously domesticates the royal mystique—"Hop in," said the Queen Mother—and normalizes the idea of the royal dream vision. Indeed, it has been suggested that the Queen features in a remarkably high number of her subjects' dreams: the concept of the royal family has penetrated deep into the nation's and the Commonwealth's subconscious.

At the beginning of the twenty-first century, the aging figure of Elizabeth II has become an icon of tradition, or more specifically, traditions that are associated with the 1950s of her accession, signaled by the pearls, sturdy-heeled court shoes, stylish hats, and white gloves that characterize her formal public attire, or the white hair curled in the permanent wave that still adorns the coinage of the Commonwealth. As the encounter with Leibovitz suggests, Elizabethan iconography in the present is almost as stable and regulated as it was in the sixteenth century. The social and cultural traditions the Queen represents also belong to this mid-century era. George VI in 1936 and his daughter Elizabeth in 1952 established and consolidated a new period of domestic-style royal family stability after the tumultuous abdication of Edward VIII. Critical or satirical voices like John Osborne's were in the minority. In one of the rapid turnarounds of modern history, this era was experienced as a renewed "Elizabethan" era of progress and economic growth, yet it is now associated with deep social conservatism. The fact that three of the Queen's four children have been divorced has had the effect of making the Queen's own marital stability look more and more as if it belongs to an outdated era.

It is possible to observe a further shift in popular feeling about the royal family and the monarchy in the past two decades, a shift that provides a telling analogy for changes in the medievalism of the Order of the Garter into the twenty-first century.

In 2001 the psychologists W. Gerrod Parrott and Rom Harré diagnosed a significant change in the "emotionology" of modern Britain. Parrott and Harré argue that in contrast to the traditional British reserve and reluctance to express emotion, the public reaction to the death of Princess Diana in 1997 reflected a substantial change in the emotional "display rules" in modern British society.[17] The scale of the reaction was huge: more than two million people came from all over the United Kingdom to London to lay flowers and to attend the funeral. There was at least one precedent, as Parrott and Harré note, following Laurence Lerner, for this kind of reaction. In 1817, after the death in childbirth of Princess Charlotte (the only legitimate grandchild of George III), there was widespread mourning. In contrast to the mourning for Diana, this was not an event magnified by the effects of globalized media or the relative ease of travel, but even so, well-attended funeral services were held all over the country, and the hapless obstetrician committed suicide the following year.

The death of Diana, who had divorced Prince Charles in 1996, did not have the dynastic implications of Charlotte's death, as Diana had given birth to two sons. Yet it was an astonishing milestone in the emotional life of the nation. Parrott and Harré argue that the event not only reflected, but in part also brought about, a cultural change in the emotional "display rules" of contemporary Britain: "Unless individuals were ready (primed perhaps) to be influenced by the media as the medium of interpersonal influence, no manifestation on so huge a scale would have been possible. In a sense, the cultural shift had already occurred in the minds of many. The death of Diana transformed it from a vague apprehension to a definite, if complex pattern of emotions and opinions."[18] One of the motives for the public display of emotion, they argue, was "to voice support for a new style of royal behavior, and to express a kind of 'censure' of the establishment." They also diagnose a shift in public attitudes to the royal family, increasingly seen as both "remote" and "drearily sleazy" in its private life. In particular, public sympathy for the princess was aroused in relation to her dealings with the royal family: "Princess Diana had, long, before her death, already come to seem to many to be the put-upon victim of an uncaring and inward looking family."[19]

Insofar as cultural and emotional changes can be an observable phenomenon, changes in British attitudes to the expression of emotion (certainly, at least, in public attitudes to its royal family) were palpable in the weeks and months following the death of the princess. The popularity of the Queen plummeted. Her apparent failure to register the depth of the nation's collective grief was the object of journalistic and popular commentary, and became the subject of the feature film *The Queen* (2006).

Six years after the death of Princess Diana, however, the pendulum had swung the other way, and the Queen's Golden Jubilee celebrations in 2002 witnessed an outpouring of national pride amid a feeling of renewed respect for this long-lived queen and her life of service. This is not to say that the republican movement is not growing in England (there have been dramatic changes in the way the royal family now pays income tax, for example), but simply to say that the House of Windsor had once more demonstrated its capacity to harness an opportune moment.

One of the more iconic images of the Jubilee celebrations was the "Party at the Palace," an outdoor pop concert that began with Brian May, lead guitarist of the band Queen, playing the national anthem on the roof of Buckingham Palace. The main stage was adorned with two large gold-painted models of a lion and a unicorn—the traditional heraldic supporters of the royal coat of arms—each sitting up and playing a huge golden guitar. Here was a willing embrace of popular culture, amid the canny, knowing incorporation of allusions of the band's name, and the memory of its beloved former singer, Freddie Mercury, who died of HIV AIDS in 1991.

The award-winning film *The King's Speech* (2010), which dramatizes the personal struggle of George VI to overcome a debilitating stammer and perform the public duties of an unwanted throne in a time of war, captures this mood of renewed interest in and sympathy for the Crown and the personal lives of the royal family. News coverage of Prince William's marriage to Catherine Middleton focused uncritically on their plans to live "like any young married couple," doing their own shopping and house cleaning in their cottage while the prince is still based with the Royal Air Force in north Wales. The royal wedding was planned for 2011, in part, we were told, so it would not clash with the London Olympics and the Queen's Diamond Jubilee in 2012.

By the time of the Jubilee, the Order of the Garter will have been led by a woman for 124 of the past 175 years. It is impossible to know what difference this made to the Order's medievalism or sense of tradition, though we may suspect it silently informs the ethos of "responsiveness to a changing world" that dominates modern official Garter discourse. The change to permit women to become full Companions, as we saw in Chapter 5, was widely regarded as a successful coup of modernity, acknowledging the equal participation of women in society, although it made very little difference to the Order's principally ceremonial function and none at all to the "real" politics of the Order, which, unlike royal honors given to rock stars and cricketers, remains finite in its numbers and restricted to those who are seen to have rendered service to the Crown, whether as former prime ministers, governors-general, members of the diplomatic and military corps, or—especially in the case of women—as philanthropists.

I have often drawn attention in this book to the ways in which the modern Order of the Garter promotes its medieval origins while also asserting its capacity to renew and remake itself. We might observe, however, that such modernizations and renovations do more than simply affirm the modernity or "relevance" of such institutions. They also demonstrate the Sovereign's control of the institution, and by extension, of the Crown. For Edward VI and Mary, the religious orientation of the Garter was a powerful sign of their own religious and political affiliations; and for Charles II, the lavish ornamentalism of his old-new Garter robes signaled a new era of royal authority. So too, when George VI reinvented the Garter procession at Windsor in 1947, he was instituting a postwar tradition to celebrate English heritage and consolidate the return to "normal" ceremonial after the privations of the war.

The dominant discourse of "responsiveness" and perpetual "relevance" masks the very great changes in the social and political meaning and significance of institutions like the Garter and the monarchy between the medieval era and the modern era. In the context of such change, it is not surprising that the increasingly vague and shifting notion of "tradition" should displace the historical specificity of the Order's medieval origins: the chivalric context of gendered behavior that the myth recalls; the distribution of honor and shame; and the radically outdated belligerence of Edward's claim to the French throne.

This dehistoricizing effect is similar to the effect of the weird cycles and temporalities of medievalism in contemporary culture, by which the medieval regularly loses all trace of its historical specificity. Sometimes it is hard to tell whether medievalism is traveling back into the past or bringing the medieval forward into the present. Time-travel fictions like Mark Twain's *Connecticut Yankee in King Arthur's Court* are increasingly being displaced by the timeless medievalism of fantasy epics or a vaguely fairy-tale world. In some contexts, great pains are taken to carry out or draw on scholarly historical research, a process that is often foregrounded in the metacommentaries of authors' afterwords or DVD features and directors' commentaries. Increasingly, however, historical accuracy is regarded as dispensable. Postmedieval culture insists on its capacity to go back and revisit the medieval, to pick and choose among its glories and its squalor, in its representations and images of the medieval past.[20] Perversely, the more that people appeal to and draw on the Middle Ages as the source of fiction, drama, cinema, clothes, and music, the more the Middle Ages are dehistoricized.

Playing with Medievalism

When the Queen is driven out in her Rolls-Royce Phantom, the little figurehead of the Spirit of Ecstasy on the front of the car is unscrewed, and an image of St. George slaying the dragon is screwed on in its place, designating the presence of the royal passenger. It is not difficult to unpack the symbolism here. St. George is the patron saint of England, so he is the appropriate guardian and representative of the head of state. As the patron saint of the Order of the Garter, St. George also represents the head of state in a decidedly chivalric mode, as the Queen "rides out" as the Sovereign of the Order.

This figurehead extends the heraldic practice of using signs and symbols to designate individual knights on the battlefield and on ceremonial occasions. On the hood of a Rolls-Royce, it seems an odd, even humorous kind of translation from a chivalric, horse-riding culture. On the other hand, the playfulness evident here is a direct inheritance from the humorous puns and rebuses of many medieval and early modern heraldic sign and images or "charges" that play on the name of the knight they symbolize, or the evocative, enigmatic mottoes of medieval heraldic and court practice.

Such playfulness remains a feature of modern heraldry. In St. George's Chapel, the guides always pointed out the heraldic achievements of Sir Edmund Hillary suspended above his stall: the banner featuring his coat of arms, and the modeled crest that appears above the ceremonial helmet and mantling. The designs of both elements referred to his climbing Mt. Everest: his coat of arms appears as three snow-covered mountain peaks on a blue background. The formal blazon reads: "Azure, a chevron embowed between two chevronels embowed in fess Argent between three prayer wheels bendwise Or." Similarly, his crest is a kiwi—the small, flightless New Zealand bird—holding an ice axe, which is blazoned thus: "A kiwi Azure grasping in the dexter foot an ice axe bendwise Or." The choice of distinctive symbols such as the Tibetan prayer wheels, the kiwi, and the ice axe remind us of the heraldic convention that coats of arms are awarded to individuals, not families, while these distinctive charges allowed spectators to experience a medieval sense of "recognizing" a knight by his coat of arms. Like Sir Edmund himself, the little bird holding the ice axe is a mountain-climbing kiwi (the popular name for New Zealanders). As with the figure of St. George and the dragon on the Queen's car, there is a playfulness about the way these birds, action figures, and animals are deployed, while there is a further pleasure on offer in decoding the semiotic and semantic conventions of heraldry in the formal blazons.

Heraldic pleasure and play can take a number of different forms. In August 2008, at Edinburgh Zoo, a King Penguin named Nils Olav was knighted by the King's Guards of Norway. Sir Nils (or a previous penguin bearing the same name) was already the mascot and colonel-in-chief of the Norwegian King's Guard, having been promoted on several previous occasions. A message was read out from King Harald: "We being well satisfied with the loyalty, courage and good endowments of our trusty and well beloved Nils Olav and reposing entire trust and confidence in you, as a penguin, in every way qualified to receive the honour and dignity of knighthood and the office aforesaid."[21] The clip available on YouTube shows Sir Nils waddling along a path, inspecting a row of soldiers, and being knighted with a sword on either side of his head—where his shoulders would be if he had them—with the badge of his knighthood tied to his right wing, a curious variant of the Garter as worn on the arm of its ladies. The connection between the Edinburgh penguins and the King of Norway dates to 1962, when Major Nils Egelien, a member of the Norwegian King's Guard, in Edinburgh for the Military Tattoo, first took an interest in the penguin colony and persuaded his regiment to adopt an Edinburgh penguin as its mascot. But we may also suspect a degree of reciprocity, or at least a consciousness of the possibility of an exchange of honors, since King Harald of Norway is a Companion of the Order of the Garter. Nils Egelien attended the ceremony at Edinburgh Zoo in 2008 and commented, "It's very, very, very important. It gives joy to the Guardsmen."

His remarks echo the Duke of Edinburgh's comments on the Order of the Garter: "It's a nice piece of pageantry which I think a lot of people enjoy. . . . Rationally it's lunatic but in practice everyone enjoys it I think."

While the playfulness of heraldic conventions represents a continuous inheritance from the Middle Ages, these appeals to the joy and the pleasure people take in such practices signal a more profound shift in the orientation of royal and chivalric ritual practice. The Order of the Garter and other medieval chivalric societies were founded to consolidate and commemorate the ties of loyalty, service, and reward that bind together a king and his knights. The politics of such honors became more and more pronounced in the postmedieval period, but it is clear now that in the modern era, despite their insistence otherwise, these traditional chivalric institutions struggle against a growing sense that they are irrelevant to contemporary society. It is not simply that they *look* outdated: the fundamental ways they bestow, withhold, and distribute shame and honor address a society very different from the one that sustains their current profile and activities. As a result, the Order of the Garter, like the monarchy itself, has had to bow to changes in the way news of its activities is broadcast and communicated, and to the ways it can fund its own activities.

Tom Nairn described the royal family's "insouciant" play with the symbols of the past, but many of the excesses of ornamentalism in the current climate are intimately bound with the commercial imperatives of contemporary tourism and heritage culture as well as medievalist play. There is nothing insouciant about the current marketing of the royal family or the Order of the Garter.

For example, on a recent trip to London, I bought a packet of twelve small blocks of chocolate: the wrapper of each one forms a composite image of a stylized cartoon drawing of the Garter procession at Windsor (figure 28). The twelve blocks are neatly packaged on gold card and labeled as coming from "The Royal Collection," St. James's Palace, London.

Windsor Castle and St. George's Chapel, like all royal buildings open to the public, offer many selling points for official souvenirs. I am also the proud owner of an engraved whiskey glass and an ornate tin plate decorated with Garter designs. At £4.95 my chocolates represent the lower end of the full range of merchandise, though the red lead pencil with the gold crown at its tip was even cheaper. At the upper range, there are many varieties of china, glassware, scarves, and other textiles available, to say nothing of the hundreds of DVDs and books for adults and children, many of which rehearse the familiar strategy of recounting the Garter myth only to suspend judgment about it and frame it as a popular fairy tale or folk story.

If royal institutions can play like this with their own symbols, signs, and rituals, examples of such play from beyond the institution can be multiplied. I considered a number of parodic examples from the end of the nineteenth century in Chapter 4. David Campbell's poem is only one of many more such examples from the twentieth.

In 1912, Jacques Futrelle published a detective novel, *My Lady's Garter*, whose plot hinges around the idea that King Edward promised to return the countess's garter by having a pair of garters rendered in gold. One of them

Figure 28. Garter chocolates. Author's collection.

"lay among the precious relics tucked away in an obscure corner of the British Museum." The novel begins a year after this garter was stolen, and the plot generates a number of concealed identities and fantasies about the "real" garter. The novel was made into a movie of the same name in 1920. Indeed, something of gallantry persisted in Futrelle's own life: he was last seen alive by his wife as she was rowed away from the *Titanic*. He had refused to climb into a lifeboat, and was seen smoking a cigar with John J. Astor.[22]

In 1944, Rex Whistler decorated the wall of his officers' billet in Brighton with a wonderful image: "Allegory: HRH the Prince Regent awakening the Spirit of Brighton" (figure 29). The prince, who had built his palace in Brighton (now the Royal Pavilion), in 1815, is shown hovering over a recumbent nude with a knowing eye leering at the viewer. He himself is naked but for his court shoes, a pair of angel's wings, the blue Garter sash with the Garter star resting on his dimpled buttock, a wisp of gauze across his genitals, and the blue Garter clearly visible around his leg.

The painting's wickedly knowing invocation of the Garter as fetish and supplement—one would feel naked without it—are telling, but the history of the painting is poignant in its own way. Whistler was killed in action just six weeks after painting this lively jeu d'esprit, but after the war, his regiment refused to buy the painting. Fortunately, the Brighton city council was not so squeamish. The contrast underlines the tension between the persistent impulse to mock the Garter, and the reluctance of official, military culture to acknowledge that impulse.

In 1978, the English poet U. A. Fanthorpe published her much-anthologized poem "Not My Best Side." Inspired by Paulo Uccello's painting *St. George and the Dragon* (c. 1470), the poem offers three monologues from the perspective of each of the main characters: dragon, girl, and knight. The girl and the dragon resent their representation and their fate. Thus, the dragon speaks:

> And why should she have me literally
> On a string? I don't mind dying
> Ritually, since I always rise again,
> But I should have liked a little more blood
> To show they were taking me seriously.

St. George is the last to speak, from a position of a confident modernity. In this perspective, the old must always make way for the new:

> My horse is the latest model, with
> Automatic transmission and built-in
> Obsolescence.

The knight addresses the reluctant girl and dragon, and their complaints:

Figure 29. *HRH The Prince Regent Awakening the Spirit of Brighton.* Artist Rex Whistler. © The Royal Pavilion, Libraries, and Museums, Brighton and Hove, U.K.

Don't you want to be killed and/or rescued
In the most contemporary way? Don't
You want to carry out the roles
That sociology and myth have designed for you?

In its celebration of these multiple points of view, and its distancing, knowing perspectives, this much-studied poem acknowledges the ritual components of the St. George story while also injecting them with the tension between tradition and modernity that characterizes the ritual life of medievalist chivalry in contemporary culture.

A chain of English-style pubs in France takes the name The Frog. The logo is printed on a drinks coaster: a green frog wearing a blue and gold tie, smoking a cigarette, and sitting on a beer keg with a plate of roast beef by his side and holding a pint of lager balanced on one jauntily raised knee. He winks lazily as he raises his bowler hat, and as the motto scrolls beneath his lower foot: "Honi soit qui peu y boit" (figure 30). Here the defiance of the "Honi soit" motto is dramatically weakened, applying only to those who don't drink enough.

In 1929 students from the University of Sydney who had been roundly condemned in the press for their boisterous Commemoration Day celebrations (an Italian student, Virgil Losciavo, was sent down from the university for allegedly desecrating the cenotaph in Martin Place), inaugurated a newsletter entitled *Honi Soit*, to defend themselves against antistudent feeling. There is no reference to the Order of the Garter in the first editorial, or anywhere in the commemorative issue published in 2006. That special issue featured a reprint of an article by Charles McCausland, who was a student at the university in 1929. The article was first published in 1989 and is called "Educated Louts: The Scandalous Origins of Honi Soit": "Why Honi Soit?— it was a matter of unity in the face of threat. The students of Sydney University felt themselves threatened by the Press reaction over the Cenotaph incident, and rallied round. The reputation of Sydney University as well as that of the undergrads was at stake and had to be defended. Ours was the deadliest of the Seven Deadly Sins—pride in Sydney University."[23] The specificity of the Order of the Garter was replaced by the vaguest notion of a general defiance. Perhaps feeling conscious of the thinness of his explanation, McCausland resorts to the more familiar medievalism of the Seven Deadly Sins to anchor his commentary.

Honi Soit remains an important newsletter for student opinion and

Figure 30. *Honi soit qui peu y boit.* Author's collection.

activism. Its enigmatic title remains so catchy and compelling that a number of former students of that university have insisted to me that *Honi soit* is the motto of the university (not its actual motto: *Sidere mens eadem mutato*). Once more, this little text has floated free of its own history.

Conclusion

Why does the modern and contemporary history of the Garter read like a series of weird examples, fragments, and half-understood allusions? Why has the preceding chapter appeared to disintegrate into a list of games, mistakes, and cheap souvenirs—a postmodern pastiche of medievalism?

The answer is simple, although it is based on complex historical changes. In spite of the Order's official protestations, this medieval chivalric order struggles to hold together its foundational mythologies in a coherent symbolic system that can compel the same kind of attention and reverence it used to. In some restricted circles its rituals and hierarchies, its genealogies, charities, and prayers no doubt seem to offer a continuity with the past; and the hierarchy of its honors no doubt continues to register deeply within some sections of English society. And to the loyal subjects and cognoscenti who line the route of the Garter procession, the Order still seems to carry forth those traditions, modeling a form of heritage culture and medievalism that is still available to contemporary generations.

But the dominant mode in which the Order of the Garter appears in contemporary culture is not the distribution of honor and shame, or as a model of social order. Rather, the Order appears most often as something that needs to be *explained*. The Order's symbolism, its origin, its motto, its internal organization, its clothing and its rituals, its methods of election have all become deeply unfamiliar. Like so many aspects of medieval culture and history, the story of the Garter survives as a series of half-remembered fragments, available for dissemination with hugely varying degrees of historical accuracy.

At the high point of European modernism, Woolf dehistoricizes and demedievalizes the medieval inheritance of ritual practice, anticipating the postmodernist pastiche by which the medieval is now chiefly known and disseminated. In other more recent scholarly contexts, tremendous energy is spent disaggregating fact from fiction about the Middle Ages, and in explaining chivalric systems like the Order of the Garter whose symbolic capital in the restricted culture of the medieval royal court depended on the instant, wordless recognition of its symbols and honors. The explanations we now give are of a very different order from the courtly guessing games inspired by the *Honi soit* motto: at every turn they insist on the alterity of medieval culture as the object of specialist knowledge. At the same time, however, the distinctions between history and mythology, between the Middle Ages and medievalism, have become almost irrevocably blurred. To the extent that the Garter and other medieval forms survive into the twenty-first century, they are regularly demedievalized, stripped of those aspects that tie them most closely to the historical period. Dissolving the power of cosmological tradition and medieval symbolism by casting doubt on the Garter myth, for example, is another typically modernist way of disabling the power of the medieval to reach into the present. As we have seen in successive chapters, however, this process began in the early modern period and is still incomplete. The work of demedievalization is never done.

I suggested in Chapter 2 that the Order's foundation myth works by making a kind of reparation for the symbolic rupture it rehearses. Not only is the dropped garter realigned into the King's symbolic and ritual economy of puissance, the very uncertainty of this myth and its truth claims are an important component of the Order's mythic capital. At a second-order historiographic level, from the longer perspective of postmedieval tradition, this uncertainty and the rival accounts of the Order's foundations threaten a different kind of rupture in their appeal to historical continuity, since we cannot track the Order's history back to the 1340s with the same accuracy we bring to historical accounts of its more recent history.

Despite its claims to preserve a continuous tradition from medieval times, the Order of the Garter's history is a very uneven one, marked by several periods of decline and revival. So much would we reasonably expect of an institution that is so closely associated with the monarchy. From the perspective of medievalism studies, the more interesting question is the changing degree to which the Order appears as medieval, or as a form of medievalism. I have worked through some of the variable possibilities here. For example, when the Order talks up its origins it stresses the medieval quaintness of the foundational myth. On the other hand, its annual procession has medieval origins but also draws on the form of the Tudor royal progress, and in its current form it encapsulates the deliberate revival or reinvention of sumptuous and precise royal pageantry after the Second World War. By contrast, elements of its ritual costume—the cloak with its long tassels, the embroidered scutcheon, the red hood—are medieval, but they are mixed with a slowly changing array of clothes worn beneath the blue mantle, from Charles II's "immutable fashion" of "the old trunk hose," to the varied conventions of "court dress." They start out looking fashionable or modern and gradually become archaic, like Winston Churchill's black stockings, or the long white pearl-encrusted dresses of the present Queen and her royal ladies. It is not difficult to conceptualize the medieval aspects of the Order on a kind of sliding scale of relative strength or weakness, and to register the extent to which the medieval is foregrounded or not in the Order, at different times, and in different aspects of its practices.

The long history of the Order of the Garter provides a register for changing attitudes to medievalism. The persistence of its traditional forms of ritual practice has had a lasting and symptomatic affect on the changing valency of the Middle Ages. The Order enjoys a long history, but it is far from a seamless or untroubled one. As we have seen, the institution is deeply riven by its own history and its own divided and troubled relation to its medieval past. Not only can the Order of the Garter not agree about its own medieval origins: it cannot agree, either, about the significance or the import of *having* medieval origins. In this it is surprisingly representative of modernity's relationship with the medieval past. The Order's rhetoric propounds an easy opposition between the old and new, between tradition and innovation, but its history shows what an impossible oversimplification that is. The ideology of continuous tradition necessitates a deep selectivity about those aspects of its past that modern ritual practice preserves, discards, and obsessively revisits. In the final irony of its long continuance, the Order of the Garter can never resolve the question of its origin, and will never be able to acknowledge the medievalism of the medieval thing at its heart.

Notes

INTRODUCTION

1. *The Queen at Eighty*.

2. Tim Cohen, author of *The Anti-Christ and a Cup of Tea*, claims that the Order of the Garter is "the secret mechanism through which the British monarchy had run the world since 1349." Interview with Andrew Brown in *The New Statesman*, 40.

3. Eco, "Dreaming of the Middle Ages," 71.

4. See Haydock, *Movie Medievalism*, 5–35.

5. See, for example, Raphael Samuel's discussion of "heritage-baiting" in *Theatres of Memory*, 259–73.

6. In this, and in so much of this book, I am indebted to work on a collaborative project with Tom Prendergast, *Medievalism and Its Discontents* (forthcoming).

7. D'Arcens, "From 'Eccentric Affiliation' to 'Corrective Medievalism,'" 304.

8. See James, *Globalism, Nationalism, Tribalism*, 65–99, for the methodological model that sits loosely behind the idea of historical layering here and throughout this book.

9. In particular, see Collins, *The Order of the Garter 1348–1461*, and Matikkala, *The Orders of Knighthood*.

10. Trigg, *Congenial Souls*.

CHAPTER I. RITUAL THEORY AND MEDIEVALISM

1. [J. J. Tierney], "As Black Rod . . . ," undated typescript in Victorian Parliamentary Library, Parliament House, Spring Street, Melbourne, Australia, 1954.

2. Begent and Chesshyre, *Order of the Garter*, 132. The Victorian Parliamentary Library document also makes this connection.

3. In 1998, *BBC News* online posted a Special Report on some changes to the rituals for the State Opening of Parliament, changes that had the effect of streamlining and shortening the ceremony. Some officials were no longer required to walk backward away from the monarch, and Black Rod was no longer to wait for the Queen to be seated before he summoned the members of the House of Commons. According to the BBC report, "In the past the MPs have kept the Queen waiting for some time as

they deliberately dawdled on the trip between the two houses, reluctant as they are to acknowledge that the Lords is, traditionally at least, the senior chamber." "State Opening Loses Some Pomp."

4. See also Trigg, "Timeless Medievalism."

5. Kafka, "Leopards in the Temple," in *Parables and Paradoxes*, 93.

6. Strohm, *England's Empty Throne*, 20–21.

7. Wagner, *Heralds of England*, 501.

8. Cannadine, "The British Monarchy," 108.

9. "Victoria's First Black Rod," undated pamphlet produced by the Victorian State Parliament.

10. There is also the possibility of confusion in the word "tip." It seems to refer to the top end of the Rod, which is affixed with a crown, though in contemporary practice, at least, the Usher of the Black Rod lifts the rod up to shoulder height, holding it parallel to the ground, and beats on the door with the lower end.

11. Begent and Chesshyre, *Order of the Garter*, 132.

12. Australian parliaments (both state and federal) have at various times vigorously debated whether to preserve or modernize their inherited traditions of costume and ritual behavior, and the extent to which such practices might, or should, accurately articulate a relationship with Britain or the medieval origins of the parliamentary system. See James and Trigg, "Rituals of Nationhood."

13. The coolamon was made by Bai Bai Napangarti, "a senior law woman from Balgo Hills in the Kimberley region of Western Australia. The coolamon was made at the Walay-irti Artists Community at Balgo Hills. Coolamons are traditionally made from hardwoods, and function as vessels for carrying babies, food, water, or other light objects." It was presented by Mrs. Lorraine Peeters.

14. Trigg, "Timeless Medievalism."

15. Collins, *Order of the Garter*, 8, 20.

16. The preeminent text here is Dinshaw, *Getting Medieval*; but see also Cohen, *Medieval Identity Machines*, especially chapter 1, "Time's Machines"; Prendergast and Trigg, "What Is Happening to the Middle Ages?" and "The Negative Erotics of Medievalism."

17. See Holsinger, *Neomedievalism, Neoconservatism, and the War on Terror*.

18. See Cannadine, "The British Monarchy."

19. Muir, *Ritual in Early Modern Europe*, 3–5.

20. Strong, *Coronation*, xxxvi–xxxvii.

21. Eliade, *Cosmos and History*, 35. See also Burke, *The Historical Anthropology of Early Modern Italy*, 183.

22. For a commanding summary of studies in the field, see Bell, *Ritual Theory, Ritual Practice*.

23. Ibid., 3.

24. For example, see Kertzer, *Ritual, Politics, and Power*, 37.

25. Grimes, *Ritual Criticism*.

26. Sellar and Yeatman, illustrated by Reynolds, *1066 and All That*, 40–41.

27. Bourdieu's concept of symbolic capital is briefly evoked in the context of the Order of the Garter by Juliet Vale, "Image and Identity," 35; and by Matikkala (following Vale) in *The Orders of Knighthood*, 286. Both scholars use this phrase to describe the strategic deployment of chivalric and symbolic honors to promote political or ideological interests.

28. Eliade, *Cosmos and History*, 46.

29. Matikkala notes that despite there being no evidence of this order's existence before 1687, the dean of the Order in 2006 still payed homage to King James II (and VII of Scotland) for "reviving" the medieval order, *The Orders of Knighthood*, 81. For the Order of the Bath, see 91–95: "Although the institution was a rhetorical revival of a medieval chivalric rite, the accompanying cultural imagery—both literary and visual—was classical and, indeed, literally Augustan," 95. See also Galloway, *The Order of the Bath*, 1–5.

30. Beltz, *Memorials*, cxxxiii. The King had previously amended the statutes so that all his sons, not just the Prince of Wales, could be admitted as members.

31. Begent and Chesshyre, *Order of the Garter*, 214, citing a letter from Sir Arthur Ellis, Comptroller of the Lord Chamberlain's Office, to Sir Alfred Scott-Gatty, Garter King of Arms, 2 October, 1906, Records of the Order of the Garter in the College of Arms, C30.

32. Begent and Chesshyre, *Order of the Garter*, 198. See also Matikkala, *The Orders of Knighthood*, 107–8.

33. Collins, *Order of the Garter*, 84.

34. Waddington, "Elizabeth I and the Order of the Garter," 101. See also my Chapter 6.

35. Adamson, "Chivalry and Political Culture in Caroline England," 174.

36. Matikkala, *The Orders of Knighthood*, 66.

37. Ibid., 89. See also the facsimile edition of Writhe's book, *Medieval Pageant, Writhe's Garter Book and the Earldom of Salisbury Roll*, ed. Wagner, Barker, and Payne.

38. Matikkala, *The Orders of Knighthood*, 176–77.

39. Ibid., 1.

40. Cannadine, "The British Monarchy," 105.

41. Bucholz, " 'Nothing but Ceremony,' " 298.

42. Ibid., 312.

43. Ibid., 314.

44. For a description of this service, see Beltz, *Memorials*, cxxv.

45. Cannadine, "The British Monarchy," 111.

46. Ibid., 116.

47. Begent and Chesshye, *Order of the Garter*, 267.

48. Ashmole, *Institution*; Anstis, *Register*; Beltz, *Memorials*.

49. Collins, *Order of the Garter*; Matikkala, *The Orders of Knighthood*.

50. Collins, *Order of the Garter*, 1.

51. Boulton, *Knights of the Crown*.

52. Collins, *Order of the Garter*, 35.

53. "Ladies of the Fraternity," 268, n.39.

54. Kertzer, *Ritual, Politics, and Power*, 66.

CHAPTER 2. ORIGINS

1. The best study here is Collins, *Order of the Garter.*

2. Jefferson, "MS Arundel 48," 356–85. The chapter she contributes to Begent and Chesshyre, *Order of the Garter,* builds on this case, 53. The original Register is lost, but various copies and fragments survive. The oldest, in French, is based on a copy of the text made for Elias Ashmole in 1660 (Bodl. MS Ashmole 1128); it includes a diatribe against Anne Boleyn, and a panegyric on Jane Seymour. There is also a fragment, in English, perhaps a series of drafts, that covers the period 1481 to 1533. The third constitutes part of "The Black Book of Windsor" (c. 1534), the first of nine volumes of the Register, which was published by John Anstis in 1724. See Begent and Chesshyre, *Order of the Garter,* 77–79; Collins, *Order of the Garter,* 1.

3. See Jefferson, "Two Fifteenth-Century Manuscripts of the Statutes of the Order of the Garter," and "MS Arundel 48," where she discusses the Ph.D. dissertation on this topic by Diethard Schneider, "Der englische Hosenbandorden: Beitrage zur Entstehung und Entwicklung des 'The Most Noble Order of the Garter' (1348–1702), mit einem Ausblick bis 1983" (4 vols., Bonn, 1983).

4. Collins, *Order of the Garter,* 6–7. Francis Ingledew suggests Froissart's confusion was in fact shared by contemporary observers, for whom the distinction was less important than for modern commentators, in *Sir Gawain and the Green Knight,* 105–6.

5. See Barber, "The Round Table Feast of 1344," 38–43 and Appendix B, texts and translations of Round Table chronicle sources, including the chronicle of Adam of Murimuth, 179–89. Jonathan Boulton points out that "round table" tournaments had been held in England at least since 1235, in *Knights of the Crown,* 107.

6. Juliet Vale, "Image and Identity," 40. See also Boulton, *Knights of the Crown,* 112.

7. Nicolas, "Observations," Latin text at p. 33, English translation at p. 119.

8. Ibid., 127; Juliet Vale, *Edward III and Chivalry,* 79–81; and Barber, *Edward, Prince of Wales,* 84. Stella Mary Newton comments that the terms *bluet/um* and *blu* are rare in the Wardrobe accounts, and in conjunction with white, seem to indicate things made for the Order of the Garter, perhaps a definite tint of blue, in *Fashion in the Age of the Black Prince,* 44.

9. Vale, *Edward III and Chivalry,* 81.

10. Collins, *Order of the Garter,* 1.

11. Ibid., 1. There is an interesting disjunction here between Collins's description of the Order's "consciously romantic associations" and his emphatic rejection of the popular story as "trivializing" the order with an "inappropriate" badge celebrating an "irrational, albeit chivalric gesture" (12).

12. Ibid., 9–10, 13.

13. Vale, *Edward III and Chivalry,* 83–84.

14. Barber, *Edward, Prince of Wales,* 91. See also Ormrod, "For Arthur and St George," 18–19.

15. Vale cites, for example, the three thousand peacock feathers used to make just one crest for the King, between 1337 and 1339 ("Image and Identity," 47).

16. Nicolas, "Observations," 125; Vale, *Edward III and Chivalry,* 86.

17. Vale, *Edward III and Chivalry,* 19, 73, 93. See also Ormrod, "For Arthur and St George," 22–23.

18. Barber, *Edward, Prince of Wales,* 89.

19. Juliet R. V. Barker describes the literary inspirations behind the tournament ceremonials, and the importance of women to these spectacles in *The Tournament in England 1100–1400,* 84–111. See also Karras, *From Boys to Men,* 47–57.

20. Pearsall, ed., *The Floure and the Leafe and the Assembly of Ladies,* 98–100.

21. Cooke and Boulton, "*Sir Gawain and the Green Knight.*" The manuscript reads "lordes and ladis þat longed to þe Table, / Each burne of þe broþerhede, a bauderyk shulde haue," though some editors amend *ladis* to *ledes,* "gentlemen."

22. See *Wynnere and Wastoure,* ed. Trigg, line 68. There is a long tradition of dating this poem quite precisely in 1352–53, but see my "Israel Gollancz's *Wynnere and Wastoure.*"

23. Smith, *Arts of Possession,* 83, 84.

24. Smith adds that the association of garters with coins offers "a metonymic sign of the initial scene's fantasy of an economic scene dominated and enfolded by the signs of aristocratic privilege," ibid., 85.

25. The making of this robe was thus budgeted at 403 working days in all, according to this record in the National Archives, E101/392/4. See Staniland, "Court Style, Painters, and the Great Wardrobe," 245.

26. See also Ormrod, "For Arthur and St. George," 28–30.

27. "Puis la prit et luy estouppa la bouche si fort qu'elle ne poeut crier que II cris ou III, et puis l'enforcha à telle doulour et à tel matire qu'onques femme ne fut ainsy villainement traittié[e]; et la laissa comme gisant toute pasmée, sanant par nez et par bouche et aultre part, de quoy ce fut grand meschief et grande pitié. Puis s'en parti l'endemain sans dire mot, et retourna à Londres, grandement couroussé de ce qu'il avoit commis." *Chronique de Jean le Bel,* ed. Viard and Déprez, 31.

28. See Chareyron, "L'amour d'Edouard III d'Angleterre pour la comtesse de salisbury." See also Gransden, "The Alleged Rape by Edward III of the Countess of Salisbury." Gransden concludes that the story is modeled closely on Livy's account of the rape of Lucretia, and should be considered "a piece of political propaganda, a deliberate 'smear' on Edward III," 341.

29. Ingledew, *Sir Gawain and the Green Knight,* 54.

30. Ibid., 125–28.

31. For text and translation of this passage in Murimuth's chronicle, see Appendix B.1 of *Edward III's Round Table at Windsor,* ed. Mundy et al., 180–81.

32. Barber, *Edward, Prince of Wales,* 86.

33. Ingledew, *Sir Gawain and the Green Knight,* 151.

34. Malcolm Vale, *The Princely Court,* 213–18.

35. Ingledew makes much of this, but the woman is described as the beautiful daughter of the Earl of Derby. In reality, the earl had two daughters, but neither became the Countess of Salisbury.

36. Ingledew, *Sir Gawain and the Green Knight,* 141. See also the discussion in Malcolm Vale, *The Princely Court,* 213–18.

37. Ingledew, *Sir Gawain and the Green Knight,* 150.

38. For a fuller reading, see my "Romance of Exchange." See also Heng, "Feminine Knots and the Other."

39. See also Ormrod, "For Arthur and St. George," 31.

40. Ingledew cites correspondence from Malcolm Parkes expressing the view that the motto was added to the poem by the same scribe, but in a different hand, in *Sir Gawain and the Green Knight,* 224, n. 10.

41. Martorell and de Galba, trans. Rosenthal, *Tirant lo Blanc,* xxviii. Rosenthal also reports that much of the *Tirant* dedication was shown by Martí de Riquer to have been plagiarized from the dedication to Don Enrique de Villena's *Los doce trabajos de Hércules* (Burgos, 1499), a work that remains unpublished, as the only known version is in possession of a bibliophile who refuses to permit its publication. Martorell, *Tirant lo Blanc,* ed. de Riquer. See also the relevant passage, with translation into French, in Colon, "Premiers echos," 445–47.

42. Martorell, and de Galba, *Tirant lo Blanc,* x–xii. Note that the translation used (Rosenthal) attributes the poem to Martorell and de Galba (who completed it); the edition edited by de Riqueur just lists Martorell.

43. Ibid., Chapter 84, 117.

44. Ibid., Chapter 85, 121.

45. The role of women in the Order is examined more thoroughly in Chapters 5 and 6.

46. "Et sunt plerique nonnulli autumantes, hunc Ordinem Exordium sumpsisse à sexu muliebri, lubricum et cauterizatum gerentes affectum quatenus credo." *Catechismus Ordinis Equitum Persiscelidis Anglicanae seu Speculum Anglorum.* The text is preserved in BL Harley MS 5415, and was published in Cologne in 1631. Barber comments, "The passage is an obscure one, and when he comes to discuss the Order's motto, he does so in conventional rhetorical terms," 86. Germán Colon suggests that this story sits behind Joan Roís de Corella's apostrophe, in his *Trihunfo de les Dones,* to the knights who wrongly compare "la desordenada regla de la Garrotera" to the apostles, "Premiers echos," 449.

47. Barber, *Edward, Prince of Wales,* 85, translating *Polydori Vergili Historiae anglicanae* (Basle, 1555; rpt. Menston, 1972), 379.

48. Hay, *Polydore Vergil,* 100. See also Barber, *Edward, Prince of Wales,* 86, who comments, "The tradition was undoubtedly genuine, for Vergil was not given to invention: and it has been claimed that he drew on popular tradition going back to the early fourteenth century: the same authority cites the Garter story as evidence that Vergil 'knew when to admit that a popular legend contained a true tradition.'" Barber also describes Jean le Bel's "propaganda" in claiming that Edward had raped the Countess of Salisbury: "If the Order's motto was perhaps Edward's reply to these shameful stories, might not the story of foundation retold by Vergil also be from a hostile source?"

49. Heylyn, *Cosmographie,* 321–22.

50. Ashmole, *Institution,* 180.

51. Anstis, *Register*, vol. I, 62.

52. Begent and Chesshyre, *Order of the Garter*, 15. See also Collins, *Order of the Garter*, 12. Leo Carruthers remarks that Vergil's account "has the appearance of a later invention whose intention is to explain and justify the motto's somewhat obscure words," in *"Honi soit qui mal y pense*," 222.

53. Ibid., 232. Carruthers also updates and corrects some of the discussion offered earlier by Margaret Galway, "Joan of Kent and the Order of the Garter." See also Packe, *King Edward III*, ed. Seaman, 170–74, for speculation that the episode may allude to Alice Montagu or Alice Perrers.

54. Carruthers, "The Duke of Clarence and the Earls of March"; Cooke and Boulton, *"Sir Gawain and the Green Knight*," 42–54. Ingledew writes, "Gawain's confrontation with his limitations at Hautdesert challenges the Arthurian-Edwardian norm: it recalls the Arthurian-Edwardian knight to the ethical framework of Christian history within which he inclines to forget his indelible inscription," *Sir Gawain and the Green Knight*, 19.

55. Ormrod, "For Arthur and St George," 33.

56. Nevinson, "The Earliest Dress and Insignia of the Knights of the Garter," 81.

57. Begent and Chesshyre, *Order of the Garter*, 16.

58. Ingledew, *Sir Gawain and the Green Knight*, 197.

59. Boulton, *Knights of the Crown*, 113.

60. Barber, *Edward, Prince of Wales*, 87. "Of þylke men of þe garteres, So com þe vsage of þe garteres," cited in the *Middle English Dictionary*, s.v. "garter" 2 (a).

61. Begent and Chesshyre, *Order of the Garter*, 16.

62. See Crowfoot, Pritchard, and Staniland, *Textiles and Clothing*, 142–44.

63. Martorell and de Galba, *Tirant lo Blanc*, 123.

64. For a comprehensive account of the symbolic resonances of Gawain's girdle, see Friedman and Osberg, "Gawain's Girdle as Traditional Symbol."

65. See the illustration of this scene in Wagner, Barker, and Payne, *Medieval Pageant*, color plate 24.

66. Keen, "Introduction," 11. For a full account of the tournament, see Hughes, *Arthurian Myths and Alchemy*, 179–82.

67. See Bentley, *Excerpta Historica*, 171ff.; and Lester, "Fifteenth-Century English Heraldic Narrative." See also Karras, *From Boys to Men*, 55–56.

68. Jackson, "Sir Gawain and the Green Knight Considered as a 'Garter' Poem."

69. Barber, *Edward, Prince of Wales*, 87.

70. Murray, *The God of the Witches*, 60–61.

71. Kraig, *Modern Magick*, 300.

72. Ormrod, "The Personal Religion of Edward III," 853–54.

73. Kennedy, "Virgin Mary's Clue to Royal Order Mystery."

74. Blackledge, *The Story of V*.

75. Jennings, *The Rosicrucian Origin of the Order of the Garter*. Jennings argues from a number of correspondences, for example, the twenty-six knights "representing the double thirteen lunations in the year" (311), to conclude "the article of dress makes it clear that the

Countess of Salisbury . . . should have rather been at home, *and at rest*, than inattentive to saltatory risks in engaging in a dance at a crowded court" (313).

76. Diski, "It's So Beautiful."

77. Anstis, *Register,* vol. I, 31.

78. Barber, *Edward, Prince of Wales,* 87.

79. Boulton, *Knights of the Crown,* 109–10; Collins, *Order of the Garter,* 8–9, 12.

80. Fox-Davies, *A Complete Guide to Heraldry,* 450.

81. Juliet Vale, *Edward III and Chivalry,* 65, 71.

82. Newton, *Fashion in the Age of the Black Prince,* 42.

83. For a comprehensive account of Edward's lavish tournaments, games, and hastiludes, see Juliet Vale, *Edward III and Chivalry,* 57–75, and Appendix 13, 175.

84. According to Caroline Shenton, the leopard was Edward's favorite symbol, displaced only by the Garter. By 1370, he had collected up to seven lions and leopards in the Tower of London. "Edward III and the Symbol of the Leopard," 77–81. See also Juliet Vale, *Edward III and Chivalry,* 68–69.

85. Juliet Vale, *Edward III and Chivalry,* 69, 73. See also Vale's "Image and Identity," 35–50.

86. Crane, *The Performance of Self,* 16–17.

87. Ibid., 17, and Baune, "Costume et pouvoir en France à la fin du Moyen Age."

88. Fradenburg, *City, Marriage, Tournament,* 179.

89. Crane, *The Performance of Self,* 222–23, n. 104. This note sits somewhat awkwardly with Crane's assertion in the text that these mottoes "assert control over interpretation and deny that multiple interpretations might have merit," 139.

90. Juliet Vale, *Edward III and Chivalry,* 65. The word "honi," or "honni" as it appears more often in French, was never common and soon became obsolete in French. While the English historians regularly translated this as "shamed," the French commentators often give a stronger reading, as "cursed," "vitupéré, laidangé." In 1694, it has become a "vieux mot François qui n'est plus en usage qu'en raillerie"—an old French word which is used only in jest—(*Dictionnaire de l'Academie française,* 570).

91. As Eve Sedgwick argues, the expression "shame on you" has a similar resonance with many of J. L. Austin's admittedly troubled examples of illocutionary speech-acts. Following Silvan Tomkins's analysis of the shame affect, Sedgwick focuses on the bodily performance of shame as she develops her own theory of performativity, to argue that shame can be productive of a kind of identity, perhaps even a queer identity: "Shame is the affect that mantles the threshold between introversion and extroversion, between absorption and theatricality, between performativity and—performativity." "Shame and Performativity," 213. See also Sedgwick and Frank, "Shame in the Cybernetic Fold."

92. My thanks to Emily Steiner, for her response to a paper given at the University of Pennsylvania in December 2005.

93. Edward's long affair with Alice Perrers is rarely mentioned in the critical literature about the Garter, but its legacy of gossip may be an important aspect of both the popularity

of and the resistance to this story. The affair began much later than the period of the Order's foundation, but there was much hostility over Alice's perceived influence over the King.

94. Jaeger, "L'Amour des rois." "L'aura du corps du roi dessine un cercle magique. Le fait de pénétrer dans ce cercle, comme celui de se retrouver en présence d'un dieu et de participer soudain de la divinité, a un effet d'enchantement" (553). The Garter is one such example where private and intimate acts lose their power to embarrass, once they are rewritten as deeds of ennobling chivalric import. The king puts the Garter "comme par magie dans la sphère de l'invulnérabilité qui lui est réservée, où le vulgaire, l'obscène et l'illicite ne sont qu'illusions et où tout est noble et digne de vénération; du même coup, il les sauve" (563).

95. Jaeger, *Ennobling Love*, 140–41.

96. Crane, *The Performance of Self*, 138–39.

97. At this tournament the King's party were all blazoned with the white harts, with "cronne3" around their necks, and chains of gold hanging thereon, "and the cronne hang-yng lowe before the hertis bodye, the which hert was the kyngis liverey, that he gaf to knyghtis and squiers and othir." "And atte firste comyng to thair justis, xxiiij. Ladie3 ladded xxiiij.kny3tis of the gartir, with cheyne3 of gold, and alle in the same sute of hertis as before is said, fro the tour of Londound, on horsbak, thorou3 the cite of Londoun in to Smyth-feld." Davies, ed., *An English Chronicle of the Reigns of Richard II, Henry IV, Henry V, and Henry VI*, 6. Anthony Wagner, Nicolas Barker, and Ann Payne offer several other examples in *Medieval Pageant*, 15–16: a tournament in Valenciennes in 1330; the Espinette feasts at Lille; and Edward III's appearance in such a procession to a tournament in Cheapside in 1331, in which the knights were dressed as Tartars, and were led by ladies with silver chains. These chains leave a heraldic legacy, too, in the silken cords (similar to the cords that hold the heraldic mantle in place) or the chains that tie knights and ladies together in the Earl-dom of Salisbury Roll, as illustrated in the same volume.

98. This last suggestion is relatively oblique, however, in contrast to the more obvi-ously embodied carnivalesque or grotesque body, or the incontinent or humoral bodies discussed by Gail Kern Paster in *The Body Embarrassed*.

99. Turner, *The Ritual Process*, 97.

100. Ibid., 102.

101. English, "Oh, what a knight! Harry and Kate have a laugh at Wills in his robes as he joins ancient Order of the Garter."

102. From the *Daily Telegraph* website (http://www.telegraph.co.uk/news/2140279/Prince-William-Order-of-the-Garter.html), accessed February 5, 2009.

103. Andersen, "The Emperor's New Suit," 21.

104. Martorell and de Galba, *Tirant lo Blanc*, 283.

105. Ashmole, *Institution*, 180–81.

106. I owe these insights to the perceptive comments of Lynn Arner.

107. Lévi-Strauss, *The Savage Mind*, 17.

108. Ibid., 21–22.

109. Muir, *Ritual in Early Modern Europe*, 4.
110. Collins, *Order of the Garter*, 12.

CHAPTER 3. HISTORIES

1. Eco, "Dreaming of the Middle Ages," 68.
2. Federico and Scala, "Introduction," 4.
3. Holsinger, *The Pre-Modern Condition*, 47.
4. Most notably, see Simpson, *Reform and Cultural Revolution*.
5. See Cohen, *Medieval Identity Machines*; and Dinshaw, "Are We Having Fun Yet?" and "Temporalities."
6. Barber, *Edward, Prince of Wales*, 85, translating Vergil, *Polydori Vergili Historiae anglicanae*.
7. British Library MS Royal 18.c.viii, ix, *The Cronicle of Polydore Vergil*, fol. 193r. Parts of this translation were edited by Henry Ellis for the Camden Society in 1845 and 1846, but not the sections covering the reign of Edward III. The British Library Catalogue describes "the minute hands of the third quarter of the sixteenth century." See also the slightly different transcription in Nicolas, "Observations," 131.
8. Segar, *The Booke of Honor and Armes*, the Fifth Book, 15–16.
9. Ashmole, *Institution*, 179–80. See also Joshua Barnes's comments below about the Garter myth "as vulgarly given."
10. Waddington, "Elizabeth I and the Order of the Garter," 109. Waddington distances himself from this courtly medievalism but offers no evidence in support of the "probably more genuine origination" of the Garter.
11. Holinshed, *Holinshed's Chronicles of England, Scotland and Ireland*, introduction by Snow. William Camden also cites this motto in his *Britannia*.
12. Vaenius, *Amorum emblemata*, introduction by Porteman, 64–65. The text was published in three polyglot versions: the Latin, English, and Italian version was dedicated to William Herbert, third Earl of Pembroke, and his brother, Philip Herbert, Earl of Montgomery.
13. Burton, *Anatomy of Melancholy*, ed. Faulkner, Kiessling, and Blair, vol. III, 192–93.
14. Puttenham, *The Arte of English Poesie*, ed. Willcock and Walker, book 2, chapter XI, 103–4.
15. *The Cronicle of Polydore Virgil*, British Library MS Royal 18.C.viii, ix, fol. 193r.
16. Peele, *The Honour of the Garter*. In the details of its procession and ceremonial, Peele's poem echoes some of the sixteenth-century accounts of processions and feasts, as, for example, the accounts of St. George's Day festivities at Windsor in the early reign of Henry VIII, in the Earl of Arundel's manuscript printed in Anstis, *Institution*, Editor's Appendix, vol. 2, xi–26.
17. "Dautant qu'Edoüard estant feru de l'Amour de la Belle Alix Comtesse de Sarisbery, un Jour devisant avec elle, la Iartiere Gauche (de Soye Bleuë) de ceste Dame estant

tombee sur son Patin, Edoüard prompt à servir sa Dame & la relever, leva quant & quant la Chemise si haut, que les Courtisans l'ayans veuë, ne se peurent tenir de rire." Favyn, *Le Theatre d'Honneur et de Chevalerie ou L'Histoire des Ordres Militaires*, 1039–40. Favyn's account is taken almost verbatim from his earlier work, *Histoire de Navarre, Contenant l'Origine, les Vies & conquestes de ses Roys, depuis leur commencement iusques à present* (Paris, 1612), 463.

18. Andrew Favin, *The Theatre of Honour and Knighthood* (London, 1623), 68.

19. Johnson, "A Gallant Song of the Garter of England."

20. E.R.M., *The Countess of Salisbury*, 253–54.

21. *Wilson's Tales of the Borders and of Scotland: Historical, Traditional and Imaginative*, rev. Leighton, vol. VII, 279.

22. Anstis, *Register*, vol. II, 24–25.

23. Ferne, *The Blazon of Gentrie*, 120.

24. See, for example, Matikkala, *The Orders of Knighthood*, 196.

25. Ibid., 313.

26. I am very grateful to Stephen Szabo for his advice on this trivet.

27. BL MS Royal 20A.IV.

28. According to Anstis, *Register*, II, 24.

29. Nichols, ed., *The Progresses, Processions, and Magnificent Festivities, of King James the First.*

30. Selden, *Titles of Honour*, part 2, chapter 5, section 40, 793.

31. Heylyn, *The History of St. George*, part 3, chapter 2, 323–24.

32. Camden, *Britain, or A chorographicall description of the most flourishing kingdomes, England, Scotland, and Ireland, and the ilands adjoyning, out of the dept of antiquitie*, trans. Holland, 278.

33. Ferne, *The Blazon of Gentrie*, 120–21.

34. Segar, *Honor Military and Ciuill*, 66.

35. Drayton, *Poly-Olbion*, ed. Hebel, 312.

36. Richard Helgerson nevertheless argues that Drayton's poem signals an important shift from the earlier Elizabethan chorographic tradition represented by Camden, in celebration of the monarch, to a celebration of "the land's revelation of itself," *Forms of Nationhood*, 145.

37. Allen, *The Battailes of Crescey and Poictiers.*

38. O Hehir, *Expans'd Hieroglyphicks*, lines 101–6, 116–17.

39. O Hehir discusses the relation between Heylyn's commentary and Denham's poem, and some of the changes Denham made after the execution of the King, 187–88, 234–35.

40. Heylyn, *Cosmographie*, 321–22. See also his *History of St. George*, 6–7.

41. J. N., *A Perfect Catalogue of all the Knights of the Most Noble Order of the Garter*, 4; Dawson, *Memoirs*, 32.

42. Ashmole, *Institution*, 181.

43. Ibid., 179.

44. Ibid., 180.

45. Ibid., 182.

46. Ibid., 182–83.

47. Barnes, *The History of Edward III*. The chapter summary for book I, chapter 19 tells how the King's love for the Countess will be "exploded," and the summary for book I, chapter 22 promises a similar demolition of the Garter myth: "The said Order is here enquired into, its Original as vulgarly given exploded, and one more Antient and Mystical asserted" (prefatory pages unnumbered).

48. Ibid., 293. The reference is to Du Chesne, *Histoire d'Angleterre, D'Ecosse, et D'Irlonde*, vol. I, 670.

49. Dawson, *Memoirs*, 30.

50. Barnes, *History*, 294.

51. Ibid.

52. Anstis, *Register*, vol. I, 62. Anstis also alludes to the theory of Micheli Marquez in his *Tesoro Militar de Cavalleria*, that the Order was "erected to the Memory of one *Periscelide*, a true fairy Queen," vol. I, 62.

53. Fradenburg, "The Wife of Bath's Passing Fancy."

54. Begent and Chesshyre, *Order of the Garter*, 15, quoting Anstis, *Register*, vol. I, 122.

55. Begent and Chesshyre, *Order of the Garter*, 15.

56. Collins, *Order of the Garter*, 12.

57. De Burgh, "The Most Noble Order of the Garter," 43.

58. Guynn, "Historicizing Shame, Shaming History," 112.

CHAPTER 4. HONOR, SHAME, AND DEGRADATION

1. Malory, *The Works of Sir Thomas Malory*, ed. Vinaver, rev. Field, vol. 1, 305. All references to Malory are taken from this edition.

2. Matikkala gives a number of examples of seventeenth- and eighteenth-century individuals who voiced their desire for the Garter in various ways, and expressed disappointment if they were rejected, *The Orders of Knighthood*, 126–29. He also cites a letter from the fourth Earl of Chesterfield, ambassador to The Hague, who wrote in 1729: "It is universally believed here that I am to have one of the vacant Garters . . . it will not be very advantageous for me here to fail of it," 136.

3. All quotations are taken from Tolkien and Gordon, eds., *Sir Gawain and the Green Knight*.

4. Lambert, *Malory*, 179–94.

5. Lynch, *Malory's Book of Arms*, 12.

6. Probyn, *Blush*, 53.

7. Kilborne, "The Disappearing Who," 39. The critical literature on shame is immense, but is principally poised between sociological and philosophical or psychological approaches.

8. See, for example, Miller, "Displaced Souls, Idle Talk, Spectacular Scenes," 632: "In

experiencing shame, we feel that we have fallen short of who we might expect ourselves to be, and the ethical impulse shame prompts is less that of the submission to punishment or the restitution of wrongs than that of an effort to change who we are."

9. For the performative quality of court life in this period, the two most useful studies are Crane, *The Performance of Self,* and Greenblatt, *Renaissance Self-Fashioning.*

10. Crane, *The Performance of Self,* 4.

11. Begent and Chesshyre, *Order of the Garter,* 269.

12. Ibid., 62. This provision appears "sporadically" in texts dating from the reign of Henry VIII, and in all texts from Edward VI's early reign, but then disappears from the tradition.

13. Lachaud, "Dress and Social Status in England Before the Sumptuary Laws," 115. The register of John Peckham, archbishop of Canterbury, also specifies Giffard should lose his "coloured clothes," though as Lachaud comments, these were not restricted to knights.

14. Fionn Pilbrow discusses the account in Warkworth's chronicle, in "The Knights of the Bath," 206. See also Keen, *Chivalry,* 175–76.

15. Keen, *Chivalry,* 175.

16. Wagner, Barker, and Payne, eds., *Medieval Pageant,* plate 18.

17. Anstis, *Observations introductory,* 104–5. Anstis is translating from the French manuscript, British Library MS Cotton Nero C.9.ii, fols. 168v–170v, "The maner of makynge Knyghtes aftyr the Custome of Engelonde." See also Wagner, Barker, and Payne, *Medieval Pageant,* 74.

18. Martorell, trans. Rosenthal, *Tirant lo Blanc,* Chapter XC, 124, and Chapter XCII, 126.

19. Segar, *The Booke of Honor,* book 5, 10–11.

20. Begent and Chesshyre, *Order of the Garter,* 123.

21. Ashmole, *Institution,* 621.

22. Strong, *The Cult of Elizabeth,* 174. *Acts of the Privy Council of England,* 180.

23. In the official guide for Garter Day 2001, we read: "(And technically The Sovereign can demote a Knight by instructing Black Rod to tap him on the shoulder with it)," *The Most Noble Order of the Garter: Garter Day, 2001.*

24. Ashmole, *Institution,* 621.

25. Begent and Chesshyre, *Order of the Garter,* 271–72; Ashmole, *Institution,* 622.

26. Ashmole, *Institution,* 622. This is how Edward VI recorded the event in his journal, in April 1552: "The lord Paget was disgraded from the order of the Garter for divers his offences, and chiefly bicause he was no gentleman of bloud, neither of father's side nor mother's side." Nichols, ed., *Literary Remains of Edward VI,* 410.

27. Paul Hammer, in e-mail correspondence (January 15, 2011), citing Masham's testimony, in State Papers 12, Domestic, Elizabeth I: 12/278/45, fol. 63v.

28. Anstis, *Register,* vol. II, 417.

29. Ashmole, *Institution,* 623.

30. Anstis, *Register,* vol. II, 441.

31. Matikkala, *The Orders of Knighthood,* 63.

32. Boulton, *Knights of the Crown*, 137–38.

33. Anstis, *Register*, vol. II, 185.

34. Begent and Chesshyre, *Order of the Garter*, 59.

35. Anstis, *Register*, vol. II, 185.

36. Begent and Chesshyre, *Order of the Garter*, 220–21.

37. Ibid., 187.

38. Boulton, *Knights of the Crown*, 138.

39. Anstis, *Register*, vol. II, 199.

40. Ibid., vol. II, vi.

41. The Aberdeen Bestiary, Aberdeen University Library MS 24, fol. 51r (http://www.abdn.ac.uk/bestiary/translat/51r.hti), accessed August 27, 2009.

42. Wheatley, *Mastering Aesop*, 85–86.

43. Anstis, *Register*, vol. I, 74–5. Anstis also remarks upon his own pleasure to find Galhard behaved honorably in his resignation of the Order: "The Editor must own that 'tis some Satisfaction to him, that this Renunciation or Resignation of the Order is thus expresly registred, which hee judged very probable from the honourable Conduct and Character of that noble Gascoigner in other Particulars," vol. II, vi.

44. Shakespeare, *The First Part of King Henry VI*, ed. Cairncross, 4.1.13–17. All subsequent quotations from this edition.

45. Compare also Queen Elizabeth's rebuke to the King in *Richard III*, 4.6.366–73.

46. Léon Daudet, "The Punishment," *Le Figaro*, January 6, 1895, in Burns, *France and the Dreyfus Affair*, 52. The officer who performs the ritual is called the executioner, but after this degradation, Dreyfus was returned to prison.

47. Keen, *Chivalry*, 176.

48. Fernie, *Shame in Shakespeare*, 24.

49. Ibid., 29.

50. Ibid., 12. Fernie here seems to be drawing on the more modulated distinction between public, institutionalized shame and private, internalized guilt offered by Bernard Williams in *Shame and Necessity*. See also Mark Miller's thoughtful review of Williams.

51. Fernie, *Shame in Shakespeare*, 42.

52. Ibid., 1.

53. Ibid., 54.

54. Walker, *Writing Under Tyranny*, 245–46.

55. Strong, *The Cult of Elizabeth*, 172.

56. Begent and Chesshyre, *Order of the Garter*, 221–22.

57. Strong, *The Cult of Elizabeth*, 173.

58. McCoy, *The Rites of Knighthood*, 19.

59. Pepys, *Diary*, vol. 8, ed. Latham and Matthews, 184–85. See also Mansfield, *Ceremonial Costume*.

60. Begent and Chesshyre, *Order of the Garter*, 172, 275.

61. Ibid., 173.

62. Rose, *The Later Cecils*, 1.

63. "Claim Royals snubbing Sir Ed dismissed," *TVNZ*, January 19, 2008.

64. For a meditation on this process, and a partial, very discreet recollection of returning the insignia of his father, Sir Paul Hasluck, see Hasluck, "The Garter Box Goes Back to England."

65. Samuel Johnson, *The Lives of the Most Eminent English Poets* ed. Lonsdale, vol. 4, 119.

66. Butler and Savage, "The Masques: Stage History" (forthcoming).

67. Garrick, *The Songs, Choruses, and Serious Dialogue of the Masque called The Institution of the Garter, or, Arthur's Round Table restored*, 9.

68. Treharne, *Old and Middle English*, 328–29.

69. *An Authentic Account of the Installation of the Knights of the Garter, at Windsor, April 23, 1805*, 24–25. See also Matikkala, *The Orders of Knighthood*, for several accounts of Garter feasts in the seventeenth and eighteenth centuries.

70. Matikkala, *The Orders of Knighthood*, 205.

71. Ibid., 297.

72. The motto was also used, more obviously, as an alternative title for the ballet *Edouard III* in the season of 1804–5.

73. Words by Richard Carle, music by Alfred E. Aarons, in *Latest Compositions by Popular Writers*.

74. Pagan, "To Mollie—A Flirt," 3.

CHAPTER 5. RITUAL, CHANGE, AND TRADITION

1. Hughes, *Arthurian Myths and Alchemy*, 176.

2. *The Most Noble Order of the Garter: Garter Day 2004*, n.p.

3. Begent, *The Most Noble Order of the Garter*.

4. Begent and Chesshyre, *Order of the Garter*, 76.

5. Ibid., 73, 74.

6. Hobsbawm and Ranger, eds., *The Invention of Tradition*, "Introduction: Inventing Traditions," by Hobsbawm, 1.

7. Cannadine, "The British Monarchy," 108, 133–38.

8. Matikkala, *The Orders of Knighthood*, 65.

9. Ibid., 296, quoting Martin Leake's critique of John Anstis Junior's management of the Garter ceremonies between 1744 and 1754.

10. Evans, "St George's Chapel," 363.

11. Ashmole, *Institution*, Preface (n.p.).

12. Bond, ed., *Inventories*, 2.

13. Ibid., 2–3.

14. Compare the similar cases recounted by Duffy, *The Stripping of the Altars*, 480–87. "In many parishes such sales were absolutely necessary to meet financial crises precipitated by the government's religious reforms," 485.

15. Bond, *Inventories*, 19.

16. Ashmole, *Institution*, 474.

17. Adamson, "Chivalry and Political Culture," 161–97.

18. Evans, "St George's Chapel," 360.

19. Jardine, *On a Grander Scale*, 33. This loss "remained a permanent source of remorse for those who had been present in St George's Chapel . . . , and who had pledged to keep these treasures safe in the dead King's memory. The items were worth a king's ransom, and if recovered would have solved the financial problems of any of those royalists impoverished by the civil wars." Ashmole quotes the Inventory of King Gustav's Garter, signed by Dr. Christopher Wren, which details how many diamonds were used to spell each letter of the motto and in the buckle (88) and hinge (12), *Institution*, 203–4.

20. Evans, "St George's Chapel," 360.

21. Ashmole, *Institution*, 136.

22. Sherwood, *Oliver Cromwell*, 61–63.

23. British Library MS Cotton Nero C.x, fol.12r.

24. Fumerton, *Cultural Aesthetics*, 4, quoting Sir Thomas Herbert, *Threnodia Carolina; or, Sir Thomas Herbert's Memoirs,* ed. Allan Fea (London: John Lane, The Bodley Head, 1905), 139.

25. Ashmole, *Institutions*, 204.

26. Jardine comments, "King Charles seem to have regarded the charmed, ceremonial Order of the Garter as his secret military weapon," *On a Grander Scale*, 40. See also Matikkala, *The Orders of Knighthood*, 62–63.

27. Matikkala, *The Orders of Knighthood*, 63.

28. Jardine, *On a Grander Scale*, 44.

29. Begent and Chesshyre, *Order of the Garter*, 119.

30. Ibid.

31. Ibid., 262.

32. Ashmole, *Institution*, 616; see also Hazard, "Absent Presence and Present Absence," 12.

33. Begent and Chesshyre, *Order of the Garter*, 137.

34. Ibid., 137.

35. Ibid., 139.

36. Ibid.

37. See, for example, Anstis's substantial *Supplement to Mr. Ashmole's History Touching Garter King of Arms,* in *Register*, vol. I, 279–488.

38. Thorndike, *Children of the Garter*, 52.

39. Begent and Chesshyre, *Order of the Garter*, 62.

40. Ibid., 62.

41. Ibid., 52.

42. Ibid., 66.

43. Ibid., 68–69.

44. MacCulloch, *Tudor Church Militant*, 31.

45. Ibid., 32.

46. Thompson, "The Revision of the Statutes," 176; and King, *Tudor Royal Iconography*, 98–101.

47. British Library MS Cotton Nero C.x, fol. 98. See Thompson, "The Revision of the Statutes," 179.

48. Thompson, "The Revision of the Statutes," 184, quoting the Windsor MS version. This manuscript belonged to John Anstis, Garter King of Arms from 1718 to 1745; it is now held in the Royal Library at Windsor.

49. Ibid., 184, 186.

50. British Library MS Cotton Nero C.x.13, fol. 98r.

51. Ibid., fol. 102r.

52. MacCulloch, *Tudor Church Militant*, 34.

53. Hoccleve, "Balade au très honourable compaignie du garter," in *Hoccleve's Works: The Minor Poems*, ed. Furnivall and Gollancz, vol. I, 41–43.

54. MacCulloch, *Tudor Church Militant*, 32.

55. British Library MS Cotton Nero C x.13, fol. 98r.

56. Thompson, "The Revision of the Statutes," 180.

57. Erasmus, *Praise of Folly*, trans. Radice, 126, 135–36.

58. Gardiner, *The Letters of Stephen Gardiner*, ed. Muller, 258.

59. Ibid., 260–61.

60. Ibid., 260.

61. Foxe, *Acts and Monuments*, ed. Reed Cattley, vol. 6, 351–52.

62. McClendon, "A Moveable Feast," 4, 7.

63. Bengston, "Saint George," 319.

64. McClendon, "A Moveable Feast," 8. Bob Stewart comments that the saint's day coincided with the final day of the May ceremonies: *Where Is Saint George?* 66. Some of the indications are a little contradictory, however, as the dragon St. George slays was also associated allegorically with the devil, heresy, and paganism, and the maiden with the church (Bengston, "Saint George," 319).

65. Bengston, "Saint George," 331–32.

66. "The King's Injunctions, restricting the number of holy days," in *Acts and Monuments*, vol. 5, 164–65, quoted in Cressy, *Bonfires and Bells*, 4–5.

67. Cressy, *Bonfires and Bells*, 7.

68. Ibid., 21, quoting Galloway, ed., *Records of Early English Drama*, 163, 178, 195. See also Bengston, "Saint George," 332. Norwich Castle Museum has three versions of the dragon, known as "Snap," one of which dates from the eighteenth century, http://www.dragonglow.co.uk/snap.htm (accessed October 26, 2009).

69. Thompson, "The Revision of the Statutes," 180.

70. Simpson, "The Rule of Medieval Imagination," 12–13.

71. Strong, *The Cult of Elizabeth*, 166.

72. *Liber Ceruleus* (Garter Register, in custody of dean of Windsor) 53, quoted in Ashmole, *Institution*, 195.

73. Ibid., 195.

74. Strong, *The Cult of Elizabeth*, 167, 168.

75. Ibid., 168. At a micro level, these reversals of policy are also played out in the mid-century records of St. George's Chapel, which alternate feverishly between "altar" and "table."

76. William Fennor, "The Originall and Continuance of the Most Noble Order of the Garter, as it was Spoken before the King's Majestie on Saint George's Day Last, anno domn. 1616," in Nichols, ed., *The Progresses, Processions, and Magnificent Festivities, of King James the First* , vol. 3, 155–56.

77. *Liber Ceruleus* 173, quoted in Ashmole, *Institution*, 195.

78. Ibid., 195.

79. Jardine, *On a Grander Scale*, 36.

80. Ashmole, *Institution*, 198.

81. Matikkala, *The Orders of Knighthood*, 262–64.

82. Ibid., 43–46.

83. Gillespie, "Ladies of the Fraternity," 259–78.

84. Ibid., 263, n. 17.

85. Ashmole, *Institution*, 218. Gillespie also comments, "That there is no record at all of the distribution of robes to the countess of Tancarville who died in 1425 and whose tomb effigy bore a Garter is an indication and a warning of the imperfect nature of the surviving evidence concerning the Ladies of the Garter," "Ladies of the Fraternity," 271.

86. Holmes, *Order of the Garter*, 174.

87. Collins, *Order of the Garter*, 301–3.

88. Begent and Chesshyre, *Order of the Garter*, 100–104.

89. Matikkala, *The Orders of Knighthood,*141, 148–49.

90. Norris and Curtis, *Nineteenth-Century Costume and Fashion*, 242.

91. Pepys, *Diary*, ed. Latham and Matthews, February 26, 1666.

92. Collins, *Order of the Garter*, 79–80.

93. McDonald, "Chaucer's *Legend of Good Women*."

94. Collins, *Order of the Garter*, 214; Barker, *Tournament in England*, 109; Keen, *Chivalry*, 212.

95. British Library MS Cotton Julius 12, fol. 46, from Gillespie, "Ladies of the Fraternity," 275. A complete text is printed by Anstis, *Register*, vol. II, 226.

96. Gillespie, "Ladies of the Fraternity," 268.

97. Ashmole, *Institution*, 218; Gillespie, "Ladies of the Fraternity," 276–78; Matikkala, *The Orders of Knighthood*, 66–67.

98. Begent and Chesshyre, *Order of the Garter*, 103.

99. Ibid.

100. Ibid., 75.

101. "It was not always thus," comments Waddington, "Elizabeth I and the Order of the Garter," 97 (footnote: commenting on UPI wire service story).

CHAPTER 6. BODIES, CLOTHES, AND MEDIEVALISM

Note to epigraph: Beerbohm, *Zuleika Dobson,* 30.

1. Begent and Chesshyre, *Order of the Garter,* 201.

2. Ibid., 159. The fine was affirmed in the statutes revised under Henry V.

3. Gardiner and Bond, *The Story of St George's Chapel,* 4. Other examples, kindly supplied by David Studham, are a painting by Elizabeth Peyton from the year 2000 and a French cigarette card from 1898, advertising *Extrait de Viande Liebig,* both offered for sale on eBay in November 2009.

4. Marshall, *An Island Story,* 280.

5. British Library MS Cotton Julius E.iv art. 6, fol.4v, was produced in the Low Countries, possibly Bruges, after 1483.

6. Kantorowicz, *The King's Two Bodies.*

7. Waddington, "Elizabeth I and the Order of the Garter," 103, citing Loades, *The Reign of Mary Tudor,* 139; Ashmole, *Institution,* 291.

8. Hazard, "Absent Presence and Present Absence," 9.

9. Ibid.

10. Ashmole, *Institution,* 571.

11. Hazard, "Absent Presence and Present Absence," 11. Hazard comments that another motivation might have been expense: if the Queen sent a lieutenant, he had to pay the bill for the feast, ceremonies, and accompanying gifts.

12. Waddington, "Elizabeth I and the Order of the Garter," 100.

13. Ibid., 100–101.

14. Ibid., 101–3.

15. Ashmole, *Institution,* 301.

16. Strong, *The Cult of Elizabeth,* 35, referring to the accounts of this feast in the transcription of the *Liber Ceruleus* in the British Library, Additional MS 36768, fols. 32–32v; Additional MS 6298, fol. 88, Harleian MS 304, fol. 168.

17. Levin, " 'Would I Could Give You Help and Succour,' " 201.

18. Ibid., 194–95.

19. Hayden, *Symbol and Privilege,* 20.

20. In her reading of Charles I's Garter jewel, Patricia Fumerton remarks: "The artifacts and ornaments that encrust the surface of history are at once peripheral and strangely central." *Cultural Aesthetics,* 21.

21. Woolf, *Orlando,* ed. Bowlby, 24–25.

22. Dinshaw, *Getting Medieval.*

23. Cf. Matikkala, *The Orders of Knighthood,* 207.

24. Rizzo, "Equivocations of Gender and Rank," 79, quoting Horace Walpole, *The Yale Edition of Horace Walpole's Correspondence,* ed. W. S. Lewis, 48 vols. (New Haven: Yale University Press, 1937–83), vol. 31, 268.

25. Taylor, "The Great Actors of England in 1775," 257. Zanerini was painted by Thomas Gainsborough, and by Sir Joshua Reynolds as a Bacchante.

26. Knighton, *Chronicon Henrici Knighton vel Cnitthon Monachi Leycestrensis*, ed. Joseph Rawson Lumby (London: Eyre and Spottiswoode, 1895), vol. 2, 58, trans. Barber, *The Black Prince*, 94.

27. Holmes, *Scanty Particulars*, 318.

28. Ibid., 53.

29. Ibid., 84.

30. See the *Guide to St. Mary's Church, Ewelme and to the Almshouse and the School* (anonymous pamphlet, no author, no date), 13.

31. See also the engraving in Anstis, *Register*, vol. I, opposite p. 126.

32. Begent and Chesshyre, *Order of the Garter*, 160.

33. William Teshe, "Verses on the Order of the Garter," in *Ballads from Manuscripts*, ed. W. R. Morfill (Ballad Society, 1873; New York: AMS Press, 1968), vol. 2, 115–29.

34. College of Arms Manuscript L.18, fols. 34r–34v.

35. The portrait of Queen Anne by Godfrey Kneller shows Anne wearing the lesser George and the Garter star (see Matikkala, *The Orders of Knighthood*, 325). See also Beltz, *Memorials*, cxxi.

36. Norris and Curtis, *Nineteenth-Century Costume and Fashion*, 100.

37. See Sweet, *Inventing the Victorians*, for a vigorous debunking of cherished notions of Victorian prudery, especially as regards the legs of pianos, ix–xv.

38. "Honi Soit Qui Mal Y Pense," (BM Prints and Drawings: 1868, 0808.9527).

39. Begent and Chessyre, *Order of the Garter*, 158.

40. Plunkett, *Queen Victoria*, 84.

41. British Library, Royal MS 20 BVI, fol. 2. See Scott, *Medieval Dress and Fashion*, 118.

42. Nicolas, "Observations," 40, 121, 160

43. British Library MS Additional 18850, fol. 256v. For a discussion of this image, see Bengtson, "Saint George," 328–30.

44. Thirsk, "The Fantastical Folly of Fashion," 53–54.

45. Available at http://www.marileecody.com/henry8/henry78holbeinsketch.jpg (accessed August 11, 2011).

46. Wardle, "The King's Embroiderer," 152.

47. For further discussion of Charles I and his renewal of the Garter, see Adamson, "Chivalry and Political Culture," 174.

48. The Garter regalia were similarly displayed in this fashion during the lying-in-state of the Queen Mother in Westminster Hall in 2002.

49. Wardle, "The King's Embroiderer," 153.

50. See, for example, Jefferson, "Gifts Given and Fees Paid."

51. Jardine, *On a Grander Scale*, 23. See also Fumerton, *Cultural Aesthetics*, 8, 19–21, and Matikkala, *The Orders of Knighthood*, 306.

52. Windsor Castle, MS X.21.F.9 (this is the version signed by the King himself).

53. Begent and Chesshyre, *Order of the Garter*, 153–55.

54. Beerbohm, *Zuleika Dobson*, 35.

55. Ibid., 27. Some editions read "aspect" for "respect" here.

56. Ibid., 30.

57. Ibid., 176.

58. Ibid., 176–77.

59. Moers, *The Dandy*, 327.

60. Beerbohm, "Dandies and Dandies," in *The Incomparable Max*, ed. Roberts, 22.

61. Hogarth, *The Analysis of Beauty*, ed. Paulson, fig. 49; plate 1, 139.

62. Wilde, *The Picture of Dorian Gray*, 10–11.

63. Stephenson and Sullivan, *The Zoo*, 13.

64. Ibid., 21.

65. At http://mrffriends.tripod.com/garter/garter.html (accessed November 17, 2009).

66. Guest, *Empire, Barbarism and Civilisation*, 89.

67. Dickens, *The Old Curiosity Shop*, ed. Brennan, 258.

CHAPTER 7. ROYALTY AND MEDIEVALISM, MEDIEVAL TO POSTMODERN

1. See also Jones and Stallybrass, "Of Busks and Bodies."

2. Woolf, *Three Guineas*, ed. Shiach, 177.

3. Ibid., 178.

4. Cannadine, "The British Monarchy," 117.

5. Cannadine, *Ornamentalism*, 95.

6. Osborne, "And They Call It Cricket," 26.

7. Ibid., 24–25.

8. Nairn, *The Enchanted Glass*, 120.

9. Baudrillard, *Simulations*, 1–13.

10. Elgood, "Long Goodbye for a Royal Favourite."

11. The relevant portion of this documentary can be viewed on YouTube, at http://www.youtube.com/watch?v=qhjeqpegvaq (accessed January 8, 2011).

12. "BBC Apologises over Queen Clips."

13. "Leibovitz: The Queen and I Did Not Fall Out in BBC 'Tantrum' Film."

14. Snowdon, *Snowdon: A Photographic Autobiography*, 14. In another picture, the parents were photographed leaning over a bridge in Buckingham Palace gardens, watching the children seated below, reading a book. Again the photograph seems to mark a new informality, yet Snowdon remarks that he based the photography on eighteenth-century romantic paintings.

15. Blumler, Brown, Ewbank, and Nossiter, "Attitudes to the Monarchy," 158.

16. Campbell, "The Australian Dream," in *Collected Poems*, ed. Kramer, 97–98.

17. Parrott and Harré, "Princess Diana and the Emotionality of Contemporary Britain."

18. Ibid., 37.

19. Ibid.

20. See Trigg, "Medievalism and Convergence Culture."

21. At http://www.youtube.com/watch?v=zr4vlmaez-e (accessed August 30, 2010).

22. Futrelle, *My Lady's Garter.*

23. McCausland, "Educated Louts," reprinted in *Honi Soit.* The same issue also re-prints, on the same page, an anonymous letter from 1930 complaining about the obscure name of the newspaper: "So far from thinking evil about those events, people have ceased to think about them at all, and your title has lost its meaning. . . . We await with interest the first humourist to identify the paper itself with the 'it' which ought to be disgraced." Six hundred years after Edward coined the motto, then, its elliptic referent continues to generate speculation.

Bibliography

MANUSCRIPTS

London, British Library, MS Add. 18850
London, British Library, MS Royal 18.C.viii, ix
London, British Library, MS Royal 20.A.iv
London, British Library, MS Royal 20.B.vi
London, British Library, MS Cotton Nero C.x
London, British Library, MS Cotton Julius E.iv
London, British Library, MS Harley 5415
London, British Library, MS Lansdowne 285
London, College of Arms, MS L.18
Melbourne. [J. J. Tierney]. "As Black Rod . . ." Typescript, Victorian Parliamentary Library, Australia, 1954.
Melbourne. Victorian State Parliament. "Victoria's First Black Rod." Undated pamphlet.
Windsor Castle, Manuscript X.21.F.9

PRINTED AND ONLINE MATERIALS

Acts of the Privy Council of England, new series, XXXI. 1906. Reprinted Nendeln: Kraus, 1974.
Adamson, J. S. A. "Chivalry and Political Culture in Caroline England." In *Culture and Politics in Early Stuart England,* edited by Kevin Sharpe and Peter Lake, 161–97. London: Macmillan, 1994.
Allen, Charles. *The Battailes of Crescey and Poictiers.* London, 1631.
Andersen, Hans Christian. *Stories and Fairy Tales.* Translated by H. Oskar Sommer. New York: Dodd, Mead, 1897.
Anstis, John. *Register of the Most Noble Order of the Garter.* London, 1724.
———. *Observations introductory to an historical essay, upon the Knighthood of the Bath.* London, 1725.
Ashmole, Elias. *The Institution, Laws & Ceremonies of the most Noble Order of the Garter.* London, 1672.

An Authentic Account of the Installation of the Knights of the Garter, at Windsor, April 23, 1805.
Strand: Kemmish, Printer, King-Street Borough, 1805.

Barber, Richard. *The Black Prince.* 1978; rpt Phoenix Mill: Sutton Publishing, 2003.

———. "The Round Table Feast of 1344." In *Edward III's Round Table at Windsor: The House of the Round Table and the Windsor Festival of 1344*, edited by Julian Munby, Richard Barber, and Richard Brown, 38–43. Arthurian Studies 68. Woodbridge, U.K.: Boydell, 2007.

Barker, Juliet R. V. *The Tournament in England 1100–1400.* Woodbridge, U.K.: Boydell, 1986.

Barnes, Joshua. *The History of that Most Victorious Monarch Edward III, King of England, France, and Lord of Ireland.* Cambridge, 1688.

Baudrillard, Jean. *Simulations.* Translated by Paul Foss, Paul Patton and Philip Beitchman. New York: Semiotext(e), 1983.

Baune, Colette. "Costume et pouvoir en France à la fin du Moyen Age: Les Devises royales vers 1400." *Revue des sciences humaines* n.s. 55 (1981): 125–46.

"BBC Apologises over Queen Clips." BBC online news, July 12, 2007. At http://news.bbc .co.uk/2/hi/entertainment/6294472.stm (accessed January 8, 2011).

Beerbohm, Max. *The Incomparable Max.* Edited by S. C. Roberts. 1962. Reprinted London: Icon Books, 1964.

———. *Zuleika Dobson.* 1911. Reprinted with introduction by Frances Hackett. New York: Random House, 1926.

Begent, Peter J. *The Most Noble Order of the Garter: Its History and Ceremonial.* Undated pamphlet. Windsor: Dean and Canons of Windsor.

Begent, Peter J., and Hubert Chesshyre. *The Most Noble Order of the Garter, 650 Years,* with a foreword by His Royal Highness the Duke of Edinburgh, KG, and a chapter on the statutes of the Order by Dr. Lisa Jefferson. London: Spink, 1999.

Bell, Catherine. *Ritual Theory, Ritual Practice.* New York: Oxford University Press, 1992.

Beltz, George. *Memorials of the Most Noble Order of the Garter, from Its Foundation to the Present Time.* London: William Pickering, 1841.

Belvaleti, Mondonus. *Belvaleti Catechismus Ordinis Equitum Persiscelidis Anglicanae seu Speculum Anglorum.* Cologne, 1631.

Bengston, Jonathan. "Saint George and the Formation of English Nationalism." *Journal of Medieval and Early Modern Studies* 27 (1997): 317–40.

Bentley, S. *Excerpta Historica, or Illustrations of English History.* London: Richard Bentley, 1831.

Blackledge, Catherine. *The Story of V: Opening Pandora's Box.* London: Weidenfeld and Nicolson, 2003.

Blumler, J. G., J. R. Brown, A. J. Ewbank, and T. J. Nossiter. "Attitudes to the Monarchy: Their Structure and Development During a Ceremonial Occasion." *Political Studies* 19 (1971): 149–71.

Bond, Maurice F., ed. *The Inventories of St. George's Chapel Windsor Castle, 1384–1667.* Historical Monographs Relating to Windsor Castle. Windsor: Dean and Canons of Windsor Castle, 1947.

Boulton, D'Arcy Jonathan Dacre. *Knights of the Crown: The Monarchical Orders of Knighthood in Later Medieval Europe 1325–1520*. Woodbridge, U.K.: Boydell, 1987.

Brown, Andrew. *The New Statesman*, October 3, 1998, 19.

Bucholz, R. O. " 'Nothing but Ceremony': Queen Anne and the Limitations of Royal Ritual." *Journal of British Studies* 30 (1991): 288–323.

Burke, Peter. *The Historical Anthropology of Early Modern Italy: Essays on Perception and Communication*. Cambridge: Cambridge University Press, 1987.

Burns, Michael. *France and the Dreyfus Affair: A Documentary History*. Boston: Bedford/St. Martin's, 1999.

Burton, Robert. *Anatomy of Melancholy*. Edited by Thomas C. Faulkner, Nicolas K. Kiessling, and Rhonda L. Blair. Oxford: Clarendon Press, 1994.

Butler, Martin, and Roger Savage. "The Masques: Stage History." In *The Cambridge Edition of the Works of Ben Jonson*, ed. David Bevington, Martin Butler and Ian Donaldson. Electronic edition forthcoming in 2013.

Camden, William. *Britain, or A chorographicall description of the most flourishing kingdomes, England, Scotland, and Ireland, and the ilands adjoyning, out of the dept of antiquitie*. Translated by Philémon Holland. Second edition. London, 1637.

Campbell, David. *Collected Poems*. Edited by Leonie Kramer. North Ryde, N.S.W: Angus and Robertson, 1989.

Cannadine, David. "The Context, Performance and Meaning of Ritual: The British Monarchy and the 'Invention of Tradition,' c. 1820–1977." In *The Invention of Tradition*, edited by E. J. Hobsbawm and Terence Ranger, 101–64. Cambridge: Cambridge University Press, 1983.

———. *Ornamentalism: How the British Saw Their Empire*. London: Allen Lane, 2001.

Carle, Richard. "Honi Soit Qui Mal Y Pense." Music by Alfred E. Aarons. In *Latest Compositions by Popular Writers*. London: M. Witmark and Sons, Chas. Sheard & Co., 1899.

Carruthers, Leo. "The Duke of Clarence and the Earls of March: Garter Knights and *Sir Gawain and the Green Knight*." *Medium Aevum* 70 (2001): 66–79.

———. "*Honi soit qui mal y pense*: The Countess of Salisbury and the 'slipt Garter.'" In *Surface et profondeur: Mélanges offerts à Guy Bourquin à l'occasion de son 75e anniversaire*, edited by Colette Stévanovitch and René Tixier, 227–33. Nancy: AMAES, 2003.

Chareyron, Nicole. "L'amour d'Edouard III d'Angleterre pour la comtesse de salisbury: Histoire, conte de fées ou tragédie?" *Revue de Littérature Comparée* 3 (1996): 341–56.

"Claim Royals Snubbing Sir Ed Dismissed." *TVNZ*, January 19, 2008. At http://tvnz.co.nz/view/page/423466/1549826 (accessed 21 June, 2008).

Cohen, Jeffrey J. *Medieval Identity Machines*. Minneapolis: University of Minnesota Press, 2003.

Cohen, Tim. *The Anti-Christ and a Cup of Tea*. N.p.: Prophecy House, 1998.

Collins, Hugh E. L. *The Order of the Garter, 1348–1461: Chivalry and Politics in Late Medieval England*. Oxford Historical Monographs. Oxford: Oxford University Press, 2000.

Colon, Germán. "Premiers echos de l'Ordre de la Jarretiére." *Zeitschrift für Romanische Philologie* 81 (1965): 441–53.

Cooke, W. G., and D'A. J. D. Boulton. "*Sir Gawain and the Green Knight:* A Poem for Henry of Grosmont?" *Medium Aevum* 68 (1999): 42–54.

Crane, Susan. *The Performance of Self: Ritual, Clothing, and Identity During the Hundred Years War.* Philadelphia: University of Pennsylvania Press, 2002.

Cressy, David. *Bonfires and Bells: National Memory and the Protestant Calendar in Elizabethan and Stuart England.* Berkeley: University of California Press, 1989.

Crowfoot, Elisabeth, Frances Pritchard, and Kay Staniland, *Textiles and Clothing, c. 1150–c. 1450.* 1993; revised ed. Woodbridge, U.K.: Boydell, 2001.

D'Arcens, Louise. "From 'Eccentric Affiliation' to 'Corrective Medievalism': Bruce Holsinger's *The Premodern Condition.*" *Postmedieval* 1. 3 (2010): 299–308.

Davies, The Rev. John Silvester, ed. *An English Chronicle of the Reigns of Richard II, Henry IV, Henry V, and Henry VI.* Camden Society, 1856.

Dawson, Thomas. *Memoirs of St George the English Patron; and of the Most Noble Order of the Garter.* London, 1714.

DeBurgh, A. "The Most Noble Order of the Garter." *Windsor Magazine* 39 (December 1908 to May 1909): 43–56, 43.

Dickens, Charles. *The Old Curiosity Shop.* Edited with an introduction by Elizabeth M. Brennan. Oxford: Oxford University Press, 1998.

Dictionnaire de l'Académie Française. Paris: Imprimérie Nationale, 1986.

Dinshaw, Carolyn. "Are We Having Fun Yet? A Response to Prendergast and Trigg." *New Medieval Literatures* 9 (2008): 231–41.

———. *Getting Medieval: Sexualities and Communities, Pre- and Postmodern.* Durham: Duke University Press, 1999.

———. "Temporalities." In *Twenty-First Century Approaches: Medieval,* edited by Paul Strohm, 107–23. Oxford: Oxford University Press, 2007.

Diski, Jenny. "It's So Beautiful." A review of Catherine Blackledge, *The Story of V, London Review of Books,* 20 November, 2003. At http://www.lrb.co.uk/v25/n22/disk01_.html (accessed 26 February 2009).

Drayton, Michael. *Poly-Olbion, being the Fourth Volume of his Works.* Edited by J. William Hebel. 1933. Corrected edition, Oxford: Shakespeare Head Press, Basil Blackwell, 1961.

Du Chesne, André. *Histoire d'Angleterre, D'Ecosse, et D'Irlonde, Contenant les Choses les plus Dignes de Memoire.* Paris, 1666.

Duffy, Eamon. *The Stripping of the Altars: Traditional Religion in England c. 1400–c.1580.* New Haven: Yale University Press, 1992.

E.R.M. *The Countess of Salisbury. To which is added The Maid of Corinth.* London: Richard Bentley, 1840.

Eco, Umberto. "Dreaming of the Middle Ages." In *Faith in Fakes: Essays,* 61–72. Translated by William Weaver. London: Secker and Warburg, 1986.

Elgood, Giles. "Long Goodbye for a Royal Favourite." *Sydney Morning Herald,* April 7, 2002. At http://www.smh.com.au/articles/2002/04/06/1017206279337.html (accessed January 8, 2011).

Eliade, Mircea. *Cosmos and History: The Myth of the Eternal Return.* New York: Garland, 1985.

English, Rebecca. "Oh, what a knight! Harry and Kate have a laugh at Wills in his robes as he joins ancient Order of the Garter." *Daily Mail,* June 17, 2008. At http://www.dailymail.co.uk/femail/article-1026847/Oh-knight-Harry-Kate-laugh-Wills-robes-joins-ancient-Order-Garter.html (accessed February 5, 2009).

Erasmus, Desiderius. *Praise of Folly.* Translated by Betty Radice, with introduction and notes by A. H. T. Levi. Harmondsworth: Penguin Books, 1971.

Evans, A. K. B. "St George's Chapel, Windsor, 1348–1975." *History Today* 25.5 (1975): 356–63.

Favin, Andrew. *The Theatre of Honour and Knighthood.* London, 1623,

Favyn, André. *Le Theatre d'Honneur et de Chevalerie ou L'Histoire des Ordres Militaires.* Paris, 1620.

Federico, Sylvia, and Elizabeth Scala. "Introduction: Getting Post-Historical." In *The Post-Historical Middle Ages,* ed. Sylvia Federico and Elizabeth Scala, 1–11. Basingstoke: Palgrave Macmillan, 2009.

Ferne, John. *The Blazon of Gentrie.* London, 1586.

Fernie, Ewan. *Shame in Shakespeare.* London: Routledge, 2002.

Fox-Davies, Arthur Charles. *A Complete Guide to Heraldry.* 1909; New York: Bonanza Books, 1978.

Foxe, John. *The Acts and Monuments of John Foxe.* Edited by Stephen Reed Cattley. London, 1838.

Fradenburg, Louise Olga. *City, Marriage, Tournament: Arts of Rule in Late Medieval Scotland.* Madison: University of Wisconsin Press, 1991.

———. "The Wife of Bath's Passing Fancy." *Studies in the Age of Chaucer* 8 (1986): 31–58.

Friedman, Albert B., and Richard H. Osberg. "Gawain's Girdle as Traditional Symbol." *Journal of American Folklore* 90 (1977): 301–15.

Fumerton, Patricia. *Cultural Aesthetics: Renaissance Literature and the Practice of Social Ornament.* Chicago: University of Chicago, 1991.

Futrelle, Jacques. *My Lady's Garter.* Illustrated by F. R. Gruger. Chicago: Rand McNally, 1912.

Galloway, David, ed. *Records of Early English Drama: Norwich 1540–1642.* Toronto: University of Toronto Press, 1984.

Galloway, Peter. *The Order of the Bath.* Chichester: Phillimore, 2006.

Galway, Margaret. "Joan of Kent and the Order of the Garter." *University of Birmingham Historical Journal* 1 (1947): 13–50.

Gardiner, Rena, and Maurice Bond. *The Story of St George's Chapel, Windsor Castle.* Windsor: Dean and Canons of Windsor, 1981.

Gardiner, Stephen. *The Letters of Stephen Gardiner.* Edited by James Arthur Muller. Cambridge: Cambridge University Press, 1933.

Garrick, David. *The Songs, Choruses, and Serious Dialogue of the Masque called The Institution of the Garter, or, Arthur's Round Table restored.* London, 1771.

Gillespie, James L. "Ladies of the Fraternity of Saint George and of the Society of the Garter." *Albion* 17.3 (1985): 259–78.

The Golden Garland of Princely Pleasures and Delicate Delights. London, 1620.

Gransden, Antonia. "The Alleged Rape by Edward III of the Countess of Salisbury." *English Historical Review* 87 (1972): 333–44.

Greenblatt, Stephen. *Renaissance Self-Fashioning: From More to Shakespeare*. Chicago: University of Chicago Press, 1980.

Grimes, Ronald L. *Ritual Criticism: Case Studies in Its Practice, Essays on Its Theory*. Columbia: University of South Carolina Press, 1990.

Guest, Harriet. *Empire, Barbarism and Civilisation: James Cook, William Hodges, and the Return to the Pacific*. Cambridge: Cambridge University Press, 2007.

Guide to St. Mary's Church, Ewelme and to the Almshouse and the School. Anonymous undated pamphlet.

Guynn, Noah D. "Historicizing Shame, Shaming History: Origination and Negativity in the *Eneas*." *L'Esprit Créateur* 39 (1999): 112–27.

Hasluck, Nicholas. *The Hasluck Banner*. Claremont, Australia: Freshwater Bay Press, 2003.

Hay, Denys. *Polydore Vergil: Renaissance Historian and Man of Letters*. Oxford: Clarendon Press, 1952.

Hayden, Ilse. *Symbol and Privilege: The Ritual Context of British Royalty*. Tucson: University of Arizona Press, 1987.

Haydock, Nickolas. *Movie Medievalism: The Imaginary Middle Ages*. Jefferson, N.C.: McFarland, 2008.

Hazard, Mary E. "Absent Presence and Present Absence: Cross-Couple Convention in Elizabethan Culture." *Texas Studies in Literature and Language* 29 (1987): 1–27.

Helgerson, Richard. *Forms of Nationhood: The Elizabethan Writing of England*. Chicago: University of Chicago Press, 1992.

Heng, Geraldine. "Feminine Knots and the Other: *Sir Gawain and the Green Knight*." *PMLA* 106 (1991): 500–14.

Heylyn, Peter. *Cosmographie*. London, 1652.

———. *The History of That Most Famous Saynt and Souldier of Christ Jesus St George of Cappadocia*. Second edition. London, 1633.

Histoire de Navarre, Contenant l'Origine, les Vies & conquestes de ses Roys, depuis leur commencement iusques a present. Paris, 1612.

Hobsbawm, E. J., and Terence Ranger, eds. *The Invention of Tradition*. Cambridge: Cambridge University Press, 1983.

Hoccleve, Thomas. *Hoccleve's Works*. Vol 1, *The Minor Poems*. Edited by F. J. Furnivall. Early English Text Society, Extra Series No. 61. London: Kegan Paul, Trench, Trübner, 1892.

Hogarth, William. *The Analysis of Beauty*. Edited with notes and introduction by Ronald Paulson. New Haven: Yale University Press, 1997.

Holinshed, Raphael. *Holinshed's Chronicles of England, Scotland and Ireland*. Introduced by Vernon F. Snow. Six volumes, 1807–8. New York: AMS Press, 1965, 1976.

Holmes, Grace. *The Order of the Garter: Its Knights and Stall Plates 1348–1984*. Historical Monographs Relating to St. George's Chapel 16. Windsor, 1984.

Holmes, Rachel. *Scanty Particulars: The Life of Dr James Barry*. London: Viking, 2002.

Holsinger, Bruce. *Neomedievalism, Neoconservatism, and the War on Terror*. Chicago: Prickly Paradigm Press, 2007.

———. *The Pre-Modern Condition: Medievalism and the Making of Theory*. Chicago: University of Chicago Press, 2005.

Hughes, Jonathan. *Arthurian Myths and Alchemy: The Kingship of Edward IV*. Stroud: Sutton, 2002.

Ingledew, Francis. *Sir Gawain and the Green Knight and the Order of the Garter*. Notre Dame: University of Notre Dame Press, 2006.

J.N. *A Perfect Catalogue of all the Knights of the Most Noble Order of the Garter*. London, 1661.

Jackson, Isaac. "Sir Gawain and the Green Knight Considered as a 'Garter' Poem." *Anglia* 37 (1913): 393–423.

Jaeger, C. Stephen. "L'Amour des rois: Structure sociale d'une forme de sensibilité aristocratique." *Annales: Economies, Sociétés, Civilisations* 46 (1991): 547–71.

———. *Ennobling Love: In Search of a Lost Sensibility*. Philadelphia: University of Pennsylvania Press, 1999.

James, Paul. *Globalism, Nationalism, Tribalism: Bringing Theory Back In*. Volume 2 of *Towards a Theory of Abstract Community*. London: Sage, 2006.

James, Paul, and Stephanie Trigg. "Rituals of Nationhood: Medievalism, Neo-Traditionalism and Republicanism." In *Medievalism and the Gothic in Australian Culture*, edited by Stephanie Trigg, 255–75. Making the Middle Ages 8. Turnhout: Brepols, 2005.

Jardine, Lisa. *On a Grander Scale: The Outstanding Career of Sir Christopher Wren*. London: HarperCollins, 2002.

Jefferson, Lisa. "Gifts Given and Fees Paid to Garter King of Arms at Installation Ceremonies of the Order of the Garter During the Sixteenth Century." *Costume* 36 (2002): 18–35.

———. "MS Arundel 48 and the Earliest Statutes of the Order of the Garter." *English Historical Review* 109 (1994): 356–85.

———. "Two Fifteenth-Century Manuscripts of the Statutes of the Order of the Garter." In *English Manuscript Studies 1100–1700*, vol. 5, edited by Peter Beal and Jeremy Griffiths, 18–35. London: British Library, 1995.

Jennings, Hargrave. *The Rosicrucian Origin of the Order of the Garter*. First published in 1870 as a chapter of *The Rosicrucians: Their Rites and Mysteries*, and reprinted as a single chapter by Kessinger Publishing, 2005.

Johnson, Samuel. *The Lives of the Most Eminent English Poets: With Critical Observations on Their Works*. Edited with an introduction and notes by Roger Lonsdale. Oxford: Oxford University Press, 2006.

Jones, Ann Rosalind, and Peter Stallybrass. "Of Busks and Bodies." In *The Forms of Renaissance Thought: New Essays in Literature and Culture*, 261–76. Basingstoke: Palgrave Macmillan, 2009.

Kafka, Franz. *Parables and Paradoxes*. New York: Schocken Books, 1975.

Kantorowicz, Ernst H. *The King's Two Bodies: A Study in Medieval Political Theology*. Princeton: Princeton University Press, 1957.

Karras, Ruth Mazo. *From Boys to Men: Formations of Masculinity in Late Medieval Europe.* Philadelphia: University of Pennsylvania Press, 2003.

Keen, Maurice. *Chivalry.* New Haven: Yale University Press, 1984.

———. "Introduction." In *Heraldry, Pageantry and Social Display in Medieval England,* edited by Peter Coss and Maurice Keen, 1–16. Woodbridge, U.K.: Boydell, 2002.

Kennedy, Maev. "Virgin Mary's Clue to Royal Order Mystery." *The Guardian,* November 23, 2002. At http://www.guardian.co.uk/uk/2002/nov/23/artsandhumanities.monarchy (accessed November 11, 2009).

Kertzer, David. *Ritual, Politics and Power.* New Haven: Yale University Press, 1988.

Kilborne, Benjamin. "The Disappearing Who: Kierkegaard, Shame, and the Self." In *Scenes of Shame: Psychoanalysis, Shame, and Writing,* edited by Joseph Adamson and Hilary Clark, 33–51. Albany: State University of New York Press, 1999.

King, John N. *Tudor Royal Iconography: Literature and Art in an Age of Religious Crisis.* Princeton: Princeton University Press, 1989.

Knighton, Henry. *Chronicon Henrici Knighton vel Cnitthon Monachi Leycestrensis.* Edited by Joseph Rawson Lumby. Two vols. London: Eyre and Spottiswoode, 1895.

Kraig, Donald Michael. *Modern Magick, Second Edition: Eleven Lessons in the High Magickal Arts.* St. Paul, Minn.: Llewellyn, 2000.

Lachaud, Frédérique. "Dress and Social Status in England Before the Sumptuary Laws." In *Heraldry, Pageantry and Social Display in Medieval England,* edited by Peter Coss and Maurice Keen, 105–23. Woodbridge, U.K.: Boydell, 2002.

Lambert, Mark. *Malory: Style and Vision in "Le Morte d'Arthur."* New Haven: Yale University Press, 1975.

Le Bel, Jean. *Chronique de Jean le Bel.* Edited by Jules Viard and Eugène Déprez. 1904. Reprint, Paris: Librairie Honoré Champion, 1977.

"Leibovitz: The Queen and I Did Not Fall Out in BBC 'Tantrum' Film. *Mail Online,* July 20, 2007. At http://www.dailymail.co.uk/news/article-467754/Leibowitz-The-Queen-I-did-fall-BBC-tantrum-film.html (accessed January 8, 2011).

Lester, G. A. "Fifteenth-Century English Heraldic Narrative." *Yearbook of English Studies* 22 (1992): 201–12.

Lévi-Strauss, Claude. *The Savage Mind.* Chicago: University of Chicago Press, 1966.

Levin, Carole. "'Would I Could Give You Help and Succour': Elizabeth I and the Politics of Touch." *Albion* 21 (1989): 191–205.

Loades, D. M. *The Reign of Mary Tudor: Politics, Government and Religion in England, 1553–1558.* London: Benn, 1979.

Lynch, Andrew. *Malory's Book of Arms: The Narrative of Combat in "Le Morte Darthur."* Cambridge: D. S. Brewer, 1977.

MacCulloch, Diarmaid. *Tudor Church Militant: Edward VI and the Protestant Reformation.* London: Allen Lane, 1999.

Malory, Thomas. *The Works of Sir Thomas Malory.* Edited by Eugène Vinaver. Third edition. Revised by P. J. C. Field. Three vols. Oxford: Clarendon Press, 1990.

Mansfield, Alan. *Ceremonial Costume: Court, Civil and Civic Costume from 1660 to the Present Day*. London: Black, 1980.

Marshall, H. E. *An Island Story: A History of England for Boys and Girls*. With pictures by A. S. Forrest. 1907. Reprinted New York: Frederick A. Stokes, 1920.

Martorell, Joanot. *Tirant lo Blanc*. Edited by Martí de Riquer. Barcelona: Biblioteca Perenne, 1947.

Martorell, Joanot, and Martí Joan de Galba. *Tirant lo Blanc*. Translated by David H. Rosenthal. London: Pan Books, 1984.

Matikkala, Antti. *The Orders of Knighthood and the Formation of the British Honours System, 1660–1760*. Woodbridge, U.K.: Boydell, 2008.

McCausland, Charles. "Educated Louts: The Scandalous Origins of *Honi Soit*." 1989. Reprinted in *Honi Soit*, Week 12, Semester 2 (2006): 6.

McClendon, Muriel. "A Moveable Feast: Saint George's Day Celebrations and Religious Change in Early Modern England." *Journal of British Studies* 38 (1999): 1–27.

McCoy, Richard C. *The Rites of Knighthood: The Literature and Politics of Elizabethan Chivalry*. Berkeley: University of California Press, 1989.

McDonald, Nicola. "Chaucer's *Legend of Good Women*, Ladies at Court and the Female Reader." *Chaucer Review* 35 (2000): 22–42.

Middle English Dictionary. Edited by Hans Kurath, Sherman A. Kuhn, John Reidy, and Robert Lewis. Ann Arbor: University of Michigan Press, 1952–1999.

Miller, Mark. "Displaced Souls, Idle Talk, Spectacular Scenes: *Handlyng Synne* and the Perspective of Agency." *Speculum* 71 (1996): 606–32.

———. Review of Bernard Williams, *Shame and Necessity*. *Modern Philology* 93.2 (1995): 217–25.

Moers, Ellen. *The Dandy: Brummell to Beerbohm*. Lincoln: University of Nebraska Press, 1978.

Morfill, W. R., ed. *Ballads from Manuscripts*. Ballad Society, 1873. Reprinted New York: AMS Press, 1968.

The Most Noble Order of the Garter. Garter Day, 2001. [Windsor:] St. George's Chapel, 2001.

The Most Noble Order of the Garter. Garter Day, 2004. [Windsor:] St. George's Chapel, 2004.

Muir, Edward. *Ritual in Early Modern Europe*. Cambridge: Cambridge University Press, 1997.

Munby, Julian, Richard Barber, and Richard Brown, ed. *Edward III's Round Table at Windsor: The House of the Round Table and the Windsor Festival of 1344*. Arthurian Studies 68. Woodbridge, U.K.: Boydell, 2007.

Nairn, Tom. *The Enchanted Glass: Britain and Its Monarchy*. London: Radius, 1988.

Nevinson, J. L. "The Earliest Dress and Insignia of the Knights of the Garter." *Apollo* 47 (1948): 81.

Newton, Stella Mary. *Fashion in the Age of the Black Prince: A Study of the Years 1340–1365*. Woodbridge, U.K.: Boydell, 1980.

Nichols, J. G., ed. *Literary Remains of Edward VI*. London: Roxburghe Club, 1857.

Nichols, John, ed. *The Progresses, Processions, and Magnificent Festivities, of King James the First.* Four vols. London, 1828.

Nicolas, Nicholas Harris. "Observations on the Institution of the Most Noble Order of the Garter: Illustrated by the Accounts of the Great Wardrobe of King Edward the Third." *Archaeologia* 31 (1845): 1–163.

Norris, Herbert, and Oswald Curtis. *Nineteenth-Century Costume and Fashion.* Originally published as *Costume and Fashion, Volume Six: The Nineteenth Century.* New York: Dutton, 1933. Reprinted Toronto: Dover, 1998.

O Hehir, Brendan. *Expans'd Hieroglyphicks: A Critical Edition of Sir John Denham's Cooper's Hill.* Berkeley: University of California Press, 1969.

Ormrod, Mark. "For Arthur and St George: Edward III, Windsor Castle and the Order of the Garter." In *St George's Chapel Windsor in the Fourteenth Century,* edited by Nigel Saul, 13–34. Woodbridge, U.K.: Boydell, 2005.

Ormrod, W. M. "The Personal Religion of Edward III." *Speculum* 64 (1982): 849–77.

Osborne, John. "And They Call It Cricket." *Encounter* 9.4 (1957): 23–30.

Packe, Michael. *King Edward III.* London: Routledge and Kegan Paul, 1983.

Pagan [Adam Cairns McCay.]. "To Mollie—A Flirt." *Bulletin,* August 21, 1901, 3.

Parrott, W. Gerrod, and Rom Harré. "Princess Diana and the Emotionality of Contemporary Britain." *International Journal of Group Tensions* 30 (2001): 29–38.

Paster, Gail Kern. *The Body Embarrassed: Drama and the Disciplines of Shame in Early Modern England.* Ithaca, N.Y.: Cornell University Press, 1993.

Pearsall, Derek, ed. *The Floure and the Leafe and the Assembly of Ladies.* Manchester: Manchester University Press, 1962.

Peele, George. *The Honour of the Garter.* London, 1593.

Pepys, Samuel. *The Diary of Samuel Pepys.* Edited by Robert Latham and William Matthews. London: G. Bell and Sons, 1974.

Pilbrow, Fionn. "The Knights of the Bath: Dubbing to Knighthood in Lancastrian and Yorkist England." In *Heraldry, Pageantry and Social Display in Medieval England,* edited by Peter Coss and Maurice Keen, 195–218. Woodbridge, U.K.: Boydell, 2002.

Plunkett, John. *Queen Victoria: First Media Monarch.* Oxford: Oxford University Press, 2003.

Potter, Sally, dir. *Orlando.* Sony Pictures, 1993.

Prendergast, Thomas A., and Stephanie Trigg. "The Negative Erotics of Medievalism." In *The Post-Historical Middle Ages,* edited by Elizabeth Scala and Sylvia Federico, 117–37. New York: Palgrave Macmillan, 2009.

———. "What Is Happening to the Middle Ages?" *New Medieval Literatures* 9 (2008): 215–29.

"Prince William: Order of the Garter." *The Telegraph,* June 17, 2008. At http://www.telegraph.co.uk/news/2140279/Prince-William-Order-of-the-Garter.html (accessed February 5, 2009).

Probyn, Elspeth. *Blush: Faces of Shame.* Minneapolis: University of Minnesota Press, 2005.

Puttenham, George. *The Arte of English Poesie.* Edited by Gladys Doidge Willcock and Alice Walker. Cambridge: Cambridge University Press, 1936.

The Queen at Eighty. Television documentary produced by BBC, 2006.

The Queen's Castle. Television documentary produced by RDF Media and History Television International, 2005.

Rizzo, Betty. "Equivocations of Gender and Rank: Eighteenth-Century Sporting Women." *Eighteenth-Century Life* 26 (2002): 70–118.

Rose, Kenneth. *The Later Cecils.* London: Weidenfeld and Nicolson, 1975.

Samuel, Raphael. *Theatres of Memory: Past and Present in Contemporary Culture.* London: Verso, 1994.

Scott, Margaret. *Medieval Dress and Fashion.* London: British Library, 2007.

Sedgwick, Eve Kosofsky. "Shame and Performativity: Henry James's New York Edition Prefaces." In *Henry James's New York Edition: The Construction of Authorship,* edited by David McWhirter, 206–39. Stanford: Stanford University Press, 1995.

Sedgwick, Eve Kosofsky, and Adam Frank. "Shame in the Cybernetic Fold: Reading Silvan Tomkins." In *Shame and Its Sisters: A Silvan Tomkins Reader,* edited by Eve Kosofsky Sedgwick and Adam Frank, 1–28. Durham: Duke University Press, 1995.

Segar, William. *The Booke of Honor and Armes.* London, 1590.

———. *Honor Military and Ciuill.* London, 1602.

Selden, John. *Titles of Honour.* Second edition. London, 1631.

Sellar, Walter Carruthers, and Robert Yeatman, illustrated by John Reynolds. *1066 and All That: A Memorable History of England, Comprising All the Parts You Can Remember, Including 103 Good Things, 5 Bad Kings and 2 Genuine Dates.* London: Methuen, 1931.

Shakespeare, William. *The First Part of King Henry VI.* Edited by Andrew S. Cairncross. Cambridge, Mass.: Harvard University Press, 1900; revised 1962.

Shenton, Caroline. "Edward III and the Symbol of the Leopard." In *Heraldry, Pageantry and Social Display in Medieval England,* edited by Peter Coss and Maurice Keen, 77–81. Woodbridge, U.K.: Boydell Press, 2002.

Sherwood, Roy. *Oliver Cromwell: King in All But Name, 1653–1658.* Phoenix Mill: Sutton, 2007.

Simpson, James. *Reform and Cultural Revolution: The Oxford Literary History,* vol. 2, *1350–1547.* Oxford: Oxford University Press, 2002.

———. "The Rule of Medieval Imagination." In *Images, Idolatry, and Iconoclasm in Late Medieval England,* edited by Jeremy Dimmick, James Simpson, and Nicolette Zeeman, 4–24. Oxford: Oxford University Press, 2002.

Smith, D. Vance. *Arts of Possession: The Middle English Household Imaginary.* Minneapolis: Minnesota University Press, 2003.

Snowdon. *Snowdon: A Photographic Autobiography.* New York: Times Books, 1979.

Staniland, Kay. "Court Style, Painters, and the Great Wardrobe." In *England in the Fourteenth Century: Proceedings of the 1985 Harlaxton Symposium,* edited by W. M. Ormrod, 236–46. Woodbridge, U.K.: Boydell, 1986.

"State Opening Loses Some Pomp." *BBC News,* November 24, 1998. At http://news.bbc .co.uk/2/hi/special_report/1998/11/98/queen_speech/216684.stm (accessed April 18, 2002).

Stephenson, B. C., and Arthur Sullivan. *The Zoo: A New and Original Musical Folly in One Act.* Kentisbeare: Ian C. Bond, 1997.

Stewart, Bob. *Where Is Saint George? Pagan Imagery in English Folksong.* Bradford-on-Avon: Moonraker Press, 1977.

Strohm, Paul. *England's Empty Throne: Usurpation and the Language of Legitimation, 1399–1422.* New Haven: Yale University Press, 1998.

Strong, Roy. *Coronation: From the Eighth to the Twenty-First Century.* London: Harper Perennial, 2005.

———. *The Cult of Elizabeth: Elizabethan Portraiture and Pageantry.* 1977. London: Pimlico, 1999.

Sweet, Matthew. *Inventing the Victorians.* London: Faber and Faber, 2001.

Taylor, Tom. "The Great Actors of England in 1775." *Victoria Magazine* 1 (1865): 83–9, 158–69, 245–59.

Thirsk, Joan. "The Fantastical Folly of Fashion: The English Stocking Knitting Industry, 1500–1700." In *Textile History and Economic History: Essays in Honour of Miss Julia de Lacy Mann,* edited by N. B. Harte and K. G. Ponting, 50–73. Manchester: Manchester University Press, 1973.

Thompson, Edward Maunde. "The Revision of the Statutes of the Order of the Garter by Edward the Sixth." *Archaeologica* 54 (1894): 173–98.

Thorndike, Russell. *Children of the Garter, Being the Memoirs of a Windsor Castle Choir-boy, during the last years of Queen Victoria.* London: Rich and Clay, 1937.

Tolkien, J. R. R., and E. V. Gordon, eds. *Sir Gawain and the Green Knight.* 1925. Second edition, revised by Norman Davis. Oxford: Clarendon Press, 1967.

Treharne, Elaine M., ed. *Old and Middle English, c. 890–c.1400.* 2000. Second edition. Oxford: Blackwell, 2004.

Trigg, Stephanie. *Congenial Souls: Reading Chaucer from Medieval to Postmodern.* Minneapolis: University of Minnesota Press, 2002.

———. "Israel Gollancz's *Wynnere and Wastoure:* Political Satire or Editorial Politics?" In *Medieval English Religious and Ethical Literature: Essays in Honour of G. H. Russell,* edited by Gregory Kratzmann and James Simpson, 115–27. Woodbridge, U.K.: Boydell and Brewer, 1986.

———. "Medievalism and Convergence Culture: Researching the Middle Ages for Fiction and Film." *Parergon* 25.2 (2008): 99–118.

———. "The Romance of Exchange: *Sir Gawain and the Green Knight.*" *Viator* 22 (1991): 251–66.

———. "Timeless Medievalism: Magna Carta and the Australian Parliament." *Australian Literary Studies* 26: 3–4 (2011): 15–26.

———, ed. *Wynnere and Wastoure.* Early English Text Society, 297. Oxford: Oxford University Press, 1990.

Turner, Victor. *The Ritual Process: Structure and Anti-Structures.* New York: Aldine, 1969.

Vaenius, Otto. *Amorum emblemata.* 1608. Facsimile edition, with introduction by Karel Porteman. Aldershot: Scolar Press, 1996.

Vale, Juliet. *Edward III and Chivalry: Chivalric Society and Its Context 1270–1350*. Woodbridge, U.K.: Boydell and Brewer, 1982.

———. "Image and Identity in the Prehistory of the Order of the Garter." In *St George's Chapel Windsor in the Fourteenth Century*, edited by Nigel Saul, 35–50. Woodbridge, U.K.: Brewer, 2005.

Vale, Malcolm. *The Princely Court: Medieval Courts and Culture in North-West Europe 1270–1380*. Oxford: Oxford University Press, 2001.

Vergil, Polydore. *Polydori Vergili Historiae anglicanae*. Basle: 1555. Reprint Menston: Scolar Press, 1972.

Waddington, Raymond B. "Elizabeth I and the Order of the Garter." *Sixteenth-Century Journal* 24 (1993): 97–113.

Wagner, Sir Anthony. *Heralds of England: History of the Office and College of Arms*. London: H.M. Stationery Office, 1967.

Wagner, Anthony, Nicolas Barker, and Ann Payne, eds. *Medieval Pageant: Writhe's Garter Book and the Earldom of Salisbury Roll*. London: Roxburghe Club, 1993.

Walker, Greg. *Writing Under Tyranny: English Literature and the Henrician Reformation*. Oxford: Oxford University Press, 2005.

Wardle, Patricia. "The King's Embroiderer: Edmund Harrison (1590–1667)." *Textile History* 26 (1995): 139–84.

Wheatley, Edward. *Mastering Aesop: Medieval Education, Chaucer and His Followers*. Gainesville: University Press of Florida, 2000.

Wilde, Oscar. *The Picture of Dorian Gray*. 1891. Harmondsworth: Penguin Books, 2000.

Williams, Bernard. *Shame and Necessity*. Berkeley: University of California Press, 1993.

Wilson, John McKay. *Wilson's Tales of the Borders and of Scotland: Historical, Traditional and Imaginative*. Revised by Alexander Leighton, vol. VII. Edinburgh: William P. Nimmo, 1888.

Woolf, Virginia. *Orlando: A Biography*. Edited with an introduction and notes by Rachel Bowlby. Oxford: Oxford University Press, 1992.

———. *A Room of One's Own and Three Guineas*. Edited with an introduction by Morag Shiach. Oxford: Oxford University Press, 1992.

Index

Acknowledgments

One of the ritual pleasures of writing a book is the gradual addition of names to the Acknowledgments. I have been writing this section almost since I began writing this book, and I offer deep gratitude to all those who have offered assistance over the years of research and writing.

I owe warm thanks to the people who have contributed Garter materials of all kinds, from gossip, anecdotes, ideas, historical allusions, references, pictures, and drinks coasters: Valerie Allen, Marion J. Campbell, Leo Carruthers, Deirdre Coleman, Kate Cregan, Louise D'Arcens, Ian Donaldson, Paul Hammond, Cameron Hazlehurst, Helen Hickey, Rachel Holmes, Irene Kearsey, Eliot Kendal, Richard Kroll, David Lawton, Caitlyn Lehmann, Peter L'Estrange, David McInnis, Sean McWilliams, Grace Moore, Peter Otto, Christine Owen, Jerry Parrott, Cyrus Patell, Kim Phillips, Tom Prendergast, William Quinn, Melissa Raine, Sarah Randles, Susan Rees-Osborne, Jessica Rosenfeld, Paul Salzman, Elaine Shaw, Peter Sherlock, Peter Stallybrass, David Studham, Marion Turner, Philip Thiel, Una Trigg, Chris Wallace-Crabbe, and Michael Wilson.

For practical assistance in England, I thank Valerie Krips, Marion Turner, and Jocelyne and Michael Wilson; and for invaluable research assistance over many years, I thank Melissa Raine, Helen Hickey, Philip Thiel, Maria O'Dwyer, Anne McKendry, Romana Byrne, and Sashi Nair, who prepared the index.

As exemplary readers and editors, I thank Lynn Arner, David Matthews, Gordon McMullan, Al Shoaf, and Paul Strohm for their advice and suggestions. A special triumvirate of scholars and friends—Tom Goodmann, Frank Grady, and Tom Prendergast—deserves warm thanks for sustained discussion, critical reading, and perfect companionship over the years. An invitation on my blog for people to read a chapter or two saw me overwhelmed with kindness and clever suggestions from Esther Chin, Jeffrey Cohen, Ryan Diehl, Melanie Duckworth, Lisa Fletcher, Helen Hickey, Melinda Johnson, Hannah Kilpatrick, Anne McKendry, Grace Moore, Paul Salzman, Julia Tan, Philip Thiel, David Thornby, and Lawrence Warner.

I would also like to thank librarians and staff at the following institutions: the British Library, the National Archives, the Baillieu Library, St. George's Chapel, the Royal Archives at Windsor Castle, and especially Mr. Robert Yorke at the College of Arms. I am also grateful for the assistance of Brien Hallett, the Usher of the Black Rod, and Kylie Scroop, director, Art Services, both of the Australian Federal Parliament.

For invaluable financial support, I thank the Australian Research Council and the Department of English and Faculty of Arts at the University of Melbourne.

I have been fortunate in my hosts and audiences at various universities where I have had the chance to present work in progress, from Paul Strohm at the University of Oxford, who urged me to breeze in with my first exploratory paper on the project, to Elizabeth Allen at the University of California, Irvine; John Ganim at the University of California, Riverside, and the Mellon Workshop in Medieval Culture and Postmodern Legacies; Rita Copeland, Emily Steiner, and David Wallace at the Medieval and Renaissance seminar at the University of Pennsylvania; David Matthews at the University of Newcastle and Gordon McMullan at King's College, London; Anthony Bale, Alcuin Blamires, and Rosalind Field at the University of London; Chris Cannon at New York University; and most recently, Jeffrey Cohen at George Washington University. I thank the Perth Medieval and Renaissance Group, and various reading groups and seminars in the Departments of English and History at the University of Melbourne; my vice-chancellor, Glyn Davis, for inviting me to speak at one of his research lunches; and the members of the Medieval Round Table at Melbourne for their patient reception of papers on the Garter over many years and for their continued fellowship. Warm thanks, too, to members of the Lyceum Club, Melbourne, to the Friends of the Baillieu Library, and to the Sydney and Melbourne branches of the Australian Heraldry Society, especially David Studham and Stephen Szabo. For their generous offers of ideas and responses to papers, drafts, and presentations, I thank especially Elizabeth Allen, Lynn Arner, Helen Cooper, Rita Copeland, Susan Crane, Louise D'Arcens, Carolyn Dinshaw, John Ganim, Tom Goodmann, Paul James, Valerie Krips, Gordon McMullan, David Matthews, Peter Otto, Tom Prendergast, Emily Steiner, Karl Steel, Paul Strohm, Clara Tuite, and David Wallace.

In 2005 I was privileged to spend four months as visiting Hurst Professor at Washington University in St. Louis. This was a singularly productive period of work on this book, and I barely know how to express my gratitude to David Lawton and the Department of English and American Literature for their generosity and fellowship. For intellectual companionship, and for providing me some critical venues to present my work at a crucial phase, I thank Lara Bovilsky, Rick Godden, Anita Hagerman, David Lawton, Joe Lowenstein, and Jessica Rosenfeld. In 2009, I spent shorter but fruitful periods at the University of Pennsylvania and New York University: my deep thanks to David Wallace and Chris Cannon for making this possible and for welcoming me so warmly into those communities.

Jerry Singerman has been an exceptionally supportive and clever editor, from an early stage of this book's development. I thank him warmly for his sympathetic good humor. It has been a delight to work with the thoughtful and efficient team at Penn, especially Noreen O'Connor-Abel and Caroline Winschel.

I would also like to thank the readers of the Humanities Researcher blog (http://stephanietrigg.blogspot.com), who have helped me deepen my sense of the various communities into which I was writing.

Work on this book came to a sudden halt in the Australian spring and summer of 2006–7 when a diagnosis of early stage breast cancer shocked me into stillness. I would like to thank Suzanne Neil, Mitchell Chipman, and the rest of the team at the Mercy Breast Clinic for their superlative and humane care. I hope I have learned something from them about how to hold on to the things that matter, and to let go of the things that don't.

Illness made me realize anew how much I depend on my networks of family and friends. I was humbled by the generosity and kindness of so many people over that difficult summer and its aftermath. Special thanks to Eva Christoff, Peter Christoff, Liz Conor, Paula Cosgrove, Kate Cregan, Robyn Eckersley, Margot Eden, Richard Finch, Kerryn Goldsworthy, Peter Kennedy, Jillian Murray, Geoff Taylor, and all who came to read *Middlemarch* to me. My colleagues in the Department of English were also generous in their support and patience during my recovery. My family in Melbourne continued to provide the loving encouragement and practical help in which they excel: warmest thanks to Fiona Trigg, Una and Wesley Trigg, and Jean and Graeme James.

Learning how to work, learning how to live, and learning how to put these things together is not always easy. I have the best companions in the world for the journey: my beloved partner, Paul, whose wisdom, love, and brilliant insight help me every step of the way; and our son, Joel, whose gracious spirit and fierce intelligence are a constant inspiration. This book is for them.

Part of Chapter 3 appeared previously in "The Vulgar History of the Order of the Garter," in *Reading the Medieval in Early Modern England*, ed. Gordon

McMullan and David Matthews, 91–105 (Cambridge: Cambridge University Press, 2007); part of Chapter 4 in "'Shamed Be . . . : Historicizing Shame in Medieval and Early Modern Courtly Ritual," *Exemplaria* 19.1 (2007): 67–89 (www.maney.co.uk/journals/exm and www.ingentaconnect.com/content/maney/exm); and parts of Chapters 6 and 7 in "Medievalism, the Queen and the Dandy," *AntiTHESIS* 19 (2009): 41–55. Permission to use these materials is acknowledged.

systems remained stable for generations. Converse (1969) argued that it took a few generations for voters to identify with parties in large numbers; in turn, partisan identification was the micro foundation of party system stability. Shefter (1994) argued that long historical patterns of state and party building shape the degree to which parties engage in clientelism. Kitschelt *et al.* (2010) asserted that the development of programmatic competition in Latin America hinged on long historical processes. Some literature on party system change in the advanced industrial democracies links it to slow, gradual processes such as secular changes in values (Inglehart 1990).

The Latin American experience raises questions about these long-term approaches for understanding this region in this time. These approaches might be right for the advanced industrial democracies, but they presume contexts of less severe stress on institutions and more solid institutions than exist in most of Latin America. More than the social science and historical literature anticipated, extraordinary stress dramatically and quickly undermined major parties (Argentina and Colombia) and even entire party systems (Bolivia, Ecuador, Peru, and Venezuela) that had been bedrocks of democratic politics, for decades (Ecuador) or generations (Argentina, Bolivia, Colombia, Peru, and Venezuela). Conversely, the transformation from an inchoate party system to an unevenly institutionalized one in Brazil also occurred over a few electoral cycles rather than generations.

In political science, sizable literature on path dependence and PSI emerged in the 1990s. They share an important commonality; both concepts rest on self-reproducing mechanisms once a system or a set of institutions has been consolidated.

Levi (1997: 28) defined path dependence as meaning that "once a country or region has started down a track, the costs of reversal are very high." Events in one historical moment greatly alter the distribution of possible and probable outcomes into the medium- and/or long-term future.[14] The two decades since the publication of *Building Democratic Institutions* undermined strong claims of path dependence in PSI in Latin America. Three systems (Argentina, Colombia, and Venezuela) became dramatically less institutionalized. The Honduran system has more recently moved in the direction of much less institutionalization. Conversely, three systems (Brazil, El Salvador, and Panama) became more institutionalized. The fact that seven countries underwent deep changes in PSI might call into question whether the concept is meaningful for Latin America and call into question how much the past shapes the present.

At the extreme, if countries' PSI fluctuated rapidly in random ways from one moment in time to the next, the concept would not be useful. A country's score for PSI in past elections would not help predict its score for the next. Systemic predictability and stability would be extremely low (0 in the event that a score

---

[14] For a similar definition, see Pierson (2004: 20–22).

for PSI in one election did not correlate at all with its score in the previous elections). Such randomness is the opposite of institutionalization.

To look at whether indicators of party system stability have predictive capacity, I turned to the large dataset on electoral volatility that Mainwaring *et al.* (2016) developed based on sixty-seven countries and 618 electoral periods that met a threshold of democracy in the period since 1945. This dataset includes all major world regions. The question is whether earlier measures (at *T*–1) of the dependent variables help to predict the dependent variable at time *T*. To test this, I used, in addition to the dependent variable in the previous electoral period (*T*–1), the same covariates as Mainwaring *et al.* (2016): per capita GDP growth, inflation (logged), the effective number of parties, district magnitude (logged), the Birth Year of Democracy (logged), Age of Democracy (logged), and per capita GDP (logged). Because electoral volatility measures change (from one election to the next) rather than level, in principle, the value at *T*–1 is independent from the value at *T*. Mainwaring *et al.* used GEE (General Estimating Equations) models, which are appropriate for estimating coefficients for entire samples; cases need not be independent.

The results (Models 1 and 2 in Table 2.8) show that the previous score for total volatility is highly statistically significant. Volatility at *T*–1 is by far the most statistically significant covariate, and it has a powerful substantive effect. Every increase of 1% point in volatility at *T*–1 is associated with a predicted increase of 0.51% at *T*. Results are very similar in the OLS model with panel corrected standard errors (PCSE), which Beck (2001) recommended as a possible alternative approach to analyzing panel data. In this model, the substantive effect is slightly greater; every increase of 1% volatility at *T*–1 is associated with an increase of 0.56% at *T*. Results with Latin American data, based on a much smaller number of countries and electoral periods, are similar (Models 3 and 4 in Table 2.8). Electoral volatility varies in systematic ways.

In contrast, with the Mainwaring *et al.* dataset for sixty-seven countries, the vote share of new parties at *T*–1 has no predictive power for the vote share at *T* (Models 1 and 2 in Table 2.9). Thus, the vote share of new parties varies randomly for this broader sample of countries. For the Latin American sample, the vote share of new parties at *T*–1 is strongly associated with the vote share of new parties at *T* in the GEE model (Model 3) but not in the OLS-PCSE model (Model 4). Strikingly, *no* covariates are statistically significant in the Latin American sample in the OLS-PCSE model.

Perhaps this lack of impact of extra-system volatility at *T*–1 on the same variable at *T* is because even in weakly institutionalized party systems, major new parties do not come along every day. They make their entrance, and in the next election, the emergence of a major new party in the previous election does not increase the probability of yet another major new contender. Although the vote share of new parties varied randomly from one electoral period to the next, for the Latin American cases, it was integrally related to other aspects of PSI.

TABLE 2.8 *Effect of Electoral Volatility (T–1) on Electoral Volatility (T) – Lower Chamber*

	Model 1 GEE (Robust GE) World	Model 2 OLS (PCSE) World	Model 3 GEE (Robust GE) Latin America	Model 4 OLS (PCSE) Latin America
Volatility (T–1)	0.509***	0.561***	0.478***	0.509***
	(0.053)	(0.094)	(0.062)	(0.083)
District magnitude (ln)	−0.044	−0.030	−0.013	−0.228
	(0.324)	(0.235)	(0.877)	(1.040)
ENP	0.978**	0.877*	0.195	0.087
	(0.354)	(0.344)	(0.543)	(0.381)
GDP growth PC	−0.636**	−0.604**	−1.034*	−1.112**
	(0.223)	(0.222)	(0.430)	(0.389)
Inflation (ln)	0.032	0.077	−0.241	−0.232
	(0.414)	(0.402)	(0.625)	(0.633)
GDP PC (ln)	−2.153**	−1.904*	−1.656	−1.042
	(0.725)	(0.842)	(1.989)	(1.849)
Age of democracy (ln)	3.293**	3.045***	6.303***	5.836**
	(1.023)	(0.876)	(1.620)	(1.824)
Birth of democracy (ln)	−6.947***	−6.225***	−6.692**	−6.655*
	(1.651)	(1.401)	(2.517)	(2.622)
Type of government (ln)	0.492	0.436	33.640	30.042
	(0.997)	(0.891)	(18.626)	(18.348)
Constant	42.201***	37.173***	0.478***	0.509***
	(8.499)	(10.379)	(0.062)	(0.083)
r2		0.603		0.442
N	544	544	140	140

Notes: Robust standard errors in parentheses * significant at 10%; ** significant at 5%; *** significant at 1%.
R2 is not reported because this statistic is not defined for GEE models.
ENP = effective number of parties.

TABLE 2.9 *Effect of Extra-System Electoral Volatility (T–1) on Extra-System Electoral Volatility (T) – Lower Chamber*

	Model 1 GEE (Robust GE) World	Model 2 OLS (PCSE) World	Model 3 GEE (Robust GE) Latin America	Model 4 OLS (PCSE) Latin America
Extra-system vol. (T–1)	0.079	0.079	0.224***	0.120
	(0.063)	(0.149)	(0.063)	(0.137)
District magnitude (ln)	0.202	0.004	0.668	0.776
	(0.493)	(0.330)	(0.901)	(0.607)
ENP	1.599**	1.347***	−0.203	−0.137
	(0.515)	(0.386)	(0.273)	(0.442)
GDP growth PC	−0.417	−0.398	−0.608*	−0.586
	(0.215)	(0.217)	(0.283)	(0.338)
Inflation (ln)	−0.170	−0.021	0.429	0.396
	(0.383)	(0.449)	(0.398)	(0.414)
GDP PC (ln)	−2.401*	−2.554**	−0.816	−0.919
	(1.013)	(0.860)	(1.622)	(1.522)
Age of democracy (ln)	2.349*	3.157***	3.421*	3.417
	(1.120)	(0.648)	(1.670)	(1.909)
Birth of democracy (ln)	−5.397***	−5.821***	−2.694	−2.424
	(1.527)	(1.029)	(2.509)	(2.784)
Type of government (ln)	−1.259	−0.482		
	(1.549)	(0.911)		
Constant	36.187***	37.137***	11.398	11.592
	(9.178)	(7.371)	(16.071)	(15.689)
r2		0.212		0.081
N	544	544	140	140

Notes: Robust standard errors in parentheses * significant at 10%; ** significant at 5%; *** significant at 1%.
R2 is not reported because this statistic is not defined for GEE models.

TABLE 2.10 *Correlations between Party System Institutionalization Indicators at T–1 and T, 1970–95 and 1990–2015 (p values in parentheses if* p<0.10)

	1970–95		1990–2015	
	Correlation (Pearson)	*p* value (2-tailed)	Correlation (Pearson)	*p* value (2-tailed)
Vote share of new parties, presidential elections	0.26	–	0.25	0.02
Vote share of new parties, lower chamber	0.30	0.02	0.22	0.02
Electoral volatility, presidential elections	0.76	0.00	0.64	0.00
Electoral volatility, lower chamber	0.73	0.00	0.67	0.00
Stability of main contenders, presidential elections	0.19	–	0.41	0.00
Stability of main contenders, lower chamber	0.23	0.09	0.46	0.00
Ideological stability, lower chamber	Nd	nd	0.04	–

Table 2.10 shows the Pearson bivariate correlations between scores at $T-1$ and T for all seven electoral period-specific variables used in this chapter for both 1970–95 and 1990–2015. Correlations for electoral volatility are consistently high for both presidential and lower chamber elections. Systems with high volatility at one time tend to continue exhibiting high volatility, and vice versa. Consistent with the regression results in Table 2.9, correlations for the vote share of new parties are much lower.

For 1990–2015 but not 1970–95, systems that had stable (or unstable) main contenders in one electoral period tended to have stability (or instability) in the next one. Finally, ideological stability varied randomly. When party systems experienced pronounced ideological shifts from one election to the next, they were not more likely to undertake another pronounced shift in the subsequent election.

In terms of institutionalization, party systems, including in Latin America, are neither immutable nor do they vary randomly. Several Latin American cases underwent deep change in PSI between the 1990s and 2015, but Table 2.8 shows that deep change in some cases is compatible with a high predictive capacity of PSI for total volatility and, to a lesser degree, the stability of main contenders.

Although levels of institutionalization tend to persist, the Latin American experience suggests shortcomings of strong claims about path dependence in contexts of weak institutions. Some of the literature on historical institutionalism overstated path dependence and assumed that institutions are strong (Levitsky and Murillo 2005, 2014). A central point of this volume is that the institutionalization of party systems in Latin America (and around the world, as can be seen in Mainwaring *et al.* 2016) varies greatly. High and low levels of institutionalization *tend* to be self-reinforcing, but party systems do not always get stuck in immutable patterns.

CONCLUSION

This chapter had three goals. First, building on the reconceptualization of PSI proposed in Chapter 1, I created indicators to measure the three attributes of the concept. These indicators are logically derived from the concept; they measure phenomena that are by definition a part of PSI. They travel seamlessly across time and space. Most of these indicators are new, and they can fruitfully be used for studying other world regions and other historical periods.

Second, I provided data for PSI for eighteen Latin American countries for the period from 1990 to 2015 and for the US as a benchmark. On almost every indicator, the range in country means across cases was huge. Most Latin American party systems are not well institutionalized, but Mexico, Chile, Uruguay, El Salvador, Brazil, and Honduras until 2013 were exceptions. At the low end of the spectrum, Peru stood out for its low PSI in a democracy that has registered many successes since 2001 (see Levitsky's chapter). Guatemala stands out for persistently low institutionalization (Sánchez 2008, 2009), and Venezuela for a party system collapse in the wake of an institutionalized system from 1968 to 1988 (Morgan 2011, and this volume; Seawright 2012). Most Latin American party systems are not well institutionalized, and that has been true for a long time, but there is great variance across countries.

Third, in light of the fact that three systems (Argentina, Colombia, and Venezuela) that were once institutionalized underwent severe erosion or collapse, and that three countries (Brazil, El Salvador, and Panama) that once had weakly institutionalized systems became more stable, I addressed whether PSI in Latin America is so transitory as to make the concept useless. The answer is a resounding no. Countries do not remain forever at the same level of institutionalization, but PSI does not fluctuate randomly. These differences in institutionalization have important consequences for democratic politics, as I show in Chapter 3.

3

Party System Institutionalization, Predictability, and Democracy

Scott Mainwaring*

This chapter focuses on consequences of differences in the level of party system institutionalization (PSI) for democracy. The reason for producing this volume is that party systems function in very different ways depending on their level of institutionalization. In one of the most famous quotes in the history of political science, Schattschneider (1942: 1) wrote that "Political parties created modern democracy and modern democracy is unthinkable save in terms of the parties." Many other prominent scholars have likewise emphasized that parties are essential for modern representative democracy (Downs 1957; Sartori 1976). What happens, then, in contexts where parties are weak, so much so that Levitsky (Chapter 11) speaks of democracy without parties in Peru? If the history of modern democracy is built on political parties, then democracy will function differently with weakly institutionalized party systems. This chapter addresses some of these differences.

I begin with some theoretical, deductively derived implications of PSI for democracy. Institutionalized party systems provide stability and predictability to important democratic outcomes and processes.[1] Greater predictability means that actors can be more confident about the range of likely future outcomes and that time horizons are typically longer. In these systems, parties serve as a major gateway to elected political office; help organize the legislature; and provide critical information cues to voters. These outcomes and processes are less stable

* Fernando Bizzarro, Jaimie Bleck, Omar Coronel, Sarah Zukerman Daly, María Victoria De Negri, Laura Gamboa, Tahir Kilavuz, Steve Levitsky, Noam Lupu, Sean McGraw, Kristin McKie, Gabriela Ippolito O'Donnell, Ana Petrova, George Tsebelis, and Samuel Valenzuela offered valuable comments. I thank Rodrigo Castro Cornejo, María Victoria De Negri, Lauran Feist, Krystin Krause, Ana Petrova, and Adriana Ramírez Baracaldo for research assistance.
[1] A different literature discusses why party institutionalization is important for authoritarian regimes. See Brownlee (2007); Geddes (1999); Hicken and Kuhonta (2015b); Smith (2005). Our volume addresses this issue only in passing.

and predictable in fluid party systems.[2] Although the empirical evidence in the chapter is limited to Latin America, the theoretical expectations about the consequences of weak PSI should hold for other regions of the world.

The chapter then presents some empirical evidence. First, institutionalized systems create high barriers for political outsiders. In weakly institutionalized systems, political outsiders can more easily win power. In turn, political outsiders are less accountable to their parties and less likely to engage in party building. They are more likely initially to be elected with weak congressional support, and, as a result, they are more likely to have severe conflict with the legislature. By temperament, they are more likely to attempt to undermine democracy.

Second, even beyond the presidency, less institutionalized party systems produce less experienced politicians. In turn, less experienced politicians are less likely to be unconditionally supportive of democracy and less likely to believe that parties are essential for democracy.

Third, as Flores Macías (2012) and O'Dwyer and Kovalcik (2007) show, policy stability tends to be greater in institutionalized party systems. This is in part because outsiders do not win presidential elections in institutionalized party systems, and outsiders are more likely to favor radical policy change. In addition, well-established parties have strong commitments to some constituencies and to programmatic positions, making radical policy change unlikely.

Fourth, weak institutions, of which fluid party systems are a prime example, are associated with shorter time horizons, with more frequent changes in the rules of the game, with less effective provision of public goods, and with greater propensity for corruption. Fifth, electoral accountability is easier in institutionalized systems because the electoral environment is more stable, allowing for clearer cues for voters. And, finally, weak PSI tends to have corrosive effects on the quality of democracy.

Institutionalized party systems do not guarantee good outcomes. Nor does weak institutionalization always produce bad outcomes. Although ever-greater institutionalization is not a blessing for the quality of democracy, the high degree of openness and instability and the low predictability of inchoate systems tend to produce some problems for democracy.

INSTITUTIONALIZED PARTY SYSTEMS, PREDICTABILITY, AND DEMOCRACY: THEORY

Institutionalized party systems give structure to the democratic competition for power. They give citizens stable and predictable vote options; actors and voters have a sense that future patterns are predictable. In inchoate party systems, past

---

[2] Levitsky and Murillo (2014) make the broader point that democratic politics functions differently in contexts of weak institutions. Along related lines, see O'Donnell (1993, 1994).

stability is lower, and actors and voters have less clarity about the likelihood of future patterns.

Because politicians win elected office through parties, and because elected politicians govern in democratic regimes,[3] institutionalized systems generate stability regarding who is likely to govern and what the range of policies is likely to be.[4] The boundaries of who is likely to govern are relatively clear. In the United States, voters and politicians can be almost certain that the next president will be a Republican or Democrat and that this president will probably adhere reasonably closely to the median position within her party or the median position in the congress. In 2016, Donald Trump flabbergasted many pundits by winning the Republican nomination despite holding positions outside the mainstream on some issues, including free trade and a few social issues such as same sex marriage. However, even this unconventional candidate hewed closely to mainstream Republican positions on most issues (for example, taxes, abortion, gun control) and depended heavily on the Republican coalition. In the US, months ahead of the actual election, skilled pollsters can predict the results of presidential elections within a few percentage points[5] – and they know with near certainty who the strongest two contenders will be.

Likewise, in the United Kingdom, voters and politicians have long known that the next prime minister would be from the Conservative, Labour, or (much less likely) the Liberal Democratic parties. In Western European countries with institutionalized but fragmented party systems, it is often not clear which party will lead a coalition government, but the general contours of policy have been fairly consistent and predictable. Change occurs within bounds established by the party system. Dramatic surprises in who holds executive power are unlikely.[6] As a result, dramatic surprises in policy are uncommon (Flores Macías 2012; O'Dwyer and Kovalcik 2007).

In weakly institutionalized party systems, there is greater uncertainty over electoral outcomes and more flux during the campaign. The turnover from one party to others is higher, and the entry barriers to new parties are lower, resulting in greater uncertainty about who will govern and what policy direction the country will take. Sometimes candidates who look strong a year

---

[3] This is not to deny the important governing powers of administrative and regulatory agencies or, in the case of the European Union, of supranational entities.

[4] In contexts of high polarization, highly divergent policy options are feasible even in institutionalized party systems. For example, in Chile, before the 1970 presidential election result was decided, it was evident that policy choices would be very different depending on who won a tight contest. However, an institutionalized system, in which it was evident that the socialist left, a left-of-center Christian Democratic party, and the right all had reasonable chances of winning, made this fact clear. With lower institutionalization, the potential variability itself is less clear.

[5] In fact, this was the case in the 2016 US presidential election. Many people were surprised by the outcome, but the 538 website accurately anticipated a close race.

[6] Przeworski (1986) famously argued that democratic elections are characterized by uncertain outcomes. This is true, but outcomes are far more predictable in institutionalized party systems.

before the election fade into oblivion, and candidates who were not on the radar screen experience a meteoric rise and win the presidency (Baker *et al.* 2006; Castro Cornejo forthcoming). For example, in December 1997, Irene Sáez, an independent presidential candidate, led Venezuelan public opinion surveys with around 40% of preferences, followed by AD dissident Claudio Fermín with 35%. Both candidates had plummeted in the polls – Sáez to 18% and Fermín to 6% – by April 1998 (McCoy 1999: 66) as outsider and former coup leader Hugo Chávez and later Henrique Salas Römer rose. Ultimately, Sáez won only 2.8% of the vote, and Fermín withdrew when his support collapsed. Chávez seemingly came from nowhere in 1997 to capture 56.2% of the vote, while Salas Römer won 40.0%.

Weak institutions reduce time horizons, increase policy instability, and make inter-temporal agreements and commitments more difficult (Garay 2016; Levitsky and Murillo 2005; Lupu and Riedl 2013; O'Donnell 1994; Simmons 2016; Spiller and Tommasi 2005, 2008). These findings presumably apply to inchoate party systems, which are defined by weak parties, sharp changes in the power of different actors (because some parties lose a high vote share while others gain it), uncertainty about future electoral prospects, and occasional profound change in who the key actors are. These systems are also more likely to experience radical change in the rules of the game.

In institutionalized systems, party labels are important to politicians and to many citizens. Attachments to institutionalized parties extend temporal horizons because politicians want to preserve the value of the party brand. With unusual exceptions under extenuating circumstances of deep crisis (Stokes 2001),[7] institutionalized parties do not abruptly radically switch positions for electoral gain (Berman 1998; Downs 1957: 103–11; Kitschelt 1994: 254–79). They function with one eye toward protecting their reputations and maintaining connections with key constituencies. Party labels, connections to key groups, and ideological commitments constrain change and hence promote predictability and longer time horizons. Politicians with strong attachments to their parties are less willing to risk burning the party label in order to eke out a short-term personal gain. In systems in which they owe their election win to the party, politicians are accountable to the organization, hence cannot act as freewheeling agents.

In personalistic parties, the organization is subordinate to the whims of the leader. The party brand is useful only insofar as it promotes the leader's agenda. Because electoral outcomes vary more from election to election, and because there is much more space for new parties and outsiders and less policy stability, it is more difficult to gauge who will be important players and what the range of likely outcomes is. Under these circumstances, time horizons shorten (O'Dwyer 2006; Simmons 2016).

In contexts of weak institutions, the absence of binding rules creates uncertainty about outcomes and reduces actors' time horizons (Flores-Macías

---

[7] See also Lupu (this volume, 2016); Roberts (2014); Weyland (2002a).

in this volume and 2012; Kitschelt and Kselman 2013; Levitsky this volume; Levitsky and Murillo 2005; Lupu and Riedl 2013; O'Donnell 1994; Simmons 2016; Spiller and Tommasi 2005). Short-term horizons favor clientelistic practices and work against the effective provision of public goods (Hicken 2015; O'Donnell 1994; O'Dwyer 2006; Simmons 2016).

With inchoate party systems, uncertainty is not limited to outcomes. As some parties fade into oblivion and others experience meteoric ascents, there is also more uncertainty about who the players will be.

PARTY SYSTEM INSTITUTIONALIZATION, ELECTORAL UNCERTAINTY, AND OUTSIDERS

Weakly institutionalized party systems make it easier for outsiders to win power. In principle, outsiders could be good for democracy, but, in practice, they more often have pernicious effects. In inchoate systems, the turnover from one party to another is high, the entry barriers to new parties are low, and the likelihood that outsiders can become the head of government is higher than in institutionalized systems. In presidential systems with inchoate party systems, new contenders can burst on the scene and win executive power (Carreras 2012; Flores-Macías 2012; Linz 1994: 26–29; Samuels and Shugart 2010: 62–93). Once powerful parties sometimes fade into oblivion.

Presidential systems usually have more personalized parties than parliamentary systems because presidents are chosen by voters and cannot (except under extraordinary circumstances such as impeachment) be removed by their parties, whereas prime ministers are chosen by, and can be removed by, their parties. Because they do not need to develop long careers within the organization to become the party leader, it is easier for outsiders to win power in presidential systems (Linz 1994: 26–29; Samuels and Shugart 2010: 62–93). Presidents are directly accountable to voters; prime ministers to their parties.

Among presidential systems, there is also a difference between institutionalized and inchoate party systems. Political outsiders do not win the presidency in institutionalized systems. In contrast, in weakly institutionalized systems, outsiders can pop up and immediately become major contenders for executive posts.

Latin American experience is rife with examples of outsiders bursting on to the scene and winning presidential elections in the context of weak party systems. Carreras (2012) developed a dataset of outsider presidential candidates in Latin America from 1980 to 2010. Sixteen of them won the presidency, including eight "full outsiders" – candidates who had never run for office before *and* who ran on new political parties: Fernando Collor de Mello in Brazil (1989),[8] Lucio

---

[8] Collor de Mello should be coded as a partial outsider – a political "maverick" in Carreras's lexicon. He had previously served as appointed mayor of the city of Maceió (1979–82) and as a federal deputy (1983–87), and governor of the state of Alagoas (1987–89), but he created a new

Gutiérrez (2002) and Rafael Correa in Ecuador (2006), Violeta Chamorro in Nicaragua (1990), Fernando Lugo in Paraguay (2008), Alberto Fujimori (1990) and Alejandro Toledo in Peru (2001), and Hugo Chávez in Venezuela (1998). In addition, Evo Morales ran in Bolivia in 2002 as a full outsider and came in second, and then ran again in 2005 and won; and Ollanta Humala ran in 2006 as a full outsider in Peru and came in second and ran again in 2011 and won. All ten outsiders ran in the context of weakly institutionalized party systems.

    Table 3.1 lists these ten presidents and shows the electoral volatility when they were elected and in the previous electoral period. Mean volatility when these presidents were elected was extraordinarily high (59.7%). Because they helped produce the extraordinary party system change, volatility in the election when they won office is not an antecedent, independent measure of PSI. Therefore, Table 3.1 also shows the level of volatility in the electoral period before they won. Although the sample is limited to eight of the winning outsider candidates,[9] mean volatility was extremely high (49.3%). Even the lowest volatility in the previous period, 37.0%, is very high. No full outsider has been elected in the context of a moderately institutionalized party system.

    Carreras also coded "political mavericks" – presidential candidates who had previously run for elected office but were running on new parties. Four political mavericks in his dataset successfully ran for the presidency: Álvaro Uribe in Colombia (2002), Sixto Durán Ballén in Ecuador (1992), Ricardo Martinelli in Panama (2009),[10] and Rafael Caldera in Venezuela (1993). With the partial exception of Caldera in 1993, these mavericks were elected in the context of weakly institutionalized or eroding party systems. Ecuador and to a lesser degree Panama had long had weakly institutionalized party systems. In Venezuela, Caldera's election in 1993 made visible the rapid erosion of the party system that led to collapse by 2000. The linchpins of the system, AD and COPEI, had already weakened significantly when Caldera was elected. In Colombia, the long-standing two-party system that dominated political life from 1910 to 1991 was greatly eroded in the 1990s (see Chapter 8 in this volume). Uribe's election in 2002 and the aftermath dealt it a deathblow, but the prior erosion was a necessary condition for his victory.

party to run for the presidency in 1989. Whether we code him as a full or partial outsider ("maverick") has no impact on the analysis that follows.
[9] In Brazil in 1989 and Nicaragua in 1990, there was no antecedent electoral period under the current competitive regime. Fernando Collor de Mello was elected in 1989 in the first popular presidential election since 1960. The first presidential election under Sandinista's rule took place in 1984. Elections under the Somoza regime (1936–79) were too controlled to be a reasonable basis for determining volatility in 1984.
[10] Martinelli was a maverick in 2004, when he first ran for the presidency on his new party label and won only 5.3% of the valid vote. He ran successfully in 2009.

TABLE 3.1 *Outsider Presidents, Electoral Volatility, and Delegative Democracy Scores*

	Successful election	Electoral volatility when they were elected	Electoral volatility in previous electoral period	Mean delegative democracy score	Change in delegative democracy score
Evo Morales	Bolivia, 2005	66.3	56.2	6.0	+6
Fernando Collor	Brazil, 1989	–	–	8.0	+2
Lucio Gutiérrez	Ecuador, 2002	58.7	43.6	8.0	+6
Rafael Correa	Ecuador, 2006	39.0	58.7	7.0	+4
Violeta Chamorro	Nicaragua, 1990	48.7	–	–	–
Fernando Lugo	Paraguay, 2008	51.8	37.0	6.0	0
Alberto Fujimori	Peru, 1990	68.0	50.4	7.2	+3
Alejandro Toledo	Peru, 2001	62.1	44.1	2.0	+1
Ollanta Humala	Peru, 2011	43.4	51.9	–	–
Hugo Chávez	Venezuela, 1998	99.4	52.8	8.0	+3
Mean		59.7	49.3	6.70	+3.1

Note: In Brazil 1989 and Nicaragua 1990, there was no previous electoral period under the new competitive regimes. Electoral volatility scores are for presidential elections. Mean delegative democracy score is based on country years, not on presidents. Change in delegative democracy score shows the change from the last year of the previous president to the first year of the outsider. *Source for delegative democracy scores*: González (2014)

Consequences of Outsider Presidents

Weak PSI paves the way for outsider presidents, who, in turn, frequently undermine democracy. Outsiders promise and deliver different styles of conducting politics. The ten outsiders who were elected under competitive political regimes railed against the establishment and promised to change the status quo in radical ways.

Outsider presidents have important consequences for presidential accountability to their parties, party building, legislative/executive relations, and democracy. As Samuels and Shugart (2010) argue, the ways in which heads of government are elected have important consequences for their relationships with their parties and for how they govern. Because they are elected by popular vote rather than chosen by their party peers, presidents generally have greater authority over and autonomy from their parties than prime ministers. Presidents are not agents of the party, but of voters.

The incentives and opportunities for presidents to have dominant authority over and autonomy from their parties are exceptionally strong with outsiders, who are not even minimally beholden to their parties. These parties emerged because of the outsider candidates, and in almost all cases were created as personalistic electoral vehicles.[11] These parties have neither the desire nor the capability to monitor these presidents, increasing the likelihood of loose cannon presidents who often have deleterious effects on democracy.

Most insider presidents care about their party brand. They have built their political careers through their party, and they need their parties' support to accomplish their legislative agendas. They usually cannot be oblivious to their party.[12] In contrast, outsider presidents have almost no incentive, and usually no disposition, to prioritize party building, at least initially.

Because they won election without a previously existing party, many outsider presidents initially see little utility to building an organization. Some view a party as more of a limitation than an asset, and they might want to reduce the probability of having a viable rival emerge within the party by keeping the organization weak. Few outsider presidents initially engage in party building, leading to the possibility of a vicious cycle: they are elected in a context of weak PSI, and they proceed to undermine the existing parties. All four cases of party system collapse in contemporary Latin America (Peru in the 1990s, Venezuela between 1998 and 2005, and Ecuador and Bolivia in the 2000s) occurred during the presidencies of full outsiders (Fujimori in Peru, Chávez in Venezuela, and Correa in Ecuador) or a partial outsider (Morales in Bolivia).

For example, Alberto Fujimori repeatedly undermined his own party and opposition parties. He ran in 1990 on the *Cambio 90* (Change 90) label. He forged a new label, NM-C90, *Nueva Mayoría-Cambio 90* (New Majority, Change 90), for the 1992 elections for a constituent assembly. Conaghan (2000: 268) summarizes, "The NM-C90 majority in the CCD (constitutional congress) exhibited no signs of being anything other than an executor of presidential directives." Fujimori never delegated power to party leaders, nor did he build an organization.

In light of the dependence of parties on outsider presidents, one would expect that when these presidents leave the scene, their parties would be vulnerable to

---

[11] MAS in Bolivia is an exception. Created in 1998, it had strong roots in Bolivia's labor movement. But even so, Evo Morales has always been the party's supreme leader.

[12] Under the stress of dire economic crises in the 1980s and 1990s, a few Latin American presidents turned their backs on their parties. See Corrales (2002); Roberts (2014); Stokes (2001); Weyland (2002a).

rapid electoral decline. This expectation is often borne out. After Fernando Collor de Mello's impeachment in 1992, his party (the *Partido de Reconstrução Nacional*, PRN) nearly vanished. In 1994, the PRN presidential candidate won 0.6% of the vote. It never fielded a presidential candidate after that. The party won only 0.4% of the vote for the Chamber of Deputies in 1994 and has never reached 1% since then. Likewise, Alberto Fujimori's party in Peru suffered a huge electoral defeat in 2001 – Fujimori had fled the country the year before. It won only 4.8% of the lower chamber vote and did not field a presidential candidate. His daughter, Keiko Fujimori, has subsequently built a party (see Steven Levitsky's chapter in this volume; Meléndez 2015), but if it were not for her, *Fujimorismo* would have evanesced. Fernando Lugo in Paraguay left almost no party legacy when he was removed from office in 2012. After Alejandro Toledo won the presidency in Peru in 2001, his party (*Perú Posible*) was not able to field a presidential candidate in 2006, and it won only 4.1% of the vote for the Chamber of Deputies. It recovered somewhat in 2011 when Toledo ran for the presidency again,[13] but as Levitsky notes in his chapter on Peru, *Perú Posible* remains closely tethered to and highly dependent on Toledo. Violeta Chamorro's UNO coalition splintered in 1992 in her second year in office in Nicaragua, never to be resurrected again.

Evo Morales and Hugo Chávez are partial exceptions to the norm that outsiders do not invest in party building. Because of its origins as a party based in a social movement that he spearheaded, from the outset, Morales was committed to building the *Movimiento al Socialismo* (Movement Toward Socialism, MAS). Chávez initially kept his party at arm's length. Later he realized that a party could be a useful way of mobilizing support. In 2007, he rebranded his party, after a merger with some minor allied parties, as the United Socialist Party of Venezuela (*Partido Socialista Unido de Venezuela*, PSUV). Although it remained strictly subordinated to Chávez, the PSUV developed some organizational capacity, as Jana Morgan shows in her chapter in this volume.

The origin of outsider presidents is likely to generate conflictual congressional/executive relationships, with potential adverse effects on democracy. In their initial successful bid, outsider presidents' coattails are rarely long enough to generate a massive vote on behalf of their congressional candidates. Table 3.2 shows the percentage of seats their parties and coalitions won in their first successful election. On average, their parties won only 18.8% of lower chamber seats and 19.4% of Senate seats. Five of the ten outsiders came to power with parties that controlled less than 10% of the seats in the lower chamber. Governing without a party (Correa and Chamorro) or with very small parties (Lugo, Collor, and Gutiérrez) is taxing. Only one of the ten outsiders – Chamorro – had a majority coalition in both chambers of congress (or in the unicameral chamber) – and it did not last for long.

---

[13] The coalition of which *Perú Posible* was part won 14.8% of the congressional vote.

TABLE 3.2 *Outsider Presidents' Share of Seats in the National Congress*

	Successful election	President's party	Party's % of seats in lower or unicameral chamber	Party's % of seats in upper chamber	Other parties in initial cabinet	Coalition's % of seats in lower or unicameral chamber	Coalition's % of seats of in upper chamber
Evo Morales	Bolivia, 2005	MAS	56	44	None	56	44
Fernando Collor	Brazil, 1989	PRN	5	5	PMDB, PFL	49	55
Lucio Gutiérrez	Ecuador, 2002*	PSP	7	unicameral	MUPP-NP PSC	41	unicameral
Rafael Correa	Ecuador, 2006*	Movimiento Alianza PAIS/PS-FA	0	unicameral	*Izquierda Democrática* (ID); *Partido Sociedad Patriótica* (PSP)	9	unicameral
Violeta Chamorro	Nicaragua, 1990*	None	0	unicameral	UNO: (APC, MDN, PALI, PAN, PC, PDCN, PLC, PLI, PNC, PSD, PSN)	55	unicameral
Fernando Lugo	Paraguay, 2008	Christian Democratic Party	2.5	0	*Partido Liberal Radical Auténtico,* Popular Movement Tekojoja (MPT), Democratic Progressive Party (PDP)	37.5	33

Alberto Fujimori	Peru, 1990	*Cambio 90*	18	23	IU-IS	29	38
Alejandro Toledo	Peru, 2001*	*Perú Posible*	37.5	unicameral		37.5	unicameral
Ollanta Humala	Peru, 2011*	*Gana Peru*	36	unicameral		36	unicameral
Hugo Chávez	Venezuela, 1998	MVR	26	25	MAS, PPT	37	35
Mean			18.8	19.4		38.7	41.0

Notes: Presidents' coalitions are defined by the parties that had cabinet positions.

*Brazil 1989: Presidential and congressional elections were not concurrent. Data for cabinet composition and congressional seat shares are from Collor's inauguration in March 1990.

Ecuador 2006: Correa's party, *Alianza País*, did not run any congressional candidates.

Nicaragua 1990: Violeta Chamorro was elected with a coalition of fourteen parties, but she was not a member of any party.

Peru: From 1979 to 1992, the Congress of Peru was bicameral. Since 1995, it has been unicameral.

Sources: See Online Appendix 3.1.

Because most outsider presidents initially have weak support in congress, they face a dilemma. They can either cultivate support among the established parties, accept limitations in accomplishing their legislative agendas, or try to circumvent congress to pursue their agendas. On the campaign trail, most outsiders railed against the existing parties. Most are reluctant to do an abrupt about face and bring them on board as partners in government,[14] and many are ideologically hostile to them. Of the ten outsider presidents listed in Table 3.1, only Gutiérrez, Toledo, and Humala from the outset cultivated the establishment parties. Nor, given their harsh criticisms of the status quo and in many cases their desire to implement radical change, are outsider presidents likely to accept protracted legislative/executive deadlock. Instead, a frequent path of outsider presidents has been to attack congress and the establishment parties and to attempt to expand presidential powers (Carreras 2014; Corrales 2014; Negretto 2013).

Eight of the ten outsiders (all but Toledo and Humala) experienced severe conflict with congress. Three (Collor in 1992, Gutiérrez in 2005, and Lugo in 2012) were removed from office by congress – an extraordinary number even in an era of a fair number of impeachments and other forms of presidential removals (Pérez-Liñán 2007). The Peruvian Chamber of Deputies nearly voted to remove Fujimori from office in December 1991 (Kenney 2004: 186), and the Ecuadoran congressional opposition attempted to impeach Gutiérrez in November 2004 before removing him the following year.

Other outsiders attacked the legislature because of difficulty working with them. Fujimori shuttered the Peruvian congress in April 1992, producing a democratic breakdown, because of his inability to win support for some proposals (Kenney 2004: 171–210). Violeta Chamorro ran into difficulties when the conservative parties within her broad electoral coalition jumped to the opposition because of her conciliatory policies toward the Sandinistas. Her own vice president, the head of the national assembly, and most of her initial coalition moved into the opposition, leading to fractious conflict within the congress and between Chamorro and the legislature (McConnell 1997).

Almost immediately after taking office, Hugo Chávez and Rafael Correa announced their desire to hold constitutional congresses to create new constitutions. The constitutional congresses diminished the capacity of the sitting congresses, and in Venezuela it replaced the existing congress. In Venezuela, the new constitution greatly expanded presidential powers, helping allow Chávez to eventually dismantle the system of checks and balances and install a competitive authoritarian regime.

Correa also experienced severe conflict with the sitting congress. When he became president, Correa announced his intention to hold a referendum to convene a constitutional assembly. The legislature voted against it on the grounds

---

[14] Lucio Gutiérrez in Ecuador (2003–05) was an exception, but his turn to the establishment parties led to a rapid rupture with the coalition that elected him and eventually led to him being ousted.

that the process was unconstitutional, leading to a sharp confrontation with Correa. The Supreme Electoral Court (*Tribunal Superior Eleitoral*) terminated the mandates of fifty-seven deputies who had voted against the constitutionality of the constituent assembly. The Supreme Court declared the decision of the Supreme Electoral Court unconstitutional, but the government proceeded with the constitutional assembly anyhow.

Unlike most outsider presidents, Evo Morales came to power with solid congressional backing, but he, too, experienced severe conflict with congress during the constitutional assembly of 2006–08. The MAS approved a new constitution only by violating an agreement it had reached with the opposition that two-thirds of the constitutional assembly would need to approve the new charter before it was submitted to a popular referendum. Lehoucq (2008) called this move a coup.

Outsider presidents are far more likely to govern in a "delegative" style (O'Donnell 1994) in which the president claims legitimacy because he was popularly elected, but regards mechanisms of horizontal accountability (legislatures, courts, and oversight agencies) as nuisances to be circumvented. González (2014) coded the degree to which eleven Latin American countries approximated a delegative democracy or its opposite ideal type, a representative democracy, for every year from 1980 or the establishment of a competitive regime, whichever came later, until 2010. Based on expert surveys, the scores range from zero (representative democracy) to eight (delegative democracy).[15] The eleven countries in his sample include all countries in Table 3.1 except for Nicaragua and all outsider presidents except Chamorro and Humala, who took office in 2011. The average score for forty-three country years for the eight outsider presidents was 6.70. The average score for all 243 country years under other presidents was 2.70.[16] Outsiders are much more likely to promote presidential supremacy and to steamroll mechanisms of horizontal accountability.

Impact on Democracy

Because political outsiders were never previously in leadership positions in the democratic process, they are likely to be less committed to preserving democracy if doing so entails sacrificing some policy preferences. They were not socialized under democratic politics, and some railed against liberal democracy before taking power. Moreover, their relative isolation in congress and other seats of power creates a situation of initial institutional weakness that generates incentives to work against established institutions. Many outsiders (such as Fujimori, Chávez, Morales, and Correa) are indifferent or hostile to democratic checks and balances in principle, and their initial institutional isolation reinforced this indifference. In contrast, insiders develop political

[15] I am grateful to Lucas González for sharing his data.
[16] The difference between these two means is significant at $p = 0.000$.

careers under liberal democracy. In the post-Cold War west, except in minor extremist parties, most insiders are loyal to democratic rules of the game.

A distinction between the eight outsider presidents who won election in the context of existing competitive political regimes and the two (Chamorro and Toledo) who won the foundational elections of new competitive regimes is useful here.[17] Chamorro and Toledo were outsiders, but they came to power with a goal of building liberal democracy where it had not existed.

All eight outsiders who came to power in the contexts of competitive regimes attempted to undermine democratic checks and balances. Chávez and Gutiérrez established their fame by leading high profile military coups (in 1992 and 2000, respectively) that, if successful, would have resulted in democratic breakdowns. This willingness of outsiders to undermine democracy is especially likely when they have radical policy agendas that could be thwarted by the establishment.

Five of the ten outsider presidents (and five of the eight elected under competitive regimes) deliberately undermined liberal democracy. They presided over some of the most important democratic erosions in contemporary Latin America. Alberto Fujimori overthrew Peruvian democracy, dismissing the congress and courts in April 1992 in a palace coup. Evo Morales (2006–present), Rafael Correa (2007–present), and Hugo Chávez (1999–2013) presided over regimes that undermined opposition rights, expanded presidential powers, and extended presidential terms. Very early in their terms, all three began efforts to circumvent the obstacles created by congressional oppositions and the judiciary. They dismantled democratic checks and balances and attacked what remained of the old party systems. All three made extensive use of state resources to create uneven electoral playing fields.[18]

Lucio Gutiérrez (2003–05) also undermined democratic checks and balances. After breaking with the left-of-center coalition that initially supported him in 2002, in December 2004 Gutiérrez unconstitutionally replaced the Supreme Court and packed it with his supporters. In April 2005, he was forced to step down in the middle of his term amidst great public dissatisfaction and mobilization, an opposition vote in congress to remove him from office, and the withdrawal of support from the armed forces.

An earlier outsider president who dismantled democracy was Juan Perón in his first presidency in Argentina (1946–55). Perón closed opposition newspapers, tolerated the destruction (by fires and bombings) of opposition organizations, changed the rules of the game so that he could run for reelection in 1951, jailed prominent political opponents, harassed the opposition,

---

[17] Although the Sandinista regime in Nicaragua allowed for elections in 1984, part of the opposition abstained. The 1990 presidential election was the first since the downfall of the authoritarian Somoza regime (1936–79) to include all opposition forces. Likewise, the 2001 presidential election in Peru was the first free and fair election since Fujimori closed congress in 1992.

[18] On the authoritarian turn in Ecuador, see de la Torre (2013) and Basabe Serrano *et al.* (2010). On Venezuela, see Corrales and Penfold (2011) and Gómez Calcaño *et al.* (2010). On all three countries, see Mayorga (forthcoming), Mazzuca (2014), and Weyland (2013). On Venezuela and the contrast with Colombia under Alvaro Uribe, see L. Gamboa (2016).

terminated the mandates of elected opposition politicians, removed judges who were not favorable to his cause and packed the courts, and changed the electoral rules to favor his party.

The ability of political outsiders to win presidential elections in weakly institutionalized party systems, and their frequent willingness to undermine democratic checks and balances, is probably one reason why Pérez-Liñán and Mainwaring (2013) found that higher democratic PSI before 1978 helps predict higher post-1978 levels of democracy in Latin America. This pattern of outsider presidents undermining democracy is not unique to Latin America, as the examples of Boris Yeltsin (1991–99) and Vladimir Putin (2000–08, 2012–present) in Russia show.

INCHOATE PARTY SYSTEMS, POLITICAL EXPERIENCE, AND DEMOCRACY

Even beyond the presidency, fluid party systems produce less experienced politicians. Outsiders are more likely to win elections, and by definition, they have less political experience. New parties are more electorally successful in less institutionalized systems, and they are more likely to bring in fresh politicians than established parties. Some new parties campaign on the basis of shaking up the political system, and this message is likely to attract newcomers. Established parties are more likely to fade, often ending the political career of veteran politicians. Moreover, institutionalized party systems tend to generate different incentives for politicians. Because party labels and organizations endure, there is a greater prospect of having a political career through the party.

Thus, deductively, it seems likely that Steven Levitsky's argument about amateur politicians in Chapter 11 should be generalizable. Levitsky argues that one consequence of weak parties in Peru has been the rise of amateur politicians, with pernicious consequences on some democratic processes. Amateur politicians are less able to build a strong congress; they lack the know-how and usually the interest. If they are not going to pursue political careers, they have little reason to invest in institution building. Because strong legislatures foster robust democracies (Fish 2006), and because a solid core of experienced legislators is almost a *sine qua non* for a strong legislature (Jones *et al.* 2002), indirectly, a large flock of amateur legislators is likely to make it more difficult to construct a robust democracy. Because they typically have short political horizons, amateurs are likely to be less committed to serving the public and more interested in using office for personal gain. If professional politicians are members of long-established parties and if their electoral and political prospects depend partly on the party label, they have incentives to pay attention to good public policy and to the medium term (Garay 2016; Simmons 2016).

Consistent with this deductive reasoning and with Levitsky's argument about Peru, the linkage between more experienced politicians and PSI holds up in a cross-national sample of seventeen Latin American legislatures (all but Cuba, Haiti, and Venezuela).[19] Fluid party systems have less experienced members of congress. In turn, less experienced members of congress are less likely to support democracy unconditionally and less likely to believe that parties are necessary for democracy.

Surveys of lower chambers (or unicameral legislatures) conducted by the University of Salamanca asked deputies about their political experience. Based on the survey questions, I constructed three variables to measure deputies' political experience. The first variable is Lower Chamber Novice, operationalized as a deputy who was serving his/her first term in the national lower chamber (see the final column of Table 3.3). The percentage of lower chamber novices was over 50% in fifteen of seventeen countries. Leaving aside Costa Rica and Mexico, which have strict term limits that ban deputies from running for reelection and therefore should exclusively have Lower Chamber Novices (Carey 1996), the countries with the highest percentage of Lower Chamber Novices had weakly institutionalized party systems. For the fifteen countries that allow reelection and for which data are available, the correlation between the summary PSI score in Table 2.6 and the percentage of Lower Chamber Novices was -0.72 (p = 0.00). As hypothesized, inchoate party systems have legislatures with less experienced members.

The second variable is Elected Novice, operationalized as a deputy who was serving in his/her first term and who had never previously held elected office. Elected novices can have held a party post or an appointed position in the past. For the same fifteen countries, the correlation between the PSI score in Table 2.6 and the percentage of elected novices is -0.46 (p = 0.08), consistent with expectations.

A political amateur is a deputy who was serving his/her first term in the national assembly *and* had no prior experience in an elected public position, an appointed public position (such as Minister or Vice-Minister), or an official party position. As Table 3.3 shows, with this stringent definition, most countries had a low percentage of political amateurs. For the seventeen countries,[20] a high summary score for PSI is modestly associated with a lower percentage of political amateurs (the Pearson's bivariate correlation is -0.33 (p = 0.19), based on the Z-scores in Table 2.6). Although this correlation is not statistically significant, higher PSI is weakly associated with fewer political amateurs.

Levitsky hypothesizes in Chapter 11 that political amateurs probably have pernicious effects on democracy. This seems likely. To function well, legislatures

---

[19] This wave was not conducted in Haiti and Cuba, and data are not available for Venezuela because the sample was not representative.

[20] For this variable, there was no clear reason to exclude Costa Rica or Mexico.

TABLE 3.3 *Prior Political Experience of Members of Lower Chamber, Latin American Countries*

Country	Number of interviews	Legislature	Political amateur (%)	Elected novice (%)	Lower chamber novice (%)
ARG	70	2007–11 and 2009–13	8.7	35.7	72.5
BOL	97	2010–13	32.0	56.7	90.7
BRA	129	2007–10	3.1	11.6	35.7
CHI	86	2010–14	10.5	25.6	44.2
COL	91	2010–14	11.0	20.9	64.8
CR	56	2010–14	9.1	55.4	82.1
Dom. Rep.	78	2010–16	5.3	49.3	57.3
ECU	95	2009–12	17.9	51.6	81.1
ELS	68	2009–11	10.3	39.7	55.9
GUA	97	2008–12	5.2	51.5	63.9
HON	91	2010–14	30.8	46.2	63.7
MEX	98	2009–11	12.4	41.2	89.6
NIC	69	2007–11	2.9	34.8	63.8
PAN	64	2009–13	15.6	54.7	62.5
PAR	72	2008–13	25.0	51.4	72.2
PER	93	2011–16	27.8	55.9	72.5
URU	79	2009–14	3.8	29.5	51.3
Mean			13.6	41.9	66.1

Notes: "Political novice": A deputy who (1) was serving in the lower chamber (or the unicameral chamber) for the first time; and (2) had no previous experience in an elected political position, as an appointed public official (Minister, Viceminister, etc.), OR in an official party position. "Elected novice": A deputy who (1) was serving in the lower chamber (or the unicameral chamber) for the first time; and (2) had no previous experience in an elected political post. "Lower chamber novice": Operationalized as a deputy who was serving in the lower chamber (or the unicameral chamber) for the first time. Source for lower chamber novice: TR3 of the PELA surveys ("Is this the first legislature in which you were elected deputy/representative?"); sources for Political Novice and Elected Novice: TR3 and TR5 of the PELA surveys (wave of 2007 to 2011) (TR3: "Is this the first legislature in which you were elected deputy/representative?"; TR5: "Have you ever served as an elected public official (mayor, city council) in addition to your current position as deputy/representative?" "Have you ever served in an appointed public position (Minister, Vice-minister, etc.)?" "And have you served in an official party position (secretary general, delegate, etc.)"); Source for mean number of years as party member: TR2 of the PELA surveys.
Source: Elites Parlamentarias de América Latina Project (PELA). Universidad de Salamanca, Manuel Alcántara, director. Wave of 2007–11.

need members who are committed to the assembly and who have the experience to help make it run.

To test two attitudinal aspects of Levitsky's hypothesis for seventeen Latin American countries, Tables 3.4, 3.5, and 3.6 show the relationship between deputies' prior political experience and their attitudes toward democracy and political parties. Consistent with Levitsky, deputies with less political experience are less likely to unconditionally support democracy and more likely to believe that democracy is possible without parties.

Table 3.4 compares Lower Chamber Novices versus all deputies on unconditional support for democracy and on whether parties are necessary for democracy. For the region as a whole, Lower Chamber Novices were much more likely to question that parties are essential for democracy (the means are 3.59 versus 3.26 on the 4-point scale). On average, Lower Chamber Novices were almost twice as far from the maximum value (0.74 away from it compared to 0.41) as deputies who had previously served in the lower chamber. The two means are statistically different at p = 0.000. Lower Chamber Novices score about the same on unconditional support for democracy; this is the only finding that does not support the hypothesis that less experienced politicians have less democratic attitudes.

Table 3.5 compares Electoral Novices to all others on these same questions, with similar results. For the region as a whole, Electoral Novices voice less unconditional support for democracy (the two samples are statistically different at p = 0.005) and show more willingness to believe that democracy is possible without parties (the two means are statistically different at p = 0.000).

Table 3.6 compares Political Amateurs to all other politicians on these same questions. For the region as a whole, 7.7% of political amateurs and only 2.4% of politicians with prior experience did not unconditionally support democracy. Although both percentages are low, the difference between the two samples is significant at p = 0.000. Likewise, politicians with prior experience were more likely to strongly agree that "Without parties there can't be democracy" (p = 0.001).

Kenney (1998: 62) reports a similar finding for an earlier Peruvian legislature (1990–95). The equivocal attitudes about liberal democracy and the indispensability of political parties for democracy found among less experienced politicians are likely to be associated with more instrumental attitudes toward democracy.

Although the percentage of deputies who question that "Democracy is always the best form of government" is low regardless of whether or not they have political experience, given social desirability bias in favor of democracy, especially among legislators in democracies, it is remarkable

TABLE 3.4 *Political Experience and Attitudes toward Democracy and Parties –*
Lower Chamber Novices versus Others

Country	Democracy is preferable (% yes)			No democracy without parties (mean)		
	Lower chamber novices	Others	*P* value if *p*<0.10	Lower chamber novices	Others	*P* value if *p*<0.10
ARG	100	100		3.76	3.65	
BOL	97.7	100		2.63	3.33	0.021
BRA	97.8	98.8		3.22	3.69	0.011
CHI	100	100		3.58	3.6	
COL	98.3	100		3.41	3.56	
CR	100	90	0.030	3.61	4.00	0.001
DOM. REP.	95.2	100		3.63	3.81	
ECU	98.7	100		3.03	3.78	0.001
ELS	84.2	93.1		3.08	3.43	
GUA	91.9	85.7		3.08	3.34	
HON	96.5	96.9		3.54	3.58	
MEX	94.2	100		2.73	2.64	
NIC	100	95.8		3.45	3.52	
PAN	97.5	95.8		3.43	3.58	
PAR	94.2	100		3.56	3.5	
PER	97	96.3		3.22	3.69	0.014
URU	100	100		3.63	3.70	
Total	97.4	96.7		3.26	3.59	0.000

Notes: "Democracy is preferable." The question is "With which of the following statements do you agree more?" (1) Democracy is preferable to any other form of government. (2) In contexts of economic crisis and political instability, an authoritarian government might be better.

"No democracy without parties." The question is "Some people say that without parties there can't be democracy. How much do you agree with that statement?" (4) a lot; (3) somewhat; (2) a little; (1) not at all.

Source: Elites Parlamentarias de América Latina Project (PELA), Universidad de Salamanca. Wave of 2007–11.

that there are statistically significant differences on this question between amateur politicians and more experienced politicians. Likewise, it is notable that less experienced politicians express less support for the statement that there can be no democracy without parties.

TABLE 3.5 *Political Experience and Attitudes toward Democracy and Parties – Electoral Novices versus Others*

Country	Democracy is preferable (% yes)			No democracy without parties (mean)		
	Electoral novices	Others	P value if p<0.10	Electoral novices	Others	P value if p<0.10
ARG	100	100		3.68	3.76	
BOL	96.3	100		2.73	2.64	
BRA	93.3	99.1	0.088	3.07	3.58	0.085
CHI	100	100		3.55	3.61	
COL	94.7	100	0.050	3.21	3.53	
CR	100	96		3.68	3.68	
DOM. REP.	94.4	100		3.57	3.84	
ECU	97.9	100		2.90	3.46	0.015
ELS	77.8	95	0.033	3.07	3.34	
GUA	90	89.4		3.20	3.15	
HON	95.2	97.9		3.50	3.60	
MEX	95	94.7		2.65	2.77	
NIC	100	97.7		3.50	3.47	
PAN	97.1	96.6		3.37	3.62	
PAR	94.6	97.1		3.51	3.57	
PER	96.2	97.6		3.37	3.32	
URU	100	100		3.70	3.65	
Total	95.3	98	0.005	3.26	3.45	0.000

Notes: "Democracy is preferable." The question is "With which of the following statements do you agree more?" (1) Democracy is preferable to any other form of government. (2) In contexts of economic crisis and political instability, an authoritarian government might be better.

"No democracy without parties." The question is "Some people say that without parties there can't be democracy. How much do you agree with that statement?" (4) a lot; (3) somewhat; (2) a little; (1) not at all.

Source: Elites Parlamentarias de América Latina Project (PELA), Universidad de Salamanca. Wave of 2007–11.

POLICY STABILITY AND STABLE RULES OF THE GAME

Institutionalized party systems tend to generate longer time horizons, greater policy stability and predictability, and greater stability in the rules of the game. In these systems, the main actors in democratic politics are stable, and their positions are

TABLE 3.6 *Political Experience and Attitudes toward Democracy and Parties – Political Novices versus Others*

Country	Democracy is preferable (% yes)			No democracy without parties (mean)		
	Political novices	Others	P value if p<0.10	Political novices	Others	P value if p<0.10
ARG	100	100		3.33	3.76	
BOL	100	96.9		2.58	2.74	
BRA	75	99.2	0.000	3.00	3.54	0.000
CHI	100	100		3.56	3.60	
COL	90	100	0.004	3.10	3.51	
CR	100	98		3.40	3.70	
DOM. REP.	100	97.2		3.25	3.74	
ECU	94.1	100	0.032	2.82	3.24	
ELS	42.9	93.3	0.000	2.86	3.28	
GUA	80	90.2		2.00	3.24	0.014
HON	92.9	98.4		3.64	3.52	
MEX	91.7	95.3		2.92	2.69	
NIC	100	98.5		4.00	3.46	0.000
PAN	90	98.1		3.40	3.50	
PAR	94.4	96.3		3.44	3.57	
PER	92	98.5		3.32	3.45	
URU	100	100		3.33	3.68	
Total	92.3	97.6	0.000	3.15	3.41	0.001

Note: "Democracy is preferable." The question is "With which of the following statements do you agree more?" (1) Democracy is preferable to any other form of government. (2) In contexts of economic crisis and political instability, an authoritarian government might be better.
"No democracy without parties." The question is "Some people say that without parties there can't be democracy. How much do you agree with that statement?" (4) a lot; (3) somewhat; (2) a little; (1) not at all.
Source: Elites Parlamentarias de América Latina Project (PELA), Universidad de Salamanca. Wave of 2007–11.

relatively stable. This stability and predictability favor longer time horizons that partially counteract the short-term electoral incentives that necessarily also drive politicians' behavior. In institutionalized parties, politicians have incentives to protect and strengthen the party label. Their own fortunes rise and fall partly on the fortunes of their party.

This is less true in inchoate systems. Mechanisms of electoral accountability are easily vitiated; politicians can escape accountability by shifting from one party to another (Zielinski *et al.* 2005). Even major parties are subject to steep electoral losses, so politicians might jump ship for opportunistic reasons. Politics is more of an amateur affair, and, for political amateurs, developing long time horizons makes little sense.

As Flores-Macías (2012) showed, an institutionalized party system favors greater policy stability than an inchoate system for two reasons.[21] First, it is easier for outsiders to win the presidency in weakly institutionalized systems. In turn, many outsider presidents favor radical policy change. For example, Collor and Fujimori on the right and Chávez, Correa, and Morales on the left were committed to radical reform.

Second, presidents from well-established parties are typically more constrained than outsiders or other presidents from weak parties. Well-established parties make it more difficult to implement radical reforms, as Carlos Andrés Pérez's (1989–93) presidency and impeachment in Venezuela showed (Corrales 2002: 121–27, 131–68). Pérez wanted to implement far-reaching neoliberal economic change, but his party, *Acción Democrática*, did not go along with this, partly because of programmatic objections, helping to sink his reform agenda and ultimately his presidency.

The prior history of ideological and programmatic commitments, connections to organized interests, the existence of experienced leaders within the party, and organizational structures in established parties constrain presidents and prime ministers. In institutionalized systems, parties generally remain faithful to long-established ideological and programmatic principles (Berman 1998; Downs 1957: 103–11; Kitschelt 1994: 254–79). Radical change tends to be costly electorally because parties would risk losing the support of organized interests, activists, and voters. The interests of funders, activists, and organized groups limit change. They hold influence within the party and contribute time, money, organizational capacity, talent, and votes. Going against these stakeholders entails potentially high costs. Established parties in institutionalized systems are usually loath to risk losing large numbers of partisans by undertaking radical shifts.

In contrast, new parties exercise little constraining effect. Political outsiders create party labels to run for the presidency, but they are not beholden to the party. To the contrary, the party owes its existence to the outsider president. Inchoate party systems "undermine political parties' ability to prevent the president from conducting drastic changes to the status quo" (Flores-Macías

---

[21] O'Dwyer and Kovalcik (2007) make a similar argument for Postcommunist Europe and O'Donnell (1994) did for delegative democracies. For a diverging perspective, see Campello (2015), who argues that more institutionalized parties did not block left-of-center presidents from implementing market-oriented economic policies and that high electoral volatility likewise did not affect the probability that presidents would announce one program as candidates and pursue another in office.

2012: 5). Programmatic principles are not yet strongly established in many young parties, so the cost of radical change is lower. The parties generally have weaker connections to organized interests, few committed activists, and fewer fund raisers and funders. Funders and organized interests are usually less attached to specific parties and more willing to support candidates of different parties. Fewer voters are partisans, so radical party shifts do not disrupt long-established bonds between the party and a strong core of partisans.

Because they were not tethered by their parties' established ties and ideological commitments, outsiders who took power in the context of inchoate party systems – Alberto Fujimori in Peru (1990–2000), Hugo Chávez in Venezuela (1999–2013), Evo Morales in Bolivia (2006–present), and Rafael Correa in Ecuador (2007–present) – were able to undertake radical change in economic policy. Conversely, leftist presidents who took office in the context of institutionalized party systems – Ricardo Lagos (2000–06) and Michelle Bachelet in Chile (2006–10, 2014–present), Luis Inácio da Silva (2003–11) and Dilma Rousseff (2011–16) in Brazil, Mauricio Funes in El Salvador (2009–14), and Tabaré Vázquez (2005–10 and 2015–present) and José Mujica in Uruguay (2010–15) – implemented modest reforms. In Latin America, stronger institutions in general, including more institutionalized party systems, helped provide greater policy stability and averted radical policy change that often proved ill-advised (O'Donnell 1994).[22]

Although policy stability is not always normatively desirable, high instability often has costs (O'Donnell 1994; Spiller and Tommasi 2005). It induces uncertainty among investors and citizens, with negative economic effects. For investors, policy instability is anathema. It makes it difficult to plan future courses of action, including decisions about investment and employment. It could raise the specter of erratic policy making and radical anti-business policies. For citizens and consumers, too, policy instability has high costs. It makes it difficult to plan major expenses and investments such as education, and it makes it difficult to figure out how to save money for the future.

In some situations, major policy change might be in order. Strong formal institutions generally, and institutionalized party systems specifically, tend to stifle radical change, which means that the possibility of radical political innovation is low. Accordingly, Coppedge (1994) warned of the perils of "partyarchy," and Schedler (1995) of the potential costs of over-institutionalization. The argument here is not that stability is always good, but rather that chronic instability shortens actors' time horizons and reduces the probability of good collective outcomes.

---

[22] An institutionalized party system does not preclude the possibility of sharp policy change. Sharp change is more likely if the main parties are programmatically polarized. In such circumstances, a change of government can produce significant policy change even in an institutionalized system. The argument here rests on an "all other things equal" clause.

Institutionalized systems also favor maintaining stable rules of the game. The set of actors is stable, and new actors are more likely than established ones to seek a radical change of the rules of the game. They might be ideologically committed to radical change in the rules, and they often have strategic reasons to change the rules. They often railed against these rules as part of the decayed and corrupt establishment. To maintain their political standing with their constituents, they want to follow through on these clamors to radically change the system. Outsider presidents typically come to power with weak congressional support, so they have strong incentives to seek to get rid of the sitting congress and to secure new rules that would help them consolidate power and weaken the old establishment forces.

One of the most radical forms of changing the rules is a new constitution. Corrales (2014) and Negretto (2013) identified twelve new constitutions in Latin America in the post-1980 period: El Salvador 1983, Guatemala 1985, Nicaragua 1987, Brazil 1988, Colombia 1991, Paraguay 1992, Peru 1993, Argentina 1994, Ecuador 1998, Venezuela 1999, Ecuador 2008, and Bolivia 2009. Four of the twelve occurred under the first president of a new democratic or semi-democratic period (Guatemala 1985, Nicaragua 1987, Brazil 1988, and Paraguay 1992) and a fifth shortly before a transition to a competitive regime (El Salvador 1983). Because the presidents in these five cases inaugurated (or were on the verge of doing so) new competitive regimes, there is no score for electoral volatility for the year when they were elected. The other seven presidents who presided over new constitutions governed in already existing competitive regimes.

Based on these seven presidents, radical constitutional change is more likely in inchoate party systems, consistent with the hypothesis that the rules tend to be more stable in institutionalized systems. Mean presidential electoral volatility when these seven presidents were elected was 54.3 compared to 31.3 for 118 elections of presidents who did not oversee the writing of new constitutions in the post-1978 period. The difference between means is statistically significant at $p < 0.06$ notwithstanding the small number (seven) of presidents who were elected and then oversaw the writing of new constitutions.

Four of the ten full outsider presidents mentioned earlier – Fujimori, Chávez, Morales, and Correa – presided over the establishment of new constitutions that enabled them to concentrate power and move toward competitive authoritarian regimes. These presidents account for every single new constitution since 1983 that expanded constitutional presidential powers according to Corrales's (2014) index. In light of Fish's (2006) evidence that strong legislatures are good for democracy, the fact that these outsiders bolstered their own powers at the expense of congress was a bad portent. The other six new constitutions that Corrales (2014) coded, introduced by insider presidents, all reduced presidential powers. All four outsiders who produced new constitutions with expanded presidential powers were impatient with the normal checks and balances of democratic politics. They sought and achieved constitutions that ended the ban on consecutive presidential terms. All ran for and won reelection. Partly because of their expanded presidential powers, they presided over the emasculation of democratic checks and balances.

EXTENDING TIME HORIZONS AND LIMITING CORRUPTION

Institutionalized party systems generate stability and predictability in electoral competition; in linkages with voters, organized interests, and the state; and in broad contours of policy. As a result, they lengthen time horizons. Conversely, more is up for grabs in weakly institutionalized systems. Parties structure the political process less than with institutionalized systems. As a result, predictability is lower and time horizons tend to be shorter (O'Donnell 1994), easily leading to policy myopia (Simmons 2016; Spiller and Tommasi 2005, 2008). Policies that pay off in the long term but not the short term, such as inclusionary and non-discretionary social policies (Garay 2016) and technology policies (Simmons 2016) are more likely with well-established parties. More generally, programmatic politics is more likely with well-established parties (Kitschelt and Kselman 2013).[23]

Although some institutionalized parties have made widespread use of clientelism, on deductive grounds, there is reason to hypothesize that institutionalized systems might be associated with less clientelism. Because institutionalized parties breed longer time horizons that are associated on average with more focus on policies that generate long-term development, they might focus less on clientelistic provision (Kitschelt and Kselman 2013). Parties have less incentive to focus on building programmatic brands in inchoate systems; they might not have the time to do so. Because less institutionalized systems have more amateur politicians with short-term horizons, they might be more conducive to clientelistic exchange. Because institutionalized systems on average feature more programmatic competition (Kitschelt *et al.* 2010), parties might rely less on clientelistic linkages. Weak formal institutions make for bastions of strong informal ones, and they more often than not protect the interests of the powerful.

If weak PSI reduces actors' time horizons and is associated with clientelistic practices, then it might correlate with a high perception of corruption because the particularistic exchange of favors that characterizes clientelism is rife with opportunities for corruption. The widely used Worldwide Governance Indicators include a measure of perception of a government's capacity to control corruption. The scores for a given country–year are the number of standard deviations above or below the world mean for a specific country in a specific year. Figure 3.1 shows the scores for Latin America for 2014. Except

---

[23] The data in Chapter 4, however, do not show an association between programmatic linkages and more institutionalized party systems.

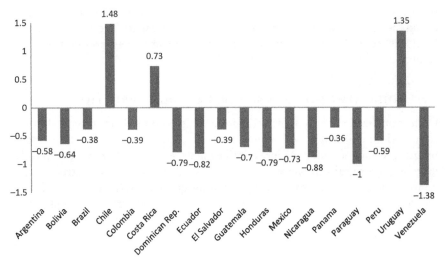

FIGURE 3.1 Perception of Control of Corruption, 2014: Worldwide Governance Indicators
Source: Worldwide Governance Indicators (2015).

Chile, Costa Rica, and Uruguay, Latin American countries scored below the world mean in 2014. Consistent with the hypothesis, institutionalized party systems are associated with better perception of control of corruption. The summary PSI score in Table 2.6 is correlated at 0.52 (p = 0.03) with the 2014 World Governance Indicator for perception of control of corruption, based on eighteen countries (all but Cuba and Haiti).

It also seems likely that, consistent with Garay (2016) and Simmons (2016), the longer time horizons that result from institutionalized party systems are conducive to a better provision of public goods. Consistent with this hypothesis, the correlation between the summary score for PSI in Table 2.6 and the 2014 World Governance Indicator for perception of government effectiveness is 0.55 (significant at p = 0.02). Of course, this correlation is merely suggestive and far from conclusive. Factors beyond an institutionalized party system (for example, a solid state and good policies) also affect government effectiveness.

THE EMERGENCE OF PARTISANSHIP AND THE POSSIBILITY OF ELECTORAL ACCOUNTABILITY

This chapter has until now focused on the effects of weak institutionalization on politicians and elite actors. Weakly institutionalized party systems also provide different environments for voters. In institutionalized systems, voters face a stable electoral landscape. The set of actors, electoral results, and parties' ideological positions are stable. As a result, it is easier for voters to get a clear sense of what the options are and which is best for them (Marinova 2016). The information environment is more stable and clearer.

The electoral environment is less stable and predictable for voters in inchoate systems. The entrance of major new parties and the exit or sharp decline of major old parties make for changing electoral alternatives. Electoral volatility is higher, so it is less predictable who the winners and losers will be. Sometimes, candidates for executive office experience meteoric rises and declines in a short time (Baker *et al.* 2006). Lower ideological and programmatic stability of the main parties make it less clear how different parties are positioned relative to one another.

For these reasons, weak PSI is inimical to partisanship. Converse (1969) argued that partisanship emerged over time as voters came to more clearly identify the main parties and what they stood for (see also Dinas 2014). In inchoate systems, the main actors change with some frequency, and the parties are less fixed ideologically. Assuming that Converse's and Dinas's arguments are correct, we should have different expectations for the emergence of partisanship in inchoate systems. Voters will not bond to ephemeral organizations; new parties are likely to take time to develop a large contingent of partisans. Voters' attachments to established parties are likely to be disrupted if those older organizations become minor contenders or undertake deep programmatic changes. The instability of the main contenders and their ideological positions creates hurdles for building partisans.[24]

This argument reverses the normal claim about partisanship, namely that partisanship is a foundation for stabilizing party systems (Converse 1969; Green *et al.* 2002). This is not to argue that the causal arrow works in only one direction or that Converse's and Green *et al.*'s classic claim is wrong. Weak partisanship makes the institutionalization of a party system more difficult and subjects it to greater future uncertainty, and it makes party systems more vulnerable to radical change (Lupu 2016; Seawright 2012).[25]

---

[24] The time series on party identification is not long enough or consistent enough to statistically test the hypothesis that lower PSI is associated with lower partisanship. A test of this hypothesis would require a measure of partisanship for the year immediately following an electoral period. Otherwise, the time gap between the data on partisanship and the electoral period is too great for a causal mechanism about the effect of PSI on partisanship to be convincing. For most Latin American countries, only one or two data points meet these criteria. Moreover, region-wide surveys often did not use the same questions about partisanship, weakening the comparability of different data points over time.

[25] The country correlation between the summary PSI score in Table 2.6 and the percentage of survey respondents who said that they sympathized with a political party in the 2014 AmericasBarometer survey was modest at 0.33 (p = 0.19). However, the AmericasBarometer question is not ideal for tapping partisanship because it asks about respondents' *current* partisan identification. Partisanship is better assessed by questions that ask about respondents' identification regardless of the immediate situation. See Castro Cornejo (forthcoming).

Other things equal,[26] low PSI might also be unfavorable to electoral accountability (Mainwaring and Torcal 2006; Moser and Scheiner 2012; O'Dwyer 2006; Zielinski *et al.* 2005). In most democracies, parties are the primary mechanism of electoral accountability.[27] In turn, electoral accountability is core to the very practice of representative democracy, whose promise hinges on the contract between voters and elected politicians. In principle, politicians should work to further the interests of voters and of the public good, and they should be voted out of office for failure to live up to this contract. Voters use parties as information short cuts to help understand what individual politicians stand for. For electoral accountability to work well, then, voters must be able to identify in broad terms what the main parties are and what they stand for (Aldrich 1995: 3; Downs 1957; Hinich and Munger 1994). In contexts where parties disappear and appear with frequency and where personalities often overshadow parties as routes to executive power, the prospects for effective electoral accountability diminish. Getting elected politicians to faithfully represent voters is challenging under the best of circumstances (Przeworski *et al.* 1999) – all the more so with weakly institutionalized systems.[28]

For electoral accountability and political representation to function well, citizens need effective information cues that enable them to vote in reasoned ways without spending inordinate time to reach these decisions.[29] In institutionalized systems, parties provide an ideological reference that gives some anchoring to voters. Voters can reduce information costs, thus enhancing electoral accountability. The limited stability of less institutionalized systems reduces the information cues that they offer voters (Moser and Scheiner 2012). The weaker information cues hamper the bounded rationality of voters, undercutting the potential for electoral accountability based on a somewhat informed evaluation of policies, governments, and leaders. Where electoral accountability is vitiated, the ideal of representative democracy, that elected politicians will serve as agents of the voters to promote good policy or public goods or to advance the interests of specific constituencies, may break down (Luna and Zechmeister 2005).

---

[26] If an institutionalized system is exclusionary or collusive, such as the Colombian system from 1958 to 1990, electoral accountability suffers for different reasons.

[27] Even in democracies in which the personal vote is important, such as the US, partisan cues and identities can be highly important (Bartels 2000; Green *et al.* 2002).

[28] Torcal and Lago (2015) correctly argue that the relationship between electoral volatility and accountability is not linear. An ideal type hyper-institutionalized party system would afford little or no accountability because vote shares would be stable regardless of how well or poorly governments performed. Accountability rests on the capacity of citizens to change their votes if they are not satisfied with the government.

[29] This paragraph comes from Mainwaring and Torcal (2006).

PARTY SYSTEM INSTITUTIONALIZATION AND THE QUALITY OF DEMOCRACY

For theoretical reasons already suggested in this chapter, we can hypothesize that low PSI would be associated with lower quality democracy. Weakly institutionalized systems make it easier for political outsiders to win power. Outsiders usually have a cavalier attitude toward representative democracy, and many attempt to undermine it. Weakly institutionalized systems have less experienced politicians, who tend to be less committed to democracy and to parties. Fluid party systems are associated with greater corruption, which can have corrosive effects on democracy. Inchoate systems hinder electoral accountability.

I leave more rigorous tests about the impact of PSI on democratic quality to subsequent scholarship and to already published work (Pérez-Liñán and Mainwaring 2013),[30] but the hypothesis holds up in a simple preliminary test of correlation. The Pearson bivariate correlation between the summary score for PSI (Table 2.6) and Freedom House scores for 2015 (based on the 2016 *Freedom in the World*) is 0.48 (p = 0.04).[31] The bivariate correlation between the summary score for PSI and *mean* Freedom House scores for 1990–2015 is 0.55 (p = 0.02).

The five cases of democratic erosion in Latin America in the new millennium have been Venezuela, Ecuador, Bolivia, Nicaragua, and Honduras (Mainwaring and Pérez-Liñán 2015). In all five countries (and in Mexico), Freedom House scores were at least two points lower in 2014 compared to their highest score during the post-1978 wave of democratization.

In Venezuela, Ecuador, and Bolivia, democratic erosion was causally connected to weak PSI (Mazzuca 2014). The election of political outsiders and the sharp erosion of the traditional party systems paved the way for the ensuing erosion of democracy. The demise of the traditional parties removed obstacles to the path from representative democracy to competitive authoritarianism in Venezuela and to a degraded representative democracy that borders on competitive authoritarianism in Ecuador and Bolivia. The absence of solid party oppositions enabled presidents with hegemonic aspirations to trample over mechanisms of accountability. All three countries had weakly institutionalized systems in the run-up to the election of the outsider presidents. All three systems show signs of becoming institutionalized in the wake of party system collapse – but under the aegis of presidents with hegemonic aspirations.

---

[30] For an interesting paired comparison along these lines, see Corrales (2001).

[31] I inverted the Freedom House scores so that a high score indicates a high quality democracy. The inverted scores range from 0 (extremely authoritarian) to 12 (very democratic). The correlation between the summary PSI score and the most recent (as of August 2016) Varieties of Democracy score for liberal democracy was 0.41 (p = 0.09) (Coppedge *et al.* 2016a).

Nicaragua's party system is fairly weakly institutionalized (its score for PSI in Table 2.6 was slightly above the Latin American average), but in its case, the relationship between weak PSI and democratic erosion is less clear-cut. The Honduran case reverses the causal direction between PSI and democratic erosion. The 2009 coup and its aftermath provoked a degradation of democracy, and subsequently a previously highly institutionalized party system eroded.

Most Latin American countries with highly institutionalized party systems have high quality democracies. According to the summary score in Table 2.6, Uruguay, Mexico, and Chile have the most institutionalized systems in the region. According to Freedom House and V-Dem, Chile, Uruguay, and Costa Rica have the highest quality democracies in Latin America. The Mexican case underscores that PSI does not ensure good democratic outcomes.

What about the relationship between change in the level of institutionalization and change in the quality of democracy? The three countries (Brazil, El Salvador, and Mexico – the latter with the qualifications discussed in Chapter 2) that experienced a clear increase in PSI since the publication of *Building Democratic Institutions* became higher quality democracies (Brazil and El Salvador) or became democratic (Mexico). The countries that maintained highly institutionalized systems, Chile and Uruguay, are high quality liberal democracies. Bolivia, Ecuador, and Peru, the cases of inchoate systems circa 1993 that later culminated in party system collapse, moved in divergent directions in the quality of democracy. Bolivia and Ecuador have experienced some erosion of democracy. Peru's party system collapse was also associated with a democratic breakdown when President Fujimori shuttered the Peruvian congress and part of the court system in 1992. Today Peru has a democracy, though as Levitsky argues (Chapter 11), not a robust one. Argentina, Colombia, and Costa Rica are cases of party system erosion without collapse, although one major party in Argentina (the Radicals) shrivelled and one in Costa Rica (the Social Christian Unity Party, PUSC) collapsed. Democracy has remained robust in Costa Rica and troubled in Colombia, with no major net gain or loss in the quality of democracy.

Overall, then, increasing PSI has been associated with increases in the quality of democracy; persistently high PSI has usually been associated with high quality democracy; and party system collapse has consistently been associated with dips in the quality of democracy – sometimes profound ones, as in Peru in the 1990s and Venezuela in the 2000s.

Notwithstanding the solid association between PSI and higher quality democracy, citizens in Latin America are not enthusiastic about parties even in institutionalized systems. Trust in parties is low in Latin America and most of the democratic world. The AmericasBarometer survey regularly asks, "How much confidence (*confianza*) do you have in political parties?" The scale ranges from 1 (no confidence at all) to 7 (a lot of confidence). In 2014, the country mean for the eighteen Latin American countries in the survey (all but Cuba and Haiti) was 2.90,[32] well below the mid-point (4) on the scale (LAPOP 2014). The country-level correlation between mean confidence in parties (based on the 2014 AmericasBarometer survey) and average PSI from 1990 to 2015 (based on Table 2.6) was modest (0.35 ($p = 0.16$)). High system institutionalization has not rescued parties from widespread negative citizen sentiment. Citizens do not share the enthusiasm of most political scientists for institutionalized party systems.

CONCLUSION

PSI has important consequences for democratic politics. The chapter has highlighted six usually negative effects of weakly institutionalized party systems. They increase electoral uncertainty and make it easier for political outsiders to win the presidency, often with deleterious consequences for democracy; they are associated with more political amateurs; they increase policy instability and instability of the rules of the game; they shorten actors' time horizons and are associated with political systems more permeated by corruption; they make electoral accountability more challenging; and, on average, they are associated with lower quality democracies.

Institutionalized party systems are not a panacea, as countless historical and contemporary cases show. When it is based on exclusion and restricted options (e.g., Colombia from 1958 until 1990), high PSI has high democratic costs. Inchoate systems do not doom a country to bad results on all dimensions, as the Peruvian example today shows (see Levitsky's chapter in this volume). High levels of PSI do not necessarily produce better democratic processes or outcomes than moderate levels. Moreover, throughout most of the region, citizens seem to dislike parties regardless of how institutionalized the system is. However, inchoate party systems are generally associated with the problematic outcomes discussed in this chapter and with lower quality democracy. A major challenge for contemporary democratic politics in Latin America and beyond is that citizens are becoming less attached to parties and more skeptical and even disdainful of them, but they remain essential agents of democratic representation and accountability

---

[32] This excludes non-respondents.

4

Democratization without Party System Institutionalization: Cross-National Correlates

Scott Mainwaring and Fernando Bizzarro*

For generations, a conventional wisdom in political science was famously captured by Schattschneider's (1942: 1) dictum that "Political parties created democracy, and modern democracy is unthinkable save in terms of the parties." By Schattschneider's logic, it is difficult to imagine a democracy without solid parties (see also Aldrich 1995: 295–96). Many other scholars have seen parties – and implicitly, institutionalized party systems – as essential underpinnings of modern representative democracy (Sartori 1976; Stokes 1999).

But as post-transition experiences in Latin America, Africa, the post-communist countries, and parts of Asia make clear, the solidity of parties and party system institutionalization (PSI) vary greatly across cases and over time. Rather than being the norm, institutionalized party systems have been the exception in third and fourth wave cases of democratization. What explains the extraordinary variance in institutionalization?

A complete answer to this question would require a different book devoted primarily to that analysis. This chapter has a more modest objective. It offers insights into average patterns for the most recent episodes of democratization in eighteen Latin American countries. Rather than exploring the process by which individual cases evolved, we search for the "average" quantifiable factors associated with variations in levels of PSI.

The chapter outlines five theoretical approaches to explaining PSI, presents hypotheses that derive from these theoretical approaches, and offers quantitative analyses that assess how compatible the results are with these theoretical approaches and hypotheses. The quantitative analysis is a crucial test of which theoretical approaches and specific hypotheses are likely to offer explanatory leverage for Latin America. Without it, it would be difficult to assess which

* We are grateful to Sarah Zukerman Daly, Steve Levitsky, Tarek Masoud, Daniel Ziblatt, and participants at the MIT Latin American politics seminar for comments and to María Victoria De Negri for helpful research assistance and comments.

theoretical approaches and hypotheses are most fruitful for further exploration. It is also perhaps the best way to consider a wide array of alternative hypotheses.

The most striking finding is the degree to which many statistical associations defied expectations and ran counter to the established literature. Neither a country's past history of democracy nor the longevity of the current semi-democratic or democratic regime had an association with PSI. In Latin America, on average, the latest wave of democratization has not induced PSI, contrary to the experience of the early democratizing countries (Lipset and Rokkan 1967) and to southern Europe after 1974. A venerable literature has postulated that in mass representative democracy, parties offer great advantages to politicians (Aldrich 1995) – but in Latin America, either politicians are not investing much in party building (see Levitsky's chapter on Peru; Hale 2006), or those investments are failing. In several party systems, outsider presidents purposefully crippled the established parties as a way of bolstering their own power (e.g., Alberto Fujimori in Peru, Hugo Chávez in Venezuela, Rafael Correa in Ecuador, Evo Morales in Bolivia).

Converse (1969) argued that as democracy survived for a longer time, voters would be more likely to develop partisan identifications, which, in turn, would stabilize electoral markets. Downs (1957) expected that electoral markets would stabilize as parties built reputations and voters learned which parties best represented their interests. But these expectations, too, have been dashed. Mainwaring *et al.* (2016) and Mainwaring and Zoco (2007) showed that electoral volatility and the vote share of new parties were on average much lower in democracies that were born a long time ago. But contrary to these two works based on a broader sample of countries, in Latin America, countries with a long prior legacy of democracy did not on average have more institutionalized party systems than countries with little history of democracy prior to the third wave. On average, democracy or semi-democracy has now lasted for two generations without PSI.

A second key finding is that, despite these and other counterintuitive null results, PSI and erosion do not occur randomly. The most important "positive" findings are associations between PSI and other party or party system characteristics. After testing the argument advanced by Zucco (2015) and Luna and Altman (2011) that PSI can occur even in the absence of programmatic connections between voters and parties and of organizationally strong parties, we find support for the first part of this argument, but not for the second. Institutionalization is much more likely when parties have strong national organizations. It is also more likely where party systems are less fragmented (i.e., where there are fewer parties).

Third, government performance has had a surprisingly weak association with PSI in Latin America. Economic growth and inflation had weak correlations with PSI. This is surprising in light of the magnitude of economic crisis and change in Latin America since the beginning of the great debt crisis in 1982, and also in light of the weight some previous literature has placed on economic distress as the major cause of party system upheaval in Latin America and the post-Soviet region.

The analysis in this chapter has several limitations. We do not offer a parsimonious theory that purports to explain PSI, but rather spell out the major theoretical approaches that might explain variance in outcomes and provide empirical tests about them. Given that the data are observational, we refrain from causal claims.

The chapter examines the plausibility of competing theories and hypotheses about PSI. It considers five different theoretical approaches to understanding PSI and twenty specific hypotheses associated with those theoretical approaches. We give evidence about theoretically important correlates that scholars have hypothesized to have a causal impact on PSI.

The chapter proceeds as follows. The first section describes the dependent variables and explains the case selection of electoral periods. The second section describes five theoretical approaches to understanding party system change, presents twenty hypotheses that correspond to these theoretical approaches, describes the operationalization of the variables, and discusses results. The third section discusses the model and presents results. The conclusion reviews the findings and their limitations.

DEPENDENT VARIABLES AND CASE SELECTION

We test for the associations between PSI and its hypothesized determinants in eighteen Latin American party systems.[1] We included all presidential and all lower chamber elections (in separate regressions) belonging to the contemporary electoral regime (as of 2015). We define an electoral regime as a continuous period in which countries score 2 or more in the Polity2 index. This criterion includes fifteen Latin American countries since (re)democratization during the third wave and the region's only three countries that democratized before the third wave and remained democratic or semi-democratic until the 2000s – Costa Rica, which has been democratic since 1953; Colombia, democratic or semi-democratic since 1958; and Venezuela, which was democratic from 1959 until the 2000s, before descending to competitive authoritarianism. We also include elections under three competitive authoritarian regimes that began as democracies or semi-democracies but then eroded: the Peruvian elections during Alberto Fujimori's presidency (1990–2000), the Venezuelan elections since 1958 despite the erosion to competitive authoritarianism in 2009, and the Nicaraguan elections since 1990 despite the erosion around 2010. In all three cases, the electoral process remained uninterrupted and elections remained highly contested except for Venezuela in 2005, when the opposition abstained.

---

[1] Coverage for Argentina's lower chamber does not extend past 2001 because of problems of data availability. As we noted in Chapter 2, after 2003 the Argentine data are available at the provincial level but not at the national level.

The unit of observation for the quantitative analyses is country electoral periods – that is, each electoral period in each country. Chapter 2 included seven indicators of PSI for which data are available for each electoral period: the vote share of new parties, the stability of the main contenders, and electoral volatility, for both presidential and lower chamber elections, and ideological change at the system level in the lower chambers of national congresses.[2] We did not include ideological stability in the analyses in this chapter because the coverage of data for this measure was more limited.

Table 4.1 reports the electoral periods included for each country and the basic descriptive statistics for the dependent variables. The 148 electoral periods for the lower chamber and 113 electoral periods for the presidency in the dataset encompass a huge range of scores for the dependent variables and most of the independent variables. This is the longest time series that has been used in quantitative analyses of electoral volatility and the vote share of new parties for Latin America.

THEORETICAL EXPECTATIONS, HYPOTHESES, AND MEASUREMENT OF VARIABLES

The literature on party system change, stability, and collapse, and party collapse contain a wide range of theoretical approaches and hypotheses. Ex-ante and post-facto, we found it difficult to adjudicate among these different theoretical approaches and hypotheses. No extant parsimonious theory satisfies us on empirical grounds, and party system change and stability are influenced by a multiplicity of variables that are difficult to boil down to a parsimonious theory. For these reasons, we tested several major theoretical approaches and included many potentially important variables at the expense of sacrificing theoretical parsimony.

The institutionalization of a party system reflects an equilibrium between the supply side (the creation, splits, mergers, and disbanding of parties by politicians; the formation and dissolution of coalitions; and defections by individual politicians from one party to another) and voters' choices. Five theoretical approaches in the literature on stability and change in parties and party systems might help explain why such an equilibrium emerges, exists, or becomes disrupted: formal rules of the game, features of parties and party systems that are not directly associated with PSI, government performance,

---

[2] We do not include the six indicators of change over a generation (1990–2015) or the summary country measures of PSI because they would limit us to cross-sectional analysis, with only seventeen or eighteen observations (countries). This is not enough observations for multivariate regression analysis with many independent variables. As a result, the dependent variables in this chapter capture only part of PSI – short-term, but not medium-term change and stability. Because of the high correlations between the six dependent variables in this chapter and the medium-term (1990–2015) values for these same indicators, the findings here should offer some guidance about the medium-term correlates of PSI.

TABLE 4.1 *Dependent Variables, Descriptive Statistics*

Country	Elections included	Lower chamber elections				Presidential elections			
		No. of EP	Volatility	New parties	Main party stab.	No. of EP	Volatility	New parties	Main party stab.
Argentina	1983–2011	9	20.7	3.5	89.0	7	46.9	10.2	67.6
Bolivia	1980–2009	8	39.9	8.7	67.5	7	42.1	11.5	62.9
Brazil	1986–2010	7	17.5	3.7	90.0	6	31.0	1.3	77.8
Chile	1989–2009	6	15.1	1.6	96.7	5	28.8	0.4	80.0
Colombia	1958–2010	18	16.4	6.4	96.8	10	33.1	20.7	71.7
Costa Rica	1953–2010	15	25.7	8.3	85.6	15	25.3	8.6	85.6
Dom. Republic	1978–2008	8	20.0	3.0	95.9	9	18.5	1.4	96.3
Ecuador	1979–2009	12	29.0	9.4	79.9	9	44.2	22.4	61.9
El Salvador	1984–2012	10	14.4	7.7	90.1	6	19.9	8.9	88.9
Guatemala	1985–2011	8	40.5	12.7	65.8	7	56.6	40.3	47.6
Honduras	1981–2009	8	12.6	5.8	100.0	8	11.5	5.5	100.0
Mexico	1988–2012	8	16.8	3.3	100.0	4	19.2	2.2	100.0
Nicaragua	1984–2006	5	31.4	1.1	66.6	5	32.0	2.7	76.7
Panama	1989–2009	5	29.0	9.5	76.8	5	43.4	5.6	70.0
Paraguay	1989–2008	5	26.0	9.8	81.8	5	42.1	13.0	70.0
Peru	1980–2006	7	47.1	12.9	53.6	7	54.9	21.0	50.0
Uruguay	1984–2009	6	12.0	1.6	100.0	6	10.8	0.7	100.0
Venezuela	1958–2012	12	34.1	14.0	78.3	12	32.6	17.7	72.9

Note: Country means. No. EP = Number of electoral periods. New Parties = Vote share of new parties. For Argentina, data for legislative elections extend to only 2003.

the political regime, and societal features. These theoretical approaches have deductive merit and have found empirical support in some studies on related issues.

H1. Open formal rules of the game are associated with lower PSI. Formal rules of the game affect the strategic incentives of politicians and voters, which, in turn, might affect their behavior and as a final result impact PSI. Rules of the game that either facilitate the entrance of new actors or that provide few incentives to stop voters changing their vote choice between elections are more likely to create the conditions for greater party system change (Carreras 2012; Cox 1997; Madrid 2005; Mainwaring *et al.* 2016; Roberts and Wibbels 1999; Su 2015; Tavits 2005). Open institutional arrangements facilitate greater supply-side changes in the party system, decreasing the system's predictability. Conversely, where rules help close systems, for example by making it harder for new parties to enter the system and become major contenders, we should see greater institutionalization.

H1a. Higher district magnitudes (the average number of seats per district) should make it easier for new parties to establish an electoral toehold in lower chamber elections (Cox 1997; Tavits 2006, 2008). Conversely, low district magnitudes might reduce volatility and set high barriers for new entrants. The effects of district magnitude operate partly through their impact on the number of parties (H2a), but district magnitude might have an independent effect on volatility.

We calculate district magnitude as the average number of seats per electoral district of a country, *District Magnitude (Log)*. We logged district magnitude because we expect a log-linear relationship between the average number of seats and PSI: if district magnitude has an effect on PSI, these effects should decrease as the average number of seats becomes larger.

H1b. Concurrent presidential and congressional elections should be associated with greater institutionalization. With concurrent presidential and legislative elections, members of congress have more at stake in the outcomes; their own political careers are immediately on the line. When presidential elections are not held concurrently with congressional elections, other politicians from the same party and coalition have weaker incentives to participate in the campaign (Cox 1997). Their own political careers are less directly tied to the outcome of the presidential election. This situation makes it easier for political outsiders to fare well (Carreras 2012) and might boost electoral volatility. This variable, *Concurrent*, is coded 1 if elections in both the first-round presidential and the lower chamber elections occurred on the same day, and 0 if otherwise.

H1c. Rules that allow candidates and parties to purchase TV and radio ads are associated with less institutionalization. If candidates can purchase TV and radio time, it makes it easier for outsiders and new parties to enter the system and expand. If they may not purchase TV and radio time, new parties have more difficulty getting their message out, which could favor the survival and stability of already established parties. *Buy TV* is an indicator of whether candidates and parties can buy television and radio ads to broadcast campaign advertising or whether ads are allocated by the state. It takes the value of 1 when candidates and parties cannot independently buy air time on national media and 0 if they can't.

H1d. Regulations that grant parties exclusive access to elected positions (and that bar independents) are associated with higher PSI. In forty-four of the legislative elections we include and forty-eight of the presidential elections, independent candidates could run without being nominated by a political party. When such a regulation is in place, non-partisan candidates can challenge the existing parties, potentially decreasing PSI. The variable *Independents can run* assumes the value of 1 when this regulation exists and of 0 when it does not. We include *Independents can run (presidential elections)* in presidential elections only; we include *Independents can run (lower chamber)* in lower chamber elections only.

H1e. More difficult registration requirements for forming a new party are associated with greater PSI. Some laws make it more difficult to create new parties, possibly increasing PSI. A high required number of signatures makes it difficult to register a new party, which might favor the existing parties and limit party system change. Consistent with this theoretical intuition, Su (2015) found that a high number of signatures favored lower electoral volatility in Latin America. We follow Su (2015) and measure the NSPR, i.e., the number of signatures required, to form a new political party. Our variable follows Su's rules, converted to a 0 to 1 scale, where 0 means that no signatures are required to register a party, and 1 is the highest value registered on Su's original scale. All intermediate values are calculated as a percentage of the highest value on Su's scale.

H1f. If public funding is generous, and if it is allocated primarily on the basis of party size, and if there is a high threshold for receiving public funding, these conditions favor the main contenders and should help stabilize the party system. This variable is calculated as the interaction between the per capita amount of public funding (in US dollars) times the allocation rule times the threshold.[3] It captures the degree to which rules for public funding favor the main contenders and make it harder for new parties to emerge and for small parties to grow. A high score means that public funding of parties is generous, that it is distributed almost exclusively based on the size of the parties and hence favors large parties, and that small parties are not eligible to receive it. A low score results from little public funding, or from allocating the public funds in a way that favors small parties. *Public Funding* is scaled from 0 to 1, where 0 is the

---

[3] For details of the construction of this variable, see Online Appendix 4.1.

lowest score of any case in the dataset, 1 is the highest score, and all intermediate scores are linear interpolations based on the original scale.

H2. *Some party and party system characteristics are associated with higher PSI.* Following a large literature, we test several hypotheses arguing for the association between some characteristics of the party system and of the parties with greater or lower institutionalization.

H2a. *A higher effective number of parties is associated with lower PSI.* In many previous studies, a higher number of parties has led to increased electoral volatility; this has been one of the most consistent findings in this literature (Bartolini and Mair 1990: 131–45; Madrid 2005: 10; Mainwaring and Zoco 2007; Mainwaring *et al.* 2016; Remmer 1991; Roberts and Wibbels 1999; Tavits 2005, 2008). A more open party system, as expressed by a higher effective number of parties, might make it less daunting for politicians to form new parties, and might particularly increase extra-system volatility for this reason. It could also affect voters' logic. If the system has many parties, the ideological difference between any two contiguous parties tends to be smaller, so that citizens might more readily switch parties from one election to the next. Moreover, voters have more options to which they can defect. Conversely, if a system affords few options, voters might be less inclined to switch to a different party.[4]

Our measure is the effective number of parties (ENP) in the lower chamber (one divided by the sum of the squares of the share of each party) (Laakso and Taagepera 1979) in the first election of an electoral period when the dependent variable is measured using legislative elections results. When the dependent variable comes from presidential elections, we use the effective number of presidential candidates (ENPC). We use the logged version because we expect diminishing effects on the dependent variables as ENP increases, *EN Parties (Log)*.

H2b and H2c test the impact of what we called underpinnings of PSI in Chapter 1. In Mainwaring and Scully (1995a), these were two dimensions of PSI.

H2b. *Systems in which large numbers of voters identify with a party should be more institutionalized.* Where large numbers of voters identify with a party, this party should have a stable electoral base (Green *et al.* 2002; Lupu 2016; Seawright 2012), and a large swath of voters will vote for the same party consistently over time. In turn, this should generate stability at the aggregate level. There are fewer floating voters. This is why Lupu's (2016) theory about

---

[4] The effective number of parties is conceptually completely independent from electoral volatility and the vote share of new parties. The latter two variables measure electoral change at *T*+1. In contrast, the effective number of parties is based on parties' vote shares (i.e., it is a variable about levels, not about change) measured at *T*. Empirically, many party systems are fragmented but stable, and some erstwhile two-party systems can unravel and experience high instability (e.g., Colombia after 1990).

party system collapse hinges critically on a prior decrease in the share of partisans.

We collected information on the percentage of respondents to Latinobarometer surveys between 1997 and 2003 and the AmericasBarometer between 2006 and 2012, which reported sympathizing with a political party (Latinobarometer 2015; LAPOP 2016). Because the years when the surveys were conducted and election years did not match exactly, we used the most recent survey conducted within an electoral period.

H2c. *Systems with solid party organizations should be more institutionalized.* Solid party organization is a fairly proximate explanatory variable that might help explain why some systems institutionalize and others do not. Solid organizations should help politicians connect in more stable ways to voters, thus reducing volatility (Samuels and Zucco 2015; Tavits 2013; Van Dyck 2016).

We use V-Dem data to measure the strength of party organizations (one year lag). V-Dem's *National Party Organizations* variable asks coders to report the share of parties in a country that have permanent national organizations.[5] Answers in the questionnaire range from "no parties" to "all parties."[6] Using a Bayesian IRT (Item Response Theory) model, these answers are translated into a continuous scale. In theory, this indicator could vary from minus infinity to plus infinity. In reality, values range from around −3 to 3. Higher values indicate countries where all parties have permanent organizations.

H2d. *Countries with more programmatic linkages between parties and voters tend to have more institutionalized systems.* Some scholars have posited that programmatic linkages are likely to be more stable than clientelistic or personalistic linkages (Hanson 2010; Kitschelt *et al.* 2010; Mainwaring and Torcal 2006). Clientelistic linkages involve an exchange: a voter gives a politician her vote in exchange for some selective or club goods (a job; access to health care, education, or retirement benefits; a local school, a paved road or street). But voters can easily defect, and in competitive political markets, they might conclude that another politician's offer is better. In contrast, programmatic linkages are built on voters' belief that a party's programmatic offer is the best available. Voters' programmatic preferences tend to be fairly stable.

We used V-Dem data to measure the types of connections between voters and parties. V-Dem asked coders to describe the predominant types of

---

[5] The V-Dem survey defines what coders should understand by "permanent organizations": "A permanent organization connotes a substantial number of personnel who are responsible for carrying out party activities outside of the election season" (Coppedge *et al.* 2016b: 125)

[6] The full text of the question is: "Question: How many political parties for national-level office have permanent organizations? Responses: 0: No parties. 1: Fewer than half of the parties. 2: About half of the parties. 3: More than half of the parties. 4: All parties" (Coppedge *et al.* 2016b: 125).

linkages established by the main parties in a polity, explicitly mentioning "clientelistic," "local collective," and "programmatic" linkages.[7] Higher values in the *Programmatic Linkages* variable indicate parties with predominantly programmatic connections between parties and voters. Scores for Programmatic linkages vary from around –3 to 3.

H2e. More polarized party systems are associated with higher PSI. With greater polarization, voters might see greater differences among parties, increasing the cost of changing options between elections. This hypothesis is consistent with recent work on Latin America. Lupu (2016) argued that programmatic or ideological convergence among parties can lead to brand dilution, which, in turn, can weaken partisanship and make parties vulnerable to collapse if they perform badly in government. If his argument applies broadly to understanding party system change and stability rather than only to party collapse, greater polarization should be associated with greater stability. Roberts (2014) argued that party systems were more stable after the neoliberal period if erstwhile left-of-center parties during the neoliberal period did not renounce their pasts by governing to the right of center. Because left-of-center parties migrating to the right would have led to reduced party system polarization, if Roberts's argument for the post-neoliberal era was applied broadly (rather than being limited to the post-neoliberal period), we would expect less polarization to be associated with greater system upheaval. We measured polarization following Singer's formula,[8] using the electoral results and ideological scores of parties in the first election of every electoral period. Values range from approximately 0.1 to 8.3, with higher values corresponding to more polarization.

H3. Poor government performance is associated with lower institutionalization. Many works have found that party systems are more likely to institutionalize when governments perform well. Bad government performance could increase politicians' willingness to abandon the governing parties and to create new parties. Poor performance might also weaken voters' support for the governing party or coalition, consistent with theories of retrospective voting.

H3a. High positive and negative rates of GDP growth are associated with less institutionalization. Some studies have found that lower rates of economic growth or high inflation are associated with higher electoral volatility – and,

---

[7] The question is: "Among the major parties, what is the main or most common form of linkage to their constituents?" Clarification: A party-constituent linkage refers to the sort of 'good' that the party offers in exchange for political support and participation in party activities. Responses: 0: Clientelistic. Constituents are rewarded with goods, cash, and/or jobs. 1: Mixed clientelistic and local collective. 2: Local collective. Constituents are rewarded with local collective goods, e.g., wells, toilets, markets, roads, bridges, and local development. 3: Mixed local collective and policy/programmatic. 4: Policy/programmatic. Constituents respond to a party's positions on national policies, general party programs, and visions for society" (Coppedge *et al.* 2016b: 126).

[8] We thank Yen-Pin Su for sharing the data.

we expect, by extension to lower PSI (Remmer 1991, 1993; Roberts and Wibbels 1999).[9] We do not expect a direct relationship between poor economic performance and an increase in within-system volatility. Positive growth can increase instability by causing large shifts toward the governing coalition. Assume a simple two-party system consisting of governing party A and opposition party B. In its first term in office, A presides over a per capita GDP growth rate of 3%, generating high public approval and producing a vote shift of 10% in its favor in the next election. In its second term, per capita GDP declines by 3% per year, producing a vote shift of 10% against it in the subsequent election. Both good and very bad growth rates (+3% versus −3%) produce the same volatility. Diametrically opposed growth rates lead to the same prediction: greater instability.

H3b. Long-term economic growth increases institutionalization. We expect that sluggish growth over an extended time will lead to dissatisfaction with existing parties and open the doors to new contenders. Political outsiders and new parties might be more able to capitalize on public dissatisfaction. Conversely, good government performance could deter the creation of new parties.

We measure economic performance with short-term and medium-term per capita GDP growth. The short-term variable, *Growth 1 year,* records the rate of GDP per capita growth in the year prior to the second election of an electoral period. To test for the non-linear association described above, we replace the linear term by the absolute value of GDP Growth (*Growth 1 year (Absolute)*). The medium-term variable for per capita growth is calculated for periods of up to ten years, *GDP Growth (10 years)* – starting 11 years before the second election of an electoral period and finishing the year before the second election of an electoral period.[10]

H3c. Higher inflation is associated with lower institutionalization. This hypothesis again follows the logic that bad government performance is associated with lower PSI. We measure inflation with the logged rate of inflation in each country prior to the second election of an electoral period.[11] The source of data on inflation and growth is The Maddison Project (2013) for 1953–2010 and IMF data for the subsequent years (IMF 2012).

---

[9] In Roberts and Wibbels's analysis, this was true in lower chamber elections, but not presidential elections.

[10] The only exceptions for this rule are for the few observations of elections between 1945 and 1955. In these cases, the averages are over the number of years between 1945 and the year previous to the second election in an electoral period.

[11] It is not possible to calculate a log from a negative value. To minimize the number of missing observations, we assumed that inflation below 1% per year including deflation has an impact on electoral volatility that is indistinguishable from that of an inflation rate of 1%. We recorded all such cases as having a logged inflation of 0.

H3d. High corruption is associated with lower PSI. Other forms of poor government performance could also affect PSI. Seawright (2012) argued that corruption scandals can destabilize party systems, and Pavão (2015) argued that corruption generates political disaffection, which could lead to greater volatility in party systems. We expect that voters are more likely to punish incumbents in contexts of more government corruption and to support new parties entering the system when corruption is rampant. Indicators of PSI, therefore, should be inversely associated with indicators of corruption.

We measure perception of corruption using two variables in the V-Dem project (Coppedge *et al.* 2016a). For legislative electoral periods, we use *Legislative Corruption*, measured in the year immediately before the second election for an electoral period. For presidential elections, we use V-Dem's *Executive Corruption* index, again measured in the year before the second election of an electoral period.[12] V-Dem indicators of corruption are more accurate and reliable than alternative measures and cover a much larger sample of country–years (McMann *et al.* 2016).

H3e. Greater state capacity is associated with higher PSI. Governments are more likely to succeed in policy implementation when state capacity is greater. State capacity is difficult to operationalize, but we follow a measure proposed by Soifer (2015), namely, the percentage of children between two and twenty-three months who were vaccinated against measles.

H4. An early history of democracy and longer-lasting democracy favor higher PSI.

H4a. An early and deeper history of democracy favors greater party system stability. Parties in long-established democracies developed strong organizations with deep connections to voters and organized interests, whereas most third and fourth wave democracies lack strong parties. Past democratic periods could have allowed for the development of many facilitators of PSI that come back to life once redemocratization happens. Some of those facilitators are the parties themselves, more robust civil societies, a population more used to voting and participating in representative democracy, or more responsive state institutions. The Uruguayan experience illustrates this argument: many organizations – including the parties – emerging during the process of redemocratization were built upon pre-existing networks and loyalties, most dating back from the democratic period that preceded the dictatorship of 1973–84. In light of these experiences, we could expect that where those organizations had more time and freedom to develop, they

---

[12] *Executive Corruption* is an index that ranges from 0 to 1, where 0 means less corrupt and 1 means more corrupt. In the original V-Dem dataset, *Legislative Corruption* varies from around −3 to 3, with lower values indicating more corruption. In order to facilitate comparisons, we multiply the values for the *Legislative Corruption* indicator by −1, so both vary in the same direction (from less to more corrupt).

facilitate PSI once redemocratization happens. Consequently, we expect that countries with a democratic past would be more likely to see greater levels of PSI contemporaneously.

We measure past experience with democracy in two ways. First, we count the number of years that countries were democratic or semi-democratic (i.e., scored at least 2 on the Polity IV scale) from 1900 until the beginning of their current electoral regime and divide by the total number of years from 1900 to the beginning of the current electoral regime. This measure emphasizes time under democracy (Prior Democracy). Alternatively, one could argue that it is not as much the time spent under democracy but the degree to which countries were democratic that allows for the development of the features that correlate to higher contemporaneous levels of PSI. Following Gerring *et al.* (2012), we measure the "stock" of previous democracy countries have. We sum the values of Polity IV scores for all years between 1900 and the year prior to the start of the current electoral regime (with an early depreciation rate of 1%). Higher values indicate countries with previous democratic experiences that were intense and long. Intermediate values indicate either short-term very democratic experiences or long-term semi-democratic histories. Low values indicate countries where authoritarianism prevailed.

H4b. Party system stability increases over time as a democracy ages. Converse (1969) argued that it takes time for voters to understand what different parties represent and therefore to identify with a party. In the early stages of a democracy, he expected a large number of floating voters who have not yet identified with a party. In turn, a large number of floating voters should generate considerable electoral volatility (Dalton and Weldon 2007). Over time, more citizens should identify with a party, leading to greater aggregate stability. Likewise, political elites might over time become more committed to party building, leading to tighter connections between voters and parties and greater PSI.[13]

Age of democracy is the number of years since the inauguration of the current "electoral regime." The expectation of a log-linear relationship between this variable and the outcomes of interest justifies the usage of the logged version of this variable.

H5a and H5b focus on the impact of societal features on PSI. Some societal features might make it more likely that voters will establish strong connections

---

[13] With cross-regional samples, however, Mainwaring and Torcal (2006), Mainwaring and Zoco (2007), and Mainwaring *et al.* (2016) argued against this hypothesis, showing that electoral volatility did not decrease over time if *Birthyear of Democracy* was also in the equation. Nevertheless, the hypothesis that stabilization occurs over time might hold for our Latin American sample. Tavits (2008) found that the vote share of new parties first decreased and then increased.

to parties, leading to more institutionalized systems. For this reason, we add two control variables.

H5a. A higher level of development is associated with greater party system stability. Wealthier countries might have more stable party systems for a variety of reasons. We treat this possibility as a control variable. Per capita GDP proxies this variable. Data come from the Maddison Project (2013) (logged).

H5b. Greater ethnic fractionalization is associated with lower party system institutionalization. Madrid (2005) argued that Latin American party systems with greater indigenous populations were beset by greater volatility because parties never established connections with the indigenous peoples, disposing them to shift support to new parties once parties that actively courted indigenous votes emerged. Arguments about ethnicity have also figured in some accounts of African party systems. We test arguments about the impact of ethnicity using a common measure of *Ethnic Fractionalization*.

The coverage of data for some variables is limited. Their overlap is even more restricted, which would make jointly testing for associations of each of these variables almost impossible; with list-wise deletion, we would end up with too few observations for statistical analysis. To circumvent this problem, we used multiple imputation to estimate values for the missing observations in the independent variables using the Amelia II software (Blackwell *et al.* 2015), estimating values for all electoral periods described above.

ESTIMATION AND RESULTS

To test for the relationship between PSI and its hypothesized covariates we use a Generalized Estimation Equations model with an AR-1 correlation structure, which is appropriate for contexts in which the dependent variable may not be independent over time from its previous values. We clustered standard errors by country. Overall, this makes for a very demanding estimation setting; it is difficult to obtain statistically significant results, and statistically significant results are probably not spurious. Given that we use ten multiply imputed datasets to overcome problems of missing data, regression results shown below are coefficients that aggregate over all datasets using the rules described by Rubin (1975).

Robustness tests (Online Appendix 4.2) use random effects with standard errors clustered by countries. These estimation strategies are in line with previous analyses of similar data (Mainwaring *et al.* 2016; Weghorst and Bernhard 2014). Results for these robustness checks mimic the conclusions of the GEE models.

Table 4.2 reports results that test most of the hypotheses listed above. We concentrate on a model that tests the hypotheses that we consider theoretically most relevant, and report results testing the other hypotheses in the Online Appendix. Below, we include all variables listed under H1, H2, and H5. From

TABLE 4.2 *Benchmark Regression Results*

	Legislative			Presidential		
	1	2	3	4	5	6
District magnitude	0.09	1.53	-1.39			
	(1.65)	(0.94)	(2.21)			
Runoff				0.27	-0.40	2.97
				(3.31)	(4.16)	(6.08)
Concurrent	3.80	3.12	-5.24	-8.06	-9.63	9.61
	(2.49)	(2.12)	(3.34)	(5.88)	(7.55)	(6.53)
Buy TV	-4.89	-4.26	16.86+	-4.53	-10.63+	-1.36
	(5.35)	(3.53)	(8.88)	(4.53)	(5.44)	(6.10)
Independents can run	-0.32	-1.03	5.90+	-1.70	-9.13**	2.58
	(3.53)	(2.11)	(3.06)	(3.01)	(3.44)	(4.30)
NSPR	-6.64	-0.65	-7.02	-13.56+	-17.18*	5.99
	(5.96)	(3.83)	(9.79)	(7.79)	(6.77)	(10.40)
Public funding	-7.86	-11.39	-23.52	-19.89*	-28.44*	16.48
	(10.13)	(7.29)	(14.26)	(9.71)	(11.35)	(18.30)
EN parties (log)	3.44	1.40	-12.08*	25.21***	8.32	-41.05***
	(4.81)	(2.30)	(4.68)	(5.34)	(5.32)	(7.02)
Party ID	0.90	0.59	-4.49	8.45	-10.96	-14.08
	(8.19)	(6.54)	(12.45)	(11.32)	(10.47)	(16.44)

Party organizations	−5.90**	−3.07**	12.80***	−10.22**	−3.01	17.01***
	(2.13)	(1.18)	(2.41)	(3.41)	(2.63)	(4.08)
Programmatic linkages	2.10	0.20	−3.68	5.12*	1.51	−8.77*
	(1.55)	(0.98)	(2.21)	(2.14)	(2.64)	(3.80)
Polarization	−0.49	−1.10	−0.81	−1.61	−0.94	0.09
	(0.95)	(0.98)	(1.55)	(1.18)	(1.13)	(1.23)
GDP growth 1 year (absolute)	0.65**	0.23	−0.65	1.23***	0.35	−2.13**
	(0.25)	(0.23)	(0.66)	(0.37)	(0.73)	(0.77)
GDP growth 10 years	−1.25	−0.57	0.75	−0.59	−0.96	0.30
	(0.82)	(0.51)	(1.01)	(0.78)	(1.09)	(1.12)
Corruption	2.22	−0.28	−3.96*	12.16	16.84*	−24.72*
	(1.58)	(0.80)	(1.62)	(7.67)	(7.50)	(11.01)
State capacity	14.76	−0.84	−24.25+	22.64+	14.47	−20.92+
	(9.18)	(5.18)	(13.66)	(11.46)	(14.13)	(11.69)
Prior democracy	4.87	−4.11	3.25	−0.37	5.15	−1.04
	(6.87)	(4.00)	(8.68)	(6.20)	(6.04)	(7.60)
Age of democracy	0.59	2.52+	3.82	1.87	1.99	−5.29
	(2.00)	(1.46)	(2.82)	(1.43)	(1.96)	(3.46)
GDP per capita	0.71	1.99	−0.96	0.31	0.57	−1.65
	(3.75)	(1.89)	(4.19)	(2.12)	(2.93)	(3.19)

TABLE 4.2 (*continued*)

	Legislative			Presidential		
	1	2	3	4	5	6
Ethnic fractionalization	26.36**	1.14	−25.65*	14.12	17.09*	−10.01
	(8.81)	(3.24)	(12.50)	(9.13)	(7.85)	(10.61)

Notes: + *p*<0.10, * *p*<0.05, ** *p*<0.01, *** *p*<0.001

Estimator: GEE. Robust standard errors in parentheses. Models 1 and 4; Volatility is the dependent variable (DV). Models 2 and 5: The Vote share of new parties is the DV. Models 3 and 6: The Stability of the main parties is the DV. For Legislative elections: Observations = 157, Countries = 18. For Presidential elections: Observations = 133, Countries = 18.

H3, we report results for the absolute measure of GDP Growth in the year prior to the election, the measure of long-term GDP growth (average over a ten year period), corruption, and state capacity measured with immunization records.

Online Appendices 4.3 to 4.8 report alternative specifications using the GEE estimator. The first and third model in each table replace our absolute measure of economic growth by the linear measure and inflation, respectively. The model in the fourth column replaces the measure of state capacity we used in the benchmark model (Immunization), by the second measure of state capacity we analyzed (Schooling). Finally, the fifth column replaces the Prior democracy indicator by the Stock of previous democracy indicator mentioned above.

Using a large number of covariates can sometimes suppress the coefficients of some of them, thus potentially obscuring statistically significant results. In order to confirm the findings, Online Appendices 4.9 and 4.10 report the coefficients for the bivariate regression of the dependent variables for each independent variable listed above. The main conclusions derived from the model reported below are supported by the analysis of bivariate associations.

Many hypotheses that were well grounded in previous work did not pan out. Moreover, a few covariates were statistically significant in the "wrong" direction. These results suggest more randomness in patterns of PSI and erosion than we expected, along the lines of what Powell and Tucker (2014) reported for electoral volatility in the post-communist countries.

Excellent work on related subjects (Lupu 2016; Morgan 2011; Riedl 2014; Roberts 2014; Seawright 2012; Tanaka 1998) provided reasonably parsimonious theoretical accounts about the causes of change in Latin American party systems. Our results do not mesh well with any of these accounts. To be clear, we did not directly test any of these theories, nor do any of these works – except Riedl's and perhaps Roberts's – focus on the same dependent variable (PSI) as we do. Still, our results speak to some ideas in these theories.

Are Some Institutional Rules Associated with Greater PSI?

For lower chamber elections, the answer is no; none of fifteen coefficients for these rules was significantly different from 0 at $p<0.05$. In presidential elections, three coefficients suggest that variations in PSI are associated with variations in the rules of the game. As hypothesized, PSI was higher on average, with less volatility and a lower vote share for new parties, where public funding was more generous and more concentrated on the main parties. A one-unit change in the measure of public funding, i.e., a comparison between the electoral period with the lowest and highest levels of public funding, was associated with a 19.9% (in absolute terms) decrease in electoral volatility and a huge 28.4% decrease in the vote share of new parties.

Contrary to expectations, if independents could run for the presidency the predicted vote share of new parties was 9.13 percentage points lower. One plausible interpretation is that if independents can run, they might see less need to form new parties.

The result for the number of signatures required (NSPR) index is also statistically different from 0. Comparing countries with the most stringent rules for new party formation to countries with the least stringent rules shows that, on average, the former had 13.5 percentage points less volatility and 17.1 percentage points lower vote share for new parties. All these results are robust to different specifications of the GEE models and to the substitution of the GEE estimator by the OLS with random effects.

The null associations for other specific institutional rules do not necessarily mean that the rules of the game do not matter for PSI. It is impossible in the cross-national analysis to systematically test for the effects of country-specific rules. Some institutional rules, for example, the de facto single non-transferable vote in Colombia, the fact that lists rarely elected more than a single candidate for the national congress, and the extraordinarily high rotation among different politicians of a single seat in the national congress created powerful incentives for politicians to act as free-wheeling individuals. As Chapter 8 argues, these rules contributed to weakening the party system.

The Connection between Party System and Party Institutionalization

Consistent with expectations, results show a consistent positive association between party organizational strength and system institutionalization in both lower chamber and presidential elections. For every unit more in the strength of party organizations, volatility was 5.9% lower in lower chamber elections and 10.2% lower in presidential elections. New parties had on average 3% fewer votes (although the coefficient was statistically significant only for lower chamber elections); and the stability of main contenders was 12.8% higher in lower chamber elections and 17% higher in presidential elections – by far the largest substantive associations in our models.

These results support the conclusions of Samuels and Zucco (2015), Tavits (2013), and Van Dyck (2016) regarding the capacity of solid organizations to stabilize individual parties' vote shares and, as a result, to help institutionalize the system. Solid organizations are no panacea; AD and COPEI in Venezuela once had dense organizations. But they give parties a way of connecting to voters and building networks of activists. They can help buffer parties from the electoral effects of bad government performance, corruption scandals, and other challenges.